SURVIVORS

Survivors tells the harrowing story of life in Warsaw under Nazi occupation. As the epicenter of Polish resistance, Warsaw was subjected to violent persecution, the ghettoization of the city's Jewish community, the suppression of multiple uprisings, and an avalanche of restrictions that killed hundreds of thousands and destroyed countless lives. In this study into the unique brutality of wartime Warsaw, Jadwiga Biskupska traces how Nazi Germany set out to dismantle the Polish nation and state for long-term occupation by targeting its intelligentsia. She explores how myriad resistance projects emerged within the intelligentsia who were bent on maintaining national traditions and rebuilding a Polish state. In contrast to other studies on the Holocaust and Second World War, this book focuses on Polish behavior and explains who was in a position to contest the occupation or collaborate with it, while answering lingering questions and addressing controversies about the Nazi empire and the Holocaust in Eastern Europe.

Jadwiga Biskupska is Assistant Professor of History at Sam Houston State University in Hunstville, Texas. She is co-director of Second World War Research Group, North America (SWWRGNA) and a former fellow of the Mandel Center at the United States Holocaust Memorial Museum.

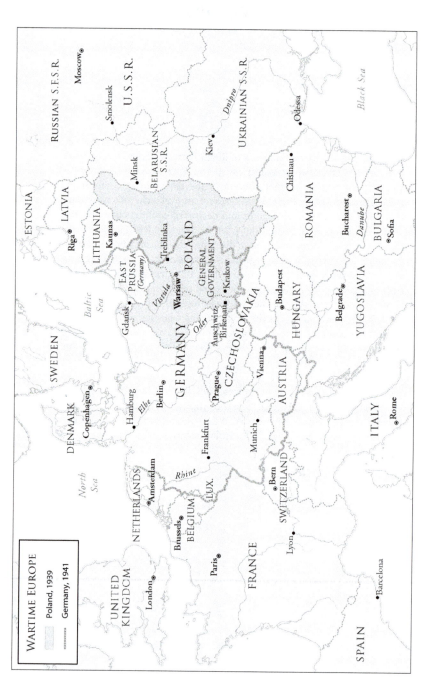

Figure 0.1 Map of Nazi-Occupied Europe

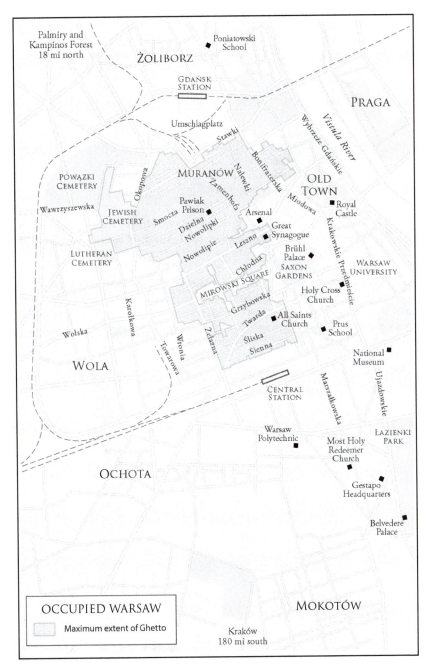

Figure 0.2 Map of Occupied Warsaw

Studies in the Social and Cultural History of Modern Warfare

General Editors
Robert Gerwarth, *University College Dublin*
Jay Winter, *Yale University*

Advisory Editors
Heather Jones, *University College London*
Rana Mitter, *University of Oxford*
Michelle Moyd, *Indiana University Bloomington*
Martin Thomas, *University of Exeter*

In recent years the field of modern history has been enriched by the exploration of two parallel histories. These are the social and cultural history of armed conflict, and the impact of military events on social and cultural history.

Studies in the Social and Cultural History of Modern Warfare presents the fruits of this growing area of research, reflecting both the colonization of military history by cultural historians and the reciprocal interest of military historians in social and cultural history, to the benefit of both. The series offers the latest scholarship in European and non-European events from the 1850s to the present day.

A full list of titles in the series can be found at:
www.cambridge.org/modernwarfare

SURVIVORS

Warsaw under Nazi Occupation

JADWIGA BISKUPSKA

Sam Houston State University

CAMBRIDGE
UNIVERSITY PRESS

University Printing House, Cambridge CB2 8BS, United Kingdom

One Liberty Plaza, 20th Floor, New York, NY 10006, USA

477 Williamstown Road, Port Melbourne, VIC 3207, Australia

314–321, 3rd Floor, Plot 3, Splendor Forum, Jasola District Centre,
New Delhi – 110025, India

103 Penang Road, #05–06/07, Visioncrest Commercial, Singapore 238467

Cambridge University Press is part of the University of Cambridge.

It furthers the University's mission by disseminating knowledge in the pursuit of
education, learning, and research at the highest international levels of excellence.

www.cambridge.org
Information on this title: www.cambridge.org/9781316515587
DOI: 10.1017/9781009026017

© Jadwiga Biskupska 2022

First published 2022

A catalogue record for this publication is available from the British Library.

ISBN 978-1-316-51558-7 Hardback

Cambridge University Press has no responsibility for the persistence or accuracy of
URLs for external or third-party internet websites referred to in this publication
and does not guarantee that any content on such websites is, or will remain,
accurate or appropriate.

I dedicate this project to the late Olga Karnauchov, who wanted me to return to graduate school. Knowing her allowed me to embark on a study of eastern Europeans upended by Hitler's war in the assurance that some of them went on to make beautiful lives out of the horror. To her and to those who did not survive: *requiescat in pace.*

CONTENTS

FIGURES

ACKNOWLEDGMENTS

This project had an unusually long gestation, and has accumulated numerous debts and obligations over the years. I will forever be grateful for the help and advice I received along the way. Thanks go first to my original Yale University dissertation committee of Timothy Snyder, Marci Shore, and Adam Tooze, for their guidance throughout my time in New Haven and since. At Cambridge University Press, I would like to thank series editor Jay Winter, editor Michael Watson, editorial assistant Emily Plater, and the anonymous readers for their comments.

To all those who have generously funded the project at different stages: the Fulbright Program and my Warsaw University hosts; the Institute of Human Sciences, Vienna; the Baden-Württemberg Exchange Fellowship; the Kościuszko Foundation; the European Studies Council at Yale University; the Jack, Joseph and Morton Mandel Center for Advanced Holocaust Studies, United States Holocaust Memorial Museum; the Smith Richardson Foundation; the Woodrow Wilson International Center for Scholars, Washington, DC; the REEEC Summer Research Laboratory at the Russian, East European, and Eurasian Center (REEEC) at the University of Illinois at Urbana-Champaign, and the College of Humanities and Social Sciences and my own history department at Sam Houston State University in Huntsville, Texas: all my thanks.

I am especially grateful to the librarians, archivists, and staff at the collections I have visited over the years in the United States and Europe who endured my garbled questions and went out of their way to make material available, often on short notice. Special thanks to those who work in the libraries and archives at the Mandel Center, whom I burdened without end. Steve Feldman's help and support during my time as a Mandel Center fellow and afterward were essential to the project's completion: I cannot thank him enough.

At an early stage, this work benefited from a manuscript review workshop created by Andrzej Kamiński's Recovering Forgotten History program. Thanks to Grzegorz Berendt, Dobrochna Kałwa, Sebastian Rejak, Bożena Szaynok, and Jakub Tyszkiewicz, who reviewed the whole manuscript and provided revision suggestions. Thanks also to Eulalia Łazarska, John Merriman, Adam Kożuchowski, Susan Ferber, Gabriel Finder, Anna Krakus, and the late Alexander Prusin and Mark von Hagen for their advice, ideas, and help during the workshop and thereafter.

Thanks also to all of the commentators who have offered criticism and suggestions on parts of this work as it developed, especially Michael David-Fox, Piotr Wróbel, Norman Naimark, Amy Elise Randall, Tarik Cyril Amar, Mark Roseman, and the late Geoffrey Megargee and Włodzimierz Borodziej. I owe a particular debt to Jesse Kauffman for his feedback and support. Thanks also to Mary Kathryn Barbier, and to my colleagues in the Second World War Research Group for the forum they have built and the camaraderie it has provided. Barbara Kalabinski and her family put me up in Warsaw and answered a thousand questions. Barbara Nowak indexed the book beautifully.

At my home institution of Sam Houston State University, I would like to thank my history department colleagues and my fellow participants in the PACE writing circles program, especially Siham Bouamer, the organizer. Special thanks to Pinar Emiralioğlu and Steve Rapp for reading and commenting on the whole manuscript, and Brian Domitrovic for his advice and help as my first departmental chair and since. And to Uzma Quraishi and Maggie Elmore: you know I would never have made it without you.

Friends and family have supported me and this project for much longer than they could have imagined without complaint. Many thanks to my entire family, but especially my siblings. I am indebted to colleagues and classmates who have become dear friends: Amanda Behm, Christian Burset, Kathleen Conti, Nicole Eaton, Kimberly Lowe Frank, Jeremy Friedman, Anna Graber, Kristy Ironside, Elana Jakel, Emily Suzanne Johnson, Marta Kalabinski, Yedida Kanfer, Nathan Kurz, Vojin Majstorović, Kathleen Minahan, Anna Müller, Iryna Vushko, Marita von Weissenberg, and Jennifer Wellington. Mattie Amanda Fitch read every word of this manuscript several times and found a way to make it coherent when it was not. Thanks to Sara Edeiken and her family, Anastasia Grivoyannis, and Matthew Menezes for their friendship. And to Meagan Fitzpatrick and Ryan Eargle, my dear friends, and Olesia and Andrew Doran, my sister and brother-in-law: thanks for feeding me, housing me, and reminding me what my life is for. All errors and eccentricities in the work are my own.

~

Introduction

The Second World War destroyed the city of Warsaw. In summer 1939, it was a thriving metropolis, the "Paris of the East." The expanding capital of a sovereign eastern European state, the Second Polish Republic, it formed the epicenter of Polish national and cultural life. By Christmas 1944 it was a mountain of rubble. Those who had built the first independent Polish state of the twentieth century and made Warsaw their home were dead, imprisoned, or exiled. They had lost their state, their city, and their home to Nazi German violence.

This book tells the story of a handful of politically conscious Poles and the world they lost under occupation, one of the most vicious in modern history.[1] It examines the intelligentsia of Warsaw and their behavior under Nazi occupation from 1939 to 1944. This elite group led responses to Nazi violence from which they were never safe. For more than five years Warsaw lived, as one Pole remembered, "under horrible terror," as if "with a gun constantly to our heads."[2] Despite enormous danger, the capital's elite embarked on a dizzying array of initiatives to capture the Polish public's loyalty, preserve their national heritage, keep themselves from going mad, and oust their hated occupiers. Some were disastrous failures and others remarkable successes. The Holocaust of Poland's – and Europe's – Jewish community unfolded simultaneously, eclipsing the persecution of the majority of non-Jewish Poles. Polish elite response to different occupation policies revealed crucial ethnic and religious fractures in the Polish national project. The final elite-led anti-occupation effort was a military uprising in summer 1944, which their occupiers crushed, razing the city that had been the center of Polish resistance since 1939.

Polish and German wartime behaviors drew on tradition. As Adolf Hitler's Germany planned its invasion of Poland, a bold attempt to secure *Lebensraum* or racial "living space," he worried that Warsaw's intelligentsia – educators, doctors, lawyers, bureaucrats, journalists, priests, military officers, intellectuals,

---

[1] In contrast to the "good" American occupations of Germany and Japan after 1945, themselves contested. Susan L. Carruthers, *The Good Occupation: American Soldiers and the Hazards of Peace* (Cambridge: Harvard University Press, 2016).

[2] PISM A.10.4.2 (I), "Wyciąg z raportu z Kraju z dnia 5. Marca 1940 r.," [1].

and their ilk – would undermine Germany's ability to control Poland in the long term. Warsaw, the largest city in the region, was key to Nazi German expansion and the extraction of Slavic labor and natural resources. The city's intelligentsia had played an integral social, cultural, and political role in interwar Poland and in Polish national tradition for generations as the Germans well knew: they were state and nation builders. If any group could mount sustained opposition, they could. They therefore became the target of a preemptive Nazi genocide at the beginning of the Second World War.

Nazi policemen killed and imprisoned the intelligentsia during their 1939 invasion of Poland, but haphazardly. Nazi planners lost track of their targets or misunderstood them; the intelligentsia were a messy tangle of individuals who embraced the Polish national project, especially when it was under threat, rather than a discrete professional or political group. In response to their first botched attempts at elite subjugation, Nazi Germany installed a draconian occupation administration in Warsaw and began an anti-intelligentsia killing campaign that continued through 1939 and 1940. This campaign filled city prisons to overflowing: "excess" victims went to concentration camps. With death tolls hovering near 100,000, Nazi killings provoked sustained military, political, and cultural resistance. By 1941, the Nazis abandoned anti-intelligentsia campaigning in favor of an unsystematic hodgepodge of retaliatory terror and bloody reprisals – a counterinsurgency campaign – that continued until the Red Army drove them out.

Early Nazi German persecution of the Warsaw intelligentsia failed and Poles concocted various ways to undermine the occupation and wrest back their state – and control over Polish society. Individuals who built the largest and most ambitious resistance projects are at the center of this argument: while many engaged in "passive resistance," "internal exile," or wait-and-see cooperation, turning a blind eye to Nazi violence against those outside the Polish national community, the focus is on those who took actions to inspire the wider population and undermine Nazi occupation.[3] In other words, the subject of this book is those individuals who continued the intelligentsia's nation-building mission under occupation and the task is understanding how successful they were. Information networks, including underground publishing and couriering, and the "secret" schooling system were especially effective; Catholic religious activities and military resistance were vulnerable to the volatile international situation and rockier in their achievements. Initiatives dependent on international support could not be controlled from Warsaw. Political independence was one such

---

[3] Holocaust scholars have developed a fine-grained model for the defiance of people with little agency, including "sanctification of life," and polemic, symbolic, and defensive resistance. Michael R. Marrus, "Jewish Resistance to the Holocaust," *Journal of Contemporary History*, Vol. 30 No. 1 (Jan. 1995), 88–90, 93.

project and thus unachievable; nation-building efforts, however, produced significant victories.[4]

This story involves a complex cast of characters, including some who will be familiar to English-language audiences and others whom they will encounter for the first time. Jan Karski, international courier and later professor at Georgetown University; Karol Wojtyła, later Pope John Paul II; and Władysław Sikorski, prime minister of the London exile government, appear alongside others unknown outside Poland, like Stefan Starzyński, the last mayor of Warsaw; Aleksander Kamiński, scout leader, insurgent, and underground publicist; Zofia Kossak, Catholic activist and Holocaust rescuer; Witold Pilecki, the army officer who snuck into Auschwitz, and Władysław Studnicki, the First World War collaborator who petitioned the Nazis to deputize him and ended up their prisoner. The intelligentsia who survived the 1939–40 killing campaigns were dynamic if frustrated people who fought against the constraints of occupation and attempted to build a better future for themselves and Poland, though they rarely agreed with one another about how to do it.

0.1 Nation-State Actors

The word "intelligentsia" is specific to eastern Europe and the development of civil society under the Russian Empire: Poles and Russians have intelligentsias and other nations generally do not.[5] The capital of the early modern Polish–Lithuanian Commonwealth, Warsaw, became the capital of the new independent Second Polish Republic in 1918, and it was the birthplace of the national intelligentsia during the partitions under Russian, Austrian, and Prussian (then German) imperial rule.[6] Beginning in 1795, the territory of the enormous Polish–Lithuanian Commonwealth was occupied – "partitioned," as it was described at the time – by its neighbors in a cooperative imperial

---

[4] Since, as David Edelstein has argued, military occupations' viability often turns on their relationship to local nation building, the German rejection of this project provided the Warsaw intelligentsia with a potential tool to build popular consensus. David Edelstein, *Occupational Hazards: Success and Failure in Military Occupation* (Ithaca: Cornell University Press, 2008), 4.

[5] Chad Bryant considers that a Czech intelligentsia emerged under Habsburg rule. Chad Bryant, *Prague in Black: Nazi Rule and Czech Nationalism* (Cambridge: Harvard University Press, 2007), 192–3. Thanks to Daniel Pratt for emphasizing this.

[6] Jerzy Jedlicki, *A Suburb of Europe: Nineteenth-Century Polish Approaches to Western Civilization* (Budapest: CEU Press, 1999); Janina Żurawicka, *Inteligencja warszawska w końcu XIX wieku* (Warsaw: Państwowe Wydawnictwo Naukowe, 1978), 12; Aleksander Gella, *Inteligencja polska* (Warsaw: Wydawnictwo AKME, 2016); Longina Jakubowska, *Patrons of History: Nobility, Capital and Political Transitions in Poland* (New York: Routledge, 2016); Maciej Janowski and Magdalena Micińska, *History of the Intelligentsia* (Frankfurt am Main: Peter Lang, 2014).

expansion they thought permanent. Because there was no independent Polish state from 1795 to 1918 and the three partitioning powers were invested in maintaining that status quo, Polish political ambition was dangerous to them. Recognizing these strictures but also chafing under them, a mixture of elites – the intelligentsia – created and maintained national traditions and debated about how to re-empower their countrymen and regain independence.

The intelligentsia were elites who identified as Polish, advocated on behalf of national causes, and maintained Polish culture under duress. In most cases, "intelligentsia" is synonymous with "elite," but it denotes a self-conscious group motivated by a sense of national mission.[7] Jan Karski called it "the term under which we [Poles] designate the educated class as a whole."[8] Jan Szczepański, sociologist of the Marxist intelligentsia, defined its early members as "those who took ideological leadership in the effort to regain independence, who maintained the cultural and social forces necessary to this purpose, who kept alive the national traditions, developed the nation's values, [and] educated the new generations for the struggle for national goals."[9] Kazimierz Brandys, a Polish *inteligent* himself and one of the objects of Szcepański's scrutiny, remarked in the 1970s that those outside eastern Europe "do not understand the nature of a country in which a hundred years ago the cause of national liberation was actively carried on by no more than a few hundred people with programs that were none too clear and had no chance for success."[10] To refer to someone as an *inteligent* meant that he – or she – felt bound to the national cause and the promotion of Polish statehood when it was absent, which it often was.

In Polish history, the growth of the intelligentsia was the product of two uncomfortable absences: that of sovereign statehood from 1795 to 1918, and that of early industrialization and its concomitant, a developing middle class.[11] An intelligentsia arose on Polish territory rather than a state bureaucracy or an educated bourgeoisie because there was no national state. Thus discussion of the intelligentsia is always already discussion of a Polish *Sonderweg* in European progress by which Polish national culture was built without the "normal" institutions supporting it in western Europe.[12] Historian Maciej Janowski pinpoints the group's origins after Napoleonic defeat, with the term acquiring fixed meaning by the January Insurrection of

---

[7] Gella, *Inteligencja polska*, 91.

[8] Jan Karski, *Story of a Secret State: My Report to the World* (Washington, DC: Georgetown University Press, 2013), 56.

[9] Jan Szczepański, "The Polish Intelligentsia: Past and Present," *World Politics*, Vol. 14, No. 3 (Apr., 1962): 408.

[10] Kazimierz Brandys, *A Warsaw Diary, 1978–1981* (New York: Random House, 1983), 147.

[11] Żurawicka, *Inteligencja warszawska w końcu XIX wieku.*, 12.

[12] Andrzej Walicki, "Poland between East and West: The Controversies over Self-Definition and Modernization in Partitioned Poland" (Cambridge: Harvard Ukrainian Research Institute, 1994).

1863, which provoked a generation of russification efforts in Warsaw.[13] Its formation was linked to the idea of armed insurrection to regain independence, whether with Napoleon's help or as the independent initiative of Warsaw insurgents, though there were always intelligentsia figures who rejected violence.[14]

Intelligentsia status turned on a nation-state mission, but members clustered in professions that came to be associated with the group. Teaching, from grammar school to university, was an intelligentsia vocation. Writers, poets, publicists, and "penmen" were included.[15] Lawyers and doctors often included themselves. Religious elites – especially Catholic clergy – had a role. Not all priests were intelligentsia (or wanted to be), but those who were had crucial authority. Physicians, scientists, industrialists, and engineers were a grey area: some were in, some out. Military officers were also elites, but they wore Russian, Austrian, and German uniforms until 1918 and contemporaries suspected their patriotism. After 1918 many opted in, and reserve officers – men with military training and civilian careers – were vital.

A nineteenth-century intelligentsia arose after the dispossession of the *szlachta*, the Polish gentry, by partitioning powers keen to reduce the economic influence of the old Commonwealth's wealthiest inhabitants.[16] Some szlachta and their descendants – especially those without significant holdings – made their way into partition-era bureaucracies.[17] These new bureaucrats, when they agitated for Polish causes, became intelligentsia. Intelligentsia clout, however, had no necessary relationship to wealth, and material resources ranged from significant means to utter pennilessness. They had, as Pierre Bourdieu would have it, cultural rather than financial capital.[18]

---

[13] An intelligentsia formed in the 1860s "with the obligation and privilege to act as the national avant-garde." Janowski, *Birth of the Intelligentsia,* 12. Bronisław Trentowski first used the term in 1844. Gella, *Inteligencja Polska*, 21; Richard Pipes, *Russia under the Old Regime* (New York: Penguin Books, 1995), 251.

[14] Slavic insurgency should not be assumed: as John Connelly's argues, only Poles and Serbs had substantive armed insurrection traditions. See John Connelly, *From Peoples into Nations: A History of Eastern Europe* (Princeton: Princeton University Press, 2020), 130–154.

[15] Writers have a privileged position here, for the same reason Poshek Fu centers them in his study of Japanese-occupied Shanghai, since they were "thinking individuals with a conscious grasp of their historical situation." Poshek Fu, *Passivity, Resistance, and Collaboration: Intellectual Choices in Occupied Shanghai, 1937-1945* (Palo Alto: Stanford University Press, 1993), xii.

[16] Jakubowska notes the gentry retained a monopoly on "the historic role of defining Polish identity." Jakubowska, *Patrons of History*, 6.

[17] Aleksander Matejko, "Status Incongruence in the Polish Intelligentsia," *Social Research*, Vol. 33, No. 4 (Winter 1966): 611–638, 612.

[18] Pierre Bourdieu, *Distinction: A Social Critique of the Judgement of Taste* (Cambridge: Harvard University Press, 1984), 260. Thanks to Mattie Fitch for noting this.

Much of the intelligentsia was Roman Catholic but religious orthodoxy was optional, however much this rankled the Catholic Church.[19] A strain of Polish nationalist thinking understood Polishness and Catholicism as intertwined and defined nationality religiously.[20] The crucial question was the relationship to Judaism (or Jewishness): could someone "of Mosaic faith" be welcome in the Polish nation? Among its intelligentsia leadership? The answer was yes and no. Intellectual historian Jerzy Jedlicki notes that "assimilated Jews were welcomed by the Polish educated classes" who embraced civic nationalism. Unassimilated Jews were another matter: one of the defining characteristics of Polish territory was the presence of religious Jews in towns and cities, including Warsaw, many of whom spoke Polish as a second language if at all. Their "welcome" changed when some Polish nationalists came to see Jews as competitors for territory and political influence rather than co-victims of partitioning oppression after 1918. The co-victimhood debate would have many afterlives: antisemitism and the assertion that Jews were not or never could be Polish – ethnic nationalism – constituted a formidable strand of intelligentsia thinking at the dawn of the twentieth century.[21]

Education was a marker of intelligentsia status. However, tertiary schooling was not always available to Poles, and the partitioning powers associated students (rightly) with radical patriotic politics. Universities were pawns of the partitioning powers, who appreciated their influence and used them to control the behavior – and the production of – Polish elites. This meant that an educated Pole had a more complicated CV than his western European peers. Warsaw University became the maternity ward of the capital's intelligentsia after its 1816 founding, but its output waxed and waned. Russian Tsar Alexander I opened it to train staff for his imperial outpost. Faculty and students thanked him by participating in the November Uprising of 1830 against his rule, and he closed it. Another tsarist thaw reopened it, and the university threw itself into the January Uprising of 1863.[22] During the 1905 Revolutions, students joined workers on the barricades, to St. Petersburg's

---

[19] Pope Gregory XVI's encyclical *Cum Primum* (On Civil Disobedience) in 1832 condemned uprising; Archbishop Zygmunt Feliński was anti-insurrection. Brian Porter-Szücs, *Faith and Fatherland: Catholicism, Modernity, and Poland* (New York: Oxford University Press, 2011), 160–161.

[20] Porter-Szücs, *Faith and Fatherland*, 328–359.

[21] Jerzy Jedlicki, "Resisting the Wave: Intellectuals against Antisemitism in the Last Years of the 'Polish Kingdom,'" *Antisemitism and Its Opponents in Modern Poland* (Ithaca: Cornell University Press, 2005), 61; Samuel D. Kassow, *Who Will Write Our History? Rediscovering A Hidden Archive from the Warsaw Ghetto* (New York: Vintage Books, 2007), 50.

[22] "The great majority of educated people were engaged in the resistance movement, though obviously to varying degree." Stefan Kieniewicz, *Trzy powstania narodowe: kościuszkowe, listopadowe, styczniowe*. (Warsaw: Książka i Wiedza, 1994), 354–357; 387–391; Connelly, *From Peoples into Nations*, 85–89.

fury. In 1914, students filled Piłsudski's Legions and fought the Russian army. In 1918, as the flagship university of a newly independent state, Warsaw University flourished. In 1939, the Nazis closed it, and the faculty reassembled it, underground.

0.2 Competing Visions

A distinct Polish elite with a national independence mission emerged from more than a century of partition, progress, and insurrection. The failure of the last substantial attempt, the January Insurrection of 1863, defined the Warsaw intelligentsia's future. For some, the romantics, the only way to gain independence was in arms – either on Polish lands or abroad.[23] For others, particularly victims of brutal Russian repression, insurrection squandered human capital and national resources. They adopted Enlightenment ideals, emphasizing education, developing infrastructure, and promoting everything from public health to women's emancipation. Such 'Warsaw Positivists' favored gradual "organic work" over rebellion.[24] Most elites were not pure romantics or positivists, but tempered idealism with pragmatism, as they would again during the Second World War.

Two men born just after the January Uprising embodied the divide between the positivist and romantic paradigms of intelligentsia nation building, inspiring the elites who would suffer under Nazi occupation. The elder was Roman Dmowski (1864–1939), born outside Warsaw in 1864 and an *inteligent* courtesy of his Warsaw University studies and lifelong political agitation. The younger was Józef Piłsudski (1867–1935), born to an impoverished gentry family in what is now Lithuania to a January Uprising veteran. Piłsudski was not much of a student, but he was a fanatical patriot from his youth.[25] The two men traveled in the same circles and were even friends in the 1890s, but their hopes for the future ran afoul of one another. They articulated the main strands of Polish national thinking, the conflict between which would define a century.[26] In rough outline, Piłsudski was a romantic and insurrectionary; Dmowski a pragmatist who thought violence foolish. Piłsudski thought the main impediment to future Polish independence was Russia; Dmowski thought Germany. Both were nominally Catholic, and Dmowski drew the

---

[23] Soldiers campaigned under the slogan "for your freedom and ours." Brian Porter-Szűcs, *Poland in the Modern World: Beyond Martyrdom* (Oxford: Wiley Blackwell, 2014), 26.

[24] Magdalena Micińska, *At the Crossroads: 1865–1918*. A History of the Polish Intelligentsia, Part 3 (Frankfurt/Main: Peter Lang, 2014), 89–106; Connelly, *From Peoples into Nations*, 278–279.

[25] Andrzej Garlicki, *Józef Piłsudski, 1867–1935* (Brookfield: Ashgate Publishing Company, 1995), 2–4, 28, 40.

[26] Andrzej Paczkowski, *The Spring Will Be Ours: Poland and the Poles from Occupation to Freedom* (University Park: Penn State University Press, 1995), 25.

Church into his camp.[27] Piłsudski joined the Polish Socialist Party (PPS) and pushed it in a nationalist direction; Dmowski founded the National Democratic Party (ND), or *Endecja*. Piłsudski imagined a large, federal state including Poles, Ukrainians, Germans, and Jews; Dmowski wanted an ethnically homogenous Poland and became a rabid antisemite.[28] Piłsudski was a civic nationalist, Dmowski an ethnic one. Both assumed the intelligentsia – their people – would lead any future sovereign Poland.

Each made allies. Dmowski spent time abroad; Piłsudski spent time in prison, including in the Tenth Pavilion of Warsaw's Citadel and in Siberian exile.[29] Both were overtaken by workers' rebellions launched outside Warsaw's All Saints Church on Grzybowski Square in November 1904 and continued into 1905.[30] In this moment, intelligentsia-led political movements were confronted with the specter of mass politics and forced to respond to urban crowds. Dmowski's Endecja weathered the moment better. After creating a trade union, Endecja cracked down on strikers, compromising with industry. When 1905 did not provide the base for an all-Polish uprising, Piłsudski revealed himself to be more nationalist than socialist. His Polish Socialist Party split between those committed to proletarian struggle and those committed to independence.

The Warsaw intelligentsia entered the twentieth century dedicated to independence, but with no consensus on what kind, where, or for whom. The international situation overtook those questions when two partitioning powers – Austria and Germany – went to war against the third, Russia, in 1914. Piłsudski raised an army, forming Polish Legions to fight Russia. Almost 21,000 men volunteered by 1917 – more than 30% students – but the Central Powers found Piłsudski and his recruits intractable. The stalwart revolutionary, Piłsudski was the example *par excellence* of the "Pandora's box opened by the national mobilization at the war's start."[31] Piłsudski's Legions became a Polish Auxiliary Corps in 1916, but shrank in 1917 when their commander refused to swear loyalty to the German Kaiser, Wilhelm II. The stunt got Piłsudski imprisoned in Saxony to wait out the First World War.[32]

Dmowski, horrified by Piłsudski's anti-Russian rebellion, spent the conflict in western Europe, negotiating.[33] Aided by his friend the pianist Ignacy Jan

---

[27] Neither was pious, though both used religion. Porter-Szücs, *Faith and Fatherland*, 181.

[28] Walicki, "Poland between East and West," 46–55; Feliks Gross, "Tolerance and Intolerance in Poland: The Two Political Traditions," *The Polish Review* Vol. 20, No. 1 (1975), 65–69.

[29] Garlicki, *Piłsudski*, 33–34.

[30] Robert E. Blobaum, *Rewolucja: Russian Poland, 1904–1907* (Ithaca: Cornell University Press, 1995), 41, 190–210.

[31] Alexander Watson, *Ring of Steel: Germany and Austria-Hungary in World War I* (New York: Basic Books, 2015), 97–99.

[32] Garlicki, *Piłsudski*, 85–87.

[33] Jesse Kauffman, *Elusive Alliance: The German Occupation of Poland in World War I* (Cambridge: Harvard University Press, 2015), 84–85.

Paderewski (1860–1941), Dmowski gave lectures, shook hands, and promoted his vision for Poland among Britons, Americans, and the French.[34] In August 1917 his efforts created the Polish National Committee (Polski Komitet Narodowy), a skeleton government. Neither man mastered the wartime situation, but Dmowski's influence got him invited to the Paris Peace Conference and meant that it was his signature – not Piłsudski's – on the Treaty of Versailles.

Warsaw beheld two of her floundering imperial masters as First World War occupiers: first the Russians, then the Germans. Russia retreated in July 1915. Departing Russians looted the city, ingratiating themselves with no one. A brutal German occupation then exploited Varsovians.[35] Hans Hartwig von Beseler, the Imperial German General Governor, ruled Warsaw with a "mix of condescension and fondness." Beseler was no Polonophile but he granted whatever self-governance spared him personnel and did not interfere with the German war effort. He reopened Warsaw University, supported Piłsudski's Legions, and formed a provisional Regency Council. Germany, however, lost the war and none of its concessions to Poland materialized, while all the wartime hardships did.[36]

Russia fell into revolution after February 1917, and in March 1918 the Peace of Brest-Litovsk pulled it from the war and out of Polish territory.[37] By October 1918, the Central Powers were also on their last legs. At the beginning of November, Austria signed an armistice with the Triple Entente and collapsed. On November 8, 1918, Germany released Piłsudski. On November 11, 1918, it signed an armistice with the victorious Entente in western Europe. The same day, Warsaw's Regency Council put Piłsudski in command of Polish soldiers, and he declared an independent Polish state. Dmowski was in Paris. Germany, Austria, and Russia were in shambles; Warsaw was in worse shape. Poland was back.

For romantics, 1918 was the end of a century-long insurrection in which the final rebellion crowned partition intelligentsia conspiracies with success. This story was simple and bloody. Approximately every generation, Warsaw intelligentsia rebelled against foreign domination, usually gunning hardest for the

---

[34] Connelly, *Peoples into Nations*, 332.

[35] Material conditions for non-Jewish Varsovians were worse in 1915–18 than 1939–44. Robert Blobaum, *A Minor Apocalypse: Warsaw during the First World War* (Ithaca: Cornell University Press, 2017), 52, 10.

[36] German conservatives thought he pandered to Poles, and Polish nationalists thought he swindled them. He inspired Władysław Studnicki. The Germans, notably, were not exactly planning an independent Poland. Vejas Gabriel Liulevicius, *War Land on the Eastern Front: Culture, National Identity and German Occupation in World War I* (New York: Cambridge University Press, 2000), 125, 196–198; Kauffman, *Elusive Alliance*, 44, 59, 84–85, quotation 36; Watson, *Ring of Steel*, 393.

[37] Connelly, *Peoples into Nations*, 327–330; Laura Engelstein, *Russia in Flames: War, Revolution, Civil War, 1914–1921* (New York: Oxford University Press, 2018), 491, 494.

Russians. Each rebellion failed. But in 1918, due to the agglomeration of effort *and* the political-military collapse of *all three* of the empires partitioning the Commonwealth, a newly independent Poland re-emerged, blinking, onto the European map.

0.3 Intelligentsia in Power: 1918–1939

Thus the Polish intelligentsia took the helm of a modern state in 1918. Piłsudski, who was popular with the masses but had a revolutionary's unorthodox approach to politics, held the reins of government. He staffed the state with Legionnaires and fellow socialist agitators.[38] Much of society filled out similarly, with elites choosing peers to begin the work of state-making. This is not to accuse the Second Polish Republic of nepotism, but to draw attention to its newness. The consequences of an absence of nineteenth-century statehood cannot be underestimated. The newly instated elite worked feverishly to inspire aristocrats, the peasantry, workers, and minorities with their political visions.[39] To the Warsaw intelligentsia the Second Polish Republic was the fulfillment of their dreams, but to Ukrainians and Germans it was an oppressive imperial state.[40]

Unsurprisingly, the intelligentsia disagreed on how to run Poland. How did their national mission democratize itself? What role would Piłsudski, "the George Washington of Poland," play?[41] State-builders were unsure, since among them numbered those who upheld a civic concept of Polishness that embraced Jews, Catholics, Ukrainians, Belarussians, and "ethnic" Poles who wished to live *po polsku* – *à la* Piłsudski.[42] There were also those in power who defined Polishness in ethno-linguistic or religious terms (excluding non-Catholics, but sometimes including converts) – *à la* Dmowski. This camp was "disassimiliationist" and treated minorities differently than "true Poles."[43] The

---

[38] Timothy Snyder, *Sketches from A Secret War: A Polish Artist's Mission to Liberate Soviet Ukraine* (New Haven: Yale University Press, 2005), 23–24.

[39] The Polishness of peasants and workers should not be assumed. Padraic Kenney claims "one could not speak of a single Polish working class in 1918 because regional identity was more powerful than national identity." Kenney, *Rebuilding Poland: Workers and Communists, 1945–1950* (Ithaca: Cornell University Press, 1997), 12.

[40] Janusz Żarnowski, *Listopad 1918* (Warsaw: Wydawnictwo Interpress, 1982), 151–157; Winson Chu, *The German Minority in Interwar Poland* (New York: Cambridge University Press, 2012), 63–113.

[41] USHMM RG-50.030.0769, Accession Number (AN): 2014.238.1, "Oral History Interview with Julian Kulski," 24:45–24:55.

[42] Paul Brykczynski calls this the "defeat of the civic nation." *Primed for Violence: Murder, Antisemitism and Democratic Politics in Interwar Poland* (Madison: University of Wisconsin Press, 2016), 131.

[43] Rogers Brubaker proposed the assimilationist–disassimilationist model noting that "ethnicity" is itself "deeply ambiguous." Brubaker, *Ethnicity without Groups* (Cambridge: Harvard

first independent Polish constitution, with weak executive powers keeping Piłsudski in check, was finalized in the shadow of these debates in 1921.

The Versailles Treaty that ended the First World War delineated Poland's western border, but this state creation method made it the target of its neighbors' revanchist jealousies. International Minorities Treaties also recognized "others" within Poland, Yugoslavia, Czechoslovakia, and Greece. New states had to recognize minority rights but older ones (including Weimar Germany) did not. The minority situation was exacerbated, ironically, by one of Piłsudski's first successes: contestation of the spreading Russian Revolution in the Polish–Soviet War (1919–20), which concluded with a Polish victory. That victory yielded territorial spoils for the Second Polish Republic: the acquisition of lands whose inhabitants were primarily Ukrainian and Belarussian speaking. This meant cool Polish–Soviet relations and potentially restive Slavic minorities.[44] Germans to the west were yet more hostile, as their 1918 defeat ushered in what Helmut Walser Smith calls a "nationalist age."[45] The Nazi *Führer*, Adolf Hitler, who became chancellor in 1933, regarded the Second Polish Republic's very existence as an affront to Germany. He called to overturn Versailles and railed about "protecting" the ethnic German minority in Poland.[46]

Internationally and domestically, the question of who was Polish resisted settlement. Polish Jews were part of cultural, intellectual, and political life in the new state and were, by law, citizens, though some religious Jews lived entirely separate lives.[47] Polish-Jewish politicians found a home in the Minorities Bloc, where they joined Germans, Belarussians, and Ukrainians.[48] Bloc success backfired: the first democratically elected president, Gabriel Narutowicz (1865–1922), was assassinated in December 1922.[49] Dmowski's

University Press, 2004), 132–146, quotation 136; Chu, *German Minority in Interwar Poland*, 63–64.

[44] Engelstein, *Russia in Flames*, 504–509.

[45] Helmut Walser Smith, *Germany, A Nation In Its Time: Before, During, and After Nationalism* (New York: W. W. Norton/Liveright, 2020), 292, 294.

[46] "Abuses [of the German minority in Poland were] often wildly exaggerated." Doris L. Bergen, "Instrumentalization of 'Volksdeutschen' in German Propaganda in 1939: Replacing/Erasing Poles, Jews, and Other Victims," *German Studies Review* 31, no. 3 (2008): 447; "Poland's Position on Minorities," *World Affairs* 97, no. 4 (1934): 204–205.

[47] Barbara Engelking, "Żydowskie wspólnoty w przededniu wybuchu wojny" in *Prowincja noc: Życie i zagłada Żydów w dystryckie warszawskim* (Warsaw: Wydawnictwo IFiS PAN, 2007), 26–29.

[48] Zionist founder Yitzhak Gruenbaum studied medicine and law at Warsaw University. Hava Eshkoli-Wagman, "Yishuv Zionism: Its Attitude to Nazism and the Third Reich Reconsidered," *Modern Judaism* 19, no. 1 (1999): 21–40.

[49] Narutowicz was not Jewish. He was Minister of Foreign Affairs and accepted the 1922 nomination; bloc support during a stalemate led to his election. He was seen therefore as a minority candidate and assassinated by an *Endek*. Brykczynski, *Primed for Violence*, 31, 100–103.

Endecja mob was enraged that minorities had not only voted – political participation they thought illegitimate – but helped elect the president.[50] This was not an auspicious start to twentieth-century Polish democracy.

Three presidents led Poland between 1918 and 1939, but politics floundered. A large number of prime ministers and coalition cabinets indicated "chronic" instability.[51] After Narutowicz's murder, Maciej Rataj of the Polish People's Party (Piast) acted as president before the election of socialist Stanisław Wojciechowski (1869–1953), who served for four years. Wojciechowski's administration was overshadowed by economic difficulties. Piłsudski ended the eight-year democratic experiment with a May 1926 coup. With "the enthusiastic approval of the political and social forces of the Polish Left," this provided a top-down solution to festering problems – but undemocratically and at the cost of human lives.[52] Piłsudski kept a president, Ignacy Mościcki (1867–1946), who stayed in the post until the Second World War. The coup did not save the economy, as the aging Piłsudski had little interest in finance. His philosemitism stabilized Polish-Jewish relations: since he favored a heavy state hand, it was possible to enforce his more tolerant views.[53] Piłsudski ruled the country as a benevolent authoritarian, allowing many aspects of the state created in 1918 to continue but without parliamentary institutions, which he rejected as "degraded" and "harmful."[54] Pilsudski's coup coddled the army and divided the country between his supporters and opponents, splitting and refashioning both the left and right.

The international situation brought the Second Polish Republic difficulties it did not need. Stalin's Soviet Union was still hostile, despite a 1932 non-aggression agreement. Hitler also negotiated a non-aggression pact with Poland but then placed Nazi Germany on an expansionist course, returning to military conscription in 1935. Piłsudski died of liver cancer months later.

---

[50] The Bloc's controversial nature had a zombie afterlife: the wartime exile government's National Council contained representatives of the major political parties but *not* the Bloc; a Jewish representative was eventually added. Anita J. Prażmowska, *Civil War in Poland, 1942–1948* (New York: Palgrave Macmillan, 2004), 5.

[51] Joseph Rothschild, *Piłsudski's Coup d'Etat* (New York: Columbia University Press, 1966), 48.

[52] Casualty numbers vary. Rothschild, *Piłsudski's Coup d'Etat*, vii; Robert Forczyk, *Case White: The Invasion of Poland 1939* (Oxford: Osprey Publishing, 2019), 34: 1,299 lives. Connelly, *From Peoples into Nations*, 385: 379 lives.

[53] Peter Hetherington, *Unvanquished: Joseph Pilsudski, Resurrected Poland, and the Struggle for Eastern Europe* (Houston: Pingora Press, 2012), 187; Kopstein and Wittenberg show that Jews voted with the government post-*coup*, and for minorities parties beforehand. Jeffrey S. Kopstein and Jason Wittenberg, "Who Voted Communist? Reconsidering the Social Bases of Radicalism in Interwar Poland," *Slavic Review*, Vol. 62, No. 1 (2003), 101–103; Anna Bikont, *The Crime and the Silence: Confronting the Massacre of Jews in Wartime Jedwabne* (New York: Farrar, Straus and Giroux, 2015), 40–41.

[54] Garlicki, *Piłsudski*, 137.

There was a massive outpouring of grief across Warsaw. Piłsudski left a country in turmoil, with aggressive western and eastern neighbors, and no obvious successor. That fall, Germany decreed its infamous Nuremberg Laws, stripping legal protections from 350,000 German Jews.[55] The precedent made antisemitism elsewhere sharper. Nazi virulence frightened the Polish-Jewish community and made them see mistreatment at home as the top of a slippery slope of Nazi-style discrimination.[56] The late 1930s were filled with ominous signs of future instability.

A "colonels' regime" of unelected leaders called *Sanacja* ran Poland from Warsaw after Piłsudski's death; they included President Mościcki and Edward Śmigły-Rydz (1886–1941), a Legionnaire who served as commander in chief. The colonels, unsurprisingly, modernized and re-equipped the army.[57] The economy lagged. Simultaneously, debates about Jews in Polish life came to a head with the introduction of "ghetto benches" segregating Polish-Jewish students, including at Warsaw University.[58] Polish universities had an increasingly antisemitic climate in the late 1930s.[59] Some Christian students protested in solidarity with their Jewish classmates, but Jewish student numbers declined.[60] University students and other youth were ready recruits for radical politics.[61] Ghetto benching was part of a wider nervousness about education and national political life. In a young and foundering society in economic straits, who deserved the dwindling available privileges, like spots at the top university?[62]

[55] Diemut Majer, *"Non-Germans" under the Third Reich: The Nazi Judicial and Administrative System in Germany and Occupied Eastern Europe, with Special Regard to Occupied Poland, 1939–1945* (Baltimore: Johns Hopkins University Press, 2003), 101–103.

[56] Szymon Rudnicki, "Anti-Jewish Legislation in Interwar Poland," in *Antisemitism and Its Opponents in Modern Poland* (Ithaca: Cornell University Press, 2005), 148, 153, 157.

[57] Forczyk claims Piłsudski stymied military reform and blames weapons obsolescence on economic difficulties, though the doctrine was updated by 1939. Forczyk, *Case White*, 55–73; Roger Moorhouse, *Poland 1939: The Outbreak of World War II* (New York: Basic Books, 2020), 56–59.

[58] Monika Natkowska, *Numerus clausus, getto ławkowe, numerus nullus, 'paragraf aryjski:' Antysemityzm na Uniwersytecie Warszawskim, 1931–1939* (Warsaw: Żydowski Instytut Historyczny IN-B, 1999), 141–160. See also Elissa Bemporad, *Legacy of Blood: Jews, Pogroms, and Ritual Murder in the Lands of the Soviets* (New York: Oxford University Press, 2019), 103–105.

[59] Natkowska, *Numerus clausus*, 160, 177.

[60] Jewish student numbers fell below 10% in 1937–1938. Israel Gutman, *Resistance: The Warsaw Ghetto Uprising* (Boston: Houghton Mifflin, 1994), 28.

[61] Endecja All-Poland Youth were part. Mikołaj Stanisław Kunicki, *Between the Brown and the Red: Nationalism, Catholicism, and Communism in 20th-Century Poland – The Politics of Bolesław Piasecki* (Athens: Ohio University Press, 2012), 11. Restrictions were introduced in April 1933 in Germany. Robert Gellately, *Backing Hitler: Consent and Coercion in Nazi Germany* (New York: Oxford University Press, 2001), 29.

[62] There were numerous antisemitic restrictions. The post-Piłsudski Camp of National Unity (*Obóz Zjednoczenia Narodowego, or "OZoN"*) proposed Jewish emigration in 1938. Natkowska, *Numerus clausus*, 167.

Though the new country was vulnerable in a Europe – and a world – fraught with economic, political, and cultural uncertainty, the view from Warsaw itself, where thorny interwar questions often found local, intimate solutions, was rosier. Warsaw housed the national government, the headquarters of the Polish army, the seat of the Polish Roman Catholic Church, and was a center of industry, finance, and culture. It was also the center of intelligentsia life and employment. A follower of Piłsudski, a soldier-turned-economist named Stefan Starzyński (1893–1939?) was the capital's last mayor, and an icon of the city's interwar transformation and the intelligentsia's multifaceted power. His biography indicates how the intelligentsia managed the Second Polish Republic and what the war took from them. Starzyński was born in Warsaw's Powiśle neighborhood into an impoverished gentry family.[63] The First World War made him a soldier, scattered his family, killed his father, got him imprisoned, and built his postwar career. Starzyński's politics were above all Piłsudski's, and he never quite put his insurgency years behind him.[64] Piłsudski got Starzyński his first civilian job at the Treasury Ministry, and Piłsudski's 1926 coup was good for his protégé.[65] In August 1934 the City Council appointed Starzyński mayor with enhanced executive powers.[66] He was an expert: a fixer. He accumulated advisers, enlarging Warsaw bureaucracy.[67] "Nobody," remembered his deputy Julian Kulski (1892–1976), "had any doubt that Starzyński was a man 'of the regime.'"[68]

Warsaw had spent the partitions as a provincial city in other states' peripheries, and the First World War under punishing occupations.[69] It was

---

[63] Drozdowski, *Stefan Starzyński*, 10–11; Marian Marek Drozdowski, "Stefan Starzyński – Żołnierz, Działacz Państwowy, Prezydent Warszawy" in *Wspomnienia o Stefanie Starzyńskim* (Warsaw: Państwowe Wydawnictwo Naukowe, 1982), 8–12.

[64] Drozdowski, *Stefan Starzyński*, 10–12; Aleksander Ivank, "Żołnierz Dobra i Honoru Polski," 80–85.

[65] The Left had little use for Starzyński, whom they saw as an establishment figure (he was), a militarist (he was), and tied to Piłsudski (he was). Norman Davies, *White Eagle, Red Star: The Polish-Soviet War, 1919–20* (New York: St. Martin's Press, 1972); Piotr Janus, *W Nurcie Polskiego Etatyzmu: Stefan Starzyński i Pierwsza Brygada Gospodarcza, 1926–1932* (Krakow: Wyd. Avalon, 2009), 113–114; Marian Marek Drozdowski, *Starzyński: Legionista, Polityk, Gospodarczy, Prezydent Warszawy* (Warsaw: Wyd. Iskry, 2006), 18–19; 32.

[66] Roman Tomczak and Zdzisław Jan Targowski, *Wspomnienia o Stefanie Starzyńskim*, 47; 94–95; 171–175.

[67] Warsaw bureaucracy was a "boys' club" of Legionnaires. Snyder, *Sketches from A Secret War*, 23–27.

[68] Julian Kulski, *Stefan Starzyński w mojej pamięci* (Warsaw: Państwowe Wyd. Naukowe, 1990), 69; Jacek Majchrowski, *Silni – zwarci – gotowi: Myśl polityczna Obozu Zjednoczenia Narodowego* (Warsaw: Państwowe Wyd. Naukowe, 1985).

[69] Main studies: Kauffman, *Elusive Alliance*; Lech Królikowski and Krzysztof Oktabiński, *Warszawa 1914–1920: Warszawa i okolice w latach walk o niepodległość i granice Rzeczypospolitej* (Warsaw: Wyd. Akademickie i Profesjonalne,

hopelessly outdated; Starzyński dragged it into the twentieth century.[70] He formed councils of technocrats, investors, economists, city planners, architects, artists, writers, and sculptors – Warsaw's intelligentsia.[71] He launched public works projects *à la* Franklin Roosevelt's concurrent "New Deal" in the United States.[72] His modernization efforts earned him re-election in 1938.[73] All this took Starzyński and his colleagues five years. In 1939 German military might would destroy it in four weeks before their eyes.

Operating in a space with profound linguistic, religious, and ethno-national diversity, the Warsaw elite wrestled for twenty years with the privileges and responsibilities of modern statehood. They ran aground against the central quandary of modern central European societies: states in this space could either be ethno-national projects *or* they could be large enough to achieve continental significance, but they could not be *both*. Polish intelligentsia attempted to square this circle. National minorities and radicals were the have-nots of this experiment: the international situation indicated they might not remain on the margins. In the center, though, were the profiteers: the intelligentsia, mellowing into statehood, expanding Polish arts and letters, absorbing and educating ambitious peasants and workers who joined them in leading Poland, and counting on their state's existence as a source of income, power, and influence.[74]

The Polish thinking classes became the Polish governing classes in 1918, explaining so many hyphenated careers. Interwar Warsaw was home to those whose lives had been happily interrupted by Polish statehood and who were rewarded with service on the government payroll.[75] There were thus a disproportionate number of minister-poets, painter-surgeons, student-activists, and Legionnaires-turned-bureaucrats. Polish cultural and social power and the Polish state were thus, as Nazi Germany observed, concentrated in a more or less coherent group. These people's lives would again be interrupted by the Nazi German invasion in 1939 and many would rehyphenate their lives, living both legal "above ground" existences and embracing forbidden "underground" opposition. The Nazi invaders viewed the Warsaw

2007); Krzysztof Dunin-Wąsowicz, *Warszawa w czasie pierwszej wojny światowej* (Warsaw: Państwowy Instytut Wydawniczy, 1974).

[70] He put 75% of the 1936 budget into transit and the riverfront, secured 1,462 new classrooms, revitalized parks, brought sewage, water, electricity, and gas to all districts and expanded hospitals, museums, and theaters. Kulski, *Stefan Starzyński*, 59; 73–82.

[71] Kulski, *Stefan Starzyński*, 59–60; 64.

[72] Unclear if FDR inspired Starzyński. Barbara Blumberg, *The New Deal and the Unemployed: The View from New York City* (Lewisburg: Bucknell University Press, 1979).

[73] Grażyna Woysznis-Terlikowska, *Wczoraj, dziś, jutro Warszawy* (Warsaw: Książka i Wiedza, 1950); Kulski, *Stefan Starzyński*, 64–65; Julian Kulski, *Z minionych lat życia, 1892–1945* (Warsaw: Państwowy Instytut Wydawniczy, 1982), 215; Norbert Konwinski, *The Mayor* (Posen, MI: Diversified Enterprises, 1978), 76.

[74] Żarnowski, *Listopad 1918*, 175.

[75] USHMM RG-50.030.0769, AN: 2014.238.1, "Interview with Julian Kulski," 10:27–11:06.

intelligentsia's twenty-year national sovereignty experiment as an impediment to German eastward expansion. The intelligentsia viewed the invasion as the theft of their state and attempted to reclaim it.

0.4   Approach and Methodology

The Warsaw intelligentsia profited uniquely from Polish independence and suffered uniquely from its destruction.[76] As the targets of early Nazi genocide, and because they were self-conscious victims capable of articulating their own experiences, what happened to them can illuminate much about human response to persecution and its effect on national communities and state projects. They have nevertheless not been the subject of their own study.[77] This work highlights the behavior of influential Polish Christians or "ethnic Poles" – no phrase is satisfactory in occupied Warsaw's complex mix – and a handful of others. Poland was the first wartime imperial conquest of Nazi Germany and Warsaw's occupation was similar to and different from others, both precedent and warning for occupiers and occupied.[78] Nazi persecution of Polish elites inspired but then departed from the Holocaust. The intelligentsia's city, Warsaw, remained within a single administrative entity, District Warsaw (*Distrikt Warschau*), under the exclusive control of Nazi Germany from its capitulation in late September 1939 until the last uprising's defeat in late 1944.[79]

---

[76] For many – especially peasants – national-political attachments were fluid and loyalty local. On borderlands: Winson Chu, *German Minority in Interwar Poland*, James Bjork, *Neither German nor Pole: Catholicism and National Indifference in a Central European Borderland* (Ann Arbor: University of Michigan Press, 2008), Kate Brown, *Biography of No Place: From Ethnic Borderland to Soviet Heartland* (Cambridge: Harvard University Press, 2004). On national commitments: Keely Stauter-Halsted, *The Nation in the Village: The Genesis of Peasant National Identity in Austrian Poland, 1848–1914* (Ithaca: Cornell University Press, 2001) and Rogers Brubaker, *Nationalism Reframed: Nationhood and the National Question in the New Europe* (New York: Cambridge University Press, 1996).

[77] These studies are the foundation: Tomasz Szarota's *Okupowanej Warszawy Dzień Powszedni* (Warsaw: Czytelnik, 1988) and Krzysztof Dunin-Wąsowicz's *Warszawa w latach 1939–1945* (Warsaw: Państwowe Wydawnictwo Naukowe, 1984). Dunin-Wąsowicz was an AB-Aktion orphan, a survivor-analyst. The third is Jan Gross's *Polish Society under German Occupation* (Princeton: Princeton University Press, 1979).

[78] Ronald Rosbottom, *When Paris Went Dark: The City of Light under German Occupation, 1940–1944* (Boston: Back Bay, 2014), Emily Greble, *Sarajevo, 1941–1945: Muslims, Christians, and Jews in Hitler's Europe* (Ithaca: Cornell University Press, 2011), and James Mace Ward, *Priest, Politician, Collaborator: Jozef Tiso and the Making of Fascist Slovakia* (Ithaca: Cornell University Press, 2013), Mark Mazower, *Inside Hitler's Greece: The Experience of Occupation, 1941–1944* (New Haven: Yale University Press, 1993), and Jozo Tomasevich, *War and Revolution in Yugoslavia: Occupation and Collaboration* (Stanford: Stanford University Press, 2001).

[79] For the General Government: Martin Winstone, *The Dark Heart of Hitler's Europe* (London: I. B. Tauris, 2015) and Gross, *Polish Society under German Occupation*.

These nationally conscious elites produced most of the sources undergirding this study. This is both problem and opportunity. Many were "participant-analysts" of events they described (another hyphenated role).[80] The difficulties of differentiating historical memory from history are exacerbated by the predominance of participants among Polish historians. Indeed, participant-analyst status is the hallmark of the Polish *inteligent*, whose social role was both to participate in politics and culture and interpret them. Elite survivors of the war and occupation created the material by which they and their society might be understood; they filtered events through their own hopes and prejudices. Interwar Poland was a young state and its franchise small, but stories of genocide and atrocity are always written as this one has been, by those who witnessed and survived it. Tales of heroism and cowardice, escapes, rescues, patriotism: uncorroborated anecdotes fill intelligentsia writings, impossible to verify. Some may be true to the letter, others might faithfully report fears and rumors, giving a flavor of the time.[81]

The intelligentsia were myopic about their own behavior – what group is not? Their comments on the peasantry and working classes are parsimonious.[82] Most were antisemites of one kind or another with few exceptions. Their understanding of what was happening outside Warsaw varied. Their sense of how much the world cared about their concerns was massively inflated. Achieving comfortable social, financial, and cultural positions during the Second Polish Republic, they were the profiteers of Polish independence. They were therefore predisposed to favor the resurrection of the Republic and the resumption of those privileges. Considering that, they were remarkably open with their criticisms of that state and creative in their reimagining of the Polish future.

There is no hard-and-fast schema for determining who engaged in what wartime behavior among the intelligentsia: widely utilized scales of collaboration and resistance or tripartite models including passivity or bystandership fit awkwardly onto Warsaw circumstances or onto the best analyses of Nazi imperialism.[83] Full-throated collaboration (sometimes called collaborationism),

Gross's thesis on how the viciousness of German exploitation prevented Polish collaboration is the enduring model; this explains its effects on the Warsaw elite.

[80] Like Władysław Bartoszewski's and Regina Hulewicz-Domańska's work; Tadeusz Manteuffel's history of the university *Uniwersytet Warszawski w latach wojny i okupacji: Kronika 1939/40–1944/45* (Warsaw: Uniwersytet Warszawski Imprint, 1948), and Tadeusz (Bór) Komorowski's *Armia Podziemna* (Warsaw: Wydawnictwo Bellona, 1994).

[81] Cf. Karen E. Fields and Barbara J. Fields, *Racecraft: The Soul of Inequality in American Life* (New York: Verso, 2014), 177–178.

[82] Jan Karski basically confined patriotism to intelligentsia circles, considering that the same sentiment "in the lower classes became chauvinism." USHMM RG-50.012.0044, AN: 1989.67.44, "Interview with Jan Karski," Part 2, 6:00–6:30.

[83] Poshek Fu's division of Shanghainese intellectuals into "passivists," resisters, and collaborators asks whether this "tripartite mode of response" might be a useful "point of

as Philippe Pétain advocated a year after this story begins, was adopted to avoid the violence in Poland, which French leaders wanted to spare their own people: the French collaborated to *avoid* Warsaw's fate; they deliberately embraced an attitude contrary to the Polish one.[84] The targeting of the intelligentsia, their economic and political marginalization, and the comprehensive economic exploitation of the wider Polish population made "passivity" or internal exile dangerous and complicated when it was possible. Moreover, such a retreat from public engagement was precisely an abandonment of the intelligentsia mission and those who attempted it of necessity depart this story.

Resistance – regarding the Nazi occupation as incompatible with their interests and rejecting, combatting, and undermining its initiatives and personnel – is therefore the category into which much intelligentsia behavior eventually fell of necessity. Nevertheless, the term is unhelpfully imprecise and laden with moral baggage. The umbrella of "resistance" covers Polish behaviors from insurgency, sabotage, and assassination to writing nostalgic poetry, and describes wildly varied levels of personal risk and much cooperation and accommodation of occupier preferences, sometimes for the moment, and sometimes for the *longue durée* in a world in which the future was uncertain. It cannot be completely avoided here because Varsovians themselves used the term, often intermingled with equally imprecise locutions like understanding themselves as "in the movement" (*w ruchu*) or "in the army" (*w armii*). In this study, the less fraught term "opposition" will be the default over "resistance" and the general Polish term "conspiracy" will be used for elite projects launched to deliberately undermine Nazi occupation.

Nazi German imperial policy, even Nazi policy in Warsaw, is impossible to conceive of in the singular: the best work on Nazi rule emphasizes its plurality, inconsistency, and ad hoc nature across Europe. The one clear consensus is on

---

reference" for occupied Europe. The model, which does not extend to armed resistance – a behavior Poles embraced – and in which the collaboration of intellectuals was actively sought and financed by Japanese authorities, does not apply in Warsaw. Fu, *Passivity, Resistance, and Collaboration*, 162. Analyses of "bystandership" often focus on German and Austrian populations; Austrian and German relationships to Nazi persecution are dramatically different than Polish ones: if Germans are "bystanders" to the Holocaust, Poles need another category. Victoria J. Barnett, *Bystanders: Conscience and Complicity during the Holocaust* (Westport: Praeger, 2000), 9–13.

[84] On the part of both occupier and occupied, as the Nazis demurred about "bringing Polish methods" to western or central Europe. Mark Mazower, *Hitler's Empire: How the Nazis Ruled Europe* (New York: Penguin Books, 2009), 103. See also: Peter Fritzsche, *An Iron Wind: Europe under Hitler* (New York: Basic Books, 2016), xvi-xvii; Robert O. Paxton, *Vichy France: Old Guard and New Order* (New York: Alfred A. Knopf, 1972), 357; Bryant, *Prague in Black*, 62; Sandra Ott, *Living with the Enemy: German Occupation, Collaboration, and Justice in the Western Pyrenees, 1940-1948* (New York: Cambridge University Press, 2017), 71; Brandys, *Warsaw Diary*, 147.

the brutality of Nazi behavior in Poland: the Third Reich was, paraphrasing Susan Carruthers, a singularly vicious overlord.[85] Peter Fritzsche writes of the experience of being buffeted by Nazi power as like that of walking into an "iron wind" that scattered those who endured it rather than uniting them.[86] Shelley Baranowski, considering the Nazi empire against earlier German ambitions, writes of "tensions," "debates," and infighting in defining occupation priorities.[87] Mark Mazower, bringing together the far-flung conquests of the Third Reich, acknowledges that "no positive vision" joined them and that "no single system of terror" dominated, the entire collection defined by an "almost limitless escalation in the use of force and a constant revision of rules and norms."[88] If one is to invoke the ideas of collaboration with or resistance to Nazi occupation, then, one must always qualify: collaboration *with what aspect* and *with which personnel* of that regime, *when*? Resistance to *what particular policy*, on *what timeline*? Indeed, oversimplifications of Nazi Germany's wartime behavior highlight its enormous war of conquest and the Holocaust against the Jewish people. For Varsovians, those "obvious" characteristics of Nazism were harder to see: in Poland's once and future capital the key thing the Nazi presence meant was defeat and persecution; what was at stake above all was Polish independence. This understanding was not wrong but powerfully right in local context. When Warsaw's elite wrangled with the question of what Nazi takeover meant and how they should respond, the question they were asking and answering was what Nazi takeover meant *for them*.

In interrogating Polish behavior, then, this work does not ask whether initiatives were motivated by acceptance or support of Nazi goals (collaboration) or rejection of them (resistance). Instead, it asks what individual Polish elites were doing, what they thought they were accomplishing in terms of the Polish nation-state project, and how their own peers responded; how Nazi occupation leadership, the wider Polish community, and Polish Jews reacted to these efforts provides context and occasionally clarification.

No one criterion predetermined intelligentsia engagement or its effectiveness. Age, gender, military service, wealth, and political and religious affiliation mattered.[89] Though many elite projects were deeply gendered, men and women often cooperated.[90] Intimate communities of trust mattered above

---

[85] Carruthers, *Good Occupation*, 1; Edelstein, *Occupational Hazards*, 49–50.

[86] Fritzsche, *Iron Wind*, xi.

[87] Shelley Baranowski, *Nazi Empire: German Colonialism from Bismarck to Hitler* (New York: Cambridge University Press, 2011), 238, 5, 259, 4.

[88] Mazower, *Hitler's Empire*, 6, 11.

[89] Karski, *Story of a Secret State*, 38.

[90] See: Ewa Bukowska, *Łączność, sabotaż, dywersja: Kobiety w Armii Krajowej* (London: Zarząd Główny Armii Krajowej, 1985); Wanda Sadurska, *Kobiety w łączności Komendy Głównej i Okręgu Warszawskiego ZWZ-AK* (Warsaw: Wydawnictwo Comandor, 2002); Anna Marcinkiewicz-Kaczmarczyk, *Kobiety w obronie Warszawy: Ochotnicza Legia*

all, as conspiracies were born amidst deadly persecution. Loyalty was necessary for survival. This intimacy requirement sustained community but not rigorous ideological purity. This study, in other words, examines Varsovians *qua intelligentsia*, reassembling Polish national-cultural life and creating the conditions for the resurrection of statehood under duress. Paraphrasing Chad Bryant's analysis of occupied Prague, this study examines Varsovian intelligentsia acting *hyper*-nationally.[91] Building off the insights of Vejas Gabriel Liulevicius' examination of German occupation in the East in the First World War, which reshaped German nationalism and identity, this study argues that the reverse was also true in the next war: the experience of *being occupied* by Germans and responding to it shaped the Polish national project.[92]

0.5   Organization

This story unfolds with four chapters on how Nazi Germany and its various personnel targeted the Warsaw intelligentsia in order to dismantle the Polish state and nation long term: Chapter 1 describes the September 1939 siege, which revealed German military brutality and provoked a Polish governance crisis. Chapter 2, "The Killing Years," explains the two-wave Nazi police genocide against the intelligentsia in 1939–1940 and its fallout. Chapter 3 places a spotlight on the main institution used to control intelligentsia behavior, Pawiak prison, and how it both symbolized but also channeled Polish elite opposition to Nazi rule. Chapter 4 considers the Warsaw Ghetto and how, when (and whether) Polish elites grappled with distinct Jewish victimhood in their midst.

The last five chapters consider how the intelligentsia responded to Nazi occupation, maintaining national and state traditions. Chapter 5, "Information Wars," is the opening case study of intelligentsia-built opposition, examining how clandestinely trafficked information sustained other conspiracies. Chapter 6 considers the other great success: underground education. Chapter 7 analyzes the Roman Catholic Church. "Matters of Faith" asks how Catholics behaved and why. It argues that a leadership crisis undermined the Church-wide response, but individual priests and lay Catholics were motivated by faith to significant activity. Chapter 8 begins a two-part examination of violence. This discussion is deliberately postponed, as much of the existing literature focuses on military activity and insurgency as a shorthand for resistance as a whole, which it was not: armed opposition projects remained fractured and hamstrung by Nazi reprisals until

---

Kobiet (1918–1922) i Wojskowa Służba Kobiet ZWZ-AK (1939–1945) (Warsaw: IPN, 2016).
[91] Bryant, *Prague in Black*, 4–6.
[92] Liulevicius focuses on *Ober Ost* but the point stands. See Liulevicius, *War Land*.

1942. Chapter 9, "Home Army on the Offensive," dissects mature insurgency in 1943–1944.

This study argues that the Nazi attack on the Polish nation-state project was a formidable one, but that the intelligentsia were able to contest and undermine parts of it. Polish nation-building endeavors focused on the intelligentsia mission narrowly thrived, those that focused on enfranchising a larger Polish community (generally excepting Polish Jews) sometimes succeeded but statehood, which required external support, was not achievable. Though many Polish elite ambitions were thwarted, the occupation of Warsaw was also a failure for Nazi Germany, which never pacified it thanks to the sustained – if varied – opposition of the intelligentsia.

***

Atrocities abounded during the Second World War. Warsaw hosted a number of the most dramatic, and its population endured persecutions that most twentieth-century peoples could not imagine let alone survive. The cumulative effect was traumatic and numbing, especially regarding the suffering of "others." City elites nevertheless believed that their experiences were vital to preserving a Polish nation state, infusing their behavior with purpose and performance.

What happened in Warsaw *was* special, and it was exceptional in Poland and exceptional in Europe. There are parallels with other places at other moments, and Varsovians were deeply conscious – even obsessed – with historical precedent. Though Leningrad was besieged longer, London and Belgrade bombarded by more *Luftwaffe* aircraft, Stalingrad and Moscow and Kiev the site of larger pitched battles, the accumulation of traumas in Warsaw, the length of Nazi occupation, and the sustained opposition despite the severity of repression, was unique even in the depths of twentieth-century violence.[93] What happened in Warsaw was also, peculiarly, never just about Warsaw, a mid-size city in the middle of a continent, the capital of a state that flickered in and out of existence. In a strange consensus, the Warsaw intelligentsia, the Nazi German occupation, and even the Soviet Union, which would claim the city at war's end, agreed that Warsaw was crucial to the control of east central Europe. Varsovians saw their conduct as important on a much larger stage. They may have been wrong on an individual level, but they behaved as if their actions were of grave historical moment, as if lives hung in the balance. They turned out to be right.

---

[93] Connelly, *From Peoples into Nations*, 450, 441. (Japanese-occupied Shanghai was held longer but its most intense phase of occupation began in 1941).

1

Warsaw Besieged

September 1939

When the Wehrmacht crossed the Polish border before dawn on September 1, 1939, a mere 200 miles of open countryside separated Warsaw from its enemy's advance guard. Varsovians had hours before the German Luftwaffe appeared in the sky and little knowledge of what lay ahead. In the fight that month, the intelligentsia joined their neighbors, trapped in the besieged capital: Luftwaffe bombers and Wehrmacht artillery did not distinguish targets based on their national-cultural role. Unlike future persecutions in which the intelligentsia would be singled out, the 1939 siege – and the 1944 uprising – obliged the intelligentsia to share others' fate. This shared experience was vitally important for elite behavior.

Despite scant consideration by military historians, the siege framed the war and occupation.[1] Varsovians discovered many things before capitulation. Most important was that their Nazi German enemy was fighting a total war for *Lebensraum* from which civilians would not be spared.[2] Poles also learned that their allies were feeble and their eastern neighbor hostile. Britain and France declared war but stayed outside the conflict, while the Soviet Union joined the German invasion from the east, complicating defense. Warsaw was politically isolated and physically surrounded, with weak-willed friends and aggressive neighbors.

Seismic shifts occurred in Warsaw and within Polish society. Prewar political parties, social classes, and ethnic groups cooperated under siege, blurring old divisions and creating new relationships; some of these were fleeting and others durable. Boundaries between "civilian" and "military" roles eroded: Varsovians did not have the privilege of observing their army's successful defense or the luxury of following a war elsewhere. Instead, city defense was hastily planned, required civilian contributions, and caused significant loss of life.

The national government evacuation on September 4–5, 1939 and of army and religious leadership shortly thereafter made a devastating impression. Public

---

[1] Excepting Forczyk's *Case White* and Moorhouse's *Poland 1939*.

[2] This spiked violence immediately, unlike spaces Germany never colonized, Cf. Alexander Prusin, *Serbia under the Swastika: A World War II Occupation* (Urbana: University of Illinois Press, 2017), 158; Mazower, *Inside Hitler's Greece*, 18, 23.

"servants" and soldiers escaped eastward. Those who remained, like Mayor Stefan Starzyński and his deputy Julian Kulski, or leaders like Wacław Lipiński (1896–1949) and Janusz Regulski (1887–1983), who organized defenses, were vital. Starzyński was of oversized importance against the backdrop of a state in flight. After evacuation, the Second Polish Republic was not the object of straightforward nostalgia: independence was mourned but not the "colonels' regime" that took flight.[3] In the absence of government and army leadership, Warsaw held out against the Wehrmacht for weeks. The stand failed, but it forged an intense Varsovian camaraderie, imbuing in them a sense of heroic – and unique – struggle. The intelligentsia shared siege-time suffering and recorded it for posterity, often tinging it with pathos. A post-1939 identity crystallized: Varsovians were people who defended themselves. The siege of Warsaw became the benchmark of suffering and violence against which its inhabitants measured later experience.[4]

1.1   Best-Laid Plans

In order to understand what Warsaw endured in 1939, one must understand the military campaign in which it was entangled. The campaign's speed exacerbated its effects and revealed crucial Polish weaknesses. Poland had two interrelated problems on which Nazi Germany capitalized in 1939: indefensible borders and weak diplomacy.[5] Interwar diplomacy under Foreign Minister Józef Beck (1894–1944) attempted to play Nazi Germany and the Soviet Union off one another while courting allies, mainly France and Great Britain.[6] The Second Polish Republic anticipated attack from the east or west. Few anticipated 1939, which involved both. In August 1939, the Nazi and Soviet foreign ministers surprised Europe with a "defensive" agreement, the Molotov–Ribbentrop Pact, dividing Poland between them.[7] At the last moment Poland secured formal guarantees from Britain and promises from France in case of German aggression.[8]

---

[3] Prażmowska claims it "left the field open for a new leadership to emerge." Prażmowska, *Civil War*, 2.

[4] Marian Porwit (1895–1988) served on the General Staff, participated in the defense, and became a German POW (*Obrona Warsawy wrzesień 1939 r.: wspomnienia i fakty* (Warsaw: Czytelnik, 1979)): a participant-analyst.

[5] Polish government "defiance" is often the explanation for Nazi brutality against Poles. Though the Second Polish Republic's refusal to accommodate Hitler provoked his rage, long-term intelligentsia defiance sustained it. Connelly, *From Peoples into Nations*, 465.

[6] Local allies were notoriously difficult for the Second Polish Republic and other new states to secure, since these "miniature Habsburg empires" had substantial minorities and Poland, Yugoslavia, Romania, Hungary, and Czechoslovakia stoked irredentist claims against one another. Connelly, *Peoples into Nations*, 364.

[7] Halik Kochanski, *The Eagle Unbowed: Poland and the Poles in the Second World War.* (Cambridge: Harvard University Press, 2012), 46–48.

[8] Jonathan Walker, *Poland Alone: Britain, SOE, and the Collapse of the Polish Resistance, 1944* (Gloucestershire: Spellmount Publishers, 2008), 20, 23; Jan Karski, *The Great Powers*

Poland's allies-dependent strategy fell apart before war began. The Polish Army (Wojsko Polskie, WP) paused mobilization at western insistence in late August, hoping to avoid "antagonizing" a volatile Hitler. This last appeasement was as effective as the previous ones and emboldened the *Führer*, indicating his opponents lacked nerve. Mobilization schedules are always sensitive, but the summer timing and underdeveloped Polish road and rail system snarled highways and train stations with soldiers. Crucial units were "secretly" mobilized (secret from the British and French) and moved to their billets.[9] Britain and France did declare war on Nazi Germany on September 3, 1939, two days after the German invasion, to wild celebration across the capital.[10] Unfortunately, these declarations devolved into a "phony war" without the aggression against Germany that Polish planning required.[11]

Geographically, Poland had difficult borders. The Treaty of Versailles drew the long western border, and 1939 was the first time it was contested.[12] International compromise gave Poland an arm of land extending to the Baltic Sea at Gdańsk, surrounded by German territory. This "Polish Corridor" was contentious and Gdańsk ("Danzig" to Germans) a "free" city owned by neither state. The splitting of Germany allowed the Wehrmacht to invade Poland from two sides without leaving its own territory in 1939.[13] Polish military planners opted for a "long border" defense with WP positions as far west as possible, extending understaffed units beyond their capacities. This decision was based on "two decades of shortsightedness" and a misunderstanding of how German combat mobility was developing.[14]

Nazi Germany understood these circumstances and had a hand in creating them. The German invasion, Case White (*Fall Weiss*), exploited Polish vulnerabilities. Walther von Brauchitsch (1881–1948) commanded the Wehrmacht in 1939, and he and Chief of the General Staff Franz Halder (1884–1972) enthusiastically carried out Hitler's orders. They eagerly reclaimed territory "lost" to Poland by Versailles.[15] Brauchitsch's army groups moved with unprecedented speed through WP defenses and swallowed western Poland, meeting across the

---

and Poland from Versailles to Yalta (Lanham: Rowman & Littlefield, 2014), 209–217; 261–268.

[9] Karski, *Story of a Secret State*, 3; Forczyk, *Case White*, 118, 121.

[10] Władysław Bartoszewski, *1859 dni Warszawy* (Krakow: Wydawnictwo Znak, 1974), 25–26.

[11] Victor Davis Hanson, *The Second World Wars: How the First Global Conflict Was Fought and Won* (New York: Basic Books, 2017), 15, 29.

[12] The eastern border was set by the 1921 Treaty of Riga. Davies, *White Eagle, Red Star*.

[13] With assistance from the Slovak Republic, avenging the earlier Polish seizure of Cieszyn. Ward, *Priest, Politician, Collaborator*, 158–162.

[14] Steven Zaloga and Victor Madej, *The Polish Campaign 1939* (New York: Hippocrene Books, 1985), 20–27.

[15] "Now, there was no sign of hesitation." Ian Kershaw, *Hitler: A Biography* (New York: W. W. Norton & Company, 2008), 483.

Vistula River behind Warsaw.[16] Army Group North, commanded by General Fedor von Bock (1880–1945), sent Georg von Küchler's Third Army to Warsaw. Army Group South, commanded by General Gerd von Rundstedt (1875–1953), sent Colonel General Johannes Blaskowitz's Eighth Army to Warsaw.[17] The Tenth Army under Artillery General Walther von Reichenau marched through Łódź to meet the Third Army in Warsaw.

These armies were well commanded, mobile, and supplemented with Luftwaffe support. Their internal communication was remarkably sophisticated. Aircraft and fast-moving light tanks reinforced each other to overwhelm Polish units, scattering them and advancing before they regrouped.[18] The commanders – von Bock, von Rundstedt, Blaskowitz, von Reichenau – were First World War veterans and went on to spectacular field victories in France and the Soviet Union. Their fast-paced, coordinated air-armor assaults were later dubbed *Blitzkrieg* or "lightning war," though military historians fret over whether 1939 was the genuine phenomenon.[19] Terminology aside, Wehrmacht speed was vital to victory: Polish defensive planning relied on its allies' intervention and desperately needed time.

Polish defenses were directed by the WP's commander in chief, Marshal Edward Śmigły-Rydz (1886–1941). Śmigły-Rydz had fought in Piłsudski's Legions and risen through the WP, becoming its commander and one of the country's leaders after Piłsudski's death in 1935. He ruled in uniform in the quasi-democratic, quasi-authoritarian twilight of the interwar alongside Ignacy Mościcki, the last president. Śmigły-Rydz's headquarters were in Warsaw, and he lost contact with border units once the invasion began.[20]

The Polish defensive plan, Plan Z (*Plan Zachód*), spread five armies along the western border with slim interior reserves.[21] The plan was to stall the enemy and

---

[16] William Russ, *Case White: The German Army in the Polish Campaign – September 1939* (Point Pleasant: Winged Hussar Publishing, 2017), 7–13; Moorhouse, *Poland 1939*, 32.

[17] Jochen Böhler, *Auftakt zum Vernichtungskrieg: Die Wehrmacht in Polen 1939* (Frankfurt: Fischer Taschenbuch Verlag, 2006), 25–36.

[18] Hanson, *Second World Wars*, 79–80; Max Boot, *War Made New: Weapons, Warriors, and the Making of the Modern World* (New York: Penguin, 2006), 224–225.

[19] "Blitzkrieg" was coined by *Time* magazine. Karl-Heinz Frieser claims *Fall Weiss* was not Blitzkrieg and the Polish army "not an equal foe." Since the French armies were also unequal the distinction is useless. Karl-Heinz Frieser, *The Blitzkrieg Legend: The 1940 Campaign in the West* (Annapolis: Naval Institute Press, 2013), 18–19. Whether Case White was Blitzkrieg is less important than whether it was achieved through air-armor assaults and speed, with consequent psychological advantage. It was. For what he thinks should rather be called *Bewegungskrieg*, see Robert M. Citino's *Quest for Decisive Victory: From Stalemate to Blitzkrieg in Europe, 1899–1940* (Lawrence: University Press of Kansas, 2002).

[20] Zaloga and Madej, *Polish Campaign 1939*, 41–45; 127; Forczyk, *Case White*, 66, 225, 244.

[21] *Polskie Siły Zbrojne w II Wojnie Światowej. Tom I: Kampania wrześniowa* (London: Wyd. Instytut Historyczny im. Gen. Sikorskiego, 1954); Michael A. Peszke, *Polish Underground Army, the Western Allies, and the Failure of Strategic Unity in World War II* (Jefferson: McFarland, 2005) and *Battle for Warsaw, 1939–1944* (New York: Columbia University Press, 1995).

then counterattack – a "hold-win-win" strategy against what turned out to be two opponents. (Counteroffensives never materialized.)[22] For the "hold" portion, Modlin Army protected Warsaw from the north. Below it, General Tadeusz Kutrzeba's (1886–1947) Poznań Army defended western Poznania and General Juliusz Rómmel's (1881–1967) Łódź Army, central Poland. Two new armies – Lublin Army and Warsaw Army – were formed on September 8, 1939 to shield the capital but were not part of the original vision; the WP had not anticipated defending Warsaw itself.[23] Rómmel received charge of Warsaw Army after his Łódź Army collapsed.[24]

Warsaw had anticipated war for years (Figure 1.1). Mayor Stefan Starzyński was cautious and his Legion days never far behind him; he was always preparing for conflict. A mandatory national reserve system cycled all the country's able-bodied men through the army, and its

Figure 1.1 Civilians walk and bicycle past a business protected by sand bags in besieged Warsaw, September 1939.
United States Holocaust Memorial Museum, Julien Bryan Archive, Photograph Number 47396.

---

[22] Forczyk, *Case White*, 48.
[23] Paweł Wieczorkiewicz, *II Wojna Światowa* (Warsaw: Bellona, 2010), 23; Porwit, *Obrona warszawy wrzesień 1939 r.*, 123–134.
[24] Forczyk, *Case White*, 260–261.

intelligentsia through the reserve officer corps, and paramilitaries, shooting clubs, and women's auxiliaries were popular.[25] In the late 1930s the WP emplaced new anti-aircraft batteries in Warsaw.[26] In 1937 the Defense Ministry offered air defense courses (*obrona przeciwlotnicza*, OPL), and 150,000 people had completed them nationally by 1938. Deputy Mayor Julian Kulski, also a Legionnaire, led civilian preparations.[27] Women were encouraged to shop carefully and not hoard food; men in trench coats put down their briefcases and dug anti-tank ditches alongside those in uniform.[28] Schoolchildren performed air raid drills and apartment blocks designated a *komendant* – the custodian or an enthusiastic veteran volunteered – to report to municipal authorities.

1.2   War Arrives

Case White unfolded dramatically. The Luftwaffe targeted military infrastructure and civilians, especially on highways into and out of Warsaw along which Poles fled before the Wehrmacht.[29] Motorized German units made for the interior, while Polish defenders struggled to communicate among themselves as forces retreated, frustrating counterattacks.[30] Jan Karski, a second lieutenant in the cavalry, remembered the collapse with bitterness: "we were now no longer an army, a detachment, or a battery, but individuals wandering collectively toward some wholly indefinite goal. We found the highways jammed ...[31]" His war had only lasted "about twenty minutes."[32] Polish soldiers like Karski congregated east of the Vistula where they were caught by Soviet forces, sometimes before engaging the Germans. The Soviet invasion on September 17 "engraved itself indelibly into Polish memory:" the country's enemies cooperated

[25] Forczyk, *Case White*, 46–63; Katarzyna Minczykowska, *Cichociemna Generał Elżbieta Zawacka "Zo," 1909-2009* (Warsaw: Oficyna Wydawnicza Rytm, 2014), 26–31; 55–57; USHMM RG-50.012.0044, AN: 1989.67.44, "Interview with Jan Karski," Part 1, 26:54.

[26] Forczyk, *Case White*, 62–63.

[27] Joanna Urbanek, *Lęk i Strach: Warszawiacy wobec zagrożeń Września 1939 r.* (Warsaw: ASPRA, 2009), 34–35; Instytut Historii PAN, *Cywilna obrona Warszawa we wrześniu 1939* (Warsaw: Państwowe Wydawnictwo Naukowe, 1965), 239–246; USHMM RG-50.030.0769, AN: 2014.238.1, "Interview with Julian Kulski [Jr.]," 6:18–6:28. This interview is not with the deputy mayor, Julian Spistosław Kulski (1892–1976), but with his son, Julian Eugeniusz Kulski (b. 1929), who discussed his father in postwar interviews.

[28] According to Julien Bryan's *Siege*, "soldiers conscripted civilians on the streets." Bryan, *Siege*, newsreel (Los Angeles: RKO Radio Pictures, 1940).

[29] Poles were the first recipients of German tactics. Wieczorkiewicz, *II Wojna Światowa*, 28–29.

[30] Kochanski, *Eagle Unbowed*, 62.

[31] Karski, *Story of a Secret State*, 7–8.

[32] USHMM RG-50.012.0044, AN: 1989.67.44, "Interview with Jan Karski," Part 2, 3:00–4:35.

better than its allies, paving the way for a fourth partition of Poland. The public mood darkened, though the army fought on.[33]

Varsovians held out, nervously following campaigning. Polish soldiers fought ferociously, surprising Germans, and providing a rallying-cry for their countrymen. German soldiers committed atrocities against Poles they had been primed to hate, seeing "bandits" and "irregulars" everywhere. Pockets of resistance lingered, despite the pace of the German advance. On the Baltic Sea's Hel Peninsula fighting continued through the month, with 180 men enduring continuous bombardment before finally surrendering on October 2.[34] On September 9, 1939 Polish forces counterattacked at the Battle of the Bzura for ten days, costing the Wehrmacht 8,000 dead. Polish units seemed everywhere in retreat; still the Germans were not victorious.[35] Warsaw became the campaign's main contest, despite Case White's and Plan Z's neglect of it. Attacking it cost more time than Wehrmacht leadership planned. Nazi propaganda disguised delays, but Dresden diarist and German-Jewish intellectual Victor Klemperer realized that "the war [wa]s being covered up ... flags are not being put out."[36] Something *had* gone awry, and Warsaw was at the heart of it.

The capital was the largest city in Poland with 1.5 million inhabitants. It was WP headquarters, an air force base, the seat of government and the Catholic Church, and the country's transportation hub.[37] The motorized Wehrmacht needed its transit links to operate. Polish soldiers gathered there and German units moved around the city, trapping them inside.[38] The Wehrmacht, like every army before it, was squeamish about besieging a fortified city: a siege risked squandering Case White's speed and giving Poland's allies time to rally.[39] It also required heavy gunnery, which took time to arrive. The Luftwaffe "softened" the city from the air, hoping it would surrender. It did not. By September 7, "a third

---

[33] Kulski, *Z minionych lat życia*, 239; Edward Kubalski, *Niemcy w Krakowie: Dziennik, I IX 1939 - 18 I 1945* (Krakow: Austeria, 2010) 29, 31. Only the Greeks also endured a substantive double invasion. Mazower, *Inside Hitler's Greece*, 16.

[34] *Museum of the Second World War: Catalogue of the Permanent Exhibition* (Gdansk: Muzeum II Wojny Światowej, 2016), 40–45.

[35] Forczyk, *Case White*, 239; Nicholas Stargardt, *The German War: A Nation under Arms, 1939–1945: Citizens and Soldiers* (New York: Basic Books, 2015), 28–31; 45; 47; BAMA RH 53–23/10, Zum Kriegstagebuch des Grenzwachtabschnitts-Kommandos (Verband v. Maltitz) A. L. F--, 3. Sept. 1939, Tagesbefehl nr. 9.

[36] Goebbels promised speedy victory. Victor Klemperer, *I Will Bear Witness: A Diary of the Nazi Years, 1933–1941* (New York: Random House, 1998), 8, 165, 264. 309.

[37] On protecting road and rail: BAMA RH 53–23/10, Zum Kriegstagebuch des Grenzwachtabschnitts-Kommandos (Verband v. Maltitz) A. L. F--, 10. Sept. 1939, Tagesbefehl Nr. 18; GUS RP, *Mały Rocznik Statystyczny: 1939* (Warsaw: Nakładem Głównego Urzędu Statystycznego, 1939), 188–190; 197.

[38] OKH estimated Warsaw held 100,000 soldiers. Russ, *Case White*, 100–102, 166, 175–176.

[39] Citino, *Quest for Decisive Victory*, 76–79; Kenneth Macksey, *Why the Germans Lose at War: The Myth of German Military Superiority* (London: Greenhill Books, 1996), 78–79.

of the city [was] already a shambles" and "the situation was far more serious than the meager censored news reports ... indicated."[40] On September 8, the newly created Warsaw Army erected defenses.[41] On September 13, the Luftwaffe targeted fortifications and public utilities, killing civilians. From mid-month Warsaw was continuously bombarded, increasingly with incendiaries.[42] Warsaw Army's soldiers launched raids, looking to break out. Tentative German assaults on the Modlin fortress and the western Mokotów neighborhood were pushed back by Polish defenders; Poles emplaced guns and tank traps as the Wehrmacht dallied.[43] When the Battle of the Bzura collapsed, however, German forces refocused on encircling the capital and launched a multi-day bombardment culminating on September 25, 1939: "horrible Monday."[44] A Wehrmacht lieutenant across the Vistula in Praga watched assembling artillery, sure that "the destruction of Warsaw is in preparation."[45] German artillery reduced the city to rubble and was followed by infantry advance into the western suburbs of Ochota and Czyste. By late September Polish soldiers were low on ammunition and civilians out of food and water. The WP knew a ceasefire was necessary, but Starzyński delayed as long as he could; on September 28, 1939 Tadeusz Kutrzeba, Warsaw Army's deputy commander, capitulated to Johannes Blaskowitz of the German Eighth Army.[46] Remaining Polish defenders – around 150,000 men – reluctantly assembled as prisoners of war (POWs), and the triumphant Wehrmacht marched into Warsaw on September 30, 1939.[47] Germans took the city's capitulation as a de facto Polish surrender.[48]

Inside the city Case White's precise operational goals dissolved into horror. Warsaw felt German bombs weeks before anyone in Wehrmacht uniform

---

[40] Julien Bryan, *Siege*, newsreel.

[41] Marian Porwit dates the defense from 14 to 21 September; Zaremba dates siege from 15 September. Porwit, *Obrona warszawy wrzesień 1939 r.*, 123–134; Zygmunt Zaremba, *"Żeby chociaż świat wiedział:" Obrona warszawy 1939; Powstanie sierpniowe 1944* (Warsaw: Bellona, 2010), 81–82.

[42] Aerial bombardment paled before later Anglo-American efforts. Boot, *War Made New*, 270–273.

[43] Forczyk, *Case White*, 281–285.

[44] The Wehrmacht dropped leaflets claiming that "continued defense is pointless." Instytut Historii PAN, *Cywilna obrona*, 121–122; Halina Regulska, *Dziennik z oblężonej Warszawy: Wrzesień – październik – listopad 1939 r.* (Warsaw: Instytut Wydawniczy Pax, 1978), 101.

[45] BAMA MSg/2/2924 Regiments-Nachrichtenzug: I. R. 94 im Polenfeldzug, 20.9.1939, 23.

[46] Russ, *Case White*, 246–254. Moorhouse, *Poland, 1939*, 294–6.

[47] Joanna Urbanek, *Codzienność w cieniu terroru: okupacja niemiecka w Polsce, 1939–1945* (Gdańsk: Muzeum II Wojny Światowej, 2014), 15–16.

[48] BAMA MSg/2/2924 Regiments-Nachrichtenzug: I. R. 94 im Polenfeldzug, 27.9.1939, 24–25; Cf. the surrender of Athens in 1941: Mazower, *Inside Hitler's Greece*, 5. On the importance of clear defeat and surrender – absent in the Polish case – for postwar stability, see Gregory P. Downs, *After Appomattox: Military Occupation and the Ends of War* (Cambridge: Harvard University Press, 2015), 11–37.

appeared on its streets: modern war was faceless. The Luftwaffe hit the
outskirts the first day, with Polish fighters contesting the attack.[49]
Reporting for duty on September 1, Colonel Julian Janowski (1886–1970)
persuaded a taxi driver to drive him to border guard headquarters. He and
the cabby bailed out as bombers passed overhead.[50] Varsovians gawked
from balconies and rooftops, but air attack put tremendous strain on
civilians.[51] Strategists of aerial bombardment had warned about what the
Luftwaffe achieved in Warsaw, the first time the technique was implemented widely in Europe.[52] Though preparations were ready – bunkers,
antitank ditches, antiaircraft stations, a nighttime blackout – Luftwaffe
superiority disturbed civilians and soldiers alike.[53] The war that arrived
was not precisely the war anticipated: Poland's allies failed to arrive, its
armies could not keep the Wehrmacht from the capital; families ran out of
food after being told it was unpatriotic to hoard it, and civilians hesitated
to buy gas masks when they appeared for sale in shops.[54] September was
full of unhappy surprises.

Overcrowding created pernicious problems. Refugees accumulated even as
some native Varsovians fled eastward. University students arrived for the fall
semester, unsure if classes were going forward. (They would, but underground). Those hoping to fight and those hoping to be defended assumed
Warsaw would hold out.[55] Because of the poor state of Poland's road and rail,
anyone going anywhere in September 1939 went *through* Warsaw. Gasoline
couldn't be had after a week, and abandoned vehicles and goods accumulated,
stuffing black markets.[56] The poet Aleksander Wat, his wife, Ola, and their
baby, Andrzej, escaped to Lwów (L'viv).[57] Socialist activist and novelist Wanda
Wasilewska (1905–64), who had lived in the capital since the mid-1930s,
headed east, eventually to Moscow where she helped Stalin build a postwar
Polish communist government, a role made possible precisely by her absence

---

[49] Forczyk, *Case White*, 148–151.

[50] Janowski was deputy border guard commander. He became Walerian Czuma's deputy in
the Warsaw Defense Command (Dowództwo Obrony Warszawy) and organized left-
bank defenses. He was an officer in three states' armies and a POW to two more. *Obrona
Warszawy 1939 we wspomnieniach*, ed. Mieczysław Cieplewicz and Eugeniusz Kozłowski
(Warsaw: Wyd. Ministerstwa Obrony Narodowej, 1984), 139–142.

[51] Porwit, *Obrona warszawy*, 28; Urbanek, *Lęk i Strach*, 73–77.

[52] Beau Grosscup, *Strategic Terror: The Politics and Ethics of Strategic Bombardment*
(London: Zed Books, 2006), 17–19, 25, 27.

[53] Forczyk, *Case White*, 155.

[54] Urbanek, *Lęk i Strach*, 45.

[55] Jadwiga Krawczyńska, *Zapiski Dziennikarki Warszawskiej, 1939–1947* (Warsaw:
Państwowy Instytut Wydawniczy, 1971), 33, 284.

[56] Wacław Lipiński, *Dziennik: wrześniowa obrona Warszawy 1939 r.* (Warsaw: Instytut
Wydawniczy Pax, 1989), 63.

[57] Ola Watowa, *Wszystko co najważniejsze...*, (Warsaw: Agora, 2011), 30–33.

from Warsaw during the war.[58] There was a distinctly leftwing aspect to the intelligentsia refugee wave, aware as they were of Hitler's intense persecution of communists and socialists. Many Polish Jews took the same route, willing to take their chances further east rather than face Nazi antisemitism.

Provincial government employees and local leadership from western Poland abandoned homes and arrived in the capital with what they could carry. Their flight reduced government function, preventing the coordination of civilian and military traffic.[59] They claimed they were pursued by murderous police gangs – an outlandish story that turned out to be true. Halina "Halszka" Donimirska (1918–2008) worked for the National Forestry Bureau. Her office in an uproar, she went to Warsaw to find out what was going on, joining a crowd on foot. Donimirska and her family, who held German and Polish citizenships, were thrown into the war's racialized violence: her brothers refused to serve in the Wehrmacht and were labelled deserters, and her surname appeared on detention lists that Nazi police carried. Warsaw's elite would soon learn more about these lists. Donimirska stayed in Warsaw and joined the underground as a nurse.[60] Aleksander Kamiński ("Hubert," 1903–78), a thirty-six-year-old teacher and scoutmaster, left his family outside Katowice and made for Warsaw by bicycle.[61] He was organizing boy scout relief efforts before the surrender.

Donimirska and Kamiński joined the capital intelligentsia: observing, recording, and organizing responses to the siege. Crowding bred unrest, violence, and disease. Government ministries, grammar schools, and parks became makeshift campsites for frightened mobs. Priests said Mass, heard confessions, and administered last rites. Spontaneous religiosity welled up from a culturally Catholic society, and diarists remembered hymns sung in darkness.[62] Frightened people thronged to sturdier buildings, the wealthy cheek-by-jowl with their neighbors in cellars and stairwells "alongside the coal and potatoes."[63] Bombardment set everything alight. Food shortages required queuing endlessly in the streets

---

[58] The firebrand daughter of Leon Wasilewski, a PPS colleague of Piłsudski's, who embraced communism. Marian Marek Drozdowski and Andrzej Zahorski, *Historia Warszawy* (Warsaw: PWN, 1981), 290–291; Marci Shore, *Caviar and Ashes: A Warsaw Generation's Life and Death in Marxism, 1918–1968* (New Haven: Yale University Press, 2009), 123–125, 154.

[59] Piotr Derdej, *Westerplatte – Oksywie – Hel 1939* (Warsaw: Wyd. Bellona, 2009); Halina Donimirska-Szyrmerowa, *Był taki świat … : Mój, Wiek XX* (Warsaw: Wyd. Cyklady, 2007), 249–254.

[60] Donimirska-Szyrmerowa, *Był taki świat*, 245, 249, 253.

[61] Aleksander Kamiński, *Zośka i Parasol* (Warsaw: Wydawnictwo Iskry, 2009), 35.

[62] Urbanek, *Lęk i Strach*, 30; Miron Białoszewski, *A Memoir of the Warsaw Uprising*. Trans. Madeline G. Levine (New York: New York Review Books), 2014, 108–112, 123, 157. Jacek Leociak, *Text in the Face of Destruction: Accounts from the Warsaw Ghetto Reconsidered* (Warsaw: Żydowski Instytut Historyczny, 2004), 219.

[63] Of 30,000 residential buildings, 69.1 percent were brick and 30.5 percent wooden or plaster. Porwit, *Obrona Warszawy*, 36; Regulska, *Dziennik*, 83.

outside shops that still had anything for sale. According to Jadwiga Krawczyńska, a journalist holed up in a friend's apartment:

> The streets became a massive throng of crowds ... the inhabitants of Warsaw made every effort to stock up their houses and apartments with foodstuffs and various provisions. This hoarding of supplies became a downright mania ... The better part of these supplies burned in the September fires ... At the same time, an unexpected wave of refugees from the western and northern regions of the country fell on Warsaw ... It was a massive wave of panic: despairing castaways from the countryside and the little towns, fleeing ahead of the Germans. Disoriented, unhappy, helpless people wandering around, looking for any sort of shelter, they camped out in public squares and city parks. Saxon Square looked like a garbage pit ... It was not just a hideous sight, but a gigantic difficulty for the city ... With each passing day securing food became more difficult, and sanitary conditions got worse. The hospitals were filled to capacity, the doctors working around the clock. A genuine state of starvation quickly dominated the besieged city, visiting its residents and the newcomers alike ...[64]

Halina Maciejowska Regulska, wife of the prominent businessman Janusz Regulski and avid diarist, agreed, calling the September streets a "scene out of Dante." (Figure 1.2)[65] When government foundered, elites filled the gaps.[66] Civic efforts flourished: ministers' wives, sewing circles, students, scouts, and seminarians darted outside between air raids, "pitching in" to tend the wounded, bury bodies, fight fires, gather horse carcasses to be butchered, prevent looting, mend blockades, or keep roads passable.[67] Regulska's family dove into defense initiatives. Socialist leaders and working-class loyalists supplied defenders, digging anti-dank ditches, and building barricades.[68] Other political parties rallied volunteers, sometimes with members of parliament and politicians at their head. The mayor formalized party efforts, appointing colleagues to lead critical initiatives.

1.3   Government and Army Evacuation

Warsaw was the seat of the national government, which might have been the key decision maker during the siege and occupation. But, on the night of

[64] Krawczyńska, *Zapiski*, 33–34.
[65] Regulska, *Dziennik*, 33.
[66] Krawczyńska, *Zapiski*, 34.
[67] The wives of intelligentsia men – political actors themselves – were crucial during the siege and occupation. USHMM RG-50.012.0046, AN: 1989.67.46, "Interview with Stefan and Sophia Korbonski," Part 2, 9:50–10:35; Krzysztof Dunin-Wąsowicz, *Na Żoliborzu, 1939–1945* (Warsaw: Książka i Wiedza, 1984), 48–50.
[68] Zaremba credited workers with more nerve than their social "betters." Zaremba, *Żeby chociaż świat wiedział*, 69, 77, 95.

Figure 1.2 A Polish family huddles in front of the Opera House in besieged Warsaw while a Polish soldier looks on, September 1939.
United States Holocaust Memorial Museum, Julien Bryan Archive, Photograph Number 47347.

September 4–5, 1939, it evacuated Warsaw eastward toward Lublin and then into Romania, an unbridgeable caesura in the legitimacy of the Second Polish Republic. Curiously, the Wehrmacht assumed the Polish government lay in their clutches, despite its escape.[69] A parade of private cars (denied to ordinary Poles since September 1) and state limousines crept across the Vistula bridges in the predawn darkness, scandalizing observers.[70] Panic ensued on the

[69] Russ, *Case White*, 82, 221.
[70] Andrzej Franaszek, *Miłosz: A Biography* (Cambridge: Harvard University Press, 2017), 180–182.

morning of September 5: offices stood empty; paper fluttered about; phones rang and rang. The evacuees were a who's who of the Second Polish Republic: bureaucrats and ambassadorial staffs, not-yet-mobilized officers, policemen, firefighters and, from September 6 on, all able-bodied men. The plan was to regroup and fight on, but it went unrealized.[71]

Defense Ministry higher-ups were not informed about evacuation: the terrible news was at first only rumor. Wacław Lipiński (1896–1949) found out from his sister, Dioniza "Dyzia" Wyszyńska, a teacher, whose husband, Antoni "Tosiek" Wyszyński, was an active-duty colonel at the Defense Ministry. Lipiński's circle was typical of the intelligentsia: he was a civil servant, historian, retired officer, and Legionnaire, and his brother-in-law was an officer. Dyzia called her brother in hysterics:

> The night from Monday to Tuesday was quite simply macabre. As usual, I went to bed late after the last of the radio programs aired, when my telephone rang at 3am. Dyzia was calling to ask if I knew what was happening. Her voice sounded different. I answered that I didn't know and asked her what had happened. She couldn't tell me over the phone, and asked that I come over immediately. Ola [his wife Aleksandra] and I got dressed and left. She was standing in her courtyard, crying that everyone in the whole house was leaving, and she didn't know why ... visibly shaken, Dyzia told us that the whole Interior and Defense Ministries and in general the whole government was evacuating. It's recommended that everyone take their families with them. Tosiek just got home and he's exhausted and sleeping and I don't want to wake him. What should I do? Do I leave with him and bring the children – or stay?[72]

Colonel Wyszyński slept as his subordinates packed, destroyed files, and fled town.

Lipiński clarified what orders had gone out to the Defense and Interior Ministries but it took all night. Selected personnel were relocating to Lublin. Many families were unwilling to be abandoned, though, and household goods, crying children, and pets joined the exodus. Lipiński learned that the Józef Piłsudski Institute for the Study of Modern Polish History had been evacuated with the Military Historical Bureau. He was the institute's director. His staff and files were en route to Lublin.

Lipiński's diary conveys the rage and frustration of Warsaw's intelligentsia during evacuation. His government gone, Lipiński mobilized himself. Before Polish High Command created the Warsaw Army, Lipiński got ahold of the situation, calmed his wife and sister, and briefed his brother-in-law – and what remained of the Defense Ministry. Together with Julian Janowski, the colonel who barely got a taxi, Lipiński came to the aid of General Walerian Czuma (1890–1962), who refused to evacuate. Commander-in-Chief Śmigły-Rydz

---

[71] WP treated *all* men as combatants: civilian-military blurring came from both sides.
[72] Lipiński, *Dziennik*, 59–61.

created a Warsaw Defense Command and gave Czuma control, evacuating days later. At the head of Warsaw Army, Czuma and Rómmel directed urban defenses. Cardinal August Hlond (1881–1948), primate of Poland, and head of the Roman Catholic Church, also evacuated mid-month and headed for Vatican City.[73] Warsaw was now missing its government, army command, and the head of its main religious denomination. Thousands more took the official evacuation as warning and left themselves, some trickling back under occupation or replaced by enthusiastic newcomers. The remainder carried on. Janowski became Czuma's deputy. Lipiński put his old uniform back on and became Czuma's propaganda chief, moving information across the city, keeping the mayor on the airwaves, preventing panic.[74]

Crisis management may have come naturally to Lipiński, but his initiative drew from the fact that he was a well-connected member of the Warsaw intelligentsia with colleagues in government, the military, and industry. He – while the phones worked – made calls, knocked on doors, and figured out what was happening. This was how Warsaw worked during the siege and afterward: intelligentsia social networks, professional contacts, and leadership experience kept them afloat. Of course, the elitist nature of government meant that "making a few calls" to solve problems hardly began in 1939; Lipiński had always functioned this way. However, in September this was the *only* way to get things done: the city functioned or collapsed according to intelligentsia initiative. As the Germans advanced, the Second Polish Republic gave way. Intelligentsia bonds preserved civil society under siege and occupation.

Civilian elites had their hands full. Halina Regulska stayed downtown with her children. She and her daughter, Hanka, volunteered at a Red Cross field hospital.[75] On September 6, Mayor Starzyński appointed Regulska's husband Janusz Regulski (1887–1983) commander of the Citizen Militia (Główna Straż Obywatelska, SO). Starzyński chose Regulski because he was not political, a prosperous, happily married father who ran an electrical conglomerate.[76] Regulski issued orders about air raid shelters, night patrols, the Red Cross, militia recruitment, human movement, shops and pharmacies, charity efforts, requisitioning private cars, and public safety, but he stole home occasionally.[77] His wife was thus well informed, and kept friends abreast of developments. On September 6, she noted in her diary that "the official order for all men to evacuate the city has come ... from the mouth of Lt. Col. Umiastowski himself. Just

[73] BABL R58 7154, EG VI 15 September, 89–90; 93–95; EG VI 30 September, 191, 207, 212; Czesław Madajczyk, *Polityka III Rzeszy w okupowanej Polsce*, Vols. I–II (Warsaw: Państwowe Wydawn. Naukowe, 1970). Tom II, 193.

[74] Porwit, *Obrona Warszawy*, 77, 175; Janowski, *Obrona Warszawy*, 139–140.

[75] Urbanek, *Lęk i Strach*, 153.

[76] Konwinski, *Mayor*, 97.

[77] Regulski's *rozkazy*: Instytut Historii PAN, *Cywilna obrona*, 22, 27, 28, 43, 48, 58, 65, 69, 95, 107, 115, 118; 341–359.

women, children, and old people are to remain here alone."[78] The national police "quickly abandoned the city" alongside "whole units of the fire department."[79] Warsaw awaited the largest incendiary bombing campaign the world had yet seen, and blocks and blocks would burn before capitulation. Umiastowski's order provoked "the most monumental traffic jam yet known in Warsaw," paralyzing evacuees in a deadlock of trucks and government limousines on the Vistula bridges.[80] Regulska was terrified, her husband not less so.

Starzyński remained at his desk, turning his relationship with Warsaw's press to good effect.[81] Radio messages emphasized civic unity and discouraged defeatism, and Lipiński kept them on the air. They also summoned volunteers and kept the city informed.[82] Starzyński used radio while the senders were in Polish hands, and then turned to newspapers and loudspeakers.[83] His familiar voice reassured the populace they were still being governed.[84] He appealed to Varsovians to "hold fast and we will be victorious," anticipating Winston Churchill's famous rallying of Londoners under bombardment the next year.[85] While German artillery blasted Warsaw into rubble, Starzyński was in city hall, trying to do something.[86]

A sense of betrayal at the government's flight united those who remained. That the Socialist Left condemned the evacuation – "the rats," prominent socialist parliamentarian Zygmunt Zaremba (1895–1967) wrote, "are escaping" – was unsurprising. In Zaremba's eyes, aristocrats were keen to flee, leaving workers and the poor to face German wrath: "The capital must be defended," he insisted,

---

[78] Umiastowski was Śmigły-Rydz's propaganda chief. Regulska, *Dziennik*, 34; Lipiński, *Dziennik*, 62; Żukowski, "Szkic Biograficzny" in Umiastowski, *Dziennik Wojenny*, 18. *IX.1939 – 19.IX.1945* (Warsaw: Wyd. DiG, 2009), 57.

[79] Warsaw firefighters evacuated; Łódź firefighters arrived later Police evacuated and many were incarcerated after capitulation. Porwit, *Obrona Warszawy*, 37–38.

[80] Rail was unreliable. Owen Gingerich, *The Book Nobody Read: Chasing the Revolutions of Nicolaus Copernicus* (New York: Penguin Books, 2005), 95; Kubalski, *Niemcy w Krakowie*, 23. The evacuation's economic fallout lingered. PISM London: MID: Dział Polski, A. 10. 4/3, Sprawozdania z Kraju, 1940: "Sprawozdanie miesięcznie Nr. 5 o stanie przemysłu w Polsce na podstawie informacyj z miesiąca kwietnia," Paris – April 1940, 2.

[81] Marian Marek Drozdowski (ed.), *Archiwum Prezydenta Warszawskiego Stefana Starzyńskiego*, 2 vols. (Warsaw: Oficyna Wydawnicza Rytm, 2004). His brother Roman Starzyński directed Polish Radio. Czesław Miłosz worked for the radio and Władysław Szpilman performed. Ron Nowicki, *Warsaw: The Cabaret Years* (San Francisco: Mercury House, 1992), 201–203.

[82] Kochanski, *Eagle Unbowed*, 66.

[83] Loudspeakers were nicknamed "*szczekaczki*" (barkers). Konwinski, *Mayor*, 94.

[84] Wojdysławski memoir, USHMM-18; 471.Ringelblum I/489; Mf. ŻIH-787 [1–2]; Regulska, *Dziennik z oblężonej Warszawy*, 78.

[85] Drozdowski, *Archiwum Prezydenta Warszawskiego Stefana Starzyńskiego* Vol. I, 298–299; Lynne Olson, *Citizens of London: The Americans Who Stood with Britain in Its Darkest, Finest Hour* (New York: Random House, 2010), 42–52, 93–94.

[86] Drozdowski, *Stefan Starzyński prezydent Warszawy*, 180.

"it can't be any other way. Every worker thinks this way, every industrial laborer, every ordinary citizen of the capital. What is the government thinking?"[87] Zaremba was too hasty; the remaining intelligentsia shared his fury. Officers hid their irritation from subordinates. Watching a colleague pack, Lipiński called high-ranking evacuees a "cowardly horde" and noted that a "nasty, unpleasant atmosphere of retreat and escape wafted about." His family stayed.[88] Even Starzyński, who refrained from criticizing his government to maintain fragile unity, referred openly to the "tragic mistake of the evacuation."[89]

Śmigły-Rydz evacuated command to Brest forty-eight hours after the government, "focused on saving the army" above all, and from Brześć he retreated to Młynów and then the Romanian border.[90] Evacuees followed Polish constitutional provisions in creating an exile government, but this was cold comfort to Varsovians. No governmental structure existed as an intermediary between them and the Wehrmacht like those that protected Prague, Belgrade, or Paris.[91] Men like Lipiński and Regulski stepped into the breach; Starzyński and Czuma rallied the city. Their wives organized soup kitchens and hospitals; intelligentsia youth rescued property and fought fires. Tales of individual heroism and pluck, however, should not distract from the fact that people took initiative because the institutions of their state had, like a rug, been pulled from beneath them. Elite agency during the siege was premised on a catastrophic failure.

1.4 Total War

Defending Warsaw *required* civilian participation. Aerial bombardment and artillery fire damaged electrical and sewage systems, cutting off water and electricity, including to hospitals.[92] Without firefighters or water, neighborhoods burned for days. Regulski's Citizen Militia fought fires, but injuries, death, and property loss mounted. Rampant looting among the hungry, panicked, and overcrowded population went unchecked due to the absence of policemen. Umiastowski's evacuations made manpower a precious commodity at a time when defender needs were legion: collecting food and

---

[87] Zaremba, *Żeby chociaż świat wiedział*, 66–67.
[88] Lipiński, *Dziennik*, 64.
[89] Less colorful than the wording he was rumored to have used behind closed doors. Porwit, *Obrona Warszawy*, 38.
[90] Zaloga and Madej, *Polish Campaign*, 127; Forczyk, *Case White*, 254, 280.
[91] Bryant, *Prague in Black*, 41–45, 62, 221; Prusin, *Serbia under the Swastika*, 61–66, 159; Julian Jackson, *France: The Dark Years, 1940–1944* (New York: Oxford University Press, 2001), 123–136.
[92] Operation Seaside. Russ, *Case White*, 155.

ammunition, digging tank traps, manning anti-aircraft posts, maintaining communications, and controlling civilians.[93]

The evacuation of government and able-bodied men begins the story of Polish scouting (*harcerstwo*) and the advance of its members into underground resistance.[94] Scouting was a patriotic activity crowded with the intelligentsia's children. The siege was their "baptism of fire" and taught youth from privileged families they were crucial to Warsaw's defenses. Scouting leaders like Stanisław Broniewski (1915–2000) and Aleksander Kamiński, freshly arrived from Katowice, assigned "their" boys to sundry tasks and memorialized their exploits.[95] Broniewski would go on to lead his scouts – the Szare Szeregi or Grey Ranks – into the London-backed military underground, citing their siege exploits as proof of their usefulness.[96]

Michał Walicki (1904–66), Warsaw University art history professor and National Museum curator, spent September frantic as art and antiques caught fire.[97] A square red-brick structure sitting at the edge of the Medieval Old Town, the Royal Castle was filled with priceless collections from Poland's long history. It was also an excellent Luftwaffe target.[98] As the cupola went up in flames, a dozen scouts turned up at Walicki's office. Walicki was unsure how word had gotten out, but Broniewski may have sent them. The boys emptied the castle into museum basements for safekeeping:[99]

> For a few days, together with the employees of the museum, they packed up the contents of the castle and loaded Canaletto paintings, bronzes, and furniture into trucks and transported it to the museum, where the valuables were hidden in the cellars. They slept and ate on the grounds of the museum the entire time. On the 17th or the 18th one of the museum's trucks, which the

[93] Łódź men 16–60 were evacuated on September 5. Gordon Horwitz, *Ghettostadt: Łódź and the Making of a Nazi City* (Cambridge: Harvard University Press, 2008), 9.

[94] Stanisław Broniewski, *Całym życiem: Szare Szeregi w relacji naczelnika* (Warsaw: Państwowe Wyd. Naukowe, 1983); Instytut Historii PAN, *Cywilna obrona*, 192–193.

[95] Scouting was national-civic education. Bogusław Śliwerski, *Harcerstwo źródłem pedagogicznej pasji* (Krakow: Impuls, 2016).

[96] Broniewski's Grey Ranks share a birthdate with Michał Karaszewicz-Tokarzewski's Polish Victory Service. APW 1716/II 27, Archiwum St. Broniewskiego, Letter, Stanisław Broniewski to Wacław [N.N.], Warszawa, dn 10 stycznia 1965 r., [6–7]; Kamiński, *Zośka i Parasol*, 36.

[97] The Old Town was rebuilt following Canaletto paintings that scouts rescued. Mariusz Czepczynski, *Cultural Landscapes of Post-Socialist Cities: Representation of Powers and Needs* (Burlington: Ashgate Publishing, 2012), 82. Walicki hid art in the museum. Michał Walicki, *Muzeum Narodowe w Warszawie: Przewodnik po dziale malarstwa obcego* (Warsaw: Nakł. Muzeum Narodowego w Warszawie, 1936).

[98] Jerzy Lileyko, *A Companion Guide to the Royal Castle in Warsaw* (Warsaw: Interpress Publishers, 1980), 20, 80–82.

[99] Art was shipped to Germany for "safekeeping." TNA GFM 33/540/1231, Hans Frank Papers, "Teilliste der sichergestellten Kunstgegenstände des GG," [1]-5.

scouts were riding in, was hit by artillery fire or an aerial bomb . . . Nobody was
killed, but a lot of the boys were injured and had to be taken to the hospital.

A handful were later wounded hauling patients and medical equipment from
a Piękna Street hospital.[100] As the occupation unfolded, September's scouts
would join the emerging underground, and some of its youth would become
Home Army combatants by 1944. The evacuation of personnel during the siege
required that those without experience or equipment – even children – do
soldiers' work. Beyond the practical problems caused by the absence of policemen, firemen, and soldiers, the evacuation triggered panic. Citizens felt abandoned. Poland's public servants, after four days of war, ceased to serve their
public. The sense of betrayal cannot be overstated and deeply affected evacuees'
and exiles' ability to understand Warsaw's war.

The defense involved civilian elites in military affairs, and vice versa. Czuma's
forces and Rómmel's Warsaw Army were inadequate before German attack. After
the government evacuation and encirclement, relieving the defenders was impossible. Civilians were recruited (or, like Lipiński and Zaremba, mobilized themselves) to guard weapons depots, direct traffic, do nighttime signaling, maintain
fortifications, and requisition supplies, especially vehicles and food. This last,
especially, was a source of tension, as people starved, hoarding and stealing food
to survive. Mayor Starzyński appealed to the citizenry to aid defenders – or stay out
of their way – on September 7. Four days later, Czuma made the same request with
teeth: "plunder, robbery, arson, damaging infrastructure, spying, and desertion . . .
would be punished with the death penalty." The city was under martial law.[101]
Military commanders hesitated to arm civilians.[102] Starzyński supported civilian
involvement, demanding defense be a "whole Warsaw" struggle. Survivors proudly
remembered a "spontaneous effort:" "society wanted this fight" and everyone
pitched in, enduring "great sacrifices."[103] Elites rubbed shoulders with neighbors
on barricades and in shop queues; Regulski, Starzyński, and deputy mayor Kulski
directed civilian defenses alongside volunteers.

Military officers – leading the still-fighting WP – helped blur boundaries
between military and civilian responsibilities. Brigadier-General Michał
Karaszewicz-Tokarzewski ("Torwid," 1893–1964), Rómmel's second-in-
command, made a clandestine plan to fight on regardless of German capitulation
terms, and he did so with the knowledge of his superiors, who ended up in captivity
or exile.[104] He and other high-ranking officers remained in Warsaw to keep

[100] APW 1716/II 27, Archiwum St. Broniewskiego, [11–12]. Letter between A. Kamiński
and Wacław [N.N.], Łódź, 18.I.1965r.
[101] Instytut Historii PAN, *Cywilna obrona*, 25–26, 41.
[102] Julien Bryan, *Siege*, newsreel.
[103] PISM London: MID: Dział Polski, A. 10. 4/1, „Sprawozdanie literata Goetla," [1].
[104] Karaszewicz-Tokarzewski was from the *kresy*, fought in Piłsudski's Legions, and participated
in the 1926 coup. AAN 2-88-44 Akta Michała Karaszewicza-Tokarzewskiego, sygn. 138.

evacuees informed and organize insurgency in civilian clothes.[105] Karaszewicz-Tokarzewski called his initiative the Polish Victory Service (Służba Zwycięstwu Polski, SZP).[106] The Service would have numerous successors and competitors, but it was born during the siege when divisions between military and civilian elites were less important than survival and preparation for resistance to come.

From initial Wehrmacht attacks on western suburbs on September 18–19, continuing through the heaviest bombardment, the Germans were held off by a combined military-civilian effort. Warsaw was not defended: it defended itself.[107] The wartime cycle of violence began during the siege, which militarized civilians. Civilians carried weapons and did soldiers' work; soldiers fought desperately and frequently escaped captivity. The Wehrmacht accused Polish soldiers entrenched around Warsaw of violations of the laws of war, which fitted Nazi stereotypes. Though tales of Polish perfidy, false "surrenders," looting of the dead, and ambushes carried out under Red Cross flags were largely fabricated, they painted a picture of Poles as dangerous and untrustworthy in the minds of German soldiers.[108] Defending Warsaw thus also radicalized German brutality even before Nazi police arrival, eroding protections for civilian noncombatants and encouraging Germans to see all Poles as enemies.

Siege intermingled Varsovians in ways unimaginable in peacetime (Figure 1.3). Less-damaged portions of the city, like the northwestern intelligentsia Żoliborz neighborhood, were crowded with internal and external refugees, mixing elite locals with working class and gentry newcomers from other cities and peasants from the countryside.[109] Barricade teams of university students, factory workers, and bureaucrats manning machine guns and "women's" work in hospitals and soup kitchens made strangers into acquaintances.[110] Old antagonisms were suspended. Polish antisemitism fluctuated as Christian and Jewish communities cooperated. Emmanuel Ringelblum (1900–44), Warsaw University historian, characterized it as an ethnic truce:

> Even the most ardent anti-Semites grasped that at this time Jews and Poles had a common enemy, and that the Jews were excellent allies who would do all they possibly could to bring destruction on the Jews' greatest enemies. The easing of tension could be felt at every step . . . The Jew, who before the war

---

[105] Bór-Komorowski, *Armia Podziemna*, 27–28.

[106] Nr. 1: "Organizacja, cele i zadania" in *Armia Krajowa 1939–1945: Wybór Źródeł*, ed. Andrzej Chmielarz, Grzegorz Jasiński, and Andrzej Krzysztof Kunert (Warsaw: Wojskowe Centrum Edukacji Obywatelskiej, 2013), 37.

[107] Konwinski, *Mayor*, 139–140.

[108] BAMA MSg/2/3232 [Infantry Lieutenant Diary], 21 48–49, 50.

[109] The Kulski family had a house in Żoliborz and took in relatives. USHMM RG-50.030.0769, AN: 2014.238.1, "Interview with Julian Kulski [Jr.]," 15:30–15:47; 18:30.

[110] Zaremba, "*Żeby chociaż świat wiedział*," 36–52.

Figure 1.3 Varsovians celebrate at the news that England and France declared war on Germany, September 1939.
United States Holocaust Memorial Museum, Julien Bryan Archive, Photograph Number 47380.

felt himself to be a second- or third-class citizen ... again became a citizen with equal rights, asked to render help to the common fatherland.[111]

Ringelblum would have the occupation to ponder how this collaboration came unglued and the "common fatherland" forgotten in favor of clannish and self-serving behavior, when Poles often turned on their Jewish neighbors.[112] The "equal rights" of September were exchanged for segregation under Nazi administration. Other new alliances endured. Friendships formed under siege often persisted, incomprehensible to outsiders and evacuees.

As first the government and then the army abandoned the capital, the mayor remained, working with soldiers, tapping elites to lead projects, keeping things intact. A myth surrounds Starzyński in Poland but he is unknown outside it. Save for Józef Piłsudski, there were few figures more important to Warsaw's 1930s than

[111] Emmanuel Ringelblum was a historian and activist – a participant-analyst. Ringelblum, *Polish-Jewish Relations during the Second World War* (Jerusalem: Yad Vashem, 1974), 24–25.

[112] There was a temporary ethnic truce in 1863. Theodore Weeks, "Assimilation, Nationalism, Modernization, Antisemitism" in *Antisemitism and Its Opponents in Modern Poland* (Ithaca: Cornell University Press, 2005), 33–34; Kassow, *Who Will Write*, 68–69.

the man who rebuilt it into the "Paris of the East."[113] Starzyński stayed at his desk with a skeleton crew. He could easily have evacuated; before capitulation a plane landed on the Mokotów Fields (Pole Mokotowskie) to fly him to Bucharest. He refused to get on.[114] Starzyński was a tangible *presence* in contrast to the absent state.[115] By 1940 he was a legend rather than a man: a squat, somber figure behind a stack of paperwork. Starzyński's career earned him critics, but his 1939 behavior separated him from the Second Polish Republic and showed that those who stayed in Warsaw had set off on their own course.

Though capitulation severed Starzyński's contact with Varsovians, he never left the city. German terms required the city to furnish twelve elite hostages during the transfer of power to the Wehrmacht, and Starzyński volunteered to be among them.[116] The incoming military occupation initially left him to his own devices: he and his deputy, Julian Kulski, remained in city hall. When Warsaw was transferred to a civilian Nazi occupation, though, the Gestapo arrested Starzyński. Kulski remained as acting mayor doing a "dual job," obediently keeping city services functioning for the Germans but also reporting to the exiles and emerging underground. Kulski was trapped and powerless. His own secret Polish-Jewish background and his boss's violent end were always on his mind if he should antagonize his Nazi masters.[117]

1.5   Effects of Siege and Bombardment

On September 28, 1939, Starzyński announced the capitulation on the pages of the *United Gazette* (*Gazeta Wspólna*), the last message some Varsovians ever received from the representative of an independent Poland:

> [...] Citizens! I thank you with my whole heart for your trust, which sustained me through the long course of the defense. I thank you for heeding my requests and for your constant, self-sacrificing fulfillment of your daily obligations, in spite of these difficult conditions. You, the people of the capital, have demonstrated boundless heroism and willingness to sacrifice. Your dedication, which required all of us to

---

[113] Drozdowski, *Stefan Starzyński prezydent Warszawy*, 5.

[114] Wacław Lenga, "W Tymczasowej Radzie Miejskiej i Komendzie Głównej Straży Obywatelskiej" in *Wspomnienia o Stefanie Starzyńskim* (Warsaw: Państwowe Wydawnictwo Naukowe, 1982), 79.

[115] Krzysztof Dunin-Wąsowicz, *Warszawa w latach 1939–1945* (Warszawa: PWN, 1984), 34–35.

[116] In parallel to Alois Eliáš in Prague, who worked for a German protectorate but remained in contact with Edvard Beneš in London. Kulski, *Stefan Starzyński*, 107–108; Connelly, *From Peoples into Nations*, 439.

[117] The Kulski family's Jewish background was secret from the deputy mayor's son. USHMM RG-50.030.0769, AN: 2014.238.1, "Interview with Julian Kulski [Jr.]," 1:08:00–1:15:25; 2:10:10–2:11:06; 2:15–4:40; 5:25–5:40.

remain at our posts to the very last, will be judged rightly by history. Much work still awaits you, including the day-to-day difficulties of bringing your lives back to normal and beginning to rebuild our city. Through the combined efforts of the whole population ... this rebuilding must and will be accomplished. Long live Poland and her capital – Warsaw.[118]

German artillery quieted and Wehrmacht commanders collected hostages, including Starzyński and Regulski (Figure 1.4). An eerie silence followed. Under bombardment Warsaw was a closed world "without a single drop of water," "an ocean of fire."[119] Starzyński and Czuma had capitulated at the last moment. A lack of water forced them, as firefighting and gun cooling had become impossible. People drank from the Vistula, which washed combat detritus to the sea. Varsovians emerged onto barely recognizable streets: towers and steeples were missing from the skyline and a flatter, smokier panorama confronted them. Downtown transitioned from burning rubble to

Figure 1.4 Stefan Starzyński (fourth from left in dark coat and hat) formalizes Warsaw's capitulation to the Wehrmacht, September 1939.
Józef Piłsudski Institute of America, 701/151/5/2486.

---

[118] *Gazeta Wspólna* nr. 2, 28.IX.1939, for which Krawczyńska wrote; Instytut Historii PAN, *Cywilna obrona*, 229–236.
[119] USHMM-18 Wojdysławski memoir; 471.Ringelblum I/489; Mf. ŻIH-787 [6].

urban cemetery. Regulska, waiting for her husband among the hostages, observed her once-pristine neighborhood:

> Everything is over. People with tragic faces wander aimlessly about the streets. They stare at the destruction of the city, searching through it for their dear ones. [...] People burst into sudden sobbing. They go crying through the streets; crying through their homes. [...] Could it be that our struggle and suffering had yielded such meager results? Was it all unnecessary?[120]

Everyone searched for family, friends, and neighbors, sometimes for years without word. Death tolls during the final bombardment were high, with many buried alive. A young Polish-Jewish man with the surname of Wojdysławski ignored evacuation orders and wandered downtown to see "streets ... filled with rubble, bricks, stone, and everything was just covered with bodies. Everything before my eyes was red. A harsh, bloody red. There was no trace of houses. No houses. Just corpses everywhere. The corpses of houses. Everywhere ran little red rivers of blood ... "[121]

Survivors had to bury strangers' corpses, rotting in the autumn sun. Starzyński had regulated burials, but by October parks and squares were festooned with makeshift crosses.[122] The wounded numbered in the tens of thousands. Polish civilian casualties emanated disproportionately from Warsaw: Lipiński calculated 16,000 military and 20,000 civilian wounded and historian Marian Porwit estimated 4,000 military and 20,000 civilian dead – depending on where the line was drawn between the two. The September Campaign cost Poland around 70,000 dead, 130,000 wounded and upwards of 700,000 prisoners to the Germans and 240,000 to the Soviets – a million men. The Wehrmacht lost 16,000 men and took 30,000 wounded, far fewer than the Poles but more than planned.[123]

Wehrmacht victory testified to Case White's clarity and the superiority of German tactics and equipment, but especially to the wealth of Poland's neighbor, which built a new army after Hitler took power in 1933. It also highlighted Poland's disastrous diplomacy, its governmental disunity, and the final failure of the Versailles order. Had the Polish armies been fully mobilized, with better communication, and backed by a government with firmer allies, their defeat might have been less devastating. Their loss was double: a military collapse and a – much greater – political collapse. Poles were also misled by their own

---

[120] Regulska, *Dziennik*, 113–115.

[121] USHMM-18 Wojdysławski memoir; 471.Ringelblum I/489; Mf. ŻIH-787 [6–7]; Leociak, *Text*, 200–201, 255

[122] Drozdowski, *Archiwum Prezydenta Warszawskiego Stefana Starzyńskiego* Tom I, 268–270.

[123] Numbers may have been manipulated to hide those dodging captivity. Lipiński, *Dziennik*, 158; Kochanski, *Eagle Unbowed*, 84; Baranowski, *Nazi Empire*, 234.

propaganda and thought they would win.[124] The legacy of deceit and defeat made it difficult to romanticize the Second Polish Republic and divided those who tried to do so from those who felt betrayed. The Nazi occupation began in a jumble of patriotism, fear, and disillusionment that humiliated Varsovians, often delaying intelligentsia opposition until occupation violence touched them personally.

The evacuated government was absent during this travail: Warsaw and the prewar Polish state split. New political alliances in occupied Warsaw were unfamiliar to evacuees and exiles who clung to the political landscape of prewar Poland and their new exile circumstances, each of which was complicated enough. The siege differentiated Warsaw from the rest of Poland; the Varsovian endured prolonged German hostility in a way that Poles elsewhere did not. This trauma fostered a perverse pride and unique identity, casting a rosy glow over the quotidian degradations of war. Writer Miron Białoszewski (1922–83) was seventeen in 1939. His family fled with the government, though they returned to Warsaw. Missing the siege made Białoszewski feel like less of a "real" Varsovian:

> ... in 1939 my parents and I had fled as far away as Zdołbunów [in Ukraine], so that I wasn't even in Warsaw after September 5 [1939], and throughout September I was disconsolate at not being [t]here. And when people told me what had happened, and wrung their hands, and mentioned September 23, 24, 25, I wanted to know about those days in particular. Throughout the entire occupation I regretted that I hadn't been there on September 25 during the famous bombardment from eight in the morning until eight at night ...

In his eyes those who missed the 1939 siege or 1944 uprising (for which he was present, to his delight) were unworthy of the city. "Every average Varsovian ... wanted to return immediately ... to this hell" to contribute to the defense.[125] For him Warsaw was the center of things, the most authentic place in Poland. This was not unique: the same sentiment drew Varsovians who fled in 1939 home despite danger, and it brought other Poles willing to contest the occupation. Just as Warsaw had been the center of politics and culture during the Second Polish Republic it would become the center of civil society and Polish national culture under occupation: the "fight inside Poland" was led from Warsaw.[126] Some soldiers slated for German captivity "melted" back into the population. This was not regarded as cowardly or unpatriotic, since to "defect" was not to abandon the fight but continue it. The city that fought in 1939 was assumed to be – and became – the center of the fight to come.

Any possibility for a peaceful occupation vanished under siege. Marching into Warsaw, Wehrmacht soldiers were awed by its destruction. Nazi Propaganda

---

[124] Kochanski, *Eagle Unbowed*, 66, 77, 81.
[125] Białoszewski, *Memoir*, 37.
[126] USHMM RG-50.012.0046, AN: 1989.67.46, "Interview with Stefan and Sophia Korbonski," Part 2, 9:50–10:35.

Minister Paul Joseph Goebbels considered Poles primitive and Warsaw "repulsive."[127] Indoctrinated to think of Warsaw as uncivilized, the brutality of the ten-day bombardment confirmed Nazi propaganda: the most elegant parts were in ruins.[128] The siege was a horror, driving inhabitants to their limits and forcing them into behavior they would never have contemplated in peacetime. The collection of elite hostages had been at their posts for weeks on end and were exhausted. The population was hungry, thirsty, and filthy. Disease was spreading, especially typhus. Varsovians presented a disgusting sight.

Physical devastation made Warsaw vulnerable to the coming occupation, and provided a standing excuse for Nazi persecution: Varsovians had, after all, held out against the Wehrmacht and stalled Case White. City elites were primed to resist: indignant at their own government, furious at the depredations of an enemy army, and invigorated by participation in city defenses, many were uneasy about life under the German thumb. They would learn that the new "normal" meant devastation. The Nazi military, civilian, and police administrations treated Warsaw as the source of Polish resistance, a role it might have volunteered for had it not been imposed.

1.6   Conclusion

In order to understand Warsaw's occupation and its intelligentsia's response it is necessary to understand what they endured during the September Campaign. The events of those weeks severed ties with the Second Polish Republic and created new – often unpleasant – possibilities. Among these foundational experiences must be understood: immense loss of life; widespread physical destruction, from housing stock to the transit system; changing loyalties and political ties; the sense of abandonment by and independence from old sources of authority, including the government, army, and Church; the escalation of violence against civilians; the importance of Starzyński and those who remained; and the conviction that Warsaw "defended itself."

Warsaw rallied in 1939, but at great cost. Historian Joanna Urbanek examines its emotions: fear, dread, surprise – but also pride and excitement.[129] Varsovians rallied because they had no choice. Before most could comprehend the situation a fast-moving, genocidal army arrived from the west to bomb them to smithereens; a rapacious ideological enemy blocked retreat to the east. Their government

---

[127] Vejas Gabriel Liulevicius, *The German Myth of the East, 1800 to the Present* (New York: Oxford University Press, 2009), 52, 154; Joseph Goebbels, *The Goebbels Diaries, 1939–1941* (New York: G. P. Putnam's Sons, 1983), 36–37.

[128] Nazi propaganda insisted Poles were dirty and violent. German soldiers, however, compared Warsaw favorably to Paris and Berlin. Stephan Lehnstaedt, "Codzienność okupanta w Warszawie w latach 1939–1944" in *Przemoc i dzień powszedni w okupowanej Polsce* (Gdańsk: Muzeum II Wojny Światowej, 2011), 496–497.

[129] Urbanek, *Lęk i Strach*, 33–49; 85–111.

and their army – save for a treasured group of defenders – withdrew, leaving them to figure things out. They documented their plight when they could do nothing more; they defended themselves because there was nobody else to defend them and they were in terrible danger. All the work of soldiering, governance, and maintaining civil society was dumped in their laps by the dual invasion and evacuation of their own state. In the coming years they both would not and could not hand over this burden, because there was nobody to hand it over to.

A handful of intelligentsia figures, some young, some old, civilians and military leaders, women and men, endured the siege, watched their state crumble, and turned to and on their neighbors. A month of bombardment invigorated their sense of mission as Polish national leaders, especially after the evacuations: those who stayed took pride in what they saw as the patriotic choice over flight. The ragged banner of patriotism fluttered over horrors and traumas, justifying dramatic and unanticipated behavior. *Being* in Warsaw under occupation was thus active, premised on *staying* in Warsaw under siege. The lieutenant, Jan Karski, was taken as a POW but got back to Warsaw as soon as he could. The mayor, Starzyński, never evacuated, nor did his deputy. Starzyński appointed Janusz Regulski to lead the Citizen Militia, and Regulski's family worked, too. Halina Donimirska and Aleksander Kamiński arrived from the provinces, pitched in with the defense, and never left. Journalist Jadwiga Krawczyńska kept the *Common Gazette* in print and scribbled a diary; she was not the only one.[130] Poet Miron Białoszewski evacuated with his parents, but raced back. Wacław Lipiński and Julian Janowski organized military defenses, Lipiński back in uniform after a long time. Zygmunt Zaremba led workers to the barricades himself; Stanisław Broniewski and Aleksander Kamiński organized scouts to help. Michał Walicki spent the next few months re-hiding museum collections as the Nazi occupation began. The German invasion interrupted their careers and changed their lives. When the Wehrmacht entered Warsaw, their prewar lives were over and new lives had begun – but their position as leaders in Polish society, culture, and politics continued. For some this was the resumption of a mantle put aside in 1918; for others this was a new and dizzying responsibility.

The Polish army had been conquered, imprisoned, or evacuated, and two foreign armies occupied Polish soil. The Varsovian nevertheless began the Nazi occupation with a sense of his own specialness: "he [wa]s proud that the fate of Warsaw was different."[131] Its future, too, would be marked by Nazi Germany's special attention, and its intelligentsia would find themselves in the crosshairs of their occupiers.

---

[130] Diary writing – encouraged by Moscow – was an intelligentsia mainstay in besieged Leningrad. Alexis Peri, *The War Within: Diaries from the Siege of Leningrad* (Cambridge, MA: Harvard University Press, 2020), 2–3.

[131] Zaremba, *Żeby chociaż świat wiedział*, 73.

The Killing Years

Warsaw's 1939 defense delayed Wehrmacht victory but also delayed the implementation of a secret, simultaneous police campaign against the intelligentsia. It was only after capitulation that the real Nazi policy to pacify Poland for long-term German domination moved forward. This genocidal targeting of the intelligentsia was police work, not a military affair. It was also the first in a series of Nazi plans to restructure eastern Europe and control its inhabitants. Two anti-intelligentsia campaigns (Operation Tannenberg and AB-Aktion, the follow-up initiative) together form a distinct genocide conducted by Nazi Germany against the leadership of the Polish national community. The elite, rather than Poles as a whole, was targeted. Pursuing this genocidal policy in Warsaw guided the creation of its occupation administration, claimed thousands of Polish lives, and provoked elite survivors' activities over the long term.

Nazi Germany sought to destroy both the Polish state and nation. During the September Campaign, there were two attacks by Nazi Germany against Poland. The first was the military invasion of September 1, Case White, which aimed to destroy the Polish *state* and its army. The second was a police campaign launched on September 6, 1939, codenamed Operation Tannenberg.[1] Tannenberg was a secret kept both from the Wehrmacht and its Polish victims. While the Wehrmacht fought the Polish army, Nazi police arrested and killed Polish civilians. This political–cultural "decapitation" fixated on the Polish "leadership stratum" (*Führungsschicht*), that is the intelligentsia. This was Nazi Germany's first wartime police-led killing spree, but not its last or most lethal: Tannenberg was a precursor to the deadlier and better-known campaign conducted against Jewish victims in eastern Europe and the Soviet Union in 1941 by the same *Einsatzgruppen* (mobile police forces).[2] Tannenberg aimed to destroy the Polish *nation*, render it incapable of

---

[1] Named for Germanic–Slavic clashes in 1410 and 1914. Liulevicius, *War Land*, 15.

[2] They had been used in Austria and Czechoslovakia (Helmut Krausnick, *Hitlers Einsatzgruppen: die Truppe des Weltanschauungskrieges, 1938–1942* (Frankfurt: Fischer Taschenbuch Verlag, 1985), 13–25; 214–218) and would be again during Barbarossa (Krausnick, *Hitlers Einsatzgruppen*, 151–178; Christopher Browning, *The Origins of the Final Solution: The Evolution of Nazi Jewish Policy, September 1939–March 1942* (Lincoln: The University of Nebraska Press, 2004), 253–294).

resistance, and "cleanse" it from the territory Germany wished to repopulate. Warsaw was besieged while this second campaign unfolded in western Poland and thus escaped the cleansing initially: the timeline of Case White and the capital's ferocious holding out stalled Nazi ideological plans. Once Warsaw's capitulation terms had been signed, police implemented Tannenberg directives. The campaign, however, was unsuccessful in preventing Polish opposition. In fact, by demonstrating their murderous intent, the Nazis created a powerful incentive for the surviving intelligentsia to oppose them.

2.1 Operation Tannenberg

Long before 1939, Nazi ideology conceived of the Polish intelligentsia as a threat to its *Lebensraum* in the east.[3] After Hitler came to power, considerable effort went into studying the Second Polish Republic's leadership.[4] Heinrich Himmler, Chief of German Police and Reichsführer-SS, head of Nazi Germany's leading paramilitary, the Schutzstaffeln (SS; protective squads), enforced conformity to National Socialism at home and on territory that the Third Reich conquered. Himmler's research staff monitored national leaders and instigators of Polish "chauvinism" (as the Nazis viewed their neighbors' patriotism).[5] Neutralizing such people would also prevent rebellion, of which Poles were historically extremely fond.

Elite "removal" was Himmler's way of ending the Polish state project and thwarting resistance, which he correctly assumed would be directed by Polish elites. Differing perspectives on the Second Polish Republic were central: Polish intelligentsia who maintained state and national traditions considered themselves leaders and patriots; Nazi police called them chauvinists. Himmler's precision de-nationalization campaign required years of research and preparation.[6] Police dossiers were compiled into *Sonderfahndungslisten* (wanted-persons lists), naming 61,000 Poles prominent in cultural, political, and national life.[7] Names included

---

[3] The experience of German soldiers deployed on the Eastern Front in the First World War produced a particular "German imperialist 'mindscape' of the East." Liulevicius, *War Land*, 151, 159. Maria Wardzyńska, *Był rok 1939: Operacji niemieckiej policji bezpieczeństwa w Polsce: Intelligenzaktion* (Warsaw: Instytut Pamięci Narodowej), 2009, 50–74.

[4] See: BABL R58 136 Die innerpolitischen Machtmittel Polens; Chu, *German Minority*, 159–199; Karski, *Secret State*, 55–56.

[5] They monitored Polish nation-building efforts, including those in German and Ukrainian communities. Michael Burleigh, *Germany Turns Eastwards: A Study of Ostforschung in the Third Reich* (New York: Cambridge University Press, 1988); for an intelligentsia campaign among Ukrainians: Snyder, *Sketches from a Secret War*, 77–79.

[6] Peter Longerich, *Heinrich Himmler* (New York: Oxford University Press, 2012), 430.

[7] The *Sonderfahndungsbuch* covered western Poland better than other regions. A snippet from the first page: Abrahamer Isidor, Abramowicz Bruno, Adamecki

politicians, judges, attorneys, industrialists, and aristocrats, and those with subtler influence like intellectuals, professors, journalists, and priests.[8]

Tannenberg was Himmler's first wartime power grab and it allowed him to attack Poles and expand police power.[9] He tasked his deputy Reinhard Heydrich, director of the Security Service (*Sicherheitsdienst*; SD), with assembling four Einsatzgruppen police squads in spring 1939.[10] Two thousand men from the SD, Gestapo, and Order Police (OrPo) assembled into 500-man groups, subdivided into 100-man commandos (Einsatzkommandos, EK).[11] Policemen were not privy to the mission, but knew they would be working in combat zones. In fact, each army group sent into Poland had a linked police task force in its rear, and the entire police campaign was conducted under the protective mantle of the Wehrmacht's war. Himmler needed a conventional war to hide the body count of his ideological campaign.[12]

Heydrich selected his policemen with care. The men in charge were thugs, deviants, and criminals. Heydrich chose SS Brigadeführer Lothar Beutel (1902–86) to head Einsatzgruppe IV (EG IV), destined for Warsaw.[13] A pharmacist from Lepizig, Beutel was too young to have fought in the First World War. He joined the Nazi party in 1929 and the SS in 1932, and was promoted to Brigadeführer in April 1939. Allegations – including of child

Teofil, Adameczewski Stefan, Adamczyk Jan, Adamczik Leon, Adamski Stanislaw, Adler Sigmund, Agacinski Jan, Ahrens Adolf, Alexandrowicz Isaak, Alijski –, Alten Viktor, and Anders – are all designated "Berlin." Four names are given for "Warschau." Śląska Biblioteka Cyfrowa, *Sonderfahndungsbuch Polen* (Berlin: Reichskriminalpolizeiamt, 1939), 3.

[8] George Mosse, "Toward a Total Culture" in *Nazi Culture: Intellectual, Cultural, and Social Life in the Third Reich* (New York: Schocken Books, 1966), 133–140.

[9] Gerhard Paul and Klaus-Michael Mallmann, *Die Gestapo im Zweiten Weltkrieg: 'Heimatfront' und besetztes Europa* (Darmstadt: Wissenschaftliche Buchgesellschaft, 2000), 11–22. British intelligence was unaware of Einsatzgruppen in Poland (TNA WO 190/884, Himmler's Private Army, 1–4).

[10] From the German perspective, understanding *which* unit was involved reveals politicization and demographic differences. From the Polish perspective, this was trivial.

[11] The distinction was between Heydrich's Security Police (Gestapo and KriPo), and Kurt Daluege's Order Police (urban police (*Schutzpolizei*), Gendarmerie, and community police (*Gemeindepolizei*)). Daluege's OrPo swelled to 131,000 and provided most Einsatzgruppe (EG) men. Michael Wildt, *An Uncompromising Generation: The Nazi Leadership of the Reich Security Main Office* (Madison: University of Wisconsin Press, 2003), 132–134, 217–221; BABL R58 242, Betr. Ministerrate für die Reichsverteidigung . . . im besetzten Gebiet, 13.Sept.1939, 233–233b.

[12] Army groups paired with an Einsatzgruppe or Polizeigruppe. We know how Einsatzgruppen operated; we have less on *Polizeigruppen*. Dorothee Weitbrecht, *Der Exekutionsauftrag der Einsatzgruppen in Polen* (Tübingen: Markstein Diskursiv, 2001), 15–16.

[13] Klaus Mallmann, Jochen Boehler, Juergen Matthaeus, eds., *Einsatzgruppen in Polen: Darstellung und Dokumentation* (Darmstadt: Wissenschaftliche Buchgesellschaft, 2008), 30–33.

molestation – later stripped Beutel of rank and consigned him to guard duty at Dachau, a telling demotion. SS-Untersturmführer Josef Meisinger (1899–1947), after battling scandalous legal trouble of his own, took command when the police settled in Warsaw. Born in Bavaria in 1899, Meisinger received the Iron Cross, 2nd Class for his First World War service and then joined the *Freikorps*. He was a notorious antisemite, an early party member, and a participant in the 1923 beerhall putsch. A bloodthirsty proponent of police violence in Poland, he was executed for war crimes in Warsaw in 1947.[14]

Operation Tannenberg competed for priority with the Wehrmacht and Joachim von Ribbentrop's foreign ministry, which was dancing around a Soviet–German demarcation line with Stalin. An SS-led *Polenpolitik* nevertheless formalized in September 1939. Days after Case White launched, Heydrich distributed arrest lists in Berlin. He informed police leadership that "the leading population stratum in Poland is to be rendered harmless."[15] Heydrich explained that "The Einsatzgruppen have made lists, from which designated leaders are to be captured, and other lists of the middle classes: teachers, clergy, gentry, Legionnaires [Pilsudskiites], reserve officers and suchlike. These types will be rounded up and sent into the leftover territory."[16] At his next briefing, Heydrich stipulated that Poland "will receive no protectorate, but a fully German administration" with a "rigorous deployment" of police.[17] To make this possible, the SS conscripted 26,000 new policemen, "despite the greatest resistance of the Wehrmacht," which objected to police expansion in wartime when men of military age were precious.[18] Days later, Heydrich's own deputy Werner Best issued a memorandum delineating the spheres of the military, civil

---

[14] Meisinger and Beutel traded duties. Beutel led the Einsatzgruppen into Poland because Meisinger was embroiled in scandal. After Beutel was himself disgraced, Meisinger replaced him. Criminality was common: these men did not uphold law in a traditional sense. Stephan Lehnstaedt, *Occupation in the East: The Daily Lives of German Occupiers in Warsaw and Minsk, 1939-1944* (New York: Berghahn Books, 2010), 2, 4, 6, 28–29. Robert Gerwarth, *Hitler's Hangman: The Life of Heydrich* (New Haven: Yale University Press, 2011), 117, 136.

[15] He added that "the remaining lower population will receive no advanced schooling, and will be comprehensively kept down." BABL R58 825, Vermerk: Amtschefbesprechung am 7.9.1939.

[16] IPN GK 704-19, Geheime Staatspolizei Poznan-EK 14/VI-SD-Posen, 2.

[17] BABL R58 825, "Amtschefbesprechung am 7.9.1939," 2–6; "Amtschefbesprechung am 8.9.1939," 1.

[18] Conscripts were under *Wehrdienstzeit* (BABL R58 825, "Amtschefbesprechung am 12.9.1939, Berlin," 1–2). On police-army tension: Martin Cüppers, *Wegbereiter der Shoah: Die Waffen-SS, der Kommandostab Reichsführer-SS und die Judenvernichtung 1939-1945* (Darmstadt: Wissenschaftliche Buchgesellschaft, 2005) and Böhler, *Auftakt zum Vernichtungskrieg*, 153.

administration, and police in Poland, with priority for the police.[19] The entire Nazi police system was reorganized, emerging as the Reich Security Main Office (RSHA) on September 27, 1939.[20] Before September ended, Heydrich reassembled police leadership to explain in cold bureaucratic language how they would run Poland:

> After the conclusion of the campaign in the east a shift in emphasis from the military to the economic-political-propagandistic sphere is to be expected . . . . The solution of the Polish problem – already in large part accomplished – varies with regard to the leadership classes (the Polish intelligentsia) and the lower working classes of *Polentum*. At most 3% of the leadership will remain in the occupied territories, and they are to be brought into concentration camps and rendered harmless . . . . The goal of all this is: that the Pole becomes and remains a kind of eternal seasonal migrant laborer with a permanent home in the area around Krakow.[21]

Historian Philipp Rutherford considers late September 1939 a turning point after which Germany was "fully committed to a policy of racial reshuffling."[22] This was not only true of the western Polish territory the Third Reich would incorporate: the police had launched a coup against the military and were planning to have their way with the territories gained through conquest. Moreover, their vision explicitly forbade Polish participation in governance: it permitted no Quisling.[23]

Despite the Berlin power grab, Tannenberg flailed in western Poland. "Securing" the intelligentsia was more complicated than anticipated, but Heydrich clung to Case White's timeline, insisting in late September that operations "would be completed in the next three to four weeks."[24] Delays allowed Poles time to flee. Tannenberg's first phase lasted from September 6, 1939 until October 6, 1939, before police entered Warsaw. Einsatzgruppen

---

[19] To "secure a frictionless continuation of the work of the whole organization." BABL R58 242, Betr. Ministerrat für die Reichsverteidigung, Reichsverteidigungskommissare, CdZ, EG und EK der SiPo, Befehlshaber der OrPo im besetzten Gebiet, 13.Sept.1939," 1.

[20] Tannenberg was part of a police power grab in fall 1939, forming the RSHA and the Waffen SS. Katrin Paehler, *The Third Reich's Intelligence Services: The Career of Walter Schellenberg* (New York: Cambridge University Press, 2017), 76–104; Longerich, *Himmler*, 426, 436–461, 469–472.

[21] BABL R58 825 "Amtschef und Einsatzgruppenleiterbesprechung am 21.9.1939," 3–4.

[22] Phillip T. Rutherford, *Prelude to the Final Solution: The Nazi Program for Deporting Ethnic Poles, 1939–1941* (Lawrence: University Press of Kansas, 2007), 50.

[23] Klaus-Peter Friedrich, "Collaboration in a 'Land without a Quisling:' Patterns of Cooperation with the Nazi German Occupation Regime in Poland during World War II," *Slavic Review* Vol. 64, No. 4 (2005), 711–746 and John Connelly's "Why the Poles Collaborated So Little: And Why That Is No Reason for Nationalist Hubris," *Slavic Review* Vol. 64, No. 4 (2005), 771–781.

[24] BABL R58 825, Vermerk: Amtschef und Einsatzgruppenleiterbesprechung [am 21.9.1939]; Amtschef u Einsatzgruppeleiterbesprechungen, 24–25.

moved from town to town, arresting and killing and reporting data back to Berlin.[25] However, as they moved eastward, the country was simultaneously destroyed by the Wehrmacht and invaded by the Red Army. Rapid Wehrmacht progress left a rear area less subdued than would have occurred with a more thorough campaign; Blitzkrieg-style victories were shocking but superficial.[26] Instead of focusing on intelligentsia, policemen found themselves disarming Polish soldiers. The Einsatzgruppen treated them as bandits rather than combatants – a racialized judgment based on the conviction that Poles lacked the right to resist.[27] Delays and distractions meant the target lists quickly became obsolete and the intelligentsia containment mission expanded. One police commando improvised a sorting checklist as replacement. If an arrested Pole was a: "a) leader or manager of any Polish organization, b) member of the Roman Catholic clergy, c) member of the Polish civil service, d) Polish academic, or e) 'other' landowner," then he (or less commonly, she) was a target.[28] The "a" category was elastic and broadly interpreted. Commandos made their own decisions on the ground.[29] Elites were the prize; most peasants were released as unobjectionable Slavic *Untermenschen*.[30] Polish Jews were assaulted, tormented, robbed, expelled from their homes, and occasionally murdered.[31] Since they were non-combatants and not conventional POWs, the law did not protect any of these people.[32] Some Poles meandered through the Nazi concentration camp system, or languished in makeshift prisons, but many were shot.[33]

---

[25] From the reports: POWs; wounded; missing: September 13 EG II in Krakow; fires: September 10 EG II in Częstochowa; plunder: September 8 EG III in Kalisch; civilians (Germans); army remnants.

[26] Citino, *Quest for Decisive Victory*, 256–259.

[27] Edward Westermann, *Hitler's Police Battalions: Enforcing Racial War in the East* (Lawrence: University Press of Kansas, 2005), 127. For "*Banden*," see: BAMA RH 53-23/10, Tages-u. Regimentsbefehle 25. Aug. 1939–Dez. 1939, Anlage 1: Zum Kriegstagebuch des Grenzwachtabschnitts-Kommandos, 5.

[28] IPN GK 704–19, Geheime Staatspolizei Poznan-EK 14/VI-SD-Posen, 2.

[29] EK 14/VI leader Lumpfenback added attorneys and judges. IPN GK 704–19, 11, 29.

[30] EK 16 captured thousands, interrogated them, and detained soldiers, targets, and "questionable" people but released Volksdeutsche and peasants. EK 16 recorded 27,834 prisoners between September 14 and October 5. EG II captured 5,329.

[31] Rossino focuses on antisemitic violence during the September Campaign, during which Jews were killed and brutalized. Alexander B Rossino, *Hitler Strikes Poland: Blitzkrieg, Ideology, and Atrocity* (Lawrence: University Press of Kansas, 2003). Pinchas Gutter, *Memories in Focus* (Toronto: Azrieli Foundation, 2018), 22–29.

[32] Geoffrey P. R. Wallace, *Life and Death in Captivity: The Abuse of Prisoners during War* (Ithaca: Cornell University Press, 2015), 125–128.

[33] These included temporary camps for Tannenberg prisoners. In late 1939, there were camps at Dobrzyca and Cerekwica. PISM London: MID: Dział Polski, A. 10. 4/2(II), "Sprawozdanie panów J. Tyszkiewicza . . . " Rome, 8.XII.1939, [1].

Einsatzgruppe IV's experiences radicalized police behavior and led to the first public knowledge of German atrocities.[34] Responding to reported violence against Volksdeutsche in Bydgoszcz (German: Bromberg), which had a significant German minority, Commander Beutel's EG IV conducted bloody reprisals, publicly executing their elite targets in the town square to terrorize the Polish population, a distinct modification of Tannenberg orders requiring secrecy.[35] The military campaign's rapidity sparked the confusion: German fifth columnists fired on Polish soldiers on September 3, 1939, and Bydgoszcz police arrested and executed some of them before the Polish army hastily retreated. Einsatzgruppe IV showed up to avenge the ethnic Germans by slaughtering Poles. News of the Bydgoszcz killings on "Bloody Sunday" ricocheted around central Europe, with reports appearing in the Nazi press and rumor lighting up Warsaw.[36]

Policing Bydgoszcz made EG IV men jumpy and encouraged them to view invasion chaos as illegitimate Polish resistance. It also delayed their advance, exacerbating their problem with "mission creep." Policemen killed anyone found armed, combing properties for weapons.[37] As Pinchas Gutter, a Polish Jewish boy, remembered the September chaos: "Nazi officials compiled a list of prominent people in Lodz, Jews and non-Jews, and immediately went about rounding them up."[38] The boy's grandfather was on the lists; policemen beat his father and robbed his family. His mother fled with him to Warsaw. Police sorted through those who remained.[39] They also "secured" antiques, art, machinery, and documents for the Reich. Jewish religious objects in particular were transported back to Germany.[40] Volksdeutsche joined German-organized *Selbstschutz* "protection" forces and enthusiastically helped Einsatzgruppen find Polish targets among their neighbors.[41]

---

[34] Wildt, *Uncompromising Generation*, 229; Longerich, *Himmler*, 430.

[35] Tomasz Chinciński and Paweł Machcewicz, *Bydgoszcz: 3–4 września 1939: Studia i dokumenty* (Warsaw: IPN, 2008).

[36] Peter Longerich, *Goebbels: A Biography* (New York: Random House, 2015), 430–431.

[37] On weapons: September 25 EG III in Łódź; September 26 EG VI in Posen.

[38] Gutter, *Memories in Focus*, 9, 23–24, 26, quotation 23.

[39] The exodus broke as the Red Army attacked on September 17. Jews feared Nazi anti-semitism above all. Germans did not prevent human movement until November 13, 1939, when SSPF Wilhelm Koppe attempted "to facilitate their arrest and expulsion." Rutherford, *Prelude to the Final Solution*, 82; Aleksander Wat, *My Century: The Odyssey of a Polish Intellectual.* Trans. Richard Lourie. Foreword Czesław Miłosz. (New York: New York Review Books, 1988), 98.

[40] Reports mention burnt synagogues (Westermann, *Hitler's Police Battalions*, 128), but the SS objected to looting so they could secure valuables themselves (September 18, EG II in Częstochowa, 124).

[41] First mention of *Selbstschutz* and *Heimatschutz* units on September 8. Many were staffed by SS-Deaths' Head Units. Martin Cüppers, *Wegbereiter der Shoah*, 28.

Poles with means fled eastward; most headed toward Warsaw, hoping for the hospitality of friends and family and the protection of their government and army.[42] The intelligentsia were not where policemen expected them to be, sending Tannenberg into a logistical tailspin, requiring police improvisation, and delaying timetables. On September 4–5, the national government evacuated.[43] Polish politicians with evacuation orders therefore had a two-day head start on policemen, who deployed on September 6.[44] Other Poles simply fled, fearing the Wehrmacht and Luftwaffe, even if they were unaware of police behavior. Police commandos repeatedly arrived in towns from which notables had departed.[45] Einsatzgruppe VI arrived too late in Poznań on September 15, losing archbishop and primate of Poland August Hlond, who had evacuated.[46] On September 17 EG II reported that its Krakow targets were nowhere to be found, and that the city was very quiet as a result: police reporters assumed that western Poland was docile because the intelligentsia had departed, reinforcing their original assumption that elites produced resistance.[47] The Einsatzgruppen conclusion was that their targets awaited them in Warsaw.[48]

2.2 Occupying Authorities

Warsaw put up a considerable fight against the Wehrmacht and Luftwaffe, and it was indeed the destination of refugee intelligentsia. Tannenberg nevertheless arrived in the capital on the heels of capitulation: Lothar Beutel's EG IV command staff entered Warsaw on the morning of October 2, 1939. They seized the Polish Ministry of Religious Affairs and Public Education, securing spacious quarters at 25 Szuch Boulevard, which they renamed *Polizeistrasse*.[49] Josef Meisinger took over from Beutel as Security Police and SD commander,

---

[42] The first of many ethnic relocations there: in 1939 ethnic Poles fled eastward; in 1944–45 ethnic Germans fled westward or faced Polonization. Norman M. Naimark, *Fires of Hatred: Ethnic Cleansing in Twentieth-Century Europe* (Cambridge, MA: Harvard University Press, 2001), 133–135.

[43] Kulski, *Z minionych lat życia*, 229; Bartoszewski, *1859 dni Warszawy*, 26–27.

[44] BABL R58 241, 4. September 1939, 2.

[45] EG III discovered Kalisz and Łódź elites had fled (BABL R58 7154 – [EG III 16 Sept.], 98); EG V noted the same for Działdowo and Łomża (BABL R58 7154 – [EG V 11, 19 Sept.], 56 and 128).

[46] Hlond would have made an excellent hostage. BABL R58 7154, EG VI September 15, 89–90; 93–95; EG VI September 30, 191, 207, 212; Madajczyk, *Polityka III Rzeszy*, Tom II, 193.

[47] BABL R58 7154, EG II September 17, 1939, 112–117; Kubalski, *Dziennik*, 24.

[48] Intelligentsia from the west congregated in Warsaw; others headed east. Wat, *My Century*, 99.

[49] BABL R58 825, "Amtschefbesprechung am 14.10.1939, Berlin," 3; R58 7154, *Tagesbericht* ending 5.10.1939 at 12:00, 201, 206.

thus becoming head of the Warsaw Gestapo.[50] Heydrich curtailed Tannenberg's mobile reporting and worked directly with the new Szuch Boulevard team. Thanks to Beutel's and Meisinger's men, their address would become a byword for Nazi terror.

By the time the Warsaw Gestapo was up and running, Nazi policymakers had a rough template for Poland. In the grander scheme of occupations, in which conquering states opt to manage populations by adopting postures of "accommodation, inducement, [or] coercion," as David Edelstein posits, ruling Poland was from the first to the last moment a matter of coercion: "ally[ing] with local elites" was rejected.[51] The violence and instability this produced is the subject of the rest of this study, and they were so clearly and quickly evident that the Polish model was not attempted in any other Nazi conquest; western and northern European states, notably, were "accommodated" and native administrations preserved by Berlin. On October 5, 1939 Hitler kicked things off with his Warsaw victory parade.[52] Poland was split between Nazi Germany and the Soviet Union, the German portion further subdivided into land incorporated into the Third Reich and the remainder designated as a "General Government."[53] This left Warsaw in German hands. A Führer decree made the General Government for the Occupied Polish Territories (GG) official from October 26, if not legal internationally.[54] Peaceful Krakow became its capital, though Warsaw and its 1,289,000 inhabitants plagued GG administrators with problems.[55]

---

[50] Until March 1941. Christian Ingrao, *Believe & Destroy: Intellectuals in the SS War Machine* (Cambridge: Polity Press, 2013), 85–87; NARA RG 242 A3343 SSO Mf306A, Meisinger Josef.

[51] The transition from Wehrmacht to civilian-SS control indicated a pure coercion approach. Edelstein, *Occupational Hazards*, 49–51.

[52] Bartoszewski, *1859 dni Warszawy*, 70.

[53] Final negotiations on September 28. BABL R58 825, "Amtschefbesprechung am 29.9.1939, Berlin," 1. According to Jan Gross, Stalin gave Warsaw to Germany for Lithuania. Jan Gross, *Revolution from Abroad: The Soviet Conquest of Poland's Western Ukraine and Western Belorussia* (Princeton: Princeton University Press, 1988), 12–13. NB: This was not a multilateral occupation but two unilateral ones. Edelstein, *Occupational Hazards*, 136.

[54] Hans Frank, *Das Diensttagebuch des deutschen Generalgouverneurs in Polen, 1939–1945* (Stuttgart: Deutsche Verlags-Anstalt, 1975), 45; Moorhouse, *Poland 1939*, 300–302.

[55] The GG encompassed 36,862 square miles and 11,542,000 people in 1939. The severing of Łódź – the "Polish Manchester" – impoverished Warsaw. Łódź, renamed Litzmannstadt, was incorporated into the Reich (Richard Breitman, *Architect of Genocide: Himmler and the Final Solution*, New York: Alfred A. Knopf, 1991, 81); Horwitz, Ghettostadt. Krakow was the second largest city with 321,000 inhabitants in a district of 3.6 million. Warsaw had 2.4 rural dwellers to feed every urban resident; Krakow had 11 for each: Warsaw was to be starved. Dieter Schenk, *Hans Frank: Hitlers Kronjurist und Generalgouverneur* (Frankfurt/Main: S. Fischer Verlag, 2006), 146. Cf. Mazower, *Inside Hitler's Greece*, 32,

Hitler sought to ensure that German GG personnel showed no sympathy towards Poles, hence his choice of the man selected to run things: Hans Frank (1900–46). [56] Hitler invited Frank to the Berlin Reich Chancellery to describe his vision for Poland. It was stark: nothing was to be rebuilt, resistance was to be crushed, and all territorial assets stripped for the Reich. "The accomplishment" of his Polish program, Hitler warned, "required a hard ethnic struggle which would not permit any legal restrictions."[57] Frank, a lawyer by training, had been part of the early Nazi movement but was a backbencher by 1939. He had served in the *Freikorps*, marched in the failed beerhall putsch, represented Hitler in the subsequent trial, served in the Reichstag after 1930, and gained positions – head of the Academy of German Law and Bavarian Minister of Justice – after Hitler's appointment as chancellor.[58] Despite a lengthy résumé, Frank never drove policymaking. It is unlikely that he knew of Himmler's and Heydrich's plans but, as General Governor in rump Poland, he became the longest-serving civilian administrator across the Nazi empire.[59] He maintained his position from the GG's creation in October 1939 until the Soviet advance in 1945, before which he fled (Figure 2.1).[60]

The Gestapo struggled with the Wehrmacht over authority in Warsaw, keen to continue Heydrich's directives and prevent resistance. Tannenberg's dysfunction, however, set the tone for the occupation, which departed from Hans von Beseler's First World War model of halting Polish–German cooperation.[61] As Case White had only just concluded, the Wehrmacht started off in charge.[62] It was hostile to Poles but focused on security in the traditional sense of the

---

44–48. Frank's GG expanded eastward in 1941. Anti-intelligentsia campaigning revived with roundups of Lwów professors (Tarik Cyril Amar, *The Paradox of Ukrainian L'viv* (Ithaca: Cornell University Press, 2015), 88, 101; DALO f. P-37 op. 4, 111 and DALO f. P-37 op. 5, 16a); Kubalski, *Niemcy w Krakowie*, 252). GG population figures are slippery. The conventional figure is 12 million, though Frank claimed 12.5–13 million in 1940 (AUJ – IDO-1, Dzieje i organizacja Instytutu 1940–1944, "Sendung u. Aufgabe deutscher Geistesführung im Osten" / Das Institut für deutsche Ostarbeit, by Hans Frank, 1940, 2; Polish Ministry of Information, *Concise Statistical Year-Book of Poland, September 1939–June 1941* (Glasgow: Robert Maclehose and Co. Ltd., 1941), 4, 26).

[56] In Poland personnel *was* policy. This practice of selecting personnel instead of detailing policy continued. Wendy Lower, *Nazi Empire-Building and the Holocaust in Ukraine.* Chapel Hill: University of North Carolina Press, 2005, 70.

[57] Martyn Housden, *Hans Frank,* Lebensraum, *and the Holocaust* (London: Palgrave Macmillan, 2003), 78–79; Schenk, *Hans Frank,* 148; Ian Kershaw, *Hitler: 1936–1945: Nemesis* (New York: W. W. Norton, 2000), 204–205.

[58] Gellately, *Backing Hitler,* 23.

[59] Frank's Nuremberg testimony: 4-18-1946. Blue Series. Examination by Alfred Seidl.

[60] NARA A3356 OKH Mf 191, Frank Hans, "Personal Nachweis," "Dienstlaufbahn" and "Beurteilung," unpaginated.

[61] Von Beseler ruled from Warsaw. Kauffman, *Elusive Alliance,* 32–48.

[62] "Nicht Heimatgebiet" and "nicht Operationsgebiet." BAMA Militärischen Rechtscharakter des GG, 23. Oktober 1940, 56–57.

Figure 2.1 Hans Frank (right) hosts Heinrich Himmler (left) at a dinner held at Wawel
Castle during his visit to Krakow, the General Government capital, 1940.
United States Holocaust Memorial Museum, Photograph Number 15074.

term. Nazi police sought harsher terms. Complaints about Tannenberg atrocities reached the ears of Field Marshal Walther von Brauchitsch,
Oberbefehlshaber des Heeres (Army Commander).[63] Generals complained
to Hitler about police behavior, despite the fact that the army was *itself*
radicalizing. Historians now trace a bright line of increasing German brutality
in eastern Europe from the launch of Case White in 1939, rather than the older
thesis of delaying wide-scale atrocity to the launch of the Barbarossa campaign
in 1941.[64] Police were disregarding traditional protections for civilians, *and*
"conventional" military forces were perpetuating numerous atrocities against
combatants. Poland and 1939 are usually considered as a "laboratory" or
"jumping off point" for the Holocaust or *Vernichtungskrieg* (war of annihilation) in the USSR, but how radicalization proceeded in Warsaw is less well

[63] Martin Broszat, *Nationalsozialistische Polenpolitik, 1939–1945* (Fischer-Bücherei, 1965),
20 and 34–35; Böhler, *Auftakt zum Vernichtungskrieg*, 237–239; Westermann, *Hitler's
Police Battalions*, 148–149; Rossino, *Hitler Strikes Poland*, 58–87; Madajczyk, *Polityka III
Rzeszy*, Tom II, 265–266.
[64] Moorhouse, *Poland 1939*, 314, 319. September 1, 1939 – and the cover of war – also
launched the euthanasia program. Breitman, *Architect of Genocide*, 89–92; Edith Sheffer,
Asperger's Children: The Origins of Autism in Nazi Vienna (New York: Norton, 2018), 20–
22, 129–130, 180–185. Gerwarth, *Hitler's Hangman*, 146–148.

explored.[65] Nazi behavior in 1939, however, was not simply a precedent for violence in other places against other populations, but in Poland against Poles: the targeting of the Warsaw intelligentsia was the first chapter in the radicalization of Nazi violence in wartime eastern Europe. Wehrmacht complaints underscore how revolutionary Himmler's 1939 plans were. The generals' protests came to nothing, but alerted Himmler that the army could not be counted on as helpmate in the prosecution of his kind of racial warfare.

Running the GG – what Tarik Amar calls a "vague, violent construct" – in the wake of military and police campaigns proved harder than Hitler's sloganeering.[66] Frank made his capital in Krakow, marginalizing Warsaw and emphasizing that this was not a Polish state. His immediate subordinate was State Secretary of the General Government Josef Bühler (1904–48) who had been a colleague since 1935. Frank appointed men he knew and trusted to positions of authority. His Warsaw staff is most important to this story. Dr. Ludwig Fischer (1905–47), Frank's Warsaw district governor, was a longtime colleague and both were "old fighters:" Fischer had joined the Nazi Party in 1926 and the SA (Sturmabteilung or Brownshirts) in 1929. He met Frank in 1931 and by 1938 Frank had promoted him to chief of staff of the National Socialist Legal Association. Fischer was from the Rhineland, married with a child, and had studied law; their backgrounds were not dissimilar.[67] Fischer served with Frank until the bitter end. He was a tireless and loyal subordinate and a remarkably uninteresting person.[68] Fischer's entire legacy consists in a few volumes of reports, likely written by underlings, and a lavishly illustrated account of his "work," *Warsaw under German Hegemony*.[69] Fischer appointed a nobody from his home town of Kaiserlautern, Ludwig Leist (1891–1967), as the German "mayor" from March 1940 to July 31, 1944. Leist worked with Julian Kulski, Starzyński's nervous replacement,[70] and ran

---

[65] For Polish atrocities as "laboratory," see Rossino, *Hitler Strikes Poland*; Böhler, *Auftakt zum Vernichtungskrieg*. For Barbarossa radicalization, see Omer Bartov, *Hitler's Army: Soldiers, Nazis, and War in the Third Reich* (New York: Oxford University Press, 1992), 105–178. Cf. Smith, *Germany*, 367.

[66] Amar, *Paradox of Ukrainian L'viv*, 89.

[67] NARA RG 242 SA Akten Mf0143, Fischer Ludwig, "Personalbogen" and "Abschrift."

[68] His defense before the Supreme National Tribunal (NTN) was that he had "signed decrees and orders without reading them." Gabriel Finder and Alexander Prusin, *Justice behind the Iron Curtain: Nazis on Trial in Communist Poland* (Toronto: University of Toronto Press, 2018), 120.

[69] *Zwei Jahre Aufbauarbeit im Distrikt Warschau*, 1941. 1942 update: *Warschau unter deutscher Herrschaft* (Krakow: Burgverlag Krakau GmbH, 1942). Herbert Hummel, who had known Fischer and Frank, became vice-governor in January 1941 (Ludwig Fischer, *Raporty Ludwiga Fischera Gubernatora Dystryktu Warszawskiego, 1939-1944* (Warsaw: Książka i Wiedza, 1987), 14–15). Assisting Fischer and Hummel was Oskar Dengel (1899–1964), Chief of the Civil Administration.

[70] Lehnstaedt, *Occupation*, 37.

the city from the Blank Palace on Senatorska Street.[71] Fischer, meanwhile, remained safely ensconced behind guards at Brühl Palace, an eighteenth-century rococo masterpiece that had housed the Polish Ministry of Foreign Affairs and sat centrally on Piłsudski Square – renamed Adolf Hitler Square.[72]

Warsaw rarely glimpsed German leadership. A handful of Varsovians had access to it, but such contact was fraught with danger. Varsovians referred to every policeman as *"esesman"* or *"gestapowiec,"* regardless of specific affiliation; Poles rarely bothered to learn the lugubrious titles of their persecutors. Nazi power was exercised through force; officials' face-lessness is underscored by their absence from caricature, the great occupa-tion art.[73] In the avalanche of Polish visual satire Hitler was omnipresent with his instantly recognizable mustache; Goebbels, Goering, and Himmler made regular appearances, and Frank appeared occasionally.[74] Germans running Warsaw were not distinct enough to earn them a place in carica-ture. As Stephen Lehnstaedt elaborates, these men were not merely faceless but "speechless," a separate community, discouraged from interaction with Poles, unable to communicate more than coercion.[75] The East was, after all, a hardship post and most Germans considered themselves there temporarily.[76] Some had not earned plum jobs and settled for GG posts – the "Reich's cast-offs," in Martin Winstone's phrase – and others hoped for spoils.[77] The "new masters," including Wehrmacht personnel (the biggest group), Reich civilians, and newly empowered Volksdeutsche, lived in the southern Mokotów neighborhood, which contained blocks of

---

[71] Tadeusz Walichnowski knew his signature but only met him in person in 1951. Walichnowski, *Rozmowy z Leistem: hitlerowskim starostą Warszawy* (Warsaw: Państwowe Wydawnictwo Naukowe, 1986), 11.

[72] Borowiec's description of Fischer as "a plump and prosperous-looking lawyer in his late thirties" is unusual (Andrew Borowiec, *Warsaw Boy: A Memoir of a Wartime Childhood* (New York: Penguin Books, 2014), 162); Leokadia Rowinski spent the occupation in Warsaw and misremembered him as *Franz* Fischer (Leokadia Rowinski, *That the Nightingale Return: A Memoir of the Polish Resistance, the Warsaw Uprising and German P.O.W. Camps* (Jefferson: McFarland & Company, Inc., 1999), 74; Walichnowski, *Rozmowy z Leistem*, 18–23; 31.

[73] Poles who denounced their neighbors to the Gestapo in 1940–41 sent letters to the "powers that be," rarely specifying Leist or Fischer. Barbara Engelking, *"Szanowny panie gistapo:" Donosy do władz niemieckich w Warszawie i okolicach w latach 1940–1941* (Warsaw: Wyd. IFiS PAN, 2003), 52–61.

[74] For two depicting Frank by "Yes" (Henryk Chmielewski) in 1942–43, see: Grzegorz Załęski, and Krzysztof Załęski, *Satyra w konspiracji, 1939–1944* (Warsaw: Wydawnictwo LTW, [2011]), 70; 78).

[75] Lehnstaedt, *Occupation*, 42, 61.

[76] PISM London: MID: Dział Polski, A. 10. 4/3, Sprawozdania z Kraju, 1940: "Sprawozdanie Gospodarcze z obszaru Polski zajętego przez Niemców," 2; Urbanek, *Codzienność w cieniu terror*, 37–38.

[77] Winstone, *Dark Heart*, 51.

new apartments finished under Starzyński's tenure and seized from their Polish owners. Germans worked downtown and lived, ate, and entertained themselves across the city, often at establishments specifically designated for their use and denied to Poles, from nightclubs to grocery stories to trams. Few brought their wives, provoking the growth of prostitution, adding another layer of exploitation to German–Polish relations.[78] Great efforts were made to keep Germans in Warsaw happy and provide them *Kultur* appropriate for the "master race," but occupation personnel were restive, touchy, and violent.[79]

Warsaw's police leadership was a nasty bunch, as should be expected from Heydrich's involvement. There were also a lot of them: each police institution had its own head and turnover was high. Himmler's direct subordinate in Krakow, Friedrich Wilhelm Krüger (1894–1945), Higher SS and Police Leader East (HSSPF-Ost), did not cooperate well with Frank.[80] Frank did not have the clout to regulate Himmler or Krüger; Fischer never tried. Police–civilian–military squabbling muddled policy and occasionally made Polish maneuvering among German interests possible.[81] Meisinger, who took over from Beutel, was Krüger's first Nazi police commander in Warsaw, but five men would lead the Gestapo from Szuch Boulevard.[82] The most infamous was Meisinger's successor, Franz Kutschera (1904–44), who policed Warsaw from September 1943 until his February 1, 1944 assassination. During those months he executed more non-Jewish Varsovians than any other Nazi – a significant achievement.[83]

---

[78] Germans numbered ca. 70,000. Lehnstaedt, *Occupation*, 20–21, 40, 47, 53–57; Maren Röger, *Wojenne związki: Polki i Niemcy podczas okupacji* (Warsaw: Świat Książki, 2016), 27–79; on the World War I template, see Liulevicius, *War Land*, 135.

[79] Housden, *Hans Frank*, 114.

[80] Himmler subordinated the police to Frank but communicated with them directly. BABL R58 241, "Führerorganisation der Polizei im Generalgouvernement," 1. November 1939, Berlin, gez. Himmler, [1]-2); NARA RG 242 A3343 SSO Mf218A, Krueger Wilhelm Friedrich.

[81] Lehnstaedt, *Occupation*, 34, 151–154, 214.

[82] Meisinger ordered the Palmiry and Wawer massacres and built the ghetto. He worked with Max Daume (1894–1947), Order Police commander (Walichnowski, *Rozmowy z Leistem*, 60–61; NARA RG 242 A3343 SSO Mf137, Daume Max). Johannes Müller (1895–1961) replaced Meisinger in March 1941; in August Ludwig Hahn (1908–86), who had led EG I in Tannenberg, replaced Müller. Himmler later gave SS-Brigadeführer Jürgen Stroop (1895–1952) the "special task" of crushing the Warsaw Ghetto Uprising (Kazimierz Moczarski, *Rozmowy z katem* (Krakow: Znak Horyzont, 2018); Finder and Prusin, *Justice*, 127; Lehnstaedt, *Occupation*, 31–32).

[83] Kutschera arrived from Eastern Front "anti-partisan" operations. Kutschera's infamy earned him an exception to the no-caricature rule: it could be his (quite ugly) face depicted in October 1943 in *Demokrata* (Załęski and Załęski, *Satyra w konspiracji, 1939-1944*, 73; Service record: NARA RG 242 A3343 SSO Mf233A, Kutschera Franz).

The men who ran the GG from Frank and Krüger down came from the Third Reich.[84] Previous German occupations had utilized Polish personnel, and other Nazi administrations during the Second World War relied on local elites, learning from the extraordinary inefficiency and violence caused by excluding Poles from administration.[85] Poles were unwelcome in government because of Himmler's anti-intelligentsia logic. Heydrich made the matter crystal clear: the territory of the Second Polish Republic would be divided and run by Germans (and their Soviet allies) for the benefit of Nazi Germany. Polish citizens of German ethnicity – Volksdeutsche – were part of the "new order," but Poles, and especially Polish Jews, were outside it.

This meant that Polish elites could not lead, not that Poles would not work for the Germans: the gap between intelligentsia experience and that of "ordinary" Poles was wide. In fact, the occupation employed "tens of thousands," though Varsovians were "mere recipients of orders."[86] Nazi police and German civilian administrators had auxiliaries for their dirtiest work. Volksdeutsche were prominent. The Hitler Youth and Labor Service pitched in with executions.[87] Polish administrative functionaries, like deputy mayor Julian Kulski and chairman of the Jewish council Adam Czerniaków, remained as hostages to German power, multilingual intermediaries between occupiers and "locals." Two institutions, however, grew and spread under Nazi occupation and were decisively Polish in their personnel and leadership, raising questions about how intimately Varsovians worked with their occupiers and how and whether Poles served German interests.

The first was a cluster of charitable or "self help" organizations born in Krakow in the GG capital, but with Warsaw branches: the Capital Social Welfare Committee (Stołeczny Komitet Sampomocy Społecznej, SKSS) and from 1940 the City Welfare Council (Rada Opiekuńcza Miejska, ROM) a branch of the Main Welfare Council (Rada Główna Opiekuńcza, RGO). These were revived First World War charities that served food, housed refugees, supplied medicine to hospitals, and petitioned on behalf of prisoners. Crucial among the people the SKSS and ROM cared for were impoverished and imprisoned intelligentsia.[88] Their

---

The last head of Warsaw's police was Paul Otto Geibel (1898–1966) (NARA RG 242 A3343 SSO Mf006A, Geibel Paul Otto).

[84] Lehnstaedt, *Occupation*, 2–6.

[85] Philip Morgan details how the intelligentsia's western European counterparts embraced collaboration. Morgan, *Hitler's Collaborators: Choosing between Bad and Worse in Nazi-Occupied Western Europe* (Oxford: Oxford University Press, 2018), 154–234.

[86] Lehnstaedt, *Occupation*, 40.

[87] Władysław Bartoszewski, *Palmiry* (Warsaw: Książka i Wiedza, 1969), 12–13.

[88] PAN III-59-97 Materiały Artura Śliwińskiego: "Sprawozdania i memoriały Rady Głównej Opiekuńczej (Rady Opiekuńczej Miejskiej składane prezesowi SKSS,") "Sprawozdanie," 15 Sept.–31 Oct. 1940, [1]-16.

organizer and patron was Artur Śliwiński (1877–1953), an old Pilsudskiite, briefly an interwar prime minister, and a member of Janusz Regulski's siege citizen militia. ROM functioned under occupation with grudging German approval – its functionaries reported to German officials, including Leist and Fischer – and through donations, including from the Polish Red Cross and Commission for Polish Relief in the United States.[89] In fact, Starzyński's office contacted Śliwiński in October 1939, warning him to remain in the city, or the occupiers would impose consequences.[90] Śliwiński, along with colleagues in Krakow like Count Adam Ronikier (1881–1952) and Cardinal Prince Adam Sapieha (1867–1951), two aristocrats who leveraged their social positions to keep such efforts afloat, therefore cooperated with the German civilian administration.[91] The reason an exception was made to the rule against Polish leadership should be obvious in this case: Śliwiński's work relieved the German occupation of burdens it happily neglected, and funneled foreign funds to reduce occupation costs.

The second collaborating institution had a much uglier profile and no charitable goals: Warsaw's city police, the "blue police" (*policja granatowa*; properly *policja państwowa*, PP), known for the color of their overcoats. The Polish government ordered policemen and what would now be called "first responders" to evacuate in September, though many stayed and 10,000 ended up as POWs; their thinned ranks necessitated civilian and scout reinforcements.[92] The Wehrmacht and German civilian administration had specific ideas of what policing meant, to which the Einsatzgruppen have already provided an introduction. Limited personnel nevertheless led Friedrich Wilhelm Krüger and the Order Police to reorganize remaining Polish police forces after October 1939.[93] Stephen Lehnstaedt, detailing German occupier demographics, counts fewer than 500 German policemen in Warsaw.[94]

---

[89] PAN III-59-97 Materiały Artura Śliwińskiego: "Sprawozdania i memoriały Rady Głównej Opiekuńczej," "Sprawozdanie," 15 Sept. – 31 Oct. 1940, 2, 4–5, 15; Sprawozdanie," 1–30 Nov. 1940, 31.

[90] PAN III-59-50 Materiały Artura Śliwińskiego: "2 pisma przez S. Starzyńskiego," 3 and 7 October 1939, 2.

[91] Kubalski, *Niemcy w Krakowie*, 24, 63, 72, 89; Adam Ronikier, *Pamiętniki, 1939–1945* (Krakow: Wydawnictwo Literackie, 2001), 7, 34–74. Ronikier was regularly harassed and arrested by Nazi police.

[92] Grabowski calculates 2,000–3,000 police casualties. Jan Grabowski, *Na posterunku: Udział polskiej policji granatowej i kryminalnej w zagładzie Żydów* (Wołowiec: Wydawnictwo Czarne, 2020), 22–23.

[93] BABL R58 136 Die innerpolitischen Machtmittel Polens, Die polnische Staatspolizei, 94–96; Robert Litwiński, "Policja Granatowa w okupacyjnej Warszawie w obronie bezpieczeństwa i porządku publicznego" in *Porządek publiczny i bezpieczeństwo w okupowanej Warszawie*, ed. Robert Spałek (Warsaw: IPN, 2018), 90.

[94] Lehnstaedt, *Occupation*, 32.

German police had "loftier" duties and were not servants of a Polish public; when Poles attempted to secure "law and order" under occupation they either turned to "indigenous local police force[s]" or, more often, took matters into their own hands.[95] "Indigenous" forces, including the blue police, criminal police, railway policemen, and gendarmes outnumbered their German superiors: blue policemen numbered 10,000–15,000 across the GG with 3,000 men and 60 commissioned officers in Warsaw by 1942.[96] As compared to 669 German policemen, Warsaw had 3,200 uniformed Polish policemen in early 1943.[97] From their first formation, the blue policemen seized occupation opportunities to terrorize Warsaw's vulnerable, especially its Jewish community, and line their own pockets. Non-Jewish Poles working against the occupation also had to fear blue policemen, though they had recourse and resources Polish Jews did not. Operating as enforcers of German directives, blue policemen patrolled the streets, arrested Varsovians, and seized property and goods on behalf of the occupation (and themselves). Historian Jan Grabowski has written a damning analysis of their GG operations, focusing on their role in Holocaust violence. Though they were most closely supervised in Warsaw, where German personnel was concentrated, they targeted Polish Jews elsewhere even without German oversight, robbing, raping, beating, and in many cases killing Jews on their own initiative. In Warsaw, too, they persecuted Jews viciously, though they tended to hand their urban victims off to the Gestapo.[98] Rank-and-file blue policemen were not members of the intelligentsia, but their leaders were. Their first commander was a holdover

---

[95] Circumstances that didn't rule out leveraging Gestapo denunciation to settle scores or betray Polish Jews. Lehnstaedt, *Occupation*, 33; Engelking, "*Szanowny panie gistapo*," 73, 86, 92, 96, 99–103.

[96] Włodzimierz Borodziej, *Terror und Politik: Die deutsche Polizei und die polnische Widerstandsbewegung im Generalgouvernement, 1939–1944* (Mainz: Verlag Philipp von Zabern, 1999), 36, 40–41.

[97] Grabowski, *Na posterunku*, 250–251.

[98] On Polish police behavior in Warsaw: Grabowski, *Na posterunku*, 257–293, 311, 317–321. On Polish police killing outside Warsaw: Grabowski, *Na posterunku*, 107–179, 359. The urban/rural distinction is one of the frontiers of Polish Holocaust scholarship: after the Polish publication in 2000 of Jan T. Gross's *Neighbors: The Destruction of the Jewish Community in Jedwabne, Poland* (New York: Penguin Books, 2002), Polish historians have worked to prove (or disprove) his larger point that non-Jewish Poles targeted Polish Jews and contributed to the lethality of the Holocaust, thus crucially focusing on areas *outside* Warsaw where German personnel were rare. Crucial here are recent arguments that Holocaust killing was driven by Polish agency in rural areas. See, especially: Jan Grabowski, *Hunt for the Jews: Betrayal and Murder in German-Occupied Poland* (Bloomington: Indiana University Press, 2013) on Poles attacking Jews in Dąbrowa Tarnowska and the two-volume *Dalej jest Noc: Losy Żydów w wybranych powiatach okupowanej Polski* (Warsaw: Stowarzyszenie Centrum Badań nad Zagładą Żydów, 2018), edited by Jan Grabowski and Barbara Engelking.

from the interwar and a subordinate of Starzyński's, Marian Kozielewski (1897–1964, "Bratkowski"), Jan (Kozielewski) Karski's older brother ("Karski" was a wartime pseudonym that the younger brother retained, and Kozielewski the original family name). Marian Kozielewski seems to have thought his policemen could serve Warsaw and tried to simultaneously build an anti-Nazi policemen's conspiracy in the emerging underground, leveraging Gestapo contacts for Polish purposes. This double game got Kozielewski arrested in summer 1940.[99] His successors, Aleksander Reszczyński (1941–1943), and Franciszek Przymusinski (March 1943–August 1944), were less ambitious. The blue policemen made controlling Warsaw easier for the occupation but their loyalty to their Nazi masters was "illusory," crumbling when the war turned against the Germans.[100] Why the Nazi occupation allowed blue policemen is more obvious still than their support of charitable efforts: Polish policemen did their dirty work.

2.3 Frank's Police Campaign

The GG's beginnings were thus a violent mess. Frank's new administration filled out, but German military officers, civilians, and policemen feuded.[101] Frank had not been in power long when Himmler undermined his authority. Himmler and Heydrich, not finished with anti-intelligentsia campaigning, nevertheless launched a massive resettlement program to immediately Germanize western Poland by dumping ethnic Poles into Frank's GG.[102] This refugee crisis compounded Tannenberg's unsolved problems as the Warsaw Gestapo was nowhere near finished "processing" prominent Varsovians.[103] To hasten things along, Krüger ordered mass executions around Warsaw and stiffened police powers to execute men without trial.

---

[99] Regina Domańska, *Pawiak: Więzienie Gestapo: Kronika 1939–1944* (Warsaw: Książka i Wiedza, 1978), 58; 79–80.

[100] Grabowski, *Na posterunku*, 54.

[101] Gross considers the police-civilian fight overblown but Frank's desire to micromanage the GG created real tension. Gross, *Polish Society*, 87.

[102] This morbid "hot potato" deportation game defined Nazi empire. Götz Aly, *Final Solution: Nazi Population Policy and the Murder of the European Jews* (London: Arnold, 1999), 88–104. Himmler planned to dump 3.4 million Poles into the GG. Longerich, *Himmler*, 408, 414, 437–449, esp. 445; Rutherford, *Prelude to the Final Solution*, 133–172;, Catherine Epstein, *Model Nazi: Arthur Greiser and the Occupation of Western Poland* (New York: Oxford University Press, 2010), 164–166; Naimark, *Fires of Hatred*, 70.

[103] Longerich claims "terror was systematized" then. Longerich, *Himmler*, 430–431; Deborah Dwork and Jan van Pelt, *Holocaust: A History* (New York: Norton & Company, 2002), 356–374; Aly, *Final Solution*, 59–87; 105–133.

The result of the violence was exactly the unrest Krüger (and Frank) feared: SS reports indicated early, isolated Polish resistance.[104]

Frank decided to take the restive security situation in hand. His new plan endorsed in-progress Nazi police roundups and added further efforts to quash opposition, coercing Polish acceptance of German rule. Anti-intelligentsia policy was therefore implemented in two waves, the first directed by Heydrich and relying on mobile personnel, the second a joint civilian–police effort directed from Krakow by Frank. Frank dubbed his new effort the Extraordinary Pacification Campaign (*Ausserordentliche Befriedungsaktion*, AB-Aktion).[105] On May 30, 1940, he called a Krakow police meeting to introduce his "extraordinary pacification campaign [against] ... the circle of politically dangerous people in the GG, the political–spiritual leadership of the Polish resistance." "The Polish leadership class that we have already secured is to be liquidated," he announced, "and what grows up in its place we will secure and dispose of at the appropriate moment."[106] AB's intelligentsia target was 3,500 people, a suspiciously round and much lower number than that set for Tannenberg. It likely did not include those already in custody. Frank noted that,

> ... the Security Police already have around 2,000 men and a few hundred women in their custody who are different kinds of officials in the leadership of the Polish resistance movement. These people are really the spiritual leadership, the inspiration of the Polish resistance movement. ... the sentencing of these people according to the stipulations of the AB-Aktion has already begun. The summary executions of this group of 2,000 is drawing to a close, and there are just a few more people to process ... In total, this Aktion will secure this entire circle of 3,500 people ... in seizing these 3,500 we have really captured the politically most dangerous portion of the resistance movement in the General Government.

For the second time an anti-intelligentsia campaign was conducted under cover of war: the AB-Aktion was timed to coincide with the invasion of France since, as Frank reminded his policemen, "the attention of the world

---

[104] BABL R58 825, Vermerk: Amtschef und Einsatzgruppenleiterbesprechung [am 21.9.1939]; Amtschef u. Einsatzgruppenleiterbesprechungen, 24–25.

[105] Wardzyńska's *Był rok 1939* considers Tannenberg and AB across Poland, and Daniel Brewing's *Im Schatten von Auschwitz: Deutsche Massaker an polnischen Zivilisten, 1939–1945* (Darmstadt: Wissenschaftliche Buchgesellschaft, 2016) places them in the context of German civilian killing. For Frank's meeting, see *Das Diensttagebuch des deutschen Generalgouverneurs in Polen, 1939–1945* (Stuttgart: Deutsche Verlags-Anstalt, 1975), 206–209.

[106] Frank, *Diensttagebuch*, 214.

[wa]s turned on that campaign."[107] In Warsaw, Meisinger's men understood AB as a kill order for remaining intelligentsia prisoners.[108]

The anti-intelligentsia campaigns therefore merged in Warsaw: EG IV, settled on Szuch Boulevard, continued to implement their Tannenberg orders until they were updated by AB. They held several hundred men, including Starzyński and his deputy, as hostages for "good behavior" during Hitler's victory parade in October 1939. They took more hostages to deter patriotic demonstrations before Polish Independence Day on 11 November. Army officers, including elderly veterans, were among them.[109] The Warsaw Gestapo then made up for lost time with mass street arrests the Poles called łapanki (roundups). When large groups were arrested, policemen sifted out elites from among them and set them aside for special treatment, releasing the rest for Wehrmacht labor.[110] The Gestapo also made arrests by professional group – reserve officers, lawyers, members of parliament, priests, university professors. At least 600 reserve officers were arrested and sent to POW camps in Germany by early 1940.[111] Prisons, like those on Daniłowiczowska and Gęsia streets, overflowed with new detainees. Dzielna street's Pawiak prison was the main holding facility for elites-turned-political-prisoners.

The Gestapo interrogated intelligentsia victims, verified their identities, grilled them for contacts and details of anti-Nazi activities, and then killed them in Warsaw and nearby forests or sent them on to concentration camps.[112] Shootings were an "everyday" occurrence: reports mentioned

---

[107] Frank, *Das Diensttagebuch*, 210–215. Peter Fritzsche's timing is off: it was not the "victory in western Europe" that allowed AB, but the campaign itself. Fritzsche, *Iron Wind*, 118. Mark Mazower credits Frank with "presid[ing] over the mass murder of the Polish elite" but he only continued it. Mazower, *Hitler's Empire*, 74.

[108] Baranowski estimated 700,000+ by capitulation. Baranowski, *Nazi Empire*, 234; Finder and Prusin, *Justice*, 71, 109.

[109] Bartoszewski, *1859 dni Warszawy*, 70, 76; Stefan Korbonski, *Fighting Warsaw: The Story of the Polish Underground State, 1939–1945*. Trans. F. B. Czarnomski (London: George Allen & Unwin, Ltd.), 1956; Wardzyńska, *Był rok 1939*, 240; USHMM – Polizei-Regiment Warschau, dem 5. November 1939, betrifft: Festnahme sämtlicher in Warschau wohnender ehem. Polnischer Offiziere am 7. November 1939, 1–2, 1.2.7.0004, ITS Digital Archive, Accessed at the USHMM November 2014.

[110] A keystone of First World War occupation. Liulevicius, *War Land*, 67–75.

[111] Some reports mention 5,000 December arrests. Officers' wives were arrested. PISM London: MID: Dział Polski, A. 10. 4/2/1, "Zarządzenia okupantów i ich stosunek do ludności," 1; A. 10. 4/4, "Jak Niemcy niszczą inteligencję polską," 8.I.1940, and "Zeznania Pani Heleny Lisowej która wyjechała z Warszawy 15 lutego 1940 r."

[112] Shifts from Tannenberg procedure to Palmiry undergirded EG re-deployment in 1941. They show development toward Holocaust killing. Vladimir Solonari, "Patterns of Violence" in *The Holocaust in the East: Local Perpetrators and Soviet Responses* (Pittsburgh: University of Pittsburgh Press, 2014), 56–60; Laurence Rees, *The Holocaust: A New History* (New York: Public Affairs, 2017), 205–240.

"8–10 daily" in "gardens and the basements of the parliament" building and elsewhere.[113] Thousands filled Gestapo prison cells. Relatives of the arrested mobbed German and Polish administrative offices for information. Social welfare institutions like Artur Śliwiński's negotiated on prisoners' behalf; pardons were occasionally granted, and bribes effective in obtaining releases.[114] Whatever the ideals of the Nazi "new order" in the east, all Poles learned very quickly that German officials were bribable. Polish police were, too.[115] Constant arrests nevertheless exacerbated early occupation chaos.[116] By late November 1939 careful observers noticed a pattern: covered trucks left Warsaw prisons at dawn, most heading north toward Kampinos forest.[117] Kampinos was a sandy pine forest northwest of Warsaw, wet and swampy in the summer and cold and snow-covered in winter.[118] No major road cut through it; along the north edge, just below the turn of the Vistula River, lay the village of Palmiry. Palmiry was twenty miles from Szuch Boulevard, an hour's drive over indirect roads.

From December 1939 until 1941, the forest became the overflow grave-yard of the Warsaw intelligentsia. Policemen shot elite prisoners over pits and ravines throughout the dense woods (Figure 2.2). Polish villagers remembered men in SS uniform with machine guns and a senior officer in neat gloves accompanied by a dog.[119] Postwar exhumation revealed that the first execution on December 7–8, 1939, killed 150 people.[120] There were twenty more mass shootings around Palmiry that year, with more in 1941, and the last in 1943. On January 22, 1940, 80 were shot; on February 26, 190. Killings resumed with the spring thaw. On April 1–2, 100; on April 23, 34; on June 14, 20; and 378 people died on the night of June 20–21, 1940.[121] On August 30, 1940, 87; on September 17, 1940, 200. There was an execution on November 11, 28 killed in December, and another 74 in

---

[113] PISM London: MID: Dział Polski, A. 10. 4/2(I), "Z raportu p. H. R. która opuściła Polskę," 18.II.40, [1].

[114] PAN III-59-97 Materiały Artura Śliwińskiego: "Sprawozdania i memoriały Rady Głównej Opiekuńczej," "Sprawozdanie," 15 Sept.–31 Oct. 1940, 14; Korbonski, *Fighting Warsaw*, 16, 26.

[115] USHMM RG-50.012.0044, AN: 1989.67.44, "Interview with Jan Karski," Part 3, 15:45–16:20.

[116] *BI* appeared regularly from May, 1940 (BN Mf. 45815, *BI*, 31 maja 1940 r.) with scattered earlier issues (Bartoszewski, *1859 dni Warszawy*, 80).

[117] Wardzyńska counted 39 sites, 6 in Warsaw. Wardzyńska, *Był rok 1939*, 270–272.

[118] Drozdowski and Zahorski, *Historia Warszawy*, 425–479.

[119] Bartoszewski, *Palmiry*, 40, 42.

[120] Red Cross exhumations began in 1946 (Bartoszewski, *Palmiry*). The cemetery contains Stars of David for Jewish victims.

[121] Simultaneously the Soviet NKVD was executing Polish reserve officers – 22,000 men – though this was unknown until 1943. Anna M. Cienciala, *Katyń: A Crime without Punishment* (New Haven: Yale University Press, 2008).

Figure 2.2 SS personnel lead a group of blindfolded Polish prisoners to an execution site in the Palmiry forest near Warsaw, fall 1939.
United States Holocaust Memorial Museum, courtesy of Instytut Pamięci Narodowej, Photograph Number 50649.

late December or early January 1941. After this the forest executions slowed, with 21 killed on March 11, 1941, and 29 on June 12, 1941, and a last execution on February 2, 1943.[122] In total, Władysław Bartoszewski, who was present at the postwar exhumations, tallied 1,793 killed at Palmiry from 1939 to 1941 and another 500 at sites around Warsaw.[123] Women and children and Polish Jews were among the victims.[124]

2.4 Elite Victims, Elite Response

Neither Tannenberg nor AB destroyed Polish civil society or prevented intelligentsia opposition. The first campaign's brutality and mission creep provoked the very reactions Himmler tried to suppress, by the very people he targeted. The second campaign compounded the first's mistakes, and began after Polish conspiracies were already growing. The fates of four noteworthy

---

[122] Bartoszewski, *Palmiry*, 12–13; 28–37; 40–42; 47.
[123] Bartoszewski, *1859 dni Warszawy*, 7; Władysław Bartoszewski, *Życie trudne, lecz nie nudne: ze wspomnień polaka w xx wieku* (Krakow: Wydawnictwo Znak, 2010), 178–180. Notably, Nazi personnel and auxiliaries buried victims' bodies. In the Holocaust, killing would escalate such that burial became a logistical problem. Smith, *Germany*, 394.
[124] Bartoszewski, *Palmiry*, 23; IPN GK 162–770 "Protokól Przesłuchania Świadka," [Bronisława Nowak], 22–25.

but very different elites, Stefan Starzyński, Maciej Rataj, Mieczysław Niedziałkowski, and Władysław Studnicki, demonstrate how anti-intelligentsia operations unfolded in Warsaw – and how they triggered reactions from their own victims.

Stefan Starzyński was quietly arrested after October 1939 and vanished from his cell in Pawiak prison on Christmas Eve of 1939. His final fate remains unclear. His Gestapo captors did *not* capitalize on his death for propaganda purposes because they were trying to keep their actions secret. "Witnesses" claimed throughout the war that they had seen the mayor, in various states of health, in locations across Germany and Poland. In a city as alive with rumor as occupied Warsaw, Starzyński sightings were frequent. He certainly spent time under interrogation on Szuch Boulevard and was held at Pawiak.[125] He was also "seen" at Dachau, Dora, Flossenburg, Sachsenhausen, Oranienburg, and at Spandau and Moabit, and rumored to have been executed in one of those camps between 1943 and 1945, or in a Warsaw park. More likely, he was shot on Szuch Boulevard or at Palmiry in late 1939 or early 1940.[126] All of his possible fortunes represent the actual fortunes of those arrested during the anti-intelligentsia years, though few had Starzyński's clout.

We know more about the fates of Maciej Rataj (1884–1940) and Mieczysław Niedziałkowski (1893–1940), both national politicians. Rataj was a leader of the People's Party (Stronnictwo Ludowe) from the eastern *kresy*, marshal of parliament, and twice briefly president of Poland; Niedziałkowski, also from the east, was an ideologue of the Polish Socialist Party (PPS) and the editor of its flagship publication, *Robotnik* (Worker).[127] They both remained in Warsaw despite the evacuation and drew Gestapo attention in fall 1939. Rataj was arrested in November 1939, interrogated, and then released. He was arrested a second time on March 30, 1940.[128] Rataj was not idle between the arrests. Niedziałkowski was arrested in December 1939 and a "courteous and understanding" Gestapo officer agreed he could spend Christmas with his family. Niedziałkowski returned to Szuch Boulevard on December 26 for the last

[125] Janusz Malinowski, "Zakładnik" and Janina Krzeczkowska, "Spotkałam prezydenta" in *Pawiak był etapem: wspomnienia* (Warsaw: Ludowa Współdzielna Wydawnicza, 1987), 43–44; 24–25.

[126] Drozdowski entertained a winter 1939/1940 execution in Natolin Park, shooting in Dachau in fall 1943, shooting in Dora in spring 1945, or death at Flossenbürg (Drozdowski, *Starzyński: Legionista*, 437–442; Drozdowski, *Starzyński prezydent Warszawy*, 324–329); Wardzyńska considered December 1939 at Palmiry likeliest (Wardzyńska, *Był rok 1939*, 245–246).

[127] Korbonski, *Fighting Warsaw*, 26; Stanisław Lato, "Marszałek Maciej Rataj" and Jan Wiktor, "Spotkanie z Maciejem Ratajem" in *Maciej Rataj we wspomnieniach współczesnych* (Warsaw: Ludowa Spółdzielnia Wydawnicza, 1984), 7; 228.

[128] Korbonski, *Fighting Warsaw*, 18; Bartoszewski, *1859 dni Warszawy*, 118; Henryk Dzendzel's "Maciej Rataj: Twórca podziemnego ruchu oporu" in *Maciej Rataj we wspomnieniach współczesnych*, 295–299; 310–314.

time.[129] Rataj and Niedziałkowski died at Palmiry the night of June 20, 1940, alongside 376 others.[130]

Rataj's and Niedziałkowski's murders demonstrate Nazi anti-intelligentsia bungling in Warsaw: the two victims had already established a political arm of Karaszewicz-Tokarzewski's Polish Victory Service when they were arrested. Stefan Korboński (1901–1989), Rataj's protégé, described his mentor's fall parlor as a veritable soirée of interwar politicians:

> Because of the throng of visitors, the doors never seemed to close ... Instinctively, men who seemed lost, who needed advice and guidance, flocked there ... I noticed how great was Rataj's political and moral authority among the numerous visitors ... one could sense that he had a clear vision of the future, a definite plan, for the fulfillment of which he was keen to labor and organize people.

Rataj shared his "clear vision" with others keeping ahead of the Gestapo, including Niedziałkowski. Korboński carried messages between them. They consulted with Polish Victory Service organizers and assembled "a supreme conspiratorial political" body, the nucleus of a "secret state," while Fischer was unpacking at Brühl Palace.[131] Even though the Gestapo cornered Rataj in November 1939, they were too late. Colleagues refused to let Niedziałkowski's and Rataj's project die. Korboński, Karaszewicz-Tokarzewski, and many who had attended Rataj's "soiree" would go on to build organized opposition to Nazi occupation, coordinating military conspiracies with civilian efforts and linking Varsovian conspirators with evacuees and emigres abroad.

Rataj and Niedziałkowski were hell-bent on undermining German tyranny. One of their peers, Władysław Studnicki (1867–1953), wanted the opposite: intelligentsia cooperation with the Wehrmacht in running Warsaw.[132] Studnicki was a devout Russophobe, had participated in von Beseler's First World War provisional council in Warsaw and saw strong relations with Germany as essential to the Polish future.[133] His Germanophilia endured Hitler's invasion,

---

[129] Korbonski, *Fighting Warsaw*, 26; Bartoszewski, *1859 dni Warszawy*, 93.

[130] Domańska, *Pawiak: więzienie Gestapo*, 65–68; Bartoszewski, *1859 dni Warszawy*, 135–136.

[131] Korbonski, *Fighting Warsaw*, 13, 19, 24; Dzendzel, "Maciej Rataj: Twórca podziemnego ruchu oporu," 281, 314–315.

[132] JPI Archiwum Władysława Studnickiego 96: 12, "Wobec nadchodzącej drugiej wojny światowej."

[133] Studnicki's Second World War behavior is the subject of silence, outside Jacek Andrzej Młynarczyk's "Pomiędzy Współpracą a Zdradą: Problem Kolaboracji w Generalnym Gubernatorstwie – Próba Syntezy," *Pamięć i Sprawiedliwość* 1, 14 (2009): 103–132. There are studies on his pre-1939 thought: Jacek Gzella's *Myśl polityczna Władysława Studnickiego na tle koncepcji konserwatystów polskich, 1918–1939* (Toruń: Uniwersytet Mikołaja Kopernika w Toruniu, 1993) and *Zaborcy i sąsiedzi Polski w myśli społeczno-politycznej Władysława Studnickiego: do 1939 roku* (Toruń: Uniwersytet Mikołaja Kopernika, 1998), Jan Sadkiewicz's "*Ci, którzy przekonać nie*

bolstered by his fervent antisemitism and his hatred of the Soviet Union.[134] Studnicki thought of himself as a logical German ally, offering advice to Nazi elites like Alfred Rosenberg and Joseph Goebbels. His pet project was a joint Polish–German army to fight the Soviets that never materialized.[135]

Studnicki was unusual but not unique: a handful of Polish fascists sought a *modus vivendi* with the Germans and Polish antisemites applauded Nazi Jewish policies as they developed. Members of the National Radical Movement (Ruch Narodowo-Radykalny, RNR) including Andrzej Świetlicki (1915–1940), also a rabid antisemite, and Bolesław Piasecki (1915–1979) approached the Wehrmacht about military–political collaboration. They got the go-ahead to form an anti-Soviet National Revolutionary Camp (Narodowy Obóz Rewolucji, NOR), which Studnicki joined. Notably, this was the Wehrmacht, always more pragmatic and less ideological than the SS, which was to run Warsaw. Nevertheless, NOR was permitted to exist until spring 1940.[136]

From the SS perspective, the hopes of Studnicki and his fascist allies were irrelevant: they were Warsaw elites and hence dangerous. Świetlicki, the brains behind NOR, was arrested by the Gestapo in June 1940 during AB.[137] Studnicki was left unmolested longer, but he, too, was arrested in July 1941 and held for more than a year in Pawiak prison.[138] Starzyński's, Rataj's, and

---

umieją:" idea porozumienia polsko-niemieckiego w publicystyce Władysława Studnickiego i wileńskiego "Słowa" (do 1939) (Krakow: Towarzystwo Autorów i Wydawców Prac Naukowych Universitas, 2012) and Gaweł Strzadała's *Niemcy w myśli politycznej Władysława Studnickiego* (Opole: Wydawnictwo Uniwersytetu Opolskiego, 2011).

[134] JPI Archiwum Władysława Studnickiego 96:10, "Ludzie, idee, i czyny,"12–13; Kauffman, *Elusive Alliance*, 64–66; Jan Sadkiewicz, "*Ci którzy,*" 17, 63.

[135] Studnicki's recommendations came to nothing. JPI Archiwum Władysława Studnickiego 96: 3, "Korespondencja," folder 1, "Memorial Betreffs Wiederaufbau der polnischen Armee," 20.XI.1939. He also prepared a hefty manuscript for Rosenberg's consideration on Polish anti-Bolshevism, "Denkschrift über die aktuelle polnische Aktion gegen den Bolschewismus," and he may have formulated it in Pawiak. It is unlikely Rosenberg read it. JPI Archiwum Władysława Studnickiego 96: 11, "Denkschrift." He met Goebbels in Berlin in 1940. Ironically, Himmler would toy with exactly such Polish–German cooperation against the USSR in the dying days of the GG. BABL R58 1002 Neuordnung der Polenpolitik, Anlage 3, "Betr. Kapitulation Warschaus," 25, 25b.

[136] Mikołaj Stanisław Kunicki, *Between the Brown and the Red: Nationalism, Catholicism, and Communism in 20th-Century Poland - The Politics of Bolesław Piasecki* (Athens: Ohio University Press, 2012), 55.

[137] Kunicki notes that NOR was "the only collaborationist projects in Nazi-occupied Poland that involved Polish fascists." Kunicki, *Brown and the Red*, 55–56; Mikołaj Kunicki, "Unwanted Collaborators: Leon Kozłowski, Wladyslaw Studnicki and the Problem of Collaboration among Polish Conservative Politicians in World War II," *European Review of History* Vol. 8, 2 (2001): 203–220.

[138] JPI Archiwum Władysława Studnickiego 96: 27, notes for "Okupacja Niemiecka i Sowiecka," 6; 96:3, "Korespondencja," folder 3, 192–193; Domańska, *Pawiak więzienie Gestapo*, 161.

Niedziałkowski's arrests and murders were brutal, but supported Nazi anti-intelligentsia logic. They did not, however, stop these men from resisting. Studnicki's unusual collaboration efforts were the exception that proved the rule: his treatment underscores that German intentions in excluding Poles from leadership were firm, and that there was no place for Polish participation, even Polish fascist participation, in occupation governance. Left without an outlet for their energies, and sure of their occupiers' brutality, they continued their prewar activities underground.

2.5   Genocide

Anti-intelligentsia campaigning shaped occupation policy in Warsaw and was unquestionably genocidal. This was in fact the definitional genocide: the man who coined the term, international legal theorist and Polish–Jewish scholar Raphael – or Rafał – Lemkin (1900–1959), hailed from the Warsaw intelligentsia and was thinking of his peers when he did so.[139] Lemkin left Warsaw, where he taught law and helped write the Polish penal code, with the evacuation, escaping to Sweden and then the United States. In his 1944 *Axis Rule in Occupied Europe*, Lemkin wrote that,

> Genocide is directed against the national group as an entity, and the actions involved are directed against individuals, not in their individual capacity, but as representatives of a national group ... The social structure of a nation being vital to its national development, the occupant also endeavors to bring about such changes as may weaken the national spiritual resources. The focal point of this attack has been the intelligentsia, because this group largely provides national leadership and organizes resistance against Nazification. This is especially true in Poland.[140]

The phrasing here hearkens back to Heydrich's and Frank's calls to "secure" the "Polish leadership class" to prevent resistance and turn Poles into Reich laborers: de-nationalization. The anti-intelligentsia campaigns targeted Lemkin personally as part of Warsaw's legal–political elite, though he escaped and survived. The German approach was not in fact new: Ottoman bureaucrats had siphoned off elites under cover of war to control the Armenian community during the First World War.[141] Joseph Stalin had

---

[139] Lemkin studied in Lwów and Heidelberg and practiced law in Warsaw. Bartolomé Clavero's *Genocide or Ethnocide, 1933–2007: How to Make, Remake, and Unmake Law with Words* (Milano: Giuffre Editore, 2008), 16; Samantha Power, *"A Problem from Hell:" America and the Age of Genocide* (New York: Harper Perennial, 2002), 42–43.

[140] Raphael Lemkin, *Axis Rule in Occupied Europe: Laws of Occupation – Analysis of Government – Proposals for Redress* (Washington: Carnegie Endowment for International Peace, 1944), 79, 83.

[141] Benny Morris and Dror Ze'evi, *The Thirty-Year Genocide: Turkey's Destruction of Its Christian Minorities, 1894–1924* (Cambridge: Harvard University Press, 2019), 244–262;

targeted the Ukrainian intelligentsia a decade earlier with arrests and show trials, repressing Ukrainian nationalism within the USSR.[142] German techniques were also not confined to one victim group: Einsatzgruppen, most importantly, were redeployed in the June 1941 German invasion of the Soviet Union, launching the first stage of the Holocaust.[143]

Lemkin's articulation of this "new" crime influenced the 1948 United Nations Genocide Convention that is now standard in international law.[144] This defined genocide as "any of the following acts committed with intent to destroy, in whole or in part, a national, ethnical, racial or religious group, as such: (a) Killing members of the group; (b) Causing serious bodily or mental harm to members of the group; (c) Deliberately inflicting on the group conditions of life calculated to bring about its physical destruction in whole or in part" and are punishable by the international community even if the destruction was incomplete.[145] Though the later targeting of the Polish-Jewish community ultimately took far more lives, the seriousness of the initial intelligentsia extermination program, and the larger aim of using it to fundamentally restructure the Polish population for Nazi purposes, cannot be doubted.[146]

Despite their genocidal character, neither Tannenberg nor AB "pacified" Poland. Tannenberg was stymied by its targets' flight and by Warsaw's resistance to the Wehrmacht. Frank's revival of anti-intelligentsia campaigning indicated he understood police goals but misfired: AB reacted to early Polish resistance rather than preventing it in the first place. This was cold comfort to its victims. The Tannenberg campaign had a death toll in the tens of thousands. The Einsatzgruppen reports are a jumping-off point for calculating lethality: they arrested

---

Norman M. Naimark, *Genocide: A World History* (New York: Oxford University Press, 2017), 70–76.

[142] Anne Applebaum, *Red Famine: Stalin's War on Ukraine* (New York: Doubleday, 2017), 98–107.

[143] Death tolls in 1941 were higher and the victims Jewish. Patrick Desbois, *The Holocaust by Bullets: A Priest's Journey to Uncover the Truth Behind the Murder of 1.5 Million Jews* (New York: Griffin, 2009); Browning, *Origins*, 244–267; Krausnick, *Hitlers Einsatzgruppen*, 121–178; Jürgen Mätthaus, Jochen Böhler, and Klaus-Michael Mallmann, *War, Pacification, and Mass Murder: The Einsatzgruppen in Poland* (Lanham: Rowman & Littlefield, 2014), 153–160; Lower, *Nazi Empire-Building*, 71–72.

[144] Power, *Problem from Hell*, 54–60; Finder and Prusin, *Justice*, 57.

[145] United Nations: Convention on the Prevention and Punishment of the Crime of Genocide, approved and proposed for signature and ratification or accession by General Assembly resolution 260 A (III) of December 9, 1948, entry into force: January 12, 1951, in accordance with article XIII.

[146] Eastern Europeanists have paid more attention to anti-intelligentsia campaigning: Naimark, *Genocide*, 78–80; Ben Kiernan, *Blood and Soil: A World History of Genocide and Extermination from Sparta to Darfur* (New Haven: Yale University Press, 2007), 430–454, quotation 438.

37,671 but admitted to executing only 411 persons. Einsatzkommando 16, operating in the Polish Corridor, indicated whether its victims appeared on the lists, but other commandos did not bother.[147] Historian Peter Longerich tallies 16,000 September victims of Einsatzgruppen auxiliaries, including Selbstschutz personnel and Wehrmacht soldiers.[148] His colleague Robert Gerwarth, concentrating on Heydrich's actions, counts "more than 40,000" killed "between September and December 1939" at Einsatzgruppen hands alone, and many more deported or killed by others. The *Sonderfahndungsbuch Polen* specified 61,000 targets and historian Maria Wardzyńska, triangulating police documentation with postwar investigations, claimed 80,000 victims.[149] Wardzyńska calculates 100,000 dead for both campaigns, the best estimate we have.[150]

After the anti-intelligentsia campaigns foundered, Polish elite behavior drove Nazi policy, which was increasingly reactive. Police brutality during Tannenberg panicked Poles, ultimately driving substantive, elite-led activities like Rataj's and Niedziałkowski's proto-state.[151] As Jan T. Gross has argued for the GG as a whole, the viciousness of Nazi behavior provided a negative motivation: since the Warsaw elite anticipated persecution at the hands of their occupiers, they had no motivation to cooperate with them.[152] Frank, Fischer, and the police built an occupation of "unlimited exploitation" with no room for Polish participation.[153] The eventual result was to channel Polish energies against their occupier, and in this the surviving intelligentsia led the way.

Arrests, interrogation, imprisonment, and murder were nevertheless formidable constraints to Polish activities. Elite opposition required good information about what was happening, which was initially sparse; anti-intelligentsia campaigns were secret.[154] Starzyński's, Rataj's, and Niedziałkowski's families were not officially informed of their deaths.

---

[147] *Polizeigruppen* numbers are unknown. Selbstschutz killings are also undocumented, and they numbered around 70,000 by October 1939, so their lethality should not be underestimated.

[148] Peter Longerich, *Hitler: A Biography* (New York: Oxford University Press, 2019), 655. Gerwarth, *Hitler's Hangman*, 144, 152.

[149] Wardzyńska, *Był rok 1939*, 49, 64.

[150] Wardzyńska asserts that Security Police were the main killers but notes Wehrmacht, Volksdeutsche, and other police participants. Wardzyńska, *Był rok 1939*, Wehrmacht: 88–99; Volksdeustsche: 28–36; Urbanek, *Lęk i Strach*, 59, 67.

[151] Morgan, *Hitler's Collaborators*, 2–4.

[152] Gross, *Polish Society*, 297.

[153] Gross distinguishes between collaboration and profiteers and spies (*Polish Society*, 119, 125–130). Later work has rejected the idea that "there was no such thing as collaboration" in favor of a more "complex relationship of Poles, Jews, and Germans" (Friedrich, "Collaboration in a 'Land without a Quisling,'" 712, 715).

[154] Wardzyńska, *Był rok 1939*, 241–242.

Violence against "ordinary" Polish targets, however, was public and shaped intelligentsia behavior. The most talked-about episode was a December 1939 massacre in the sleepy Wawer district of Warsaw, where killings spread "panic" and "terror."[155] A few days after Christmas two Polish thugs ("znanych w przedmieściu łobuzów") shot two German non-commissioned officers after some dispute between them at a local bar. Nazi Order Police retaliated massively, arresting 120 Poles and executing 107 of them.[156] The episode paralleled events in Bydgoszcz, and both responses were designed to cow Poles and protect German personnel – especially where they were in "absurdly small numbers" on the ground.[157] Wawer's victims were *not* elites but unlucky bystanders and Christmas visitors. Nevertheless, Wawer had a profound effect on Polish elite thinking. Compounded with rumors of other killings, it confirmed Nazi willingness to execute civilians. For those pondering resistance, especially armed resistance, it was a valuable lesson in the costs of directly targeting occupation personnel. The first Polish elite conspirators would monitor German personnel but rarely risk killing them, focusing instead on sabotage and intelligence gathering in the hope of avoiding reprisals.[158]

2.6   Chaos and Terror

1940 was the last year during which the "Polish question" preoccupied Nazi leadership in Berlin: despite mistreatment and terror, German behavior in Warsaw after the anti-intelligentsia campaigns was derivative: an amalgam of antisemitism, the original Tannenberg guidelines, Frank's 1940 updates, military requirements, and Reich labor demands. In 1939, the fate of Poles had been central to Nazi planning, the first step in securing Poland as *Lebensraum*. But the nature of Nazi violence in the GG changed radically,

---

[155] Ludwik Landau, *Kronika lat wojny i okupacji*, Tom I (Warsaw: Państwowe Wydawnictwo Naukowe, 1962), 158. IPN GK 162-770 Materiały dochodzeniowe w sprawy egzekucji ... 1946–1951, "Protokól," Stefan Krzywoszewski – Długie Życie – Wspomnienie, 37–38.

[156] IPN GK 162-770 Materiały dochodzeniowe w sprawy egzekucji ... 1946–1951, "Protokól," Stefan Krzywoszewski – Długie Życie – Wspomnienie, 37–38; Max Daume ordered the massacres. Descriptions were collected by the Main Commission for the Investigation of Nazi Crimes in Poland in 1946–51 (Główna Komisja Badania Zbrodni Hitlerowskich w Polsce, GKBZHP) which was the basis of the IPN (IPN GK 162-770 Materiały dochodzeniowe w sprawy egzekucji ... 1946–1951, "Protokól," Wacław Klemensiewicz, 31 lipca 1946, 34–36 of file; "Protokól," Stanisław Krupka, 20 stycznia 1951, 41–45).

[157] Housden, *Hans Frank*, 114.

[158] Killing Volksdeutsche constituted an exception, like the spring 1941 assassination of actor Karol "Igo" Sym. Wardzyńska, *Był rok 1939*, 240.

toward retaliation designed not to *prevent* elite resistance but *punish* it in gruesome and exemplary ways.[159] Poles did not cease being persecuted or killed: on the contrary, violence in Warsaw increased, especially from mid-1942 on. Tannenberg and AB had a zombie afterlife, though: as Warsaw's police realized they could not kill the entire intelligentsia, they refocused on controlling and criminalizing their behavior.

The Gestapo became a resistance-combating counterinsurgency organization, tracking elite conspiracies and destroying them. Its manpower was supplemented by native Polish police forces and a quiet army of Polish informers, denouncers, and those turned under torture.[160] Traditional intelligentsia activities were the focus of Gestapo monitoring: mass media, schools and universities, churches, the military. These were restricted or closed. The crackdown on elite behavior – political and military organization, education, intellectual life, religious and cultural leadership – lumped it together with violent crime, which was rampant.[161] This collective criminalization kept the intelligentsia the victims of violence, while obliging them to differentiate their "crimes" (which they saw as patriotic opposition) from the "ordinary" crimes of other Poles, undermining citywide solidarity. The result was a continual but evolving occupation persecution of the Polish elite, who expanded their struggle against the regime within a broadening net of Nazi terror.

By 1943, the preventative killing campaign was clearly over, and GG memoranda even indicate some reconsideration of intelligentsia removal from power. The following comment appears in an SS report on the "Polish Question" handed to Ludwig Fischer: "The solution of the Polish Question, that is to say, the elimination of Polish nationalism through the exclusive destruction of the intelligentsia, is not possible … The members of the intelligentsia are also needed for the administration and maintenance of the territory."[162] Almost four years after the GG's founding, German administrators acknowledged that the Polish elite was not going anywhere and tentatively considered re-empowering

---

[159] Borodziej considers "terror" and "policy" as alternating occupation modes. Borodziej, *Terror und Politik*, 162–190.

[160] Blue police and private citizens helped. Barbara Engelking notes that a disproportion of those who denounced their neighbors were older or poorly educated, but all classes pitched in. Engelking, *"Szanowny panie gistapo,"* 62–64.

[161] Sebastian Piątkowski, "Przestępczość w okupowanej Warszawie" in *Porządek publiczny i bezpieczeństwo w okupowanej Warszawie*, ed. Robert Spałek (Warsaw: IPN, 2018), 295–308, 318.

[162] SS-Sturmbannführer Schenk weighed Slavic nationalisms; he was not looking to rehabilitate the intelligentsia generally. BABL R102/II/11, Gouverneur des Distrikts Warschau, "Die ukrainische Frage," Lemberg, 12. Mai 1943; "Die Polenfrage," Lemberg, den 21. April 1943, 5–6, 12. This demonstrates Nazi recognition of the failure of the coercion model. Edelstein, *Occupational Hazards*, 50.

them.[163] Times had changed.[164] Between the abandonment of anti-intelligentsia campaigning in late 1940 and defeat in late 1944 – most of the occupation – Varsovians existed in a morass of retaliatory violence meant to intimidate them into submission.

2.7   Conclusion

This killing campaign – conducted as a two-wave anti-intelligentsia killing spree – happened differently in Warsaw than elsewhere. Both campaigns were launched under the "cover" of war to hide the number and nature of casualties, underscoring the murderous intentions of Nazi police.[165] The first wave (Tannenberg) largely missed the capital because the siege kept German soldiers and policemen outside Warsaw until the end of operations. The campaigns therefore began in Warsaw after the cessation of military hostilities and proceeded half-secretly, with mass arrests of elites. Those arrested in Warsaw disappeared into Gestapo custody for long-term imprisonment, execution, or transfer to concentration camps. From the launch of the first anti-intelligentsia campaign, genocide was linked to occupation planning and the imposition of a "new order" in the east; no Polish puppet state was allowed, as anything of the sort would have re-empowered those the anti-intelligentsia campaigns dispossessed. Hans Frank's GG administration was ushered in under SS guidance as a civilian "front" for radical police population control. That Frank misunderstood the nature of his power was neither here nor there, but police–civilian squabbles opened some spaces for Polish maneuvering between fluctuating German interests.

In Warsaw, the heart of Polish opposition, police control was firmly felt. Frank's first effort as general governor, the AB-Aktion, rebooted anti-intelligentsia campaigning. In Warsaw, this required "processing" prisoners taken after capitulation. Arrested Warsaw elites went to Pawiak prison and the Gestapo interrogated them on Szuch Boulevard, executed some in the Kampinos forest, and transferred other prisoners onward to concentration camps in the Third Reich including, after 1940, a new camp at Auschwitz. With AB, Frank made police policy his own and strangled any possibility for the co-optation of the surviving elite in governance. When anti-intelligentsia genocide failed at preventing

---

[163] Unattempted. BABL R102/II/11, Gouverneur des Distrikts Warschau, "Die Polenfrage, 5–6; 23–24.

[164] GG memoranda on a "new order for Polish policy" toyed with involving Poles in administration in 1944 – and dismissed it. BABL R58 1002, Neuordnung der Polenpolitik (etc.), 15–42; 218–221.

[165] Thanks to Yedida Kanfer for her comments on this point.

opposition and in fact provoked it, German anti-Polish policy collapsed, sliding from preventative targeting to punishment and reprisal.

Before turning to the systems of elite response that developed after the failure of the anti-intelligentsia killing campaigns, we must understand what persecution was still in play and how the Nazi occupation controlled the city's inhabitants. Nazi authority hinged on two institutions: Pawiak prison and the Warsaw Ghetto. Each gives us a privileged window onto the perspectives of the Warsaw intelligentsia, the prison as their primary site of persecution, and the ghetto as a demonstration of the limits of Polish solidarity in the face of the Holocaust.

3

Pawiak Prison

As the anti-intelligentsia campaigns waxed and waned in Warsaw and the Nazi occupation shifted toward a strategy of reprisal and punishment, one institution came to symbolize the continuity of Nazi hostility toward the Polish national project in Warsaw: Pawiak prison (Figure 3.1). Pawiak became a byword for terror, a shorthand for brutality. Originally seized as an intelligentsia-holding facility, the prison became the occupation's central counterinsurgency institution. It was entwined, practically and symbolically, with nearly every aspect of Nazi persecution of Polish resistance in Warsaw. During the occupation the prison (enclosed within the ghetto in 1940) held nearly 100,000 prisoners. Tens of thousands of anti-Nazi conspirators and myriad opposition projects died inside. Its persistent overcrowding was the result of the viciousness and ineffectiveness of Nazi anti-insurgency efforts and its cells a melting pot of those who had run afoul of a tyrannical regime: Polish political "criminals" would rub elbows in Pawiak with Polish Jews, a few foreigners, and a stable of guards including Poles, Ukrainian *Hilfswilliger*, and German personnel.[1] Unmanageable prisoner numbers linked Pawiak to the Auschwitz concentration camp, which was used as an overflow facility, further intertwining Polish with Polish–Jewish persecution, and spreading Warsaw's political opposition across the Nazi camp system.[2]

---

[1] Reuben Nowak, a Polish Jew, was held in Pawiak as a Polish political prisoner. His comrades "helped" but "not all of them knew [his] true identity, only a few." Fortunoff Yale HVT-1021, interviewed by Nina Taus and Sandy Hoffman, 1987, ca. 36:50 and 44:40; Joshua D. Zimmerman, *The Polish Underground and the Jews, 1939–1945* (New York: Cambridge University Press, 2015), 350–381.

[2] Pawiak was not the only Warsaw prison. "Gęsiówka" was inside the ghetto and in 1943 its ruins became the site of KL Warschau, later KL Lublin-Arbeitslager Warschau (Gabriel N. Finder, "Jewish Prisoner Labour in Warsaw After the Ghetto Uprising, 1943–1944" in *Polin: Studies in Polish Jewry, Vol. 17: The Shtetl: Myth and Reality*, ed. A. Polonsky (Liverpool: Liverpool University Press,2004), 325; Barbara Engelking and Jacek Leociak, *Getto warszawskie: przewodnik po nieistniejącym mieście* (Warsaw: Stowarzyszenie Centrum Badań nad Zagładą Żydow, 2013), 821–826. Until the 1942 liquidation, ghetto Jews were imprisoned in Gęsiówka; Jews caught outside the ghetto were held in Pawiak when not immediately executed (Bogusław Kopka, *Konzentrationslager Warschau: Historia i Następstwa* (Warsaw: IPN, 2007), 45). "Centralniak" lay near city hall. There was also the citadel and a Mokotów prison (Jacek Pawłowicz's "Więzienie Warszawa-Mokotów w latach 1945–1956" in *Warszawa miasto w opresji: Warszawa nie?pokonana* (Warsaw: IPN, 2010), 163–192).

Figure 3.1 Pawiak Prison under Russian partition viewed from Dzielna Street, 1906. Wikimedia Commons.

Tsarist authorities built the prison in the 1830s to punish participants in the November Insurrection, a Polish uprising that aimed at independence from Russia and failed. For Poland's various conquerors, it was a political prison for dangerous insurrectionaries; among Poles, it was a site of martyrdom. The prison stayed open in the interwar, but its symbolic power lay in its earlier and later use by foreigners.[3] It was only lightly damaged during the bombardment and conveniently located in central Warsaw; the Nazi Security Police (*Sicherheitspolizei*) requisitioned the building and its staff in fall 1939. Nazis simply repurposed Pawiak – redubbed *Gefängnis Warschau* – when they brought their persecution system eastward into Poland. Their early camp system had involved "converting existing structures" rather than later purpose-built facilities; the pattern repeated itself in Warsaw.[4] The GG persecution system would connect to the one in the Reich itself, drawing on the camp

---

[3] The focus is *political* prisoners. Just before evacuation, President Igancy Mościcki offered a prisoner amnesty. Piątkowski, "Przestępczość w okupowanej Warszawie" in *Porządek publiczny i bezpieczeństwo*, 279.

[4] Nikolaus Wachsmann, *KL: A History of the Nazi Concentration Camps* (New York: Farrar, Straus & Giroux, 2015), 19, 22, 202. And continued elsewhere, as in Belgrade's Banjica prison (Prusin, *Serbia under the Swastika*, 66–69) and Prague's Pankrác prison (Bryant, *Prague in Black*, 186).

system when the city ran out of prison space. Far from a *tabula rasa* or "new order" in the east, Nazi persecution felt familiar to Poles, filtered through memories of previous occupations.[5] The prison's pre-Second World War legacy lent it power: Poles who spent time in Pawiak and its sister prison, Serbia, for conspiring against the Führer traced a lineage of fathers and grandfathers held there for rebelling against the tsar. The sense of multi-generational continuity undermined synchronic identification with Polish–Jewish victims of Nazi violence; this continued even though the ghetto surrounded the prison in 1940. That subject – the Warsaw Ghetto's tangled history – occupies Chapter 4. Only the prison's final destruction in 1944 cut this long thread of continuity.[6]

Good information about what happened inside Pawiak was hard to get during the war and painstaking to reconstruct thereafter: early Nazi policy in Warsaw confused both perpetrators and victims. Tannenberg and AB direct-ives, after all, were strict secrets. Rumors of violence produced fear and confusion, and the regime's official information organs, the so-called "reptile press," clarified nothing.[7] Ludwik Landau (1902–44), a well-connected Polish–Jewish economist, kept a diary of occupation life that indicates when the prison's reputation became established among the intelligentsia. Landau's diary documented the arrests of friends and colleagues from fall 1939, but it was not until April 1940 that he suspected the arrested were ending up in Pawiak; by July, he had some notion of their fate.[8] In spring 1940, Aleksander Kamiński began regularly printing his underground *Biuletyn Informacyjny* (Information Bulletin), which became Warsaw's central underground newspaper. He discussed Nazi political arrests in the first issue and named Pawiak in July 1940 as the destination of those taken; the prison was mentioned frequently thereafter.[9] Other underground groups tracked movement into and out of Pawiak.[10] Pawiak's inner workings nevertheless remained mysterious and contact with the imprisoned was difficult.

---

[5] In Polish-language scholarship there is thus an emphasis on denoting this as a(nother) German occupation, and the term "German" is preferred to "Nazi," emphasizing continuities in German encroachment on Polish territory. Mazower, *Hitler's Empire*, 179–222.

[6] Anna Müller, *If the Walls Could Speak: Inside a Women's Prison in Communist Poland* (New York: Oxford University Press, 2018), 55.

[7] *Prasa gadzinowa* (reptile press), a twist on *prasa godzinowa* (hourly press). Lucjan Dobroszycki, *Reptile Journalism: The Official Polish-Language Press under the Nazis, 1939–1945* (New Haven: Yale University Press, 1994), 30–31.

[8] Landau, *Kronika*, 63, 97, 27, 66, 442, 567, 583.

[9] SZP was a Home Army predecessor. See chapter 8. BN, Mf. 45815, *BI*, July 6, 1940, "Warszawa," 6, as "Dzielna St. prison"; BN, Mf. 45815, *BI*, July 19, 1940, "Warszawa," 5, by name.

[10] AAN AK, s. 203-III-131, Mf. 2375-18 (1940-1943); AAN AK, s. 203-X-59, Mf. 2394-5.

Records smuggled from the prison and survivor memoirs are the basis of spotty current knowledge.[11] Pawiak was a Gestapo (Security Police and SD) prison from 1939 to 1943 and from mid-1943 it abutted a Majdanek satellite camp called KL Warschau, which was under separate jurisdiction and is itself little understood.[12] The demolition of the prison after the crushing of the city-wide uprising in 1944 destroyed physical evidence.[13] No complete Nazi German records of its operations exist. Coupled with exhumations around Warsaw, information about prisoner fates has been reconstructed from underground documents by surviving Varsovian elites, especially Władysław Bartoszewski (1922–2015) and Regina Hulewicz-Domańska (b. 1922). Domańska's brothers Witold and Jerzy Hulewicz were tortured there and executed on June 12, 1941 for writing an underground newspaper.[14] Her own radio broadcasting work and investigations into her brothers' disappearance got her arrested in 1943 and imprisoned in Serbia and then Ravensbrück, which she survived. Domańska became the director of the postwar memorial museum and published a book in 1978 compiling 65,000 inmate names.[15] Władysław Bartoszewski did *not* spend time in Pawiak but was also a Nazi political prisoner in Auschwitz. Working with the underground, he monitored the prison after 1941 and became an official observer of the postwar exhumations around Palmiry, where many Pawiak prisoners were executed.[16]

---

[11] Leon Wanat, *Za murami Pawiaka* (Warsaw: Książka i Wiedza, 1967); Zygmunt Śliwicki, *Meldunek z Pawiaka* (Warsaw: Państwowe Wyd. Naukowe, 1974); Julien Hirshaut, *Jewish Martyrs of Pawiak* (New York: Holocaust Library, 1982); Anna Czuperska-Śliwicka, *Cztery lata ostrego dyżuru: wspomnienia z Pawiaka, 1940–1944* (Warsaw: Czytelnik, 1965).

[12] Gabriel Finder, "Warschau Main Camp" in *Encyclopedia of Camps and Ghettos, 1933–1945* Vol. I, Part B, ed. Geoffrey Megargee (Bloomington: Indiana University Press, 2009), 1512–1515.

[13] Yitzhak Zuckerman, *A Surplus of Memory: Chronicle of the Warsaw Ghetto Uprising* (Berkeley: University of California Press, 1993), 612; Bartoszewski, *Warsaw Death Ring, 1939–1944* (Warsaw: Interpress Publishers, 1968); 361; 12.

[14] Regina Hulewicz-Domańska published under her married name. AAN 2–1230–0 sygn. 76-III-57, "Uwagi Z. Kossak-Szczuckiej o prasie podziemnej Polski w czasie okupacji niemieckiej. Co wiem o prasie podziemnej," [1]; Domańska, *Pawiak Więzienie Gestapo*, 101; Regina Hulewicz-Domańska, "Najtrudniejszy rozdział mojego życia (14 IX 1943 – 1 III 1944)," in *Wspomnienia więźniów Pawiaka*, ed. Anna Czuperska-Śliwicka (Warsaw: Ludowa Spółdzielnia Wydawnicza, 1964), 357–374.

[15] *Wspomnienia więźniów Pawiaka* (Warsaw: Ludowa Spółdzielnia Wydawnicza, 1978); *A droga ich wiodła przez Pawiak* (Warsaw: Książka i Wiedza, 1981); *Pawiak – kaźń i heroizm* (Warsaw: Wydawnicto Książka i Wiedza, 1988). On Pawiak there is only Andrzej Ossibach-Budzyński's *Pawiak więzienie polityczne, 1880–1915* (Warsaw: Muzeum Niepodległości, 2016).

[16] Bartoszewski, 361; *1859 dni Warszawy* (Krakow: Wyd. Znak, 1974); *Palmiry* (Warsaw: Książka i Wiedza, 1969). His papers undergirded daughter in law Alexandra Richie's *Warsaw 1944: Hitler, Himmler, and the Warsaw Uprising* (New York: Farrar, Straus and Giroux, 2013).

The most extensive survivor memoirs belong to two Poles with uniquely long stays in the prison and privileged access to its inner workings, and to a Polish–Jewish escapee. Teacher Leon Wanat (1906–77) and physician Zygmunt Śliwicki (1903–82) were arrested for anti-Nazi activities and then employed as inmates. Wanat was arrested in March 1940 and escaped in 1944, working meanwhile in the prison clerk's office. Śliwicki was arrested in September 1940, released in 1944, and employed as a prisoner-doctor in the clinic. The Polish-Jewish prisoner, Julien Hirshaut, was caught in hiding in "Aryan" Warsaw late in the occupation and one of the few Polish-Jewish prisoners to successfully escape.[17] All three memoirists were intelligentsia, and Wanat and Śliwicki were embroiled in activities the Nazi occupation had forbidden; Hirshaut's very existence was criminalized by antisemitic regulation. Their writings together reveal that life in Pawiak was brutal but that community – and conspiracy – developed inside.[18]

3.1   Prison Evolution

Pawiak was under Nazi police control from October 1939 and utilized for Tannenberg and AB.[19] After the anti-intelligentsia campaigns foundered, the prisoner population shifted from Tanennberg's "potential" resisters to actual conspirators, suspected conspirators, and Polish Jews. In parallel, Polish guards were removed and replaced with Germans and Ukrainians. As Nazi police focused on destroying Warsaw's Jewish community, the prison, surrounded by the ghetto, was intertwined with the Holocaust.

Pawiak remained full as the anti-intelligentsia campaigns waned. Life in the prison had many parallels to life in the concentration camp system, though the individual nature of interrogation kept prisoners in intimate contact with their occupiers.[20] The purpose of Pawiak was to control political threats, yet since occupation authorities had a flexible definition of "political," denoting anyone who might undermine their rule, a wide variety of people ended up inside. Lawyers, doctors, students, actors, musicians, professors, member of parliament, priests, communists, and journalists were common. Families arrived

---

[17] The term "Aryan" is problematic because ethnic Poles were not considered "Aryans" except in this phrasing. For the complexity of the term for Polish Jews, see: Małgorzata Melchior, "Uciekinierzy z gett po 'stronie aryjskiej' na prowincji dystryktu warszaws- kiego – sposoby przetrwania" in *Prowincja noc*, 325–327.

[18] The best records are: AAN 203/III/131, Mf. 2375/18; AAN 203/X/59, Mf. 2394/5 and AAN 203/X/83, Mf. 2394/17; lists appear in the USHMM Ghetto Fighters' House, USHMM RG 68.112M.11623.

[19] Paul and Mallmann, *Gestapo im Zweiten Weltkrieg*, 30–41; Brewing, *Im Schatten*, 158– 175; Wardzyńska, *Był rok 1939*.

[20] Pawiak extended the logic that built Dachau and Sachsenhausen, interning political "threats" to Nazi Germany. Wachsmann, *KL*, 79–83; 97–100.

with children in pajamas, husbands and wives, the female relatives of a man on the run, the employees of a factory floor, the students of a secret university seminar, the residents of an apartment building with their custodian, betrayed Jews with the Pole who had hidden them, priests and nuns, even the occasional bewildered foreigner.[21] Controlling Warsaw meant criminalizing activities from reading the "wrong" newspaper to studying, to say nothing of assassinations, espionage, sabotage, or weapons stockpiling.[22] Being Jewish in "Aryan" Warsaw also became a crime when the ghetto was enclosed, as Polish Jews were forbidden to live outside the ghetto area. Punishments for criminalized activities included labor deportation, imprisonment, and execution, but they were doled out inconsistently. The Gestapo suspected individual offenders (including hidden Jews) were part of larger networks and interrogated inmates to get them to reveal their co-conspirators.

Most prisoners spent too little time there to understand its evolution; Śliwicki was an exception and noted distinct phases in prison life.[23] The first stage, from the beginning of the occupation until November 1940, when the ghetto around the prison was sealed, was nearly over when the doctor arrived. It encompassed the anti-intelligentsia campaigns and was mildest, with prewar Polish guards still in place. Himmler's spring 1940 inspection assessed this arrangement and found it wanting. The second phase began with the sealing of the ghetto and the SS takeover of guard duties, and it lasted from mid-November 1940 to March 1942, "times of physical and psychological terror," with constant beatings and little food.[24] From this phase on, an SS officer and his deputies ran the prison.[25] Prisoners interacted with the deputies, who set the tone. The longest-serving of these was Franz Bürkl (September 1941 to April 1943). Bürkl's brutality made him one of the most hated men in Warsaw and a target for the armed underground, which eventually assassinated him in spring 1943.[26]

---

[21] Domańska, *Pawiak więzienie gestapo*, 15, 134, 90, 92, 416; Engelking, "*Szanowny panie gistapo*," 92.

[22] On October 18, 1939 the GG required registering phones, radio, and telegraph equipment which was thereafter confiscated, PISM London: MID: Dział Polski, A. 10. 4/3, Sprawozdania z Kraju, 1940: "Sprawozdanie Gospodarcze z obszaru Polski zajętego przez Niemców," 1–2.

[23] Bartoszewski, *Warsaw Death Ring*, 13.

[24] Serbia kept Polish guards longer. Wanat, *Za murami*, 26; Domańska, *Pawiak więzienie gestapo*, 237.

[25] Otto Gotschalk was first commandant (until March 1941). Commandants Herbert Junk (Aug. 1942–Feb. 1943) and Erich Pietsch (Apr. 1943–May 1944) stayed longer, and Norbert Bergh-Trips oversaw its 1944 dissolution.

[26] Part of Operation Heads. On Bürkl's sadism: Zdzisław Żołądkiewicz, "Gwoździe"; Zuzanna Zawadzka, "Kurierka"; Stanisław Piwowarski, "Z łapanki na Pawiak" in *Pawiak był etapem*, 244, 250, 271; Hirshaut, *Jewish Martyrs*, 73 and Kazimierz Leski, *Życie niewłaściwie urozmaicone: Wspomnienia oficera wywiadu i kontrwywiadu AK* (Warsaw: Państwowe Wyd. Naukowe, 1989), 286.

In March 1942, the third phase began when the last Polish staff was replaced by *Volksdeutsche* and Ukrainian *Hilfswilliger*, who mistreated the prisoners.[27] Ukrainian guards were notoriously bribable and at lower prices than German supervisors. Memoirists noted the shift in guard structure as a sea change in prison life.[28] Jewish prisoners, however, remembered Ukrainian *and* Polish guards who brutalized them.[29] The third phase continued through the *Grossaktion* of summer 1942 (the ghetto liquidation), the Ghetto Uprisings of January and April 1943, and ghetto demolition thereafter. Though Śliwicki did not differentiate it, the transformation of the ghetto into a work camp and execution site designated another shift in the prison's role. The last phase Śliwicki described began as the prison was dismantled on May 1, 1944, and coincided with the operation of neighboring KL Warschau, developed to exploit Jewish labor. Medical staff, including Śliwicki, was released in summer 1944, though Jewish KL Warschau prisoners were forced into a death march westward ahead of the Red Army's arrival.[30]

3.2   Life Inside

The prison lay in the Muranów district, a Polish-Jewish neighborhood. Its three-story structure contained an interior courtyard and two gates, one onto Pawia Street, for which it was named, and the main entrance on Dzielna Street. According to the nineteenth-century design by Enrico "Henryk" Marconi, its Italian architect, its capacity was 428 prisoners, with guard billets, offices, and a records room. The basement level, where the kitchens, laundry, and storage were, had space for 20 prisoners; the ground floor, where the administration was, held 80, the second floor held 80 and offices, and the third held 248 prisoners and a clinic.[31] Besides isolation units, cells were built for ten or fourteen people.[32] The Gestapo considered holding capacity for Pawiak to be 700 men, and neighboring Serbia 250 women. At its maximum, even while transferring prisoners out to ease overcrowding, Serbia held 700 prisoners and Pawiak 2,000 – five times as many as Marconi intended.[33] Arrests were so numerous that those totals were maintained even with constant deaths and

---

[27] Giving Ukrainians who had endured Polonization power encouraged violence. Fischer noted Polish-Ukrainian tension in summer 1941. From the Report of the Chief of Distrikt Warschau [Fischer to Frank] for the Month of June 1941, dated July 12, 1941 (Fischer, *Raporty*, 339–340); USHMM 15.165.

[28] Hulewicz-Domańska, "Najtrudniejszy rozdział mojego życia," 374.

[29] Hirshaut, *Jewish Martyrs*, 75, 109.

[30] Bernard Nissenbaum was among those in this death march. USHMM RG 02.005.01, "My Deportation," Bernard Nissenbaum, 30–33); Kopka, *Konzentrationslager Warschau*, 43–56; Śliwicki, *Meldunek z Pawiaka*, 7–9; 31–32.

[31] Ossibach-Budzyński, *Pawiak: więzienie polityczne*, 40–41.

[32] Domańska, *A droga ich wiodła przez Pawiak*, 11.

[33] Domańska, *Pawiak – Kaźń i Heroizm*, 17.

transfers. From late 1941 until early 1942, Domańska's calculations noted transfers to Auschwitz: 108 on October 15, 1941; another 174 on November 19; 62 on January 8, 1942; another 65 on January 14 and 176 on February 2. In five months, Pawiak transferred 585 prisoners to Auschwitz alone, substantially more than Marconi's original holding capacity of 428. Easily twice as many were brought in as transferred out. The prisoner problem, and the political opposition in Warsaw that produced it, never abated.[34]

Arrival in Pawiak was accompanied by violence. The yard and basement quarantine cells saw a grisly carousel of badly beaten prisoners of all ages – the administration's "new guests."[35] Men were brought in trucks with canvas-covered windows. Some had been taken in labor roundups and deemed suspicious while others had heard a knock at the door in the early hours of the morning. When families were arrested, women and children were separated from men, either to be held in Serbia or sometimes released. Some arrived so badly beaten that they died before facing Gestapo interrogation, while others committed suicide to avoid betraying anyone under torture. Attorney Mieczysław Grygosiński poisoned himself en route to Pawiak and "died within 15 minutes after arriving at the prison."[36]

Upon arrival, guards shaved prisoners' heads and confiscated their possessions. They were beaten, stripped naked, and forced into basement quarantine, where they stayed for fourteen days. Nakedness and a medical examination meant that circumcised men were re-categorized as Jewish and segregated, blowing the cover of Polish Jews caught in hiding, who formed the prison's main Polish-Jewish population.[37] Prisoners froze in the winter and boiled in the summer. Basement cells designed for 4 held 18–20 men while larger ones meant for 10 held 40–50. Prisoners got soup and coffee – or something like them – in filthy tin bowls without spoons. There were a few cots in the basement but no mattresses or blankets. Cells were alive with fleas and lice, and disease was rampant.

After quarantine, the most dangerous suspects were isolated with frequent shuttling to the Gestapo and "normal" prisoners went upstairs to regular cells. Regular cells had mattresses, a wash basin but no soap, a bucket toilet, larger windows, and better heating.[38] Each cell had an elder – *starosta* – who verified cellmates at roll call (*apel*). In theory, prisoners could receive packages, especially at Christmas, but mail was censored. Polish welfare institutions like Artur Śliwiński's ROM and SKSS attempted to secure communication and

---

[34] Domańska, *Pawiak więzienie gestapo*, 175–196.
[35] Wanat, *Za murami Pawiaka*, 12.
[36] Domańska, *Pawiak więzienie gestapo*, 171.
[37] This blew Hirshaut's cover. Hirshaut, *Jewish Martyrs*, 21–22; Zuckerman, *Surplus of Memory*, 340; Grabowski, *Na posterunku*, 182, 259, 306.
[38] Domańska, *A droga ich*, 62–67, 70.

provide food and necessities to prisoners with limited success.[39] Some of the first elite Polish opposition to Nazi control developed from the basic human desire to contact imprisoned family members.[40] Official correspondence consisted of fill-in-the-blank bilingual postcards that informed families of prisoner good health – sometimes after death or deportation.

The Gestapo forbade communication among prisoners and restricted it with the city outside. Discussion in the corridors or during exercise provoked brutal beatings. Cell friendships were undermined by the presence of informers – often turned Poles hoping for release – and eavesdropping guards. In response, prisoners developed an intricate message system, *grypsy*, notes written in code on tightly rolled cigarette paper. Before ghetto enclosure, *grypsy* were thrown out windows to Poles thronging the gates.[41] Afterwards, they were passed out through bribed guards, medical personnel, and laundry workers.[42] A particularly important rendezvous point was the toilet tank at the end of each corridor where prisoners left messages, mementos, keys, and occasionally, vials of poison for one another.[43]

Guards beat prisoners, which German and Ukrainian guards did more than the Polish guards, who were bribable or even sympathetic.[44] Some guards were known for sadism and others for stupidity. The daily schedule involved a 5:30 a.m. wake up, 6:00 a.m. roll call with release for interrogations, washing, breakfast, walks (forbidden for men after 1942), medical rounds, lunch, another release for interrogations, dinner, the return of the interrogated, roll call, and lights out at 8 p.m.[45] When prisoners encountered each other moving among cells – to interrogation, exercise, or toilets – they were required to stand silently facing the wall so that those passing could not interact with them.[46] Prisoners were therefore uncertain about others' identity unless they shared cells. Regulations were designed to prevent communication, though there was

---

[39] PAN III-59-97 Materiały Artura Śliwińskiego: "Sprawozdania i memoriały RGO," "Sprawozdanie," 15 Sept. – 31 Oct. 1940, 14.

[40] Irena Sendler was involved in early aid to the imprisoned, especially POWs like her husband. Anna Bikont, *Sendlerowa w ukryciu* (Wołowiec: Wydawnictwo Czarne, 2017), 71–73.

[41] Jacek Leociak reminds that letters are "built on foundations of hope." Leociak, *Text*, 119.

[42] Wanda Lewandowska, *Pawiak był etapem*, 215.

[43] Irena Lipińska, *Wspomnienia więźniów Pawiaka*, 306–308; Domańska, *Pawiak – Kaźń i Heroizm*, 224–320. Since toilets could not be denied prisoners, they were often a – fetid – communications hub.

[44] Polish guards were arrested in fall 1940 for aiding prisoners. Domańska, *Pawiak – Kaźń i Heroizm*, 140–142; Józef Garliński, *Survival of Love: Memoirs of a Resistance Officer* (Oxford: Basil Blackwell, 1991), 16–26. Pitting ethnicities against one another continued postwar: ethnic Germans "cleansed" from Poland in were housed in Nazi camps and "camp directors were often Poles of Jewish origin." Naimark, *Fires of Hatred*, 129.

[45] Domańska, *Pawiak więzienie gestapo*, 18–19.

[46] Dom Spotkań z Historią (DSH), *Przetrwałam: doświadczenia kobiet więzionych w czasach nazizmu i stalninizmu*, 188–189.

a dangerous workaround for each one. Meals were 120–250 grams of bread and half a liter of ersatz coffee for breakfast at 7 a.m., a liter of meatless soup, usually cabbage, at 12 p.m., and coffee and leftover soup at 5 p.m.[47] Prisoners' caloric intake was lowest from late 1941 through 1942 at around 500–800 calories per day, and around 1000 daily calories the rest of the time. Men sickened, though death by starvation alone was rare. Instead, weakened prisoners succumbed to disease and broke under interrogation. Existence in the prison paralleled life in the ghetto outside, where starvation levels climbed dangerously from 1940 to 1942, leading to epidemics of typhus.[48]

Extraction of information was the purpose of imprisonment in Pawiak. It took place at Gestapo headquarters at Szuch Boulevard No. 25 – then *Polizeistrasse* or Police Street in the German district. Prisoners moldered in their cells for weeks, and long stretches passed between interrogations. Those to be interrogated were named at morning roll call and driven across the city at 8 a.m. in covered trucks. Interrogation sessions began in the Szuch Boulevard basements, where a series of joined cells served as a waiting room called "the streetcar" (*tramwaj*) for its rows of forward-facing wooden benches. Those who moved, spoke, or looked askance were beaten by guards pacing the hallway behind a metal grid. The dread of awaiting an actual confrontation with the Gestapo in these seats became one of the defining experiences of Polish political persecution. When interrogators finally summoned prisoners, they were required to recite a brief biography (*życiorys*) and answer questions. A translator and secretary were present and those who knew German hid it to buy time to formulate answers. Prisoners were beaten with rubber truncheons, but some policemen focused their efforts, smashing fingertips, crushing hands, "breaking ribs, or beating the groin and kidneys."[49] Interrogators asked questions about prisoner activities, families, and known contacts. Teenager Julian Kulski, the deputy mayor's son, remembered a "very thick book" placed before him during his first interrogation, filled with photographs of Poles the Gestapo sought but could not identify. He paged through friends' faces and "innocently" pointed out a man already captured who shared his Pawiak cell. The guard bludgeoned him in the back of the head.[50] Prisoners returned to their cells in a condition that petrified newcomers. After interrogation, they were forced to sign confessions and might then be informed of their sentences, which could include release, forced labor in the *Reich*, transfer to a camp, or execution (at Palmiry, or, later, in the ghetto ruins). Those to be executed were called at dawn and handed a slice of bread.[51]

[47] Domańska, *A droga ich*, 77.
[48] Engelking and Leociak, *Getto warszawskie*, 278–282.
[49] Domańska, *Pawiak więzienie gestapo*, 104–105, 108.
[50] USHMM RG-50.030.0769, AN: 2014.238.1, "Interview with Julian Kulski [Jr.]," 2:00:00–2:03:10.
[51] Domańska, *Pawiak – Kaźń i Heroizm*, 148.

The Gestapo developed a system of processing prisoners and tens of thousands of people went through it, some to return to "normal" life, but many never to be seen again. Jewish prisoners were treated most harshly and most likely to be executed. The Gestapo believed Polish-Jewish children could deserve execution, sparing most imprisoned Polish children this fate. Young men were prominent among the inmates, but elderly men who had entered politics in the nineteenth century under the Russian partition also found themselves inside – sometimes for the second time.[52] Previous experience with political persecution lent authority, even in privileged company: the *starosta* of cell 210 in late 1942, which contained the director of the Krakow agricultural bank, a former senator, an actor, and a collection of priests and religious, was a man named Józef Jakimiak who had done twenty years of hard labor in Siberia and was considered something of an expert, an honorary "professor of prison law and custom" to whom his cellmates deferred.[53]

The majority of prisoners and those executed were men. Women were more likely to be released or held hostage to be exchanged for husbands, fathers, or brothers. Nevertheless, there was a dedicated women's facility, Serbia, and women were interrogated, tortured, transferred to camps – primarily Ravensbrück, Auschwitz, and Majdanek – and executed.[54] Pregnancy, sickness, and youth or old age did not guarantee clemency.[55] Maria Rutkiewicz (1917–2007), a Polish communist activist from a privileged family in eastern Poland, was arrested visibly pregnant in September 1943 and held in isolation. Despite torture, she gave birth to healthy fraternal twins on February 16, 1944 in prison, Jaś and Malgosia.[56] Other women gave birth, having been arrested pregnant or sexually assaulted in custody, and there were always children in Serbia.[57] In fall 1943, executions increased, and so did the percentage of women among them, including a thirteen-year-old girl. Women were executed sick with typhus and tuberculosis, so badly beaten they could not stand, and, on at least three occasions in 1944, into their ninth month of pregnancy. Executions were so gruesome that one member of the execution squad committed suicide rather than continue.[58]

---

[52] Hirshaut's cellmate thought "life in Pawiak under the Czars was a bed of roses compared with what we endured under the Nazis." Hirshaut, *Jewish Martyrs*, 27.

[53] Kazimierz Wzdzięczny, *Pawiak był etapem*, 273.

[54] Bór-Komorowski, *Armia Podziemna*, 189; "Króliki z Ravensbrück" in *Przetrwałam*, 16–29; Madajczyk, *Polityka III Rzeszy*, Tom II, 273–305.

[55] On February 25, 1944 they contained 1809 men, 715 women, and 9 children. Domańska, *Pawiak więzienie gestapo*, 427.

[56] Rutkiewiczowa and Domańska were cellmates and wrote its history together. Domańska, *Pawiak więzienie gestapo*, 32, 353, 423.

[57] There is little data on sexual relationships between Germans and Poles. Maren Röger notes a Polish woman whose relationship with a policeman began at her arrest. Röger, *Wojenne związki*, 98; Lehnstaedt, *Occupation*, 8, 129.

[58] Domańska, *Pawiak więzienie gestapo*, 448, 366, 363.

How many people moved through the Pawiak–Serbia complex? German records, including the prisoner card file, which sat in a set of dark green metal boxes atop a table in the interior guards' office – and from which the Polish prisoner staff frequently stole or "adjusted" information – were damaged, lost, or destroyed in 1943 and 1944.[59] However, based on Domańska's work, data collected by underground networks, and prisoner memoirs, it can be concluded that around 100,000 people were imprisoned in Pawiak, 97,000 of whom can be accounted for specifically. Hirshaut, the Polish-Jewish escapee, calculated 8,000 Polish Jews killed in Pawiak of the approximately 40,000 prisoners between 1942 and 1944, a breakdown other sources cannot corroborate.[60] Some were arrested on forged identity papers (*Kennkarten*) or using pseudonyms and remain unidentifiable; others may have been Polish Jews successfully passing as non-Jews. Around 37,000 were executed, 60,000 transferred to other camps (where a substantial number died), and a few hundred released.[61]

The majority of Pawiak prisoners were Polish with a robust minority of Polish Jews, but exceptions were telling. Surviving prisoners remembered foreign nationals, including Soviet soldiers held alongside Polish communists in cell 125.[62] One of the designated Jewish cells (Hirshaut's) may also have housed Roma prisoners.[63] A British soldier, warrant officer G. P. Hickman, wandered into Gestapo clutches on December 10, 1943 in murky circumstances. He was tortured on Szuch Boulevard and killed at Pawiak "some time between December 20, 1943 and January 1, 1944." Considering this a war crime, the British Foreign Office pursued the matter postwar to obtain information about Hickman and "conditions in the prison." A Polish female witness described the guard who killed Hickman as "about forty years of age, tall, dark, clean-shaven and w[earing] spectacles." The British eventually abandoned their inquiries in light of "determined obstructionism from official quarters": Pawiak would remain a mystery.[64] Notably, Hickman was an unusual prisoner in that he was British, but not unusual in that he was murdered in a Pawiak cell. Most of those who shared that fate, though, were Varsovian intelligentsia.

[59] Wanat, *Za murami*, 14; Wachsmann, *KL*, 19.

[60] Hirshaut, *Jewish Martyrs*, 76.

[61] Wanat gives 90,000, naming 60,000. Jews shot immediately were not counted. Wanat, *Za murami*, 68, 206; Domańska, *A droga ich*, 6.

[62] Janusz Krzywicki, *Pawiak był etapem*, 218.

[63] Hirshaut remembers "the other five [of 28 cellmates] were the usual Gypsies or idlers with no profession" – perhaps a reference to Roma. Hirshaut, *Jewish Martyrs*, 40.

[64] TNA FO 371/57600 Death of Warrant Officer G. P. Hickman in Pawiak Prison, Warsaw (unpaginated). Foreign Office War Crimes Section letter to Warsaw Chancery, February 27, 1946; F. F. Garner to Colonel R. C. Halse, 2 October 1946; Warsaw Chancery to War Crimes Section, 18 September 1946.

3.3   From Pawiak to Auschwitz

Pawiak did have a limit beyond which it could not house further prisoners: 2,000 men could not be kept there indefinitely. Guards crammed the cells beyond capacity, especially the basement ones in sections VII and VIII, which were for quarantine and Jews, and the filthiest and most crowded. By spring 1940 during the AB-Aktion, Pawiak was overflowing, and prison administrators sent thousands into Nazi Germany's most elastic detention system: the Reich concentration camps.[65] Poles sent by rail to Dachau, Sachsenhausen, and Ravensbrück brought their politics and their grievances with them, embroiling prisoners of other nationalities.[66] In Ravensbrück, French-speaking Józefa Kęszycka (1920–42, "Józia") talked to western European POWs and relayed information back to Poland until her 1942 execution.[67] Large-scale executions of transferred Poles were some of the first mass killings in the camp system, numbering hundreds of Polish victims: even within the larger Nazi persecution system, Polish intelligentsia were selected for particular violence.[68] A huge backlog of Warsaw political prisoners still piled up.[69]

The long-term solution to Pawiak overcrowding was the opening of a new concentration camp accessible to Warsaw. The "Warsaw problem," however, was carried to the new camp: political prisoners from the city organized opposition there. Himmler ordered the SS to scout a site around the railroad town of Oświęcim in early 1940. Buggy, damp, and shabby, SS staff rejected it, but an ambitious officer named Rudolf Hoess revisited the site in spring – a place "far away, in the back of beyond" – and deemed the old military and prison buildings serviceable.[70] Like many Nazis working in Poland, Hoess had a rocky career. Once considered "Hitler's appointed successor," he spent the war far from Berlin running Auschwitz.[71]

---

[65] Versus *Aktion Reinhard* death camps built after the Wannsee Conference.

[66] Pawiak women went to Ravensbrück. Sarah Helm, *Ravensbrück: Life and Death in Hitler's Concentration Camp for Women* (New York: Anchor Books, 2015), 162–163; 170–171.

[67] Kęszycka joined TAP in fall 1939 as Pilecki's courier. She was arrested in July 1940, held in Serbia, and then sent to Ravensbrück and executed in July 1942. Krystyna Śmigiel, "Kęszycka Józefa" in *Sylwetki Kobiet-Żolnierzy*, ed. Krystyna Kabzińska, Służba Polek na Frontach II Wojny Światowej – 7 (Toruń: Fundacja Archiwum i Muzeum Pomorskie Armii Krajowej oraz Wojskowej Służby Polek, 2003), 162–165; Domańska, *Pawiak więzienie gestapo*, 171.

[68] The largest executions were in Sachsenhausen, Mauthausen, and Auschwitz in November 1940. Wachsmann, *KL*, 218–219.

[69] Danuta Olesiuk and Tomasz Kranz, *Listy z Majdanka* (Lublin: Państwowe Muzeum na Majdanku, 2009), 31; 36; 38–39; 45.

[70] Rudolf Hoess, *Commandant of Auschwitz* (London: Phoenix Press, 2000), 106; Madajczyk, *Polityka III Rzeszy*, Tom II, 287.

[71] Louis L. Snyder called Hoess a "paladin extraordinary." Snyder, *Hitler's Elite: Biographical Sketches of Nazis who Shaped the Third Reich* (New York: Hippocrene Books, 1989), 77.

The camp was out of the way and right in the center of things: the eastern-most bastion of the SS concentration camp empire, but at the westernmost edge of what had been Poland, on territory incorporated directly into the Reich and outside Frank's civilian jurisdiction. It thus served both Germany and what remained of Poland by rail, connecting the persecution system built after 1933 with the one expanding to subdue eastern Europe. Unable to wait for Auschwitz to open, Pawiak sent 823 men to Sachsenhausen on May 2, 1940. At the end of June 1940 Pawiak was still hopelessly overcrowded.[72] Auschwitz's first prisoner transports came not from Pawiak, but from a much closer Polish town, Tarnów, on June 14, 1940, mostly "students and soldiers" – Polish political threats.[73] On August 14, 1940 Pawiak sent its first transport of 513 men, including "lawyers, doctors, officers of the Polish Army, social and political activists, and priests" to Auschwitz.[74] By the end of the year, almost 8,000 Pawiak prisoners had been sent to the camp. By March 1941, it held almost 11,000 inmates, and by early 1942, when it transitioned to accommo-date new prisoners – Jews from countries across Nazi-occupied Europe – it still held 12,000 men, more than 75% of whom were Polish and the majority of whom were from Warsaw.[75]

The injection of Pawiak prisoners brought Polish opposition to Auschwitz. Such "recalcitrant Poles," too dangerous to be used as unsupervised slave labor in the Reich, did not cease to conspire against German power after transfer to Auschwitz.[76] In fact, the looser and less-regulated structure of the growing camp provided more opportunities for those who knew how to use them. Captain Witold Pilecki (1901–48), a Polish Army officer and the co-founder of an early underground military group, built an opposition organization inside the camp (Figure 3.2). Pilecki grew up in Vilnius before the First World War. There he joined one of the kresy's scouting organizations and was just old enough to fight in the Polish–Bolshevik War. In newly independent Poland, Pilecki was demo-bilized but not depoliticized, and he continued his education in the fine arts – some of his paintings are still extant – married a teacher, had two children, mastered French and German in addition to his native Polish and Russian, and became a reserve officer. In 1939 he fought in the September Campaign as a second lieutenant in the cavalry and, when his unit was scattered, made his way to Warsaw. He found himself in the apartment of a fellow reserve officer,

---

[72] Domańska, *Pawiak więzienie gestapo*, 52–57; 68–70.

[73] Sławomir Kapralski, *The Nazi Genocide of the Roma* (New York: Berghahn Books, 2013), 244; Wachsmann, *KL*, 202–203.

[74] The *Bulletin* mentioned a "concentration camp" but not Auschwitz. BN, Mf. 45815, *BI*, August 16, 1940, 7; Wachsmann, *KL*, 79–83.

[75] Yisrael Gutman, "Auschwitz – An Overview" in *Anatomy of the Auschwitz Death Camp* (Washington, DC: United States Holocaust Memorial Museum, 1994), 16. Here "Polish" means *not* Jewish.

[76] Dwork and van Pelt, *Auschwitz*, 173.

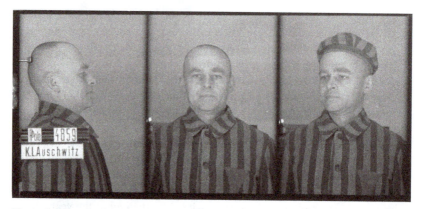

Figure 3.2 Auschwitz prisoner intake photographs for Witold Pilecki, prisoner 4859, September 1940.
Archive of the Auschwitz-Birkenau State Museum.

a man who had gone into hiding, and Pilecki used his name – Tomasz Serafiński – to establish a new occupation identity for himself.[77]

Pilecki connected with other restless officers in hiding in the circles of a fledgling military conspiracy that called itself the Secret Polish Army (*Tajna Armia Polska*, TAP). As part of TAP, Pilecki saw the devastating effects of Tannenberg and AB on comrades and friends. In spring 1940 several TAP members were arrested, including Dr. Śliwicki and his courier-assistant, "Józia."[78] Their disappearances led to Pilecki's fall 1940 project: to figure out what the Germans were doing to their victims. An "Auschwitz volunteer," Pilecki deliberately walked into an SS roundup in Warsaw's Żoliborz neighborhood and became Auschwitz prisoner 4859. Over three years, Pilecki smuggled out reports, building a group he called the United Military Organization (ZOW, *Związek Organizacji Wojskowej*). This was dangerous work conducted on top of the travails of prisoner life, to which many succumbed without any of Pilecki's additional burdens.[79] He was aided by his military training and the continuous influx of men from Pawiak. He mentioned with particular relief arrivals in 1942: "a transport from Warsaw (March of '42) again brought in a great number of friends as well as information about what was going on" and, later in the year, "a new transport from Pawiak in Warsaw which included my friends and former colleagues in

---

[77] Though they had not met, Pilecki stayed with Serafiński's parents after escaping Auschwitz. Jacek Pawłowicz, *Rotmistrz Witold Pilecki (1901–1948)* (Warsaw: IPN, 2008), 17–41; 82–83; 116–117.

[78] The Gestapo arrested TAP in February and September 1940.

[79] AAN 2-2840-0 Akta Bogny Lewtak sygn1, [Letter 2016], 3.

the TAP ... they brought me some interesting news."[80] To Pilecki's frustra-tion, "no one in Warsaw had seriously considered that Auschwitz could represent an active asset; for the most part people felt that everyone there was a skeleton:" too physically weak and psychologically cowed to continue opposition. He saw his job as changing that, and putting Auschwitz prisoners in contact with friends in Warsaw, and vice versa, expanding the network of those combatting the Germans. Józef Garliński, historian of Polish Auschwitz resistance, considers Pilecki's work central. Building secret cells of five patriotic, trustworthy, like-minded men – *piątki* – (the model for armed opposition outside the camp), good luck reconnected Pilecki with Warsaw: the Gestapo, which had certainly been bribed, requested one of his first recruits' release.[81] This freed prisoner carried Pilecki's report to Warsaw in November 1940, the first of many painstakingly smuggled out.[82] These detailed prisoner demographics and later the mass murder of Jews. Opposition in Warsaw paired with opposition in Auschwitz: interconnecting Polish victims helped conspirators understand what was happening and how to contest it.[83]

Pilecki's ultimate goal in Auschwitz was to organize a camp-wide revolt, but someone's confession – or denunciation, it is unclear – undermined the plan.[84] Pilecki escaped in April 1943. This escape demonstrated enduring intelligentsia influence, as it relied on Polish support across the countryside, anonymous supporters who aided him or did not betray him to occupation authorities. Traveling over 200 miles through the GG, Pilecki rejoined the Warsaw underground equipped with knowledge of expanding Nazi exter-mination facilities.[85]

Auschwitz, most often associated with its post-1942 role as the largest concentration camp of the Holocaust, spread the opposition that had earned

---

[80] Witold Pilecki, *The Auschwitz Volunteer: Beyond Bravery* (Los Angeles: Aquila Polonica, 2012), 165; 239, 240–241. On Auschwitz's intelligentsia, see Kubalski, *Niemcy w Krakowie*, 210.

[81] Pilecki recruited those with similar backgrounds to his own. Sebastian Pawlina, *Praca w dywersji: Codzienność żołnierzy Kedywu Okręgu Warszawskiego Armii Krajowej* (Gdańsk: Muzeum II Wojny Światowej, 2016), 201–211.

[82] Józef Garliński, *Fighting Auschwitz: The Resistance Movement in the Concentration Camp* (Los Angeles: Aquila Polonica, 2018), 39, 41, 45, 47.

[83] Pilecki's projects relied on women. Müller, *If The Walls*, 165; 174.

[84] The revolt never happened. Jewish resisters felt exploited by Poles, who had more agency (Tzipora Hager Halivni, "The Birkenau Revolt: Poles Prevent a Timely Insurrection," *Jewish Social Studies* Vol. 41 No. 2 (Spring, 1979): 126). Halivni noted that "the experi-enced Poles were potential soldiers; the neophyte Jews ... disoriented." See further: Shmuel Krakowski, *The War of the Doomed: Jewish Armed Resistance in Poland, 1942–1944* (New York: Holmes & Meier Publishers, 1984), 234–273.

[85] Pilecki, *Auschwitz Volunteer*, 274–275; Pawłowicz, *Rotmistrz Witold Pilecki (1901-1948)*, 110–111; Pawłowicz, "Więzienie Warszawa-Mokotów w latach 1945-1956," 190.

so many a cell in Pawiak.[86] Pawiak morning roll call sent men and women to execution, to Szuch Boulevard, to Auschwitz, to Majdanek or, occasionally, to release. Some of those fates left the possibility of continuing opposition – albeit with difficulty. The transfer of prisoners out was also the long-term solution to the problem created by the unresolved anti-intelligentsia campaigns: Germans did not have sufficient capacity to quarantine the "threat" such people posed as potential and then actual promoters of resistance unless they were prepared to kill them all, which Tannenberg and AB revealed to be impossible.

3.4 Imprisonment as Motivator

Pawiak prisoners were political, albeit broadly so. Their captors assumed they were linked to networks that could aid them in captivity and upon release or escape, which was sometimes but not always the case. Though arrest, interrogation, and execution buried some conspiracies, Gestapo brutality invigorated other efforts. Pilecki's Auschwitz activities demonstrated this. The experience of persecution could radicalize whole families, exciting behavior the Nazis hoped to curtail and intertwining individuals in webs of opposition. That the concentration of political "criminals" in the prison actually expanded political conspiracy should not have surprised the Nazis: the early anti-intelligentsia campaigns had been secret to prevent making martyrs of their victims.[87] Of course, the community of prisoners was a fraught one: informers, guards, and interrogators fractured bonds of trust, and communication bans made planning difficult. Nevertheless, a remarkably tight-knit community formed that persisted among survivors.[88]

Though many prisoners confessed under torture, and their anti-Nazi opposition work – of which a great deal more later – crumbled with their arrest, other projects were invigorated by imprisonment. Arrest records and prison stays themselves testify to the diversity and ubiquity of intelligentsia opposition and occupier paranoia about its dangers. Opposition that required face-to-face interaction, like teaching secret classes, was badly disrupted by arrest – though

---

[86] In time, the link would be reinforced in the other direction: Jewish Auschwitz prisoners, heavily Italians and Greeks, were transported to Warsaw from late 1943 in order to sort and clear the rubble of the destroyed ghetto after its uprising. They were held in KL Warschau, nicknamed "Gęsiówka," a destroyed ghetto prison that abutted Pawiak. These prisoners were sometimes forced to aid in burning the bodies of executed Pawiak prisoners. Finder, "Jewish Prisoner Labour" and Edward Kossoy, "The Gęsiówka Story: A Little-Known Page of Jewish Resistance," both in *Polin: Studies in Polish Jewry Vol 17: The Shtetl: Myth and Reality*, ed. A. Polonsky (Liverpool: Liverpool University Press, 2004), 327–328; 354–355.

[87] Müller, *If the Walls*, 3; Padraic Kenney, *Dance in Chains: Political Imprisonment in the Modern World* (New York: Oxford University Press, 2017).

[88] Kenney calls Pawiak prisoners "well-coordinated" and communication "well oiled." Kenney, *Dance in Chains*, 92.

some teachers took up instructing their cellmates. Other work, like data gathering to suss out Nazi capacities, was aided by imprisonment, since it allowed conspirators to verify information about the prison itself. The experience of elite prisoners and the effect of arrests reveal the close-knit nature of intelligentsia life and the vitality of networks that made elite opposition possible.

Intelligentsia family histories were pockmarked with arrests and imprisonments. Stanisław Michał Jankowski (1911–2002, "Agaton") lost his father, his brother, and nearly his mother to Pawiak in circumstances that took him years to unravel. Jankowski had studied architecture at the Warsaw Polytechnic before the war. He was mobilized by the WP on September 3, 1939 and his father Czesław Jankowski saw him off on the platform of Warsaw's main train station. Czesław took the family signet ring from his son's finger and wore it on a chain around his neck. The ring was still around Czesław's neck when he was executed at Palmiry in 1940, and made it back to his wife, Elżbieta, after the exhumation of his body in 1946.[89] In that sense the family was lucky, because the ring made Czesław Jankowski's corpse identifiable. Arrested with other intelligentsia during AB roundups, Czesław and his other son Andrzej were held in Pawiak. They left the prison on June 20, 1940, heading north toward the Kampinos forest in covered trucks. The first transport left at 7 a.m., and the last at 7 p.m., hauling 368 prisoners, including 82 women and both Jankowskis. It was an intelligentsia transport that included "prominent social and political activists, publicists, doctors, lawyers, and engineers."[90]

Polish summer days are long; those 368 people were buried before dark on June 20, 1940. Stanisław found out about his father's and brother's fate from his mother, who had waited and hoped after their arrest. The Gestapo informed her of her husband's death in September 1940. This was three months late and misleading: father and son had been shot the same day, side by side over the same pit. The announcement was for one death, and Elżbieta hoped her son Andrzej was still alive. By August 1941, with one son abroad (Stanisław), a dead husband (Czesław), a dead son (Andrzej) about whom she was unaware, a daughter on the run, and two grandchildren to mind, the Gestapo called again. She was taken to Serbia when she would not – or could not – reveal her daughter's whereabouts.[91] She endured four months inside with eight interrogations at Szuch Boulevard, but was finally released by a well-bribed guard. She spent the rest of the occupation in hiding. Her daughter was surely engaged in conspiracy, though the mother may have been unclear about

---

[89] Stanisław Jankowski, *Z fałszywym ausweisem w prawdziwej Warszawie: Wspomnienie 1939–1946*, Tom 2 (Warsaw: Państwowy Instytut Wydawniczy, 1985), 19–20.

[90] Domańska, *Pawiak więzienie gestapo*, 64–66.

[91] See: "Maria Dzierżawska" and "Jadwiga Bodych" on male relatives in *Chronicles of Terror: Warsaw* (Warsaw: Witold Pilecki Center for Totalitarian Studies, 2017), 144–145, 147.

the details. Stanisław, her son, was in Soviet captivity and then escaped to join Polish military forces in western Europe. He was thus outside Warsaw while the Gestapo killed his father and brother and hunted his mother and sister. He would sneak back into Warsaw in 1942, find his mother, join the underground, and fight in the Warsaw Uprising in 1944.[92] The Jankowskis were an extreme case, but loyalty entangled numerous families in Nazi persecution.

Peter (Piotr Florian) Dembowski (1925–, "Syn") was the son of a politically active Catholic family, and knee-deep in paramilitary conspiracy in 1942, hiding Home Army weapons. When his cache of contraband was found, he was sent to Pawiak and his mother and sister to Ravensbrück. Arrest confirmed Dembowski's sense of generational baton-passing, a coming-of-age moment. "In the fall of 1913, Włodek [Włodzimierz, his father] spent some time in the czarist Pawiak prison in Warsaw (built in 1835). I would get to know the same prison building in April and May 1944."[93] The Gestapo was unsure if the weapons belonged to the teenage Dembowski and he was released; his mother and sister died.

Like Jankowski and Dembowski, the Szuch family also fell afoul of the occupation. A gentry clan from the *kresy*, patriarch Aleksander Szuch had been a cavalry officer during the First World War and earned the Virtuti Militari during the Polish–Bolshevik War. His children, Teresa and Janusz, were young but their home at No. 12 Noakowski Street near the Warsaw Polytechnic became the hub of multiple conspiracies. Aleksander Szuch was part of a paramilitary effort and was aiding Jews, one or the other of which earned him a trip to Pawiak and extensive torture at Szuch Boulevard. He was transferred to Auschwitz with 875 men and 141 women in August 1943, where he was subjected to medical experimentation.[94]

Undeterred, Szuch's arrest set his wife and children along the same path. Teenage Janusz found his way into the *Kedyw*, a saboteur group, and worked in the "Parasol" Battalion under General Leopold Okulicki ("Niedźwiadek"), one of the members of Michał Tokarzewski-Karaszewicz's Polish Victory Service (SZP), and the last commander of the Home Army before its disbanding in 1945. Though the three "free" Szuchs scattered, persecution forged new ties: Aleksander met four relatives in Auschwitz. Janusz and Teresa both fell in love – and then lost their sweethearts to violence.[95] The Gestapo intended Aleksander Szuch's 1943 deportation to intimidate Poles. From 1941 on arrest announcements like the one with his name on it were published on streets and squares as warning to potential conspirators. Szuch underscored the accuracy of Nazi assumptions about Polish

---

[92] Jankowski, *Z Fałszywym ausweisem*, Tom 2, 21, 207–352; Leski, *Życie niewłaściwie urozmaicone*, 110–111; 135.
[93] Peter F. Dembowski, *Memoirs Red and White: Poland, the War, and After* (South Bend: University of Notre Dame Press, 2015), 13, 27–31.
[94] Domańska, *Pawiak więzienie gestapo*, 346–347.
[95] AAN 2-2840-0 Akta Bogny Lewtak sygn1, [Bogna Lewtak-Baczyńska Letter 2016], 1–4; [Życiorys], 1–3; [Obituary *Gazeta Wyborcza*].

intelligentsia behavior: his First World War service and social status targeted him up for Tannenberg persecution, but he dodged it and did exactly what the Nazis feared: foment rebellion. Arresting the father, however, left behind a wife and two teenagers, each of whom joined other conspiracies.

The last example of how imprisonment provoked opposition in the intelligentsia community is, strangely enough, Władysław Studnicki's. Studnicki, interwar rabble-rouser and Germanophile, tried to persuade the Wehrmacht to include him in German rule; the SS quashed these plans. Studnicki was indefatigable, reaching out to Goebbels and Goering.[96] His politicking irritated the SS, and they arrested him in summer 1941, during a week when Polish politicians from right and left arrived at Pawiak in another wave of crackdowns.[97] By 1941, Studnicki had come out against Poles using violence and sabotage, believing such anti-Nazi methods were inspired by "the provocation of Soviet agents."[98] Prison experience – he was held for fourteen months – might have turned him against the Germans, but it did not. In fact, his unfinished memoirs called the arrest "perfectly comprehensible," attributing it to SS corruption:[99] "A few days after my arrest a Gestapo official communicated to me," he wrote, "that I had been arrested on the orders of the Gestapo commander in Krakow at the request of the governor [Frank] and that I had to remain in prison or be transferred to Germany. I immediately chose transfer to Germany." The Wehrmacht finally "rescued" him after an avalanche of letters to Frank, the Wehrmacht, and German colleagues.[100] While he waited for his "inevitable" release, Studnicki's imprisonment gestated multiple political treatises, each as fiery as his prewar work. Once free, he returned to a comparative study of Nazi–Soviet occupation, coming out against Soviet occupation as more destructive to Polish national life.[101] Though Studnicki was unusual in his Nazi sympathies, he behaved like other prisoners: his persecution honed his commitments, despite the risks.

3.5 Privileged Prisoners

Szuch spent weeks traveling between Pawiak and Gestapo headquarters for interrogation before transfer to Auschwitz; Studnicki wrote to every

---

[96] JPI Archiwum Władysława Studnickiego 96: 27, "Okupacja Niemiecka i Sowiecka," 6; 96:3, "Korespondencja," folder 3, 192–193.

[97] Domańska, *Pawiak więzienie gestapo*, 161.

[98] JPI Archiwum Władysława Studnickiego 96: 3 "Do rozdziału 'Aneksja i wojna z Sowietami,'" 3 (246 of file).

[99] "Dla mnie całkiem zrozumiałe." JPI Archiwum Władysława Studnickiego 96: 3 "Do rozdziału 'Aneksja i wojna z Sowietami,'" 3 (246).

[100] JPI Archiwum Władysława Studnickiego 96: 3 "Do rozdziału 'Aneksja i wojna z Sowietami,'" 4-[5] (247–248).

[101] JPI Archiwum Władysława Studnickiego 96: 27, "Okupacja Niemiecka i Sowiecka."

Wehrmacht officer he knew. Most of those in Pawiak hoped for release but "arrests did not often end happily."[102] A handful spent years inside: Leon Wanat and Zygmunt Śliwicki were in this long-haul prisoner category. Both men revived the activities that had gotten them imprisoned in the first place, linking "free" and imprisoned conspirators, and thwarting German attempts to keep Pawiak affairs secret. Wanat was arrested on March 30, 1940, another AB victim. Originally from Krakow, he studied in Warsaw and was mobilized there as an officer in 1939. When his unit disintegrated, Wanat returned to Warsaw to teach, but leapt into underground intrigues as well. Military service protected him from the first anti-intelligentsia campaign but not AB. After his arrest, Wanat went to Centralniak prison on Danilowicz Street and then to Pawiak. "Thanks to his beautiful handwriting and know-ledge of German," the clerk put him to work in the records office, where he overheard staff and guard conversations. The cushy post shielded him from transfer.[103] Records that Wanat "worked on" somehow ended up in conspir-ators' hands outside the prison, confirming colleagues' arrests and aiding release and escape arrangements. It also made Wanat one of the best-informed observers of the internal operations of Nazi persecution in Warsaw, and he testified against policemen Josef Meisinger and Ludwig Hahn postwar.

Wanat studied the staff, from the sadistic morphine addict Bürkl with his riding crop, to the impossibly vain Engelberth Frühwirth, who spent hours doing his hair. He watched guards set dogs on prisoners, order bizarre gym-nastics exercises, string men up in their cells "for sport," and subject them to medical "experiments."[104] Wanat's records, like Regina Domańska's, meticu-lously listed names, but also noted details that might otherwise have been lost – jokes condemned men told to cellmates; the sounds of nighttime beatings in pitch darkness; the escapes, including ten Polish-Jewish prisoners who slipped out one night; the personal foibles of people condemned to die.[105] Wanat's explicit documentation undergirded a Polish counternarrative in contrast to German propaganda.

Pawiak also put Zygmunt Śliwicki's skills to use. A physician, Śliwicki had gotten his medical degree at Warsaw University. He was tending to the wounded as a WP regimental doctor when Polish defenses broke in 1939. Ordered to evacuate to Romania, Śliwicki found the road to Bucharest blocked. Still in civilian clothing – he had not been issued a uniform – he returned to practice in Pruszków, outside Warsaw. His

---

[102] Zofia Kossakowska-Szanacja, *Zapiski dla wnuków* (Warsaw: Biblioteka Więzi, 2009), 241–242.
[103] Wanat, *Za murami*, 9–10; Domańska, *Pawiak więzienie gestapo*, 60.
[104] Wanat, *Za murami*, 38, 41, 56, 62–63.
[105] Wanat, *Za murami*, 184, 255, 140, 358.

consulting room served as a meeting point for "patients" building the Secret Polish Army (Tajna Armia Polska, TAP), which included Witold Pilecki.[106] The Gestapo got wind of Śliwicki's machinations (he may have been betrayed) and arrested him on September 26, 1940. He went straight to the "streetcars" at Szuch Boulevard and then joined six others in a Pawiak cell.[107]

Because Pawiak had many people needing medical attention, and because a previous physician had just been released, Śliwicki became prisoner-doctor under "free" physician Stefan Baczyński.[108] The compound hospital in Serbia turned out to be a nexus of communication. Śliwicki even refused an arranged escape in 1941, thinking he was more useful to his country inside.[109] He was joined by Anna Czuperska (née Krawecka ("Dr. Podkowa," 1908–88)), who also studied at Warsaw University. She and her husband Henryk Czuperski joined Karaszewicz-Tokarzewski's Polish Victory Service and were betrayed in November 1940. Separated from her husband, who was transported to Auschwitz and killed, Czuperska went to Serbia. She spent four years there as a prisoner-doctor and organized a women's spy ring codenamed "998." She worked with Śliwicki until her July 1944 release and the two married in 1946.[110]

No one – not even a prisoner-doctor – was safe from deportation. Śliwicki's name appeared on the Auschwitz transport lists seventeen times. A German doctor removed it each time, but Śliwicki never knew if the privilege would last. Śliwicki watched guards "take gravely ill prisoners, often a few hours after major surgery, and even women nine months pregnant" for transfer. His patients betrayed prolonged torture and some were beyond saving. Clinic staff was forbidden to provide painkillers to Jews, no matter their injuries.[111] Their torment reminded Śliwicki – lest he forget – that he was trapped inside a hospital inside a prison inside the ghetto. Śliwicki's imprisonment reveals the complex fate of intelligentsia whose training and connections were useful to both their countrymen and their occupiers: the doctor's medical knowledge kept him alive and useful to the Gestapo, and simultaneously allowed him to help injured co-conspirators and smuggle information back to TAP and its successors. Was this collaboration or resistance? For Śliwicki the answer was obvious.

---

[106] The same subterfuge is used in Fritz Lang's *Hangmen Also Die!* (1943): Dr. Svoboda uses his examination rooms for conspiracy.

[107] Śliwicki, *Meldunek z Pawiaka*, 9–13.

[108] The man released was Dr. Alfred Fiderkiewicz, communist physician. Nothing was pinned on him in 1940 but he was arrested again on June 28, 1943. Domańska, *Pawiak więzienie gestapo*, 95, 103, 332, 347.

[109] Śliwicki, *Meldunek z Pawiaka*, 76–77.

[110] Domańska, *Pawiak więzienie gestapo*, 112.

[111] Śliwicki, *Meldunek z Pawiaka*, 36–38; 54; 80.

3.6   Operation Arsenal and Escape

The enclosure of the prison within the ghetto had practical significance for both escape and rescue, attempted frequently but rarely successful.[112] Escape was the consummate act of group behavior, even if attempted by an individual, since it drew on a community of helpers and observers. An escaping prisoner put his cellmates at risk for retaliation and had to break through both Pawiak and ghetto walls to return to "Aryan" Warsaw. Escaping Polish-Jewish inmates achieved little if they only escaped into the ghetto, where they were still prisoners. Most breakouts, therefore, were attempted in transit between Pawiak and Szuch Boulevard or between Pawiak and a camp.[113] Kazimierz Andrzej Kott pulled off the first successful escape in January 1940, from Gestapo headquarters. He climbed out the window of the men's toilets between beatings and into the city, where he was helped by passersby.[114]

Sickness could be a ticket out, as Śliwicki's clinic was small and contagious diseases (especially typhus) required treatment at "free" hospitals, usually the Catholic Hospital of the Child Jesus.[115] Escape required friends, money, and good luck. It meant contacts in the prison, the ghetto, and in "Aryan" Warsaw, and access to transport such as a laundry cart, an ambulance, or delivery vehicle. This was significantly more difficult for Polish-Jewish prisoners. It was also easier for established conspirators since they had connections with skills and motivation to spring them.

Stanisław Tomaszewski (1913–2000), a photographer, landed in Pawiak in 1941 because he was caught attempting to build a photographic record of Nazi atrocities. His well-connected colleagues launched an intricate escape plan. This involved a prisoner-dentist "deliberately infect[ing] him with typhus," a transfer to the infectious disease hospital, and "faked appendicitis and a borrowed corpse" to cover up his disappearance from the hospital.[116] Prisoner-doctors and dentists provided diagnoses of prisoner-patients who needed treatment but could not escape and fakers who could use the opportunity to get free.[117] This was a viable escape route for only a few and a plan this complex endangered the whole chain of conspirators, and genuinely ill patients besides.[118]

Life inside Pawiak was keyed to conspiracies outside. This meant that as conspirators turned to violent confrontation late in the occupation, they grew

---

[112] Kenney, *Dance in Chains*, 97, 150–153.
[113] Janusz Byliński, *Pawiak był etapem*, 221.
[114] Domańska, *Pawiak – Kaźń i Heroizm*, 194–195.
[115] Run by Vincentians since its opening in 1901, staff engaged in anti-Nazi conspiracies.
[116] Prisoner-doctors arranged transfer on October 22, 1941 to Wojewódzki Szpital Zakaźny. Kenney, *Dance in Chains*, 152; Domańska, *Pawiak więzienie gestapo*, 177.
[117] Śliwicki, *Meldunek z Pawiaka*, 73–77.
[118] Ossibach-Budzyński, *Pawiak: więzienie polityczne*, 211; 216–217.

more ambitious about rescuing imprisoned comrades.[119] Escapes became legend. The most famous was the rescue of Jan "Rudy" Bytnar (1921–43) in March 1943. An underground assault team sprang Bytnar and provoked police crackdowns.[120] Crucially, this occurred in spring 1943 when his comrades were toying with open insurgency.[121] Bytnar's escape, codenamed Operation Arsenal, involved characters familiar from the siege. Scout leader Stanisław Broniewski, directing the Grey Ranks of underground scouts, sprung Bytnar and twenty-four other political prisoners headed back to Pawiak from Szuch Boulevard.[122] Working alongside him was Tadeusz Zawadzki ("Zośka" 1921–43), six years Broniewski's junior but rising through the underground scouting ranks and in and out of prison himself. Zawadzki's friend Bytnar, the Gestapo prize, had been arrested with his father on March 23, 1943 in a middle-of-the-night raid. Men, weapons, and explosives seized earlier pointed to Bytnar's handiwork.[123] Bytnar, who had started as a scout, was trafficking weapons when the Gestapo caught him.[124] Execution awaited him. To free Bytnar, Broniewski formed a plan code-named "Mexico II." A recently released prisoner informed conspirators of the exact route vehicles took between Gestapo headquarters in the German district and Pawiak in the ghetto. Broniewski's twenty-eight-member crew picked an intersection they knew well, the corner of Bielański and Długa Streets in front of the old arsenal: a neighborhood filled with friends and colleagues. On the afternoon of March 28, 1943, they ambushed the prisoner transport with benzene-filled Molotov cocktails, grenades, and machine pistols. Overwhelming the driver, killing several SS men and wounding two women, the operation freed twenty-five prisoners, including Bytnar, and vanished into the city.[125] Though Bytnar later died of his wounds, Operation Arsenal was a triumph for the underground – of which Bytnar and Broniewski were members – "in broad daylight in the middle of the capital."[126] Friendly doctors patched up the wounded, and Bytnar was hidden

[119] Home Army rules: not to aid the enemy, to talk as little as possible, and to focus on self-improvement. Komisja Historyczna Polskiego Sztabu Głównego w Londynie, *Polskie Siły Zbrojne w Drugiej Wojnie Światowej*, Tom III: *Armia Krajowa* (London: Instytut Historyczny im. Gen. Sikorskiego, 1950) 93–96.

[120] Landau, *Kronika*, Tom II, 297.

[121] Borodziej, *Terror und Politik*, 206–209.

[122] APmstW Zespół 1716/II: Archiwum Stanisława Broniewskiego, Naczelnika Szarych Szeregów, s. 55; Stanisław Broniewski, *Akcja pod Arsenałem* (Warsaw: Ksiażka i Wiedza, 1972); Aleksander Kamiński, *Stones for the Rampart* (London: Polish Boy Scouts and Girl Guides' Association, 1945).

[123] Families were arrested for leverage. Domańska, *Pawiak więzienie gestapo*, 321.

[124] Leski, *Życie niewłaściwie urozmaicone*, 310–311.

[125] Leszek Wysznacki, *Warszawa Zbrojna: 1794–1918, 1939–1945* (Warsaw: Krajowa Agencja Wydawnicza, 1979), 62–63.

[126] BN, Mf. 45818, *BI*, April 1, 1943, Nr. 13 (1688), "Warszawa," [1] and 7.

in the apartment of Professor Jan Wuttke ("Jaś Czarny" or "Black Johnny"), a conspirator who later died in the 1944 Uprising.

Diarist Ludwik Landau, not one for violent confrontation himself, called Arsenal a "sensation:" "What happened yesterday evening, just before the start of the curfew," he confided to his diary, "was the sensation of Warsaw: an attack on a transport of prisoners from Pawiak." Immediately afterward "panic spread in the whole quarter, and men began to escape," because "the Germans ... began apprehending passers-by. Who knows if there will be a repression in Pawiak?[127]" The German administration's "repression" was swift and limited only by the outbreak of the Ghetto Uprising shortly thereafter, when Nazi police focused on destroying Polish-Jewish resisters over Polish ones.[128] Successful escapes required the functioning of networks that reached through Pawiak's walls, into Śliwicki's clinic and Wanat's record office, connecting conspirators inside and outside the Nazi persecution system. In 1943, some of the city's armed conspirators were powerful and well-connected enough to contest the prison, and the Gestapo power it represented, directly.

3.7   Conclusion

When the anti-intelligentsia campaigns failed, the Gestapo chased resistance it had not prevented, arresting those suspected of working against the regime or for Polish national culture. Pawiak was the central tool in these efforts and reminded Warsaw that the consequences of opposition were dire. The pale walls of the prison stood as a testament to Nazi willingness to crush Polish efforts and, though it was often out of sight during those years, it was never out of mind. Pawiak's function demonstrates concretely how Nazi German *Polenpolitik* was implemented and its limitations once opposition behavior spread. Pawiak was also a testament to segregation and its failures. It drew power both because of its prewar history and because of its "removal" behind ghetto walls in 1940, separating it from the daily life of non-Jewish Varsovians. Inmates like Śliwicki thus became some of the most intimate non-Jewish witnesses of antisemitic persecution in the surrounding ghetto in 1942 and 1943. Ironically – but unsurprising considering the effects of other political prisons – Pawiak galvanized opposition. It angered and terrified "apolitical" Varsovians, became a rite of passage for conspirators (some of whom met inside), and tested the mettle of underground groups who monitored it, assassinated its deputy commander, and freed its last prisoners during the 1944 uprising.

---

[127] Landau, *Kronika*, Tom II, 297; Franciszek Wyszyński, *Dzienniki z lat 1941–1944* (Warsaw: Sowa, 2007), 330.
[128] Domańska, *Pawiak więzienie gestapo*, 304–305, 309.

The Warsaw Ghetto

A People Set Apart

Warsaw's surviving intelligentsia grappled with their own persecution, responding with significant opposition. They were simultaneously crucial witnesses and some of the first responders to the Nazi persecution of their Jewish neighbors.[1] The creation of the Warsaw Ghetto in 1940, the "liquidation" and murder of its inhabitants at the Treblinka death camp in 1942, and the resistance of survivors in the 1943 Ghetto Uprisings destroyed the Polish-Jewish elite and transfixed their Polish peers.[2] The Holocaust is crucial to Warsaw's history and observing it affected intelligentsia behavior, even though Poles did not substantially alter the situation. Nazi antisemitic persecution was distinct from anti-intelligentsia policy but overlapped in time. Upon the creation of the ghetto, Jews were subjected to restrictions never attempted on majority Poles, even the intelligentsia. How the Warsaw Ghetto operated and how the Polish intelligentsia reacted – or did not react – to Jewish victimhood reveals much about the circumstances of occupied Warsaw and the successes and failures of Nazi experiments there.

Nazi policy "divided and conquered" Warsaw ethnically. Germans – Volksdeutsche and GG administration carpetbaggers – cordoned off the main boulevards downtown and most of Mokotów for their use (Figure 4.1). Poles were allowed to live where it was habitable in areas Germans had not claimed, and Polish Jews were eventually restricted entirely to an enclosed ghetto in the northwest. Segregation facilitated differential treatment, privileging Volksdeutsche and punishing Polish Jews above all.[3] It also allowed Nazis to play antagonistic groups off one another, using Volksdeutsche and the Ukrainian minority as Pawiak guards, or Polish blue police to rob and kill Jews. This stifled solidarity and reduced German personnel needs. Nazi policy

---

[1] Jan Grabowski questions the use of "witness" and "bystander." Grabowski, *Na posterunku*, 219; Barnett, *Bystanders*, 128–130.

[2] Jan T. Gross, *Fear: Anti-Semitism in Poland after Auschwitz* (New York: Random House, 2007), 32.

[3] Following the earlier segregation bureaucracy built in the Warthegau – also designed to undermine Polish solidarity. Epstein, *Model Nazi*, 193–230; Tim Cole, "Placing the Ghetto: Warsaw and Budapest, 1939–1945" in *Polin Studies in Polish Jewry, Vol. 31: Poland and Hungary: Jewish Realities Compared*, ed. F. L. Guesnet, H. Lupovitch, and A. Polonsky (Liverpool: Liverpool University Press, 2019), 367, 371, 376.

Figure 4.1 Soldiers exiting a segregated "O" tram reserved for German use in downtown Warsaw, 1941.
Narodowe Archiwum Cyfrowe, 3/2/0/-/7941.

segregated Jews from "ethnic" Poles according to Nazi racial definitions, but they did so on territory where Poles and Jews had co-existed for centuries. This meant that Polish-Jewish occupation relations were based on wartime policy *and* pre-war experience. Nazi measures turned genocidal in 1942, but anti-semitism was not new at all.

As Nazi policies vis-à-vis Poles and Polish Jews diverged after 1940, they widened gulfs between Polish and Polish-Jewish elites, undermining solidarity forged during the siege. The Warsaw intelligentsia remarked on "the Jewish Question" but in a manner that indicated they saw Polish-Jewish suffering as outside their concerns. Polish intelligentsia's response to Jewish persecution did not emerge until the ghetto liquidation in 1942, and was most significant during the 1943 ghetto uprisings, when it occurred at all. Growing Polish antisemitism, the trauma of anti-intelligentsia campaigning, and the high level of occupation violence muted and delayed Polish response, part of the "eras[ure of] whole horizons of empathy" that Peter Fritzsche sees as the defining characteristic of civilian life under Nazi tyranny.[4] Polish-Jewish elites thought their Warsaw neighbors had betrayed them, though they knew Poles could not protect them.[5] Polish elite silence appeared to the ghetto as complicity, support for Nazi murder. Still, the Polish intelligentsia responses that did occur are notable, from Jerzy Andrzejewski's guilt-ridden novella *Holy Week* to Zofia Kossak's creation of Żegota, the Council to Aid the Jews. These efforts illuminate the intelligentsia's evolving definitions of Polishness and its wartime power.

4.1 Antisemitic Persecution

When the Wehrmacht invaded Poland the whole country was in danger, but not everyone was in the same danger.[6] This inequity widened under occupation. On September 23, 1939, with Warsaw surrounded, Starzyński appointed Adam Czerniaków (1880–1942) chairman of the city Jewish community.[7] As the GG formed, Himmler's adjutants formed a *Judenrat* (Jewish council) to control Warsaw's Jews, and retained Czerniaków as chairman.[8] Czerniaków was part of the Warsaw intelligentsia, from a family prominent in Jewish charitable organizations. Trained as a chemical engineer at the Warsaw Polytechnic, he spoke Polish, Russian, German, and Yiddish and wrote his diary in Polish. He had served in the Polish senate as a representative from the Minorities' Bloc and was a longstanding member of the Gmina Żydowska or Kehillah, the Warsaw Jewish community. Czerniaków had a strong sense of social consciousness. He and his wife Felicja (née Cwajer), an educator, devoted themselves to causes on behalf of poor Jewish children. The couple's only son, Jan, would die in the Soviet Union and Felicja would survive her husband, hidden by Polish friends. Czerniaków's stolid demeanor, cautious temperament, knowledge of German and Germans, and connections to prominent Poles shaped the Jewish community between 1939 and 1942, even though Nazi policy thwarted his efforts at every turn. His tenure was controversial, with some ghetto inhabitants seeing him as a collaborator, and others fierce defenders of his attempts to protect the community.[9]

---

[4] Fritzsche, *Iron Wind, xiii.*
[5] "One bad apple might cost them their lives." Martin Dean, "Where Did All the Collaborators Go? *Slavic Review* Vol. 64, No. 4 (Winter, 2005), 795.
[6] Madajczyk, *Polityka III Rzeszy*, Tom II, 384–392.
[7] Adam Czerniaków, *Prelude to Doom: The Warsaw Diary of Adam Czerniaków* (New York: Ivan R. Dee, 1999), 76.
[8] Breitman, *Architect of Genocide*, 81; Engelking and Leociak, *Getto warszawskie*, 186–202.
[9] Leociak, *Text*, 73; Zuckerman, *Surplus of Memory*, 59; Jerzy Lewiński, "The Death of Adam Czerniaków and Janusz Korczak's Last Journey" in *Polin Studies in Polish Jewry*

Nazi antisemitic persecution in Warsaw emerged out of anti-intelligentsia campaigning and the developing war. It had not been distilled into policy when the war began, and the GG had no unified plan for the Jewish population, ten times the size of the German one. Warsaw, the second largest Jewish city in the world, had around 375,000 Jewish inhabitants on the eve of war. During the September Campaign, the Jewish community – like the city population generally – swelled beyond the capacity of municipal institutions to manage. Jewish refugees camped out in parks and schools, but settled mainly in Jewish neighborhoods in the northwest, where they joined friends and relatives, uncertain of what was to come.[10] The Gutter family, who were winemakers, and the Wattenberg family of Łódź art dealers relocated to Warsaw by late 1939: Polish-Jewish elites from western Poland, like Polish elites more generally, went to Warsaw.[11] Appointing a Jewish Council and retaining Czerniaków indicated that the Gestapo prioritized streamlining communication with the Yiddish-speaking Jewish community and that they were content to adapt existing institutions. Though Starzyński was arrested and much city government shut-tered, Jewish self-administration continued.[12] The transition to GG control under Hans Frank and Ludwig Fischer was rocky, and the vacuum of power created in the wake of the Polish government evacuation and then Starzyński's arrest fed lawlessness, exacerbated by Gestapo and Wehrmacht rampaging.[13] Frank, a pronounced antisemite, was unconcerned about the "temporary prob-lem" of Polish Jews, squabbling less with the police about radicalizing antisemit-ism than he had about Polish deportations or anti-intelligentsia campaigning.[14]

Circumstances in Warsaw differed from other Polish cities. From the moment the Wehrmacht arrived in October 1939, Warsaw Jews witnessed Nazi persecu-tions visited on the intelligentsia *and* suffered antisemitism from Polish neigh-bors and their new occupiers.[15] Left-leaning Warsaw Jews with means like Aleksander Wat's family opted for life under Soviet communist rather than Nazi German control, moving to eastern Poland or into the Soviet interior.[16]

Vol. 7: Jewish Life in Nazi-Occupied Warsaw, ed. A. Polonsky (Liverpool: Liverpool University Press, 2008), 236, 238.

[10] Jews from outside Warsaw faced a particularly dangerous future in the later ghetto, where they had fewer material resources and local contacts. Andrzej Żbikowski, "Żydowscy przesiedleńcy z dystryktu warszawskiego w getcie warszawskim, 1939–1942" in *Prowincja noc*, 228, 238–249.

[11] Gutter, *Memories in Focus*, 23–26; Mary [Watten]Berg, *The Diary of Mary Berg: Growing up in the Warsaw Ghetto* (New York: OneWorld Oxford, 2007), xx–xxi.

[12] Cooperation was demanded of Polish-Jewish elites. On the councils: Hannah Arendt, *Eichmann in Jerusalem: A Report on the Banality of Evil* (New York: Penguin Books, 2006), 91, 117–118.

[13] Rossino, *Hitler Strikes Poland*, 88–120.

[14] Housden, *Hans Frank*, 127–128.

[15] Madajczyk, *Polityka III Rzeszy*, Tom II, 214.

[16] Wat, *My Century*, 97–99.

Since Łódź was incorporated into the Third Reich, many Łódź Jews fled across the GG border into Warsaw. Nazi planners contemplated an enclosure of the Jewish quarter in Łódź in late 1939, and the first ghetto was created there in spring 1940, trapping 200,000 people inside.[17] Despite this shocking development, Warsaw Jews did not assume that Łódź precedent was relevant to them: Frank's GG was a dumping ground for racial "undesirables" and German policy in territories incorporated into the Reich like Łódź differed from those in Warsaw.[18]

Indications for Jewish life in Warsaw were nevertheless ominous. Nazi anti-semitism was already infamous. The Gestapo persecuted Jews as they consolidated their hold on the intelligentsia, and Varsovians frequently made Jews into scapegoats for the instability Nazi rule provoked. Attacks on persons during Tannenberg and AB were accompanied by attacks on property as Poland was plundered for the German war economy. Those fleeing Warsaw lost property to the occupiers and their own neighbors. Thefts were rampant and the remnants of the Polish legal system unequipped to prosecute them; Polish policemen more often pitched in than put a halt to such problems.[19] Fischer's appointment as district governor did not stabilize matters. In November 1939, shortly after Fischer's installation, a Polish blue policeman was murdered: a known Polish-Jewish criminal shot the policeman in an apartment on Nalewki Street. Case White had only recently concluded, Tannenberg roundups were proceeding, and Poles were officially disarmed, so the shooting sparked a hasty reaction.[20] The Gestapo added fresh Nalewki Street hostages to its Polish prisoner haul and executed fifty three without trial. They also claimed a 300,000-zloty "ransom" from the Jewish community, the first of many.[21] The next day, the occupation regime's paper the *New Warsaw Courier* (NKW) announced that Jews had to display a blue-and-white Star of David on their clothing in public. Despite protests, those who walked the streets of Warsaw were thenceforward distinguished by race: Jews with stars, Poles without, Germans with uniforms.[22]

---

[17] Horwitz, *Ghettostadt*, 62–90.

[18] Czerniaków, *Prelude*, 89.

[19] General disruption and prisoner releases led to thefts; ordinary citizens were also desperate to replace things lost during the bombardment. Piątkowski, "Przestępczość w okupowanej Warszawie" in *Porządek publiczny i bezpieczeństwo*, 281–282; 296–297. Jewish property was targeted. Martin Dean, *Robbing the Jews: The Confiscation of Jewish Property in the Holocaust* (New York: Cambridge University Press, 2010), 177; Czerniaków, *Prelude*, 77; Lehnstaedt, *Occupation*, 133.

[20] Piątkowski, "Przestępczość w okupowanej Warszawie" in *Porządek publiczny i bezpieczeństwo*, 288–294.

[21] Czerniaków, *Prelude*, 93, 90; Bartoszewski, *1859 dni Warszawy*, 70, 76.

[22] Announced in *NKW* on November 23, 1939. Mary [Watten]Berg, *Diary of Mary Berg*, 11; Czerniaków, *Prelude*, 93; Władysław Szpilman, *Pianista: Warszawskie wspomnienia, 1939-1945* (Krakow: Wyd. Znak, 2000); Lehnstaedt, *Occupation*, 45, 64, 133–137; Mazower, *Hitler's Empire*, 92–95.

The November 1939 ordinance was a watershed. Armbands indicated the limitations of Nazi categorization in eastern Europe: the occupiers needed a visible marker to enable race-based persecution, since Germans could not always distinguish Jews from Poles.[23] The armbands – refusal to wear them was punishable by steep community fines – escalated *divide et impera* strategy, drawing non-Jewish Poles into policing Jewishness: it was Poles who implicated Jews without armbands since they recognized markers of Jewishness their occupiers did not.[24] A wave of attacks by predatory Varsovians and Volksdeutsche on armband-wearing Jews followed, escalating into pogroms.[25] Holy Week and Easter of 1940 were especially violent, after allegations that Jewish shopkeepers murdered a Polish boy swirled about and Poles attacked and robbed city Jews.[26] Antisemitic violence served Nazi interests, frightening the Jewish community and keeping them confined to their homes.[27] Urban crime, real and rumored, radicalized Nazi antisemitic policy which, in turn, triggered further crime, escalating street violence and hardening its ethnic dimensions.

4.2   Ghettoization

GG administrators contemplated segregating Warsaw completely in late 1939 through the creation of a Jewish ghetto; separate residential areas had already been secured for the occupying community.[28] For the Germans, the debate

---

[23] Visible markers of ethnic difference continued: Germans would wear an "N" (for *Niemiec*) postwar and be subjected to ghettoization. Naimark, *Fires of Hatred*, 117, 128–30; Grabowski, *Na posterunku*, 93, 256; Carruthers, *Good Occupation*, 123.

[24] Nazi segregation demonstrates what Karen and Barbara Fields call "racecraft." "Passing" was regarded by the occupation "as a particularly insidious form of deceit." Fields and Fields, *Racecraft*, 108, 210.

[25] Czerniaków mentioned pogroms on March 25 and 27, 1940. Czerniaków, *Prelude*, 132; Tec mentions the first in February 1940. Nechama Tec, *When Light Pierced the Darkness: Christian Rescue of Jews in Nazi-Occupied Poland* (New York: Oxford University Press, 1986), 18. For the drawing of neighbors and acquaintances into genocidal violence, sometimes for material gain, see: Gross, *Neighbors*, 48–55, 66–70; Applebaum, *Red Famine*, 233–240. Marek Edelman noted antisemitic violence in Warsaw also before the invasion. Bikont, *Crime and the Silence*, 108. Poland was not the only place that saw pogroms led by local agents alongside and simultaneous with Nazi antisemitism, see: Bemporad, *Legacy of Blood*, 114–125.

[26] Based on an incident at the Mirowski Square market, though the child was unharmed. The script of the accusations followed age-old antisemitic ritual muder tropes. Leociak, *Text*, 241–242; Bemporad, *Legacy of Blood*, 2, 8-9. 91, 96.

[27] Berg, *Diary of Mary Berg*, 15, 17; Czerniaków, *Prelude*, 100–107, 132; Emanuel Ringelblum, *Kronika getta warszawskiego, wrzesień 1939–styczeń 1943* (Warsaw: Czytelnik: 1983), 76.

[28] Carl H. Nightingale recognizes segregation in Nazi-occupied eastern Europe, "the outermost extreme of racist imagination and racial politics," but fails to realize that it was tripartite in Warsaw, separating Jews, Poles, and Germans. Nightingale, *Segregation: A Global History of Divided Cities* (Chicago: The University of Chicago Press, 2012), 339.

turned on whether ghettoization would aid wealth extraction and labor exploitation, how complex it would be to implement, and where a ghetto should be located in or around Warsaw. For its Jewish victims, ghettoization meant dislocation, property loss, and increasing Nazi control over daily life: terrifying prospects. Poles who lived alongside Jews were opposed to the idea, as dividing the city ruptured family and business relationships further, exacerbating siege destruction and German property confiscation.[29]

Czerniaków was the official intermediary between the Jewish community and the GG, attempting to stop and then ameliorate ghettoization. It was initially unclear whether Czerniaków was subordinate to Julian Kulski (Starzyński's deputy), or reported to Ludwig Leist, head of the German city administration.[30] When Heinz Auerswald (1908–70) became ghetto commissioner in spring 1941, he was Czerniaków's main contact, but the Jewish chairman was bandied among German administrators for years.[31] Czerniaków met with Kulski, Leist, Auerswald, and the Gestapo to air Jewish petitions and was threatened and arrested. Along with fellow intelligentsia, he spent a night in Pawiak, sat in the "streetcars" of Szuch Boulevard, and was beaten. The next morning, he was handed his hat and coat and limped, bleeding, home. SS officers declared Czerniaków's numerous offers to resign "inadvisable."[32] He crisscrossed Warsaw looking for clarification, organizing aid, and subduing panic. Clarification was not forthcoming: German plans were in flux and Leist, Fischer, and the Gestapo kept Czerniaków on tenterhooks. German disorganization undermined Judenrat authority, and well-connected Jews circumvented Czerniaków. Czerniaków worked to prevent ghettoization, and then, when it was inevitable, to ensure the ghetto was as open as possible. A strand of Nazi antisemitic propaganda associated Jews with disease – especially typhus – and proposed their segregation to protect "healthy" non-Jewish populations. This disease threat was the final justification for the creation of a closed Jewish residential district, realized in late 1940. It also provided a ready-made excuse to "quarantine" the supposedly ill, allowing the blue police to trap people in their apartments, search their homes, and rob them.[33]

From late 1939 through summer 1940, as Warsaw suffered Tannenberg and AB, ghettoization was debated and Jewish persecution escalated. The use of mikvahs (ritual baths), synagogues, and public gatherings were all restricted.

---

[29] Tim Cole, "Placing the Ghetto" 367–371, 380; Lehnstaedt, *Occupation*, 50, 53; Jörg Friedrich, *The Fire: The Bombing of Germany, 1940–1945* (New York: Columbia University Press, 2006), 386.

[30] Kulski and Czerniaków were Jewish under Nuremberg Laws: Kulski's father's family came from a line of Krakow rabbis. USHMM RG-50.030.0769, AN: 2014.238.1, "Interview with Julian Kulski [Jr.]," 2:15–4:40; 5:25–5:40; Engelking and Leociak, *Getto warszawskie*, 55.

[31] Leociak and Engelking, *Getto warszawskie*, 99.

[32] Czerniaków, *Prelude*, 212–213; 111.

[33] Grabowski, *Na posterunku*, 257.

Fines for not wearing armbands, failing to respectfully acknowledge passing Germans, speaking "foreign" languages (including Yiddish), selling books, changing currency, using trams not designated for Jewish passengers, being out after curfew, or attempting to emigrate, fell hard, and especially hard on the poor, the religious, and those dependent on trade. Warsaw's Jews were terrified. Non-Jewish Poles also felt many of these restrictions, though less harshly: both groups had curfews, but the Polish "police hour" was later.[34] Holocaust historian Barbara Engelking tallies this different accumulation of persecutions and the primary result of it, a ruptured community and a "problem of rivalry in martyrology between the victims."[35]

On October 12, 1940 the Judenrat was informed that a closed ghetto would be created in northwest Warsaw. Poles, Jews, and Germans bargained for and against the inclusion of particular streets and boundaries moved back and forth for weeks. October 1940 was a chaos of real estate transactions. Non-Jewish Poles were usually the profiteers of panicked speculation, and far fewer of them had to move – 70,000 versus 150,000 Polish Jews.[36] Wealthier Polish Jewish families were best able to secure lodgings, usually in the "little" or intelligentsia ghetto to the south, separated from the main ghetto by Chłodna Street and the triangular wedge of the Mirowska Square market. This was the nicest ghetto real estate, with wider streets and larger apartments. Still, population density in the ghetto was astronomically higher than in "Aryan" designated streets for Poles and Germans outside. All Warsaw Jews were required to be in residence inside the designated area by November 12, 1940, and on November 15, 1940 the space was gated and a police guard installed. Polish underground press noted "great chaos" and "the bestial treatment of Jews by the German police" in the process.[37] The whole affair put enormous strain on Czerniaków and his unpaid administration.[38] Watching the trajectory of Nazi policy, there were those Jews – especially the assimilated, well-connected, and wealthy – who decided to take their chances on the "other side" of the wall, hiding amongst Varsovians or attempting to emigrate.[39]

Once enclosed, the Warsaw Ghetto was the largest Jewish community under Nazi control.[40] The ghetto gates – twenty-three, dwindling to four as

---

[34] This occasionally went the other way: in spring 1940 Poles wore Jewish armbands to avoid labor deportation. Czerniaków, *Prelude*, 147; PISM London: MID: Dział Polski, A. 10. 4/4, „Germany's Death Space:" Str. 181; Str. 184–185.

[35] Engelking, *Holocaust and Memory*, 71–72.

[36] BN Mf. 4581X, *BI*, 25 października 1940 r., 6.

[37] BN Mf. 4581X, *BI*, 21 listopada 1940 r., 6; Finder and Prusin, *Justice*, 64–65.

[38] Berg, *Diary*, 27.

[39] Poles hid Jews and resisters in higher numbers than other occupied peoples, despite draconian punishments. Prusin, *Serbia under the Swastika*, 136–138; Bryant, *Prague in Black*, 186–189.

[40] Engelking and Leociak, *Getto warszawskie*, 69–70.

its footprint shrank – and the German, Polish, and Jewish "yellow" police-men (*Ordnungsdienst*), named for the gold braid on their caps, guarding them maintained an ever-present threat of violence.[41] The "seal" on the ghetto, however, was imperfect and "Polish Warsaw" never unaware of happenings within: a tram line ran through the original ghetto territory, and numerous buildings had exits into the ghetto – and onto the other side. Smuggling was omnipresent. In Nazi eyes, the ghetto was a source of conta-gion and money. Despite the poverty of many Warsaw Jews, the arrival of penniless refugees, and the expense of forced relocation, Nazis remained confident that Jewish wealth could be obtained with the "right" methods.[42] This assumption led to eighteen months of attempts to extract money, labor, and goods from the ghetto with hideous consequences for its inhabitants. Fischer used Czerniaków to levy taxes for the supposed expense of ghetto administration. The ghetto population was confined to an area that had previously held half as many, and there were sanitation problems, food shortages, and disease.[43] The Nazi-controlled Transfer Office (*Transferstelle*) regulated trade between the ghetto and Warsaw, limiting prices Jews obtained for the sale of possessions and wares, and what they could buy, including food.[44] Overcrowding and the lack of green space prevented growing kitchen gardens, as Poles outside did.[45] Because the "legal" Transfer Office was exploitative, most food consumed in the ghetto was brought in illegally and trade across ghetto walls involved Poles in Jewish daily life, despite draconian punishments.[46]

These conditions spelled catastrophe by winter 1940–41. Because of sanita-tion problems and bans on importing medicines, typhus reached epidemic proportions and the starving and dying littered the crowded streets, the corpses of those who had succumbed covered with newspaper until they were carted off.[47] Czerniaków's charity collections earned him enemies

---

[41] Czerniaków *Prelude*, 250; Gunnar S. Paulsson, *Secret City: The Hidden Jews of Warsaw, 1940-1945* (New Haven: Yale University Press, 2002), xv.

[42] In *Mein Kampf* Hitler ominously articulated the role of the Jewish community in German history as financially predatory – "to squeeze, yes, to grind, more and more money out of the[ir] plundered subjects" – a justification in advance for ruthlessly extracting funds from Jewish communities. Adolf Hitler, *Mein Kampf*, translated by Ralph Manheim (Boston: Houghton Mifflin Company, 1971), 311.

[43] The *Judenrat* thought there were 359,827 before enclosure. Breitman, *Architect of Genocide*, 81.

[44] Zuckerman, *Surplus of Memory*, 129; Madajczyk, *Polityka III Rzeszy*, Tom II, 225–231.

[45] Poles grew vegetables, imported food from the countryside, and raised rabbits for meat. Aleksandra Zaprutko-Janicka, *Okupacja od Kuchni: Kobieca sztuka przetrwania* (Krakow: Ciekawostki Historyczne, 2015), 51–74; 125–129.

[46] PISM London: MID: Dział Polski, A.10.4/1, „Warszawa pod koniec 1939 r.," [1]-2; Kassow, *Who Will Write*, 93; Grabowski, *Na posterunku*, 361.

[47] Kassow, *Who Will Write*, 135, 139; Cole, "Placing the Ghetto," 370.

among the rich, but the situation for the poor was increasingly precarious, with climbing death tolls in 1941.[48]

Misery inside the ghetto reinvigorated old animosities and revealed the enormous diversity of Warsaw Jewry, ghettoized according to Nazi definitions of Jewishness. Emanuel Ringelblum, the Polish-Jewish historian who had participated in the 1939 defense, organized various initiatives, including a community archive, *Oneg Shabbat*. A Polish-Jewish intelligentsia project, the archive painstakingly collected periodicals, diaries, surveys, scientific publications, folklore, and children's drawings from the ghetto – and solicited studies, research, and reports – in Polish, Yiddish, and Hebrew using the services of underemployed intelligentsia.[49] Ringelblum was overworked and exhausted and wrote angrily about dealing with a diverse population under terrible strain: "Religious Jews and rabbis," he complained, "don't make the slightest preparation for suffering, and they do so in the name of faith.[50]" Differing community leaders' priorities placed them in competition with one another. Polish elites outside the wall, too, competed with one another in their opposition initiatives and desire to direct community behavior, but not with the threats or material limitations their Jewish peers faced. Jewish converts to Christianity were another source of tension, as they had identified with Catholic Poles rather than Polish Jews before the war. They were marginalized in the ghetto, outsiders for reason of their conversion but required by the Nazis to live as Jews.[51] After a year of attempting to balance ghetto finances and keep the poor alive, Czerniaków applied "severe sanctions against the rich" in 1942.[52] "The rich" was by then a comparative designation: Warsaw's Jews had begun to starve.

Ghettoization produced enormous suffering but preceded any specific plans to murder Warsaw Jewry.[53] The physical segregation served the double purpose of undermining Polish-Jewish solidarity and extracting wealth and labor from Jewish communities.[54] This exploitation nevertheless "contributed to the gathering genocide."[55] Nazi persecution became a self-fulfilling prophecy: when

---

[48] ROM and SKSS also supported the Polish-Jewish community up to ghetto enclosure, but much less effectively thereafter. PAN III-59-97 Materiały Artura Śliwińskiego: "Sprawozdania i memoriały Rady Głównej Opiekuńczej," "Sprawozdanie," 1–30 Nov. 1940, 9.

[49] Much – but not all – was recovered, making reconstruction of the cultural-intellectual life of the ghetto possible. Kassow, *Who Will Write*, 169, 209–224, 374.

[50] Leociak and Engelking, *Getto warszawskie*, 683–694; Ringelblum, *Kronika*, 206.

[51] They numbered around 5,000 and attended All Saints' Church. Berg, *Diary*, 111–113; Dembowski, *Christians in the Warsaw Ghetto: An Epitaph for the Unremembered* (South Bend: University of Notre Dame Press, 2005); Leociak, *Text*, 217.

[52] Czerniaków, *Prelude*, 320–321.

[53] Ghettoization was about "control," not yet murder. Browning, *Origins*, 111. Smith, *Germany*, 363–364.

[54] "Mieczysław Maślanko" in *Chronicles of Terror*, 159.

[55] Dean, *Robbing the Jews*, 175.

Germans made exorbitant demands the ghetto inhabitants, fearing further torment, impoverished themselves to fulfill them, "proving" to their tormentors that they were concealing "secret" wealth.[56]

A handful of Jewish families became the patrons of numerous ghetto projects, from Ringelblum's archive to a school system.[57] Even they succumbed to intensifying persecution. Miriam Wattenberg, born in 1924 (Figure 4.2), the daughter of an affluent family from Łódź, lived in the ghetto until liquidation. She was a privileged teenager, protected by her father's business connections as an art dealer and her mother's status as an American citizen – which ultimately saved the family. The Wattenbergs lived on "aristocratic" Chłodna Street, and Mary kept a diary. Though affected by increasing privation, Mary dated, took architecture classes, and socialized with the children of the ghetto elite. Compared to the life her parents had expected for her, the ghetto was misery. Her generation of Polish-speaking, patriotically Polish elite urban Jews perished in 1942. Her boyfriend, Romek, ended their last New Year's Eve together with a solemn performance of Friedrich Chopin's Funeral March (Piano Sonata No. 2).[58] Her friends died the next year. Mary did not. In the end, it was American passports and not wealth or social connections that saved the Wattenbergs: even privileged Jewish families were unable to escape Nazi persecution in Warsaw.

Hunger and disease stalked the ghetto elite by late 1941. Czerniaków, fastidiously well-dressed, found a louse on his nightshirt – the harbinger of typhus. In December the disease was "raging." "Friends and acquaintances," he wrote, "are dying all around me – all of them members of the intelligentsia." By February 1942 hunger encroached everywhere: Czerniaków mourned his wife's lapdog, Kikuś. "The little fellow has disappeared," he mourned – onto his neighbors' dinnerplates.[59]

4.3 Holocaust Murder

As Nazi antisemitic persecution proceeded in Warsaw and ghetto circumstances deteriorated, Polish sympathy on the "Aryan" side of the walls wavered and in some cases disappeared entirely.[60] Occupied Poland, as reports from

---

[56] What Timothy Snyder calls the "magic of racial thinking" (Timothy Snyder, *Bloodlands: Europe between Hitler and Stalin* (New York: Basic Books, 2010), 216) and Barbara Engelking calls a "retrospective alibi" (Engelking, *Holocaust and Memory: The Experience of the Holocaust and Its Consequences: An Investigation Based on Personal Narratives* (London: Leicester University Press, 2001), 83).

[57] Leociak and Engelking, *Getto Warszawskie*, 557–623; Hannah Schmidt-Holländer's "Ghetto Schools: Jewish Education in Nazi-Occupied Poland" PhD diss., Universität Hamburg, 2017: http://ediss.sub.uni-hamburg.de/volltexte/2017/8531/.

[58] Berg, *Diary*, 119–121.

[59] Czerniaków, *Prelude*, 257, 305, 325; Kassow, *Who Will Write*, 92.

[60] Contrasting with occupations where native antisemitism had less influence, such as Serbia and Greece, and comparing to those where it had plenty, like Prague. Prusin, *Serbia under*

Figure 4.2 Polish-Jewish diarist Miriam Wattenberg (Mary Berg) walks down a street in the Warsaw Ghetto alongside boyfriend Romek Kowalski, March 1942.
United States Holocaust Memorial Museum, Photograph Number 75311

1939 through 1941 put it, had a "Jewish problem."[61] Despite siege solidarity, some Polish intelligentsia accused Polish Jews of "panic" during the September

---

the Swastika, 126–128; Mazower, *Inside Hitler's Greece*, 257–261; Bryant, *Prague in Black*, 224; generally: Connelly, *From Peoples into Nations*, 467–470.

[61] PISM London: MID: Dział Polski, A.10.4/2(I), "Problem żydowski w Polsce okupowanej," 14. Arguably, so did the Second Polish Republic. For evolving antisemitism, see: Ireneusz Krzemiński, "Polish National Antisemitism" *Polin Studies in Polish Jewry, Vol. 31: Poland and Hungary: Jewish Realities Compared*, ed. F. L. Guesnet, H. Lupovitch, Howard, and A. Polonsky (Liverpool: Liverpool University Press, 2019), 515–542.

Campaign, and remembered their flight eastward toward the "Bolshevik armies" with lingering bitterness.[62] Nazi appropriation of Jewish property and the shuttering of Jewish-owned businesses threw city life into chaos.[63] Fischer's administration pandered to Polish antisemites, announcing ghetto-ization as the "heartfelt wish" of Varsovians, claiming "the Jews of Warsaw have always been a heavy burden on the city, especially where moral and hygienic questions were concerned."[64] The pandering was, at least in some cases, successful, forming a "narrow bridge" on which Nazi administrators and antisemitic Polish elites met.[65] Endecja leaders, in particular, praised ghetto-ization, embarrassing the London exiles, who were repeatedly accused of antisemitism – or at least of including antisemites in their deliberations, which they did – by the European Jewish press.[66] Ringelblum and his peers thought their Polish neighbors had little sympathy for their plight: "It is said of Poles, who look quite content riding along in the trams, that their dream of a Warsaw without Jews is coming true."[67] It was in this unfriendly climate that Nazi antisemitism in Warsaw took a genocidal turn.

In 1941 and 1942, the Holocaust began: Nazi Germany started to kill Jews within its imperial control en masse. Warsaw Jews were not, however, the first Holocaust victims. The larger war drove events: the opening of the Eastern Front in 1941 raised anew the possibility of deporting Polish Jews from the GG, abandoned in 1939.[68] The Holocaust would not arrive in Warsaw until 1942, but events in 1941 set the stage for the murder of Warsaw Jewry.

East of Warsaw, Jewish communities were scattered across towns and cities. Again using the cover of a military campaign to conduct genocide, Heydrich's Einsatzgruppen were re-deployed during Operation Barbarossa in another secret killing campaign, this time targeting Soviet Jews rather than Polish intelligentsia, employing the same murderous methods on a wider scale.[69]

---

[62] Józef Milej, engineer and Warsaw Polytechnic graduate, reported on his social circle. PISM London: MID: Dział Polski, A.10.4/4, "Wyciąg ze sprawozdania inż. Józefa Mileja: Nastroje wśród ludności," [before 20.II.1940], [1].

[63] PISM London: MID: Dział Polski, A.10.4/1, "Warszawa pod koniec 1939 r.," [1].

[64] PISM London: MID: Dział Polski, A.10.4/4, "Germany's Death Space: Str. 176," 4.

[65] Quoting Karski. David Engel, "An Early Account of Polish Jewry under Nazi and Soviet Occupation Presented to the Polish Government-in-Exile," February 1940, *Jewish Social Studies*, Vol. 45 no. 1, 1983: 12–13. *Cf.* Fields and Fields, *Racecraft*, 136.

[66] There were accusations that "the legal representations of the Polish Nation and State have been drawn or are being drawn into an anti-Semitic attitude [by antisemites' actions in Poland] . . . no member of the [exile] Government . . . has ever expressed either in word or in print anything of an anti-Semitic character or tone" (PISM London: MID: Dział Polski, A.10.4/4, „Opening Remarks," 4). Such accusations were frequent during and after the war. Finder and Prusin, *Justice*, 55.

[67] Ringelblum, *Kronika*, 206.

[68] Kershaw, *Hitler*, 669; Connelly, *From Peoples into Nations*, 466.

[69] Mallmann, "Aufgeräumt und abgebrannt," in *Gestapo im Zweiten Weltkrieg*, 503–520.

This redeployment, though it did not touch Warsaw, indicated that genocidal plans against the Polish intelligentsia had escalated as eastern European Jews became targets: Wardzyńska estimated 100,000 victims for the anti-intelligentsia campaigns, but during Barbarossa Einsatzgruppen killed much, much faster. Einsatzgruppe A in Belorussia killed 190,000 Jews before the end of 1941; Einsatzgruppe D reported 55,000 victims; police and soldiers in Ukraine claimed 100,000 victims by mid-October 1941, including 33,000 Kiev Jews murdered at Babi Yar; Einsatzgruppe B expanded its initial orders to include Jewish women and children among its victims.[70] Wehrmacht soldiers abandoned their 1939 squeamishness and helped enthusiastically, killing Jewish civilians while prosecuting a military campaign.[71] Though numbers must be approximate, historians agree that Einsatzgruppen, Order Police, Waffen-SS personnel, and soldiers killed around 500,000 eastern European Jews by late 1941 and over a million before their second campaign concluded. Perhaps as many as two million victims, including other Soviet civilians, would die at the hands of Nazi police in eastern Europe and the Soviet Union.[72]

Operation Barbarossa captured the western Soviet Union but did not defeat the Red Army in 1941.[73] This military setback shifted antisemitic policy decisively, since the failure to secure victory meant an ongoing military campaign during which all Polish and some Soviet Jews were under German control (western Polish Jews had been since 1939). In other words, the state of war that Himmler and Heydrich had intermittently used as cover to conduct smaller genocides would now be ongoing. Nazi Party elites and GG personnel began 1942 outside of Berlin at the Wannsee Conference listening to SS plans for a "Final Solution of the Jewish Question" made possible – to them necessary – by the expanding war.[74] Josef Bühler, GG Secretary of State, represented Warsaw and Krakow. At Wannsee, Heydrich unveiled a plan to systematically murder ghettoized Polish Jews in new facilities – the Operation Reinhard death camps – along GG rail lines. Camps were under construction in Chełmno, Bełżec, Sobibór, Treblinka, and at Birkenau, expanding Auschwitz.[75] Treblinka would "serve" the Warsaw and Białystok ghettoes.

In Warsaw, Einsatzgruppen killings and the Operation Reinhard facilities were secret from Polish and Polish-Jewish elites. Rumors nevertheless unsettled the ghetto in early 1942. The arrival of Jewish survivors from further east

---

[70] Browning, *Origins*, 287–292; Rees, *Holocaust*, 208.

[71] Krausnick, *Hitlers Einsatzgruppen*, 179–183.

[72] Rees, *Holocaust*, 206; Longerich, *Hitler*, 759–760; Kershaw, *Hitler*, 675.

[73] David Stahel, *Battle for Moscow* (New York: Cambridge University Press, 2015), 24–51.

[74] Browning, *Origins*, 410–415.

[75] Op. Reinhard was named for Heydrich, assassinated in June 1942. Paul and Mallmann, *Gestapo im Zweiten Weltkrieg*, 416–421; Yitzhak Arad, *Belzec, Sobibor, Treblinka: The Operation Reinhard Death Camps* (Bloomington: Indiana University Press, 1987).

with horrifying stories about mass murders escalated fears.[76] Poles followed these measures closely. The April 30, 1942 *Bulletin* featured a story on the ghetto. Jewish affairs were usually covered in local news, but in April 1942 they were on the front-page: "Warsaw Ghetto. Poverty, hunger, cold, and horrible hygienic circumstances have created a nightmarish situation." Poles read death statistics for ghetto poorhouses, where losses reached half the inhabitants. Climbing ghetto death tolls across 1941 trumped losses in "Aryan" Warsaw:

January	898
February	1023
March	1608
April	2601
May	3821
June	4290
July	5550
August	5560
September	4545
October	4614
November	4801
December	4966
Total:	44,277

Despite fatalities approaching 10% of the ghetto population, the article noted that "Germans are deliberately trying to *worsen* the already horrible existing circumstances," and were reducing the ghetto's size.[77]

In May and June 1942, Varsovians outside the ghetto were rounded up and sent to do heavy labor at Straflager Treblinka (Treblinka I).[78] Polish diarists mentioned arrests but did not understand their purpose, which was to utilize Polish labor to facilitate the murder of Polish Jews. Strange rumors circulated of mass resettlements; Polish Jews lived with their bags packed.[79] Word reached Warsaw about the deportation of the Krakow ghetto, everyone loaded onto cattle cars and sent to an unknown destination in May and June 1942.[80] News of "liquidations"

---

[76] Zuckerman, *Surplus of Memory*, 172–173.
[77] BN Mf. 45817, *BI*, 30 kwietnia 1942 r., Rok IV, Nr. 17 (121), "Żydzi," [1]-2.
[78] Bartoszewski mentions roundups, with hundreds held at the Skaryszewska street camp. Bartoszewski, *1859 dni Warszawy*, 275, 286.
[79] Wyszyński, *Dzienniki*, 111.
[80] Kubalski, *Niemcy w Krakowie*, 209, 215; Jan Grabowski, *Hunt for the Jews: Betrayal and Murder in German-Occupied Poland* (Bloomington: Indiana University Press, 2013), 31.

in Krakow and Lublin, coupled with executions in the ghetto and Pawiak, led to panic.[81]

On July 21, 1942, killing started in the Warsaw Ghetto with a reprise of the Tannenberg and AB logic: Jewish yellow police launched an anti-intelligentsia *Aktion* targeting the Judenrat and other notables. Sixty men were dragged from their beds to Pawiak prison to serve as hostages for the good behavior of the masses, just as "Aryan" Warsaw suffered in October 1939 when the Wehrmacht arrived.[82] On July 22, 1942, the Jewish day of mourning for the Destruction of the Temple, Tisha B'Av, Czerniaków learned the ghetto would be resettled "in the east" and he was to organize transports: 6,000 people that afternoon; 9,000 the next day. The transports were in fact destined for Treblinka's gas chambers. That this was not like "other" Nazi camps, which were merely horrible, became clear shortly, as Polish villagers around Małkinia glimpsed heaps of putrifying corpses and the continuous smoke of crematoria: Treblinka meant murder, not imprisonment.[83] Czerniaków, who had accommodated Nazi antisemitic policy for years in the hopes of protecting his community, poisoned himself rather than organize the deportations.[84] Despite his suicide, all the quotas were fulfilled.[85]

Between July 22 and August 18, 1942, the Gestapo ordered half a million people to assemble with their luggage at the *Umschlagsplatz* (collection point) on Stawki Street in the north corner of the ghetto.[86] Ola Watowa's parents went to the Umschlagsplatz in September 1942 – she did not know the date – to die at Treblinka.[87] In a final flourish on Yom Kippur, the last day of the deportations, "the Germans collected hundreds of Jewish policemen, on the pretext that they were supposed to receive medals, and took them and their families to Treblinka."[88] Jewish community leaders who facilitated the process fell victim to it.[89] Warsaw's Jews were crammed into cattle cars at the railyard abutting the Umschlagsplatz and taken to the village of Małkinia and then to Treblinka, where 265,000 were gassed to death within hours of arrival. In the hideous confusion, with families separated, Czerniaków dead, and community leaders assisting or held hostage, there was no organized Jewish resistance.

---

[81] Wyszyński writes that "a sense of unease connected to the rumors ... predominated" and Bartoszewski notes murders on May 29–30 and June 8–9. Wyszyński, *Dzienniki*, 111; Bartoszewski, *1859 dni Warszawy*, 282; 285.

[82] Berg, *Diary*, 163; Czerniaków *Prelude*, 383.

[83] Smith, *Germany*, 400; Arad, *Belzec, Sobibor, Treblinka*, 81–99, esp. 92–94.

[84] Czerniaków, *Prelude*, 385.

[85] Zuckerman, *Surplus of Memory*, 194.

[86] Madajczyk, *Polityka III Rzeszy*, Tom II, 344, 346.

[87] Watowa, *Wszystko co najważniejsze*, 14.

[88] Zuckerman, *Surplus of Memory*, 245; 190–192.

[89] Kassow, *Who Will Write*, 172.

Władysław Szpilman, one of Poland's finest pianists and a frequent radio performer, was separated from his family on the Umschlagsplatz and spared, retained with other young people for forced labor.[90] Somewhere between 50,000 and 80,000 Jews like Szpilman remained alive, mostly working at German-owned "shops" or tasked with clearing the homes of the dead.[91] From this remnant opposition emerged, overtaking Polish insurgents outside the ghetto in their plans for armed uprising. Yitzhak Zuckerman ("Antek," 1915–81), in particular, a firebrand activist from the *kresy* who dodged the Treblinka roundups, considered what options Warsaw Jews still had. Zuckerman, born in Vilnius during the First World War, had embraced Zionism young. From Soviet-occupied Vilnius, he made his way westward from Soviet territory to Warsaw in 1940 to intrigue: Warsaw was the center of both Polish and Polish-Jewish resistance.[92] Together with his girlfriend (later wife) Zivia Lubetkin (1914–76), Mordechai Anielewicz (1919–43), and others, Zuckerman built a military conspiracy in the ghetto connected to parts of the Warsaw underground. These young Polish-Jewish leaders were in every way unusual: in their politics, in their willingness to use violence, in their manifold connections to other Jewish activists and to Polish conspiracies. Nevertheless, like other intelligentsia efforts, their actions had disproportionate consequence for their communities. Unlike most of those who joined him in that venture, Zuckerman survived the war to tell the story.

4.4   Polish (In)action in 1942

Varsovians were aware of the Grossaktion: the scale of the deportations and the rush of Jewish escapees affected "Aryan" Warsaw. Jewish "inaction" nevertheless fed antisemitic Polish stereotypes that would only be dislodged by the outbreak of ghetto resistance in 1943.[93] Inside the ghetto, the Grossaktion meant life and death; outside, it made less of an impression. Though in retrospect the murder of the largest ghetto in Europe looms ever larger in importance, at the time, intermingled with terror and conspiracy on "their" side, few Poles comprehended its distinct genocidal nature.

---

[90] Szpilman had played piano in the ghetto's cafes and escaped to friends in "Aryan" Warsaw in February 1943. Władysław Szpilman, *The Pianist: The Extraordinary Story of One Man's Survival in Warsaw, 1939–45* (London: Victor Gollancz, 1999), 131, 134–135; Bikont, *Sendlerowa w ukryciu*, 14.

[91] The "shops period." Zuckerman claims 70,00–80,000 left on "both sides of the wall" after the *Grossaktion*. Zuckerman, *Surplus of Memory*, 263; Gutman, *Resistance*, 145, 197.

[92] Left-wing Polish Jews who had fled east in 1939 and returned launched ghetto resistance. Krakowski, *War of the Doomed*, 161; Engelking and Leociak, *Getto warszawskie*, 696–698.

[93] Despite the fact that most Warsaw conspiracies were uninterested in insurgency – but interested in assassination – then.

Varsovian intelligentsia who had already taken up organized opposition better appreciated what was happening in the ghetto. Underground press monitored German movements, focusing on how antisemitic persecution affected Poles: that summer the *Bulletin* bristled about street arrests and the pressganging of Polish labor. On July 23, 1942, the first issue published after the *Grossaktion*, the front page was devoted to an essay on Polish political unity.[94] Deportations were mentioned in the next issue under local news: "the beginning of ghetto liquidation." The paper called the deportations a "pogrom" "carried out with the whole of Prussian bestiality," and noted 6,000 people were being relocated "to the east" daily, with rumors their destination lay "in the region around Małkinia." (This was correct, and indicated Warsaw conspirators had contacts in the ghetto and outside the city.) Though the article mentioned Czerniaków's suicide, the brutality of German, Ukrainian, and Lithuanian police at the Umschlagsplatz, and many deaths, the issue of mass murder was not raised: the last sentence claimed only that "in the course of the murder of the Jews, a few Poles working there were also killed."[95] "In the course of the murder of the Jews" was ambiguous and the Polish reader would not necessarily have taken it to mean that the deportations were murderous. In 1942, after the Einsatzgruppen had killed many of the Jews of Ukraine, Belarus, and Russia, and as the SS were killing Poland's Jews, Warsaw's elite slowly began to understand that their Jewish neighbors were the victims of a distinct genocide.

Confusion and uncertainty had haunted Warsaw from 1939 and the intelligentsia struggled to comprehend the Grossaktion in 1942. Zuckerman, no friend of "Aryan" Warsaw, noted that, "If the Jews didn't understand the meaning of their transport to Treblinka, you can't blame the Poles of that time who didn't do anything." Certain of Polish hostility, he thought Polish inaction in 1942 was more about ignorance. He failed to understand the genocidal turn immediately: the development of the Holocaust was enormously confusing for both Jewish victims and observers. Zuckerman was sure, however, that Poles did not come to their neighbors' aid in 1942.[96]

For Zuckerman and his colleagues, the realization that "annihilation [was] beginning" came from the east. News trickled into the Warsaw Ghetto in early 1942 about Einsatzgruppen killings. The testimony of a "gravedigger" – a Baltic Jewish man forced to bury gassing victims outside Chełmno – supplied detail.

---

[94] Likely written beforehand. On roundups: BN Mf. 45817, *BI*, 25 czerwca 1942 r., Rok IV, Nr. 25 (129), "Chłopi," [1]; on political unity: BN Mf. 45817, *BI*, 23 lipca 1942 r., Rok IV, Nr. 29 (133), "W Poszukiwaniu Siły," [1].

[95] Polish blue policemen were unmentioned. BN Mf. 45817, *BI*, 30 lipca 1942 r., Rok IV, Nr. 30 (134), "Warszawa: Początek Likwidacji Ghetta," 6–7; Grabowski, *Na posterunku*, 110–112, 269–277.

[96] Zuckerman, *Surplus of Memory*, 260; 186; Kassow, *Who Will Write*, 133; Lewiński, "Death of Adam Czerniaków," 225.

The man made it to Warsaw and told his story, but was largely dismissed. His tale was corroborated by reports of vanished shtetls in the old Polish border-lands. Some ghetto youth took the reports as indication of a sea change in Nazi policy and demanded action. Zuckerman remembered the counter-argument of an older Bundist colleague who pointed out that "Jews weren't the only ones being killed, so were Poles," and that a wait-and-see attitude was preferable to dangerous armed resistance.[97] The comparison would turn out to be hollow, but the generational divide separating insurgents from their kin was durable.

Polish elites also largely failed to appreciate what was happening. This was true despite the fact that they generally had better access to information than ghetto inhabitants. Details of liquidations and rumors of early death camps appeared in the *Bulletin* in summer 1942, with hints beforehand.[98] Most Warsaw intelligentsia response to the Nazi genocide of the Jews nevertheless came very late: spring 1943 was the main moment of Varsovian confrontation with the Holocaust. Those who appreciated the genocidal nature of what was happening before 1943 were unusual. The most important was a woman vital to the Warsaw underground, Zofia Kossak ("Weronika," 1889–1968). A prewar novelist, Kossak was from a renowned family of artists and intellectuals, and her many novels (including a biography of Saint Francis of Assisi) ended up on the Nazi index of banned books, cementing her sterling reputation as a Catholic patriot.[99] Kossak, unusual among her peers, and unusual among antisemites, took a stand. Distributed in fall 1942, Kossak's Front for the Rebirth of Poland (FOP) published a leaflet signed with the organization's crest.[100] It protested Polish inactivity during ghetto liquidation, and it called Warsaw Catholics to account for neglecting their Jewish neighbors:

> In the Warsaw Ghetto, behind walls that divide them from the rest of the world, several thousand condemned people await death. For them, there is no hope of rescue, nobody to help them … The total number of those killed has already passed one million, and that number grows daily … The slaughter of millions of defenseless people is met with a universal, ominous silence … Poles also remain silent. Those Polish politicians who are friendly to Jews restrict themselves to mere diary notations. Those Poles who are antagonistic to Jews declare that they are disinterested and that

---

[97] Zuckerman, *Surplus of Memory*, 172–173; 155–158; Arad, *Belzec, Sobibor, Treblinka*, 24–25.

[98] Discussions of murdered Poles were frequent. In the June 3, 1942 issue there was mention of Jewish deaths at Bełżec. BN Mf. 45817, *BI*, 3 czerwca 1942 r., Rok IV, Nr. 22 (126), "Kraj: Obóz w Bełżcu," 6.

[99] Her uncle was painter Wojciech Kossak (1856–1942). She grew up in her parents' literary soiree. She had two children from her first marriage, and two from her second. Her daughter, Anna Szatkowska (1928–2015), published memoirs. Szatkowska, *Był dom … Wspomnienia* (Krakow: Wydawnictwo Literackie, 2013), 61; Szarota, *Okupowanej Warszawy*, 365.

[100] Bartoszewski, *1859 dni Warszawy*, 137.

the matter does not concern them ... We, Polish Catholics, are speaking up. Our feelings about the Jews have not changed. We will continue to consider them as political, economic, and ideological enemies of Poland ... Whoever does not understand this and ties the proud, independent Polish future to a despicable joy at the misfortune of his [Jewish] neighbor – is therefore neither a Catholic nor a Pole.[101]

Kossak's use of "we" was crucial: she was writing as an *inteligent*, a leader of the Polish national community, and chastising her countrymen for their passivity and bad behavior; she was demanding change.[102] Alongside better known German Protestant clergymen Martin Niemöller and Dietrich Bonhoeffer, Kossak asked Warsaw Catholics to protest Jewish mistreatment.[103] Kossak's leaflet had a print run of 5,000, but like all illegal publications the practice was to read it and pass it along. Czesław Miłosz read it, and composed poetry about the ghetto, accusing himself and his fellow Poles – "the helpers of death: the uncircumcised" – of ignoring Jewish persecution.[104]

Watching the deportations, Kossak and her FOP colleagues built an organization to aid Jews in hiding.[105] The Council to Aid the Jews (Rada Pomocy Żydom) that emerged took the codename "Konrad Żegota," and formalized quickly. Drawing in Catholic contacts and intelligentsia across the political spectrum, Żegota leadership included Kossak's circle and socialists, communists, and Bund members: the only cooperative Polish-Jewish wartime opposition effort. Wanda Krahelska-Filipowicz (1886–1968), a fellow Catholic and the wife of a diplomat – but a committed socialist – joined Kossak in building the project. Adolf Berman (1906–78), a Varsovian from a prominent family of left-wing Polish-Jewish intellectuals and Emanuel Ringelblum's colleague organizing public welfare projects in the ghetto, became its general secretary.[106] There was little on which Berman and Kossak agreed, but Żegota was their common endeavor. From its formation in late 1942 until the outbreak of the 1944 citywide

---

[101] Polin: Museum of the History of Polish Jews: "Polish Righteous:" "Protest! – 75 Years Ago Zofia Kossak Condemned the Holocaust" by Mateusz Szczepaniak, trans. Andrew Rajcher, August 11, 2017 [accessed March 14, 2018]." Władysław Bartoszewski, *O Żegocie: relacja poufna sprzed pół wieku* (Warsaw: Literatura Faktu PWN, 2013), 63.

[102] Jacek Leociak considers that "speaking in the first-person plural is a demonstration of a community of fate:" the "we" matters. Leociak, *Text*, 127.

[103] Like Kossak, Niemöller was antisemitic. Eberhard Bethge, *Dietrich Bonhoeffer: Theologian, Christian, Man for His Times: A Biography* (Minneapolis: Fortress Press, 2000); Michael Heymel, *Martin Niemöller: vom Marineoffizier zum Friedenskämpfer* (Darmstadt: Lambert Schneider Verlag, 2017), 184–192.

[104] Czesław Miłosz's 1943 poem "A Poor Christian Looks at the Ghetto," was published by Żegota. Miłosz, *Selected Poems* (New York: Seabury Press, 1973); Franaszek, *Miłosz*, 216–217.

[105] What Catholics call a "corporal work of mercy." Grabowski, *Na posterunku*, 187.

[106] Shore, *Caviar and Ashes*, 226–227, 360–361; Grabowski, *Na posterunku*, 303–307; Bikont, *Sendlerowa w ukryciu*, 135.

uprising, Żegota smuggled food, medicine, identity papers, and information to Jews hiding across Warsaw. It drew funds from multiple sources, including the London Poles, and was most effective at saving Jewish children, who were easiest to disguise as "Polish" – in other words, to have their Jewishness hidden in a non-Jewish context. Kossak recruited the woman who ran the children's aid program, Irena Krzyżanowska-Sendler ("Jolanta," 1910–2008).[107] Sendler, a Catholic social worker from a family prominent in Polish socialist circles, continued her prewar work with the poor and marginalized, while her husband moldered in a POW camp. Sendler was one of many intelligentsia figures who thus "cultivated a conspiracy within a conspiracy," as her biographer Anna Bikont put it. She snuck around 2,500 Jewish children out of the ghetto and hid them in families, orphanages, and convents using the Żegota network.[108] There is some debate about how many Żegota saved, but the number exceeded 3,500 people.[109] Kossak launched a dizzying variety of dangerous and overlapping efforts, delegating tasks to confidantes – even those across prewar political lines. Despite her enduring antisemitism, Kossak's protest helped launch the largest Jewish aid organization in Nazi-occupied Europe in the name of the faith she shared with "Aryan" Warsaw.

At the same moment another member of the Warsaw intelligentsia attempted to transmit news of ghetto liquidation outside Poland. In the west, still-fighting belligerents might be in a position to intervene. Jan Karski, like his compatriot Witold Pilecki, snuck into the Nazi antisemitic persecution system. Karski queried ghetto leaders in October 1942, one a Zionist like Zuckerman, the other a Bundist.[110] They stole Karski into the ghetto where he saw suffering, starvation, and murder.[111] The Bundist revealed insurgency plans that became the uprisings of 1943, and asked for Polish and broader Allied support,

---

[107] On women's role in aid to Jews, see: Joanna B. Michlic, "Gender Perspectives on the Rescue of Jews in Poland: Preliminary Observations," *Polin Studies in Polish Jewry, Vol. 30: Jewish Education in Eastern Europe,* eds. E. R. Adler and A. Polonsky (Liverpool: Liverpool University Press, 2018), 407–426.

[108] Born Irena Krzyżanowska in Otwock, she took husband Mieczysław Sendler's name. A Catholic, Sendler was the daughter of an atheist socialist physician with many poor Jewish patients. Anna Mieszkowska, *Die Mutter der Holocaust-Kinder: Irena Sendler und die geretteten Kinder aus dem Warschauer Ghetto* (Munich: Deutsche Verlags Anstalt, 2006); Anna M. Littke, "Polnische 'Gerechte Unter den Völkern' Zwischen Moral und Politik" *Jahrbücher für Geschichte Osteuropas,* Neue Folge, 60, no. 3 (2012): 350–72; Engelking and Leociak, *Getto warszawskie,* 272; Bikont, *Sendlerowa w ukryciu,* 51, 55, 71, 73, 84.

[109] Bartoszewski, *O Żegocie,* 74, 80, 91; Grabowski, *Na posterunku,* 303; Bikont, *Sendlerowa w ukryciu.* Bikont's study discusses several dozen Polish Jews with whom Sendler worked and whom she aided, among them Michał Głowiński, Estera Sztajn/Teresa Körner, and Margarta Turkow.

[110] The Bundist was Leon Feiner (1885–1945) who later joined Żegota. Karski, *Secret State,* 302.

[111] Karski, *Secret State,* 314–315.

particularly weapons.[112] Asking what he should relay to the Western Allies, they demanded retaliation: "the cities of Germany ought to be bombed mercilessly and with every bombing, leaflets should be dropped informing the Germans fully of the fate of the Polish Jews."[113] Polish Jews and Gentiles shared hopes for an Allied bombing of Germany – "we pray for it every day."[114]

Karski was also taken to a death camp.[115] Contacts smuggled him into a Bełżec transit camp in a guard's uniform to observe what "deportation to the East" actually meant.[116] Karski watched 250 Jews crammed into cattle cars filled with quicklime, sealed inside, and borne off to die, "their inhuman screams ... echoes from the moving train." He personally abhorred war and violence and described himself even late in life as a "mama's boy"; he had undertaken military service as a young man because it was required, not because he had any taste for soldiering.[117] The experience so unnerved him that Karski – who had served as an officer, been both a Nazi and Soviet prisoner, and survived Gestapo torture – succumbed to a multi-day bout of terrified vomiting until he drank himself into a stupor and limped back to Warsaw.[118] Karski carried Emmanuel Ringelblum's reports of Jewish murder in all their gory detail to the London exiles and Western Allied leadership.[119] They did not respond, let alone retaliate. In late 1942 the few Warsaw elites who reacted to ghetto liquidation could not stop it.

4.5   Jewish Resistance

The remnant of the Jewish community who survived 1942 lived a traumatized existence from day to day. Many were the only surviving members of their families, neighborhoods, or synagogues. Nazi intentions could no longer doubted: Polish Jews were going to die. Those who had advocated for violence,

---

[112] Feiner wanted aid, which Karski discussed with Rowecki; Rowecki opposed a Jewish uprising but reversed course in 1943. Władysław Bartoszewski and Marek Edelman, *I była dzielnica żydowska w Warszawie* (Warsaw: Literatura Faktu PWN), 2010, 116–127; Zimmerman, *Polish Underground*, 170–171.

[113] Karski, *Secret State*, 307. German civilians saw the Anglo-American bombing campaign as retaliation for the Holocaust (Stargardt, *German War*, 345–381), though its destruction merely intensified German antisemitism (Friedrich, *Fire*, 386, 428).

[114] PISM London: MID: Dział Polski, A. 10. 4/1, "Odpis: List młodej dziewczyny z Warszawy do matki z dnia 2 lutego 1940 r.," [2 Feb. 1940], 2.

[115] Arad, *Belzec, Sobibor, Treblinka*, 359.

[116] Warsaw Ghetto inhabitants were murdered at Treblinka, not Bełżec. Arad, *Belzec, Sobibor, Treblinka*, 326.

[117] USHMM RG-50.012.0044, AN: 1989.67.44, "Interview with Jan Karski," Part 2, 7:30; Part 3, 1:19–2:51.

[118] Arad, *Belzec, Sobibor, Treblinka*, 329–332.

[119] Jewish elite agency was central to specifying the persecution Karski did not see, and ghetto elites filled their report with evidence, "full of charts and tables." Leociak, *Text*, 142.

a ghetto underground dominated by the young, Zionists, and Bundists, planned aggressive action. Between the Grossaktion's start and October 1942, Yitzhak Zuckerman, Mordechai Anielewicz, Marek Edelman, and other Zionist and communist leaders assembled a Jewish National Committee (Żydowski Komitet Narodowy, ŻKN), a confederation of eager insurgents acting as a single political entity – paralleling institutions Polish conspirators called the Home Army and "secret state" after 1942. Anielewicz had been advocating for Jewish opposition and making contacts with the Polish underground since 1941. In fact, he had been liaising between Polish and Polish-Jewish conspiracies in Silesia in summer 1942 and thus escaped deportation. The committee, which was young and secular in outlook, welcomed Jews of varying politics, but all agreed that violence was the only answer to continued deportation. By December they built a military force, the Jewish Fighting Organization (Żydowska Organizacja Bojowa, ŻOB).[120] So did some of their political rivals, who built a parallel group, fracturing Jewish military unity.[121] Working as a team, Anielewicz became ŻOB commander and Zuckerman and Marek Edelman his deputies. Though poorly armed, it planned an uprising. This required weapons, for which the Polish underground was the only nearby source.[122] The consolidating military arm of the Warsaw underground in late 1942, the Home Army, was not easy to persuade, and unwilling to coordinate attacks with Jewish fighters. Polish communists were more generous, but there were few of them and they were lightly armed. A firm predilection for secrecy, antisemitism, skepticism about the efficacy of Jewish resistance, and a crucial weapons shortage made Home Army commander Stefan "Grot" Rowecki (1895–1944) hesitant to aid the ŻOB. This was not merely the position of the Home Army but of the Grand Alliance more broadly, which supported resistance under Nazi occupation only if it had concrete strategic value; militarily Warsaw's Jews "had nothing to offer."[123] Polish conspirators were divided, with some seeing Jewish efforts as aiding a common struggle against Nazi occupation, and others seeing them as a distraction that would consume resources and blow their cover. Rowecki, ordered by the London exiles (who took a more sympathetic attitude toward

---

[120] Zuckerman dated it from July 28, 1942, Krakowski from October 20, 1942. Bartoszewski and Edelman, *I była dzielnica żydowska*, 119–123; Zuckerman, *Surplus of Memory*, 197; Krakowski, *War of the Doomed*, 168.

[121] Most importantly the Jewish Military Union, though they made a truce in early 1943. The presence of multiple militaries fractured potential strength, an important parallel with Polish insurgency. Krakowski, *War of the Doomed*, 168–171.

[122] Frank Golczewski, "Die Heimatarmee und die Juden" in Bernhard Chiari, ed. *Die polnische Heimatarmee: Geschichte und Mythos der Armia Krajowa seit dem Zweiten Weltkrieg*. (Munich: Oldenbourg, 2003), 635–676; Krakowski, *War of the Doomed*, 164, 167.

[123] USHMM RG-50.012.0044, AN: 1989.67.44, "Interview with Jan Karski," Part 3, 15:15–15:45.

Polish Jews), and impressed with the four-day January Uprising in 1943, provided the ŻOB with around fifty pistols, hand grenades, and explosives. ŻOB members also received training from Varsovians, but not weapons in the quantities they requested.[124]

Ghetto fighter frustration with Polish conspirators was emblematic of the chasm that opened between Polish-Jewish and Polish opposition priorities. Though persecution of Poles and Jews had been intertwined at points, ghetto liquidation meant that the groups' most pressing concerns were on different scales. The ŻOB wanted first of all to survive, and then Zionists wanted a new home in Palestine, whereas the Warsaw underground and exile government wanted to recreate an independent Polish state – after the war.[125] Despite their common methods, those willing to fight within the ghetto and those willing to fight in Warsaw outside it had different timelines: ghetto fighters faced deportation and had to act immediately; Varsovians outside timed efforts to coincide with Allied help. Poles watched the progression of the Eastern Front, which in early 1943 seemed perilously far away. To them haste meant disaster; to the Jews waiting meant annihilation. That disconnect – that the Poles had the luxury of time while Polish Jews did not – reveals the distinctly separate fates of these populations at Nazi hands, even if there was overlap in how they were initially persecuted.

On the Eastern Front, the Germans were mired around Stalingrad, and 1943 would see the first significant German military defeat: an enormous morale boost for those under Nazi control. Propaganda Minister Goebbels was unable to hide the news, which reached Warsaw with lightning speed.[126] In mid-January, the Gestapo launched the largest *łapanka* to date, snatching almost 70,000 Poles from Warsaw and surrounding towns. This *Grosssäuberungsaktion* or "Mass Cleansing Action" threw Warsaw into uproar. While that "action" progressed, the Gestapo implemented another ghetto deportation on January 18, 1943. The ŻOB attacked police units organizing the deportations and killed a number: the January Ghetto Uprising.[127] The Gestapo scoured the city looking for fighters and hidden Jews. There was a new curfew, stiff fines, and a citywide census. Pianist Władysław Szpilman fled the ghetto at this moment, taken in by Polish friends on Noakowski street near the polytechnic, passed off for more

---

[124] Zimmerman, *Polish Underground,* 196–197; 202–205; Finder and Prusin, *Justice,* 65.

[125] Early Home Army histories barely mention ŻOB. From the section on "Other Nationalities:" "The Home Army established contact with the ŻOB and provided the help when armed conflict broke out in Warsaw, supplying a certain quantity of weapons and ammunition." Komisja Historyczna Polskiego Sztabu Głównego w Londynie, *Polskie Siły Zbrojne,* Tom III, 47.

[126] Landau, *Kronika,* Tom II, 161–166.

[127] In Jewish history, this is the January Uprising, distinguished from the April Uprising. For Poles, "January Uprising" denotes 1863. Zuckerman, *Surplus of Memory,* 263–347; Engelking and Leociak, *Getto warszawskie,* 782–784.

than a year among musicians, conductors, Polish Radio contacts, and Żegota conspirators.[128]

On April 19, 1943, a large force of policemen gathered at the ghetto gates, including Polish blue police, SS men, and auxiliaries. The timing followed the Nazi practice of coordinating persecutions with Jewish holidays: final liquidation was prepared during the Passover seder. It was a holiday for both Christians and Jews: in 1943, Passover and Holy Week, the preparation for Catholic Easter, coincided. Policemen attacked the ghetto and the ŻOB held out for almost a month.[129] Knowing the territory, and lightly armed, ghetto fighters contested every building, forcing the police to take casualties. Himmler, outraged, sent SS Polizeiführer Jürgen Stroop to crush Jewish resistance and kill everyone in the ghetto.[130] Reinforced with heavy equipment, Stroop's men emptied buildings one by one and set everything aflame (Figure 4.3). Fire spelled the fighters' defeat. Fighting ended on May 16, 1943, when the SS blew up the Great Synagogue on Tłomackie Street. Around 13,000 Jews were killed, and 50,000 more imprisoned. By mid-May, Stroop had destroyed the ŻOB and then the ghetto, mining its ruins. It remained a site of persecution, though: Pawiak still functioned. Abutting Pawiak, the SS turned the remnants of Gęsiówka prison into a concentration camp to house Auschwitz prisoners, forced to collect bricks and look for valuables, the last traces of legendary Jewish wealth.[131] A few ŻOB fighters, miraculously, escaped: Zuckerman, who was in Polish Warsaw securing weapons, survived.[132] People hid in the ruins, a few until the citywide uprising of 1944. One of the most congested places in Europe in November 1940, by summer 1943 the ghetto was a ghost town.

The ghetto persecuted Poland's Jews *as Jews* and its destruction was part of the genocide against them. When Nazis considered Warsaw Jewish policy, they thought about the ghetto. But, not *all* Warsaw's Jews lived within it: an uncertain number lived in hiding or openly "on Aryan papers." Historian Gunnar Paulsson estimates 28,000 hidden Warsaw Jews comprising a "secret city" with its own norms and dangers.[133] At a number of points, Jews in hiding outside the walls entered the ghetto, or were caught and arrested and ended up,

---

[128] Szpilman, *Pianist*, 134–135; Filip Mazurczak, "Władysław Szpilman's Postwar Career in Poland," *Polin Studies in Polish Jewry, Vol. 32: Jews and Music-Making in the Polish Lands*, ed. F. L. Guesnet, H. Lupovitch, and A. Polonsky (Liverpool: Liverpool University Press, 2020): 222.

[129] Landau, *Kronika*, Tom III, 352.

[130] During Stroop's reign of terror, Soviet air raids targeted Warsaw. Rumors circulated that the Soviets were aiding Jews – an indicator of how non-Jewish Poles conflated Jewishness with communism. Landau, *Kronika*, Tom III, 410–413.

[131] Finder, "Jewish Prisoner Labour in Warsaw," 325–326.

[132] Zuckerman, *Surplus of Memory*, 348–376.

[133] Paulsson, *Secret City*, 2.

Figure 4.3 Surrounded by SS and SD personnel, Juergen Stroop (center), watches the Warsaw ghetto burn, spring 1943.
United States Holocaust Memorial Museum, Photograph Number 26572.

for a time, inside Pawiak. After the Grossaktion, the numbers of those fleeing the ghetto spiked, and after the collapse of the 1943 uprisings, survivors again moved to the "other side."[134]

Polish-Jewish life had a different trajectory outside than inside the ghetto.[135] Most importantly, those who lived outside the ghetto were severed from Jewish community and at the mercy of the Polish population, which was often hostile. Their companions, protectors, and exploiters were Polish, not Jewish.[136] In order to keep their identity secret, it was safest to live singly or in small groups. Julien Hirshaut, the Polish-Jewish attorney who escaped Pawiak, split from his brother to survive – and his brother died alone.[137] Women, because they were not circumcised, were at less risk than men if they

---

[134] This required Polish contacts and steep bribes. "Łazarz Menes" in *Chronicles of Terror: Warsaw*, 170–171.

[135] Jewish survival depended on the support of non-Jewish Poles and assimilated elites had advantages. For Polish rescuer motivation: Tec, *When Light Pierced the Darkness*.

[136] Poles of various classes hid Jews, including some who were paid for their efforts. Ghetto fighter Marek Edelman estimated "probably about a hundred thousand Poles" aided Jews in Warsaw, though not all those aided survived. Bikont, *Crime and the Silence*, 108; on what is known and still unclear, see: Melchior, "Uciekinierzy z gett" in *Prowincja noc*, 321–372.

[137] Hirshaut, *Jewish Martyrs*, 76.

spoke Polish well.[138] This meant divided families and life among Catholic Varsovians. Even those Poles who had committed themselves steadfastly to opposing Nazi occupation knew that their abilities to hide and protect Jews was limited: Jan Karski repeatedly noted that even committed Poles "could save only individuals" and not thwart the larger genocide.[139] Zofia Korbońska remembered seven Jewish children who had appeared in their apartment courtyard in 1942, ghetto escapees; she fed them and hid them on their veranda. When she and her husband were themselves forced to flee their apartment, the children stayed behind. She never knew whether the children, one of whom plaintively asked her for cocoa, had survived. Her husband remembered several Polish-Jewish acquaintances who had reached out to him, often requesting forged documents. Notably, Polish-Jewish acquaintances contacted *him*, knowing his politics, his sympathies, and his power in the underground: Polish Jews outside the circle of the intelligentsia who did not have friends like Korboński were stuck.[140] Psychologically, Polish-Jewish life in hiding was haunted by fear of discovery, betrayal, and extortion, compounded by worry about the fate of family members and friends elsewhere. Isolation was difficult: Zuckerman, who left the ghetto just before the final uprising, almost returned: "Although I had been gone only six days, I was terribly lonely. I hated being in a strange place on Passover, for the Seder."[141] This loneliness captures the separation between Jewish and Polish fates: surrounded by Poles, Jews felt alone; in Warsaw they felt themselves "in a strange place."

Ludwik Landau was one of the Polish-Jewish intelligentsia "on the Aryan side." Landau was an economist and a member of Piłsudski's Polish Socialist Party (PPS), a civic nationalist and Polish patriot. He had spent the 1930s as a government bureaucrat working for the Main Statistical Bureau (GUS), researching relationships between state economics and social class. He continued his research during occupation, editing a newsletter called *Occupation Chronicle*, which tabulated demographic data. Landau lived with Polish intelligentsia friends. Financial means and a tight-knit network of colleagues from Main Statistical Bureau and the underground Institute for Social Work, alongside participation in the work of the mature Home Army, kept him alive. His last diary entry, dated February 28, 1944, noted that, for the moment, "It's quiet here with us and in the world."[142] Landau survived the 1939 invasion, both

---

138 Grabowski, *Na posterunku*, 180–181, 197.
139 Karski maintained until his death that the only effective aid could have come from the Allies. USHMM RG-50.012.0044, AN: 1989.67.44, "Interview with Jan Karski," Part 4, 18:05–18:25.
140 USHMM RG-50.012.0046, AN: 1989.67.46, "Interview with Stefan and Sophia Korbonski," Part 3, 1:05–3:45; Part 2, 27:20.
141 Zuckerman, *Surplus of Memory*, 350.
142 Landau, *Kronika*, Tom III, 674, 672, demographics: 679–763.

anti-intelligentsia campaigns, ghetto enclosure, ghetto liquidation, and the 1943 uprisings, but the Gestapo caught him in early 1944. Ultimately, his Jewishness condemned him to death, despite Polish colleagues' help.[143] His years of survival in hiding, however, underlines Polish-Jewish intelligentsia vulnerability and reveals the importance of continued Polish support for even their temporary survival, support that even some of the most committed elite resisters were unwilling or unable to provide.

4.6   Intelligentsia Response in 1943

Kossak, Karski, and their peers observed ghetto resistance. Elite eyewitnesses to Jewish genocide had themselves been victims of Nazi atrocity, and they were not neutral bystanders to Jewish persecution. As historian of religion Victoria Barnett remarks, "people are changed by what they see and do, and they are often moved to act."[144] These people saw in Jewish persecution something intimately interwoven with their own lives and fates. Though Polish underground press covered the ghetto, the event which stamped Jewish persecution on the minds of the Polish intelligentsia was the 1943 uprisings: violence, unsurprisingly, drew intelligentsia conspirators' attention.

Czesław Milosz's (1911–2004) poem, "Campo dei Fiori," captured the despair of a segment of the philosemitic Varsovian intelligentsia at wider Polish indifference. His poem described young Poles on a spring night riding a city carousel as "The bright melody drowned/the salvos from the ghetto wall.[145]

Miłosz wrote it in 1943, struggling with his obligations as an artist, a Pole, and a "Jew of the New Testament." Originally from the eastern borderlands, Miłosz finished his education in Vilnius and moved to Warsaw in the late 1930s where his early poetry made him a reputation in the capital's left-leaning literary circles, and where he befriended Zionists and Bundists. The Jewish Fighting Organization hoped for Polish support from people like him. Bundist Ignacy Samsonowicz ("Samson," 1902–56) penned a call to arms:

> Poles! Citizens! Soldiers of Freedom! . . .
> The struggle for your freedom and ours continues.
> For yours and our – human, social, national – honor and dignity. We avenge the
>   crimes of Auschwitz, Treblinka, Belzec, and Majdanek.
> Long live Fighting Poland's [Walczącej Polski] brotherhood of arms and blood!
> Long live freedom! Death to the butchers and murderers![146]

[143] Grabowski, Na posterunku, 330.

[144] Barnett, Bystanders, 9.

[145] Louis Iribarne translation: https://www.poetryfoundation.org/poems-and-poets/poems/detail/49751

[146] Ignacy Samsonowicz wrote as "Tadeusz Leszczyński" and was hidden by Żegota member Eugenia Wasowska-Leszczyńska. Bartoszewski and Edelman, I była dzielnica żydowska, 131–132.

The brotherhood Samsonowicz hoped for did not materialize. Polish Warsaw did not join the Jewish Fighting Organization, and a citywide uprising was not launched until August 1944, when Polish conspirators seized a window of opportunity between the retreat of the Wehrmacht and the arrival of the Red Army. Polish support to the ghetto was limited and the uprising failed.[147]

Varsovian reactions varied, including expressions of passionate support, the indifference Miłosz alluded to, and antisemitic hostility. Franciszek Wyszyński, an *Endek*, assumed ghetto fighters were launching a communist takeover, and he was not the only person who thought so.[148] Longstanding conflations of Jewishness and communism undergirded wartime suspicions, encouraging Poles to think of their Jewish neighbors as supporting the Soviet Union and its 1939 co-invasion of the country.[149] This mental leap allowed Poles to center their own persecution as victims of Nazi and Soviet persecution, betrayed again by the communist sympathies of their Jewish neighbors, rather than to see Poland's Jews as particular victims of Nazism or assess their own role in that persecution. Nevertheless, even Wyszyński expressed a note of pride on May 8, 1943: "It seems that the fight is finished and the whole ghetto is under the control of the Germans. If that's true, then their fight with the Jews lasted 19 days. And so the Jews in the Warsaw Ghetto defended themselves two days longer than the English in Singapore!"[150] For the intelligentsia, who often lived in Muranów and Żoliborz near the ghetto, reactions ranged from solidarity to curiosity, from condemnation of Jewish motivations, to the ubiquitous impulse to document events.

Aurelia Wyleżyńska (1881–1944), a major literary talent whose diaries wander between Polish and French, wrote for underground periodicals, volunteered as a nurse, and aided hidden Jews. The ghetto uprising overwhelmed her.[151] For Wyleżyńska the fight, partially visible from her balcony, provoked fear and irritation. Her concern at the time was the fate of friends with whom she had lost contact, one of whom was imprisoned in Pawiak. Ghetto fighting was mentioned in her diary but overshadowed by "new waves of street arrests"

---

[147] Some Poles helped ŻOB who escaped through the sewers. Polish sources indicate substantial Home Army support, and Jewish ones that Poles rooted against them. Paulsson, *Secret City*, 91–92.

[148] A right-wing Home Army soldier told Zuckerman "it was a communist uprising … designed to serve the interests of Moscow." Zuckerman was no communist, though he took weapons from the People's Army. Zuckerman, *Surplus of Memory*, 360.

[149] For actual Jewish political behavior, see: Kopstein and Wittenberg, "Who Voted Communist?" Polish Jews logically preferred Soviet to Nazi occupation during the war because of the intensity of Nazi antisemitism.

[150] Little is known about Wyszyński (1876–1944). He lived in Żoliborz. Wyszyński, *Dzienniki*, 348; 362.

[151] Rachel Feldhay Brenner's assessment of Wyleżyńska as a philo-Semite in her *The Ethics of Witnessing: The Holocaust in Polish Writers' Diaries from Warsaw, 1939–1945* (Chicago: Northwestern University Press), 71–101, is sympathetic.

that made her afraid to leave her apartment. She discussed the "Jewish struggle" with her secretary, Hanka, whom she considered a "personification of the conscience of the youth," who was unsympathetic. "Is it worth it," Hanka mused, "to sacrifice one's strength … for people who aren't worth it?" On the third day of the ghetto uprising during Holy Week, Wyleżyńska's diary was uncharacteristically brief. It ended: "The fight in the ghetto continues. For your freedom and ours?" She had read Samsonowicz's call to action, quoting the nineteenth-century slogan of Polish romantics, substituting his exclamation point for a question mark. The next day, Good Friday, she mentioned a rumor – the one Wyszyński had heard – that "Jews had stockpiled weapons against us [Poles], waiting for the arrival of the Bolsheviks to settle accounts." The violence frightened her and she was increasingly suspicious of the motivations of her Jewish countrymen. On Easter Sunday, April 24, she wrote only: "I shut my window on the shooting in the ghetto."[152] Though Wyleżyńska assisted hidden Jews until her death, the ghetto uprising was not a cause she felt obliged to support.

For Zygmunt Śliwicki, Pawiak's prisoner-doctor, the uprising was closer: it raged around him, surrounding the prison. Most of the Warsaw intelligentsia, though close enough to see smoke rise and hear gunfire and explosions, did not *see* insurrection. Śliwicki saw Jewish fighters in action.[153] The windows of the operating room faced onto ghetto streets, where Śliwicki saw Jewish fighters tortured and shot in "nightmarish scenes … burned into his memory." He saw Stroop ordering living men into the flames. Some Jewish fighters froze in terror while others yelled "Niech żyje Polska!" (Long live Poland) or "Deutschland kaput!" while the SS shot them.[154]

Wyleżyńska and Śliwicki were adults under occupation; the war ended Wyleżyńska's life. Both remembered the partitions. The Polish–Soviet War was Śliwicki's political baptism. By 1943, however, politics were in the hands of those who came of age under occupation. Though the generational divide between those who attempted to survive occupation by cooperating and those who actively opposed it was not as stark as among Polish Jews, younger people were increasingly active. Michał Wojewódzki ("Andrzej," 1914–90), was part of this. Wojewódzki was four when Piłsudski proclaimed an independent Poland. Twenty-five when Hitler invaded, he was part of the young intelligentsia: he studied law at Warsaw University, completed reserve officer training, and worked for the postal service. He fought in the September Campaign in 1939, and joined clandestine press efforts in 1940.[155]

---

[152] BN Mf. 48171 Sygn. IV. 6456, manuscript pages: 367, 370, 371, 374, 376, 381.
[153] Śliwicki, *Meldunek z Pawiaka*, 10–12.
[154] The Ghetto Uprising is a few pages. Śliwicki, *Meldunek z Pawiaka*, 117–118.
[155] Michał Wojewódzki, *W Tajnych Drukarniach Warszawy, 1939–1944: Wspomnienia* (Warsaw: Państwowy Instytut Wydawniczy, 1978), 5, 15–16.

Wojewódzki followed fluctuating wartime circumstances nervously. He spent Easter 1943 at his parents' house "100–150 meters" from the ghetto wall in Muranów. The ghetto uprising impressed Wojewódzki, who was rooting for the ŻOB, but his attention was preoccupied with military planning: "I saw the tragedy of the ghetto every day from close up, unhappily for me from much too close ... When the uprising broke out in the ghetto, we found ourselves suddenly within range of the guns ... It was a nightmare ... an inhuman struggle.[156]" For Wojewódzki, ghetto violence and the Nazi police it drew risked exposing Polish conspiracies. On Holy Thursday, April 22, 1943, Wojewódzki's father raised the alarm as policemen raced into their courtyard, screaming, "Where are the bandits? Where are the Jews, where are the bandits?" The Gestapo was pursuing escaping ghetto fighters into buildings abutting the ghetto wall. In order to canvas the area, all residents were dragged from their homes and interrogated. Policemen – likely Poles, though Wojewódzki does not specify – examined everyone's *Kennkarten*, and shot a houseful of Wojewódzki's neighbors with improper paperwork in the street. "Jews or other people hiding, who were not properly registered at that address," were arrested.[157]

Conspirators like Wojewódzki were subject to execution. Wojewódzki admired the Jewish fighters, but when the police turned up his primary concern was that his own operations not be uncovered. The ghetto ruins became the site of execution of Jewish fighters and then Poles, both victims of "mass street executions" by "Hitlerite bandits." Wojewódzki was part of the Warsaw underground that supported the ŻOB, but found Samsonowicz's plea for Poles to "join the fight" strange: he had already been fighting for three years and his priority was continuing that work.[158]

Warsaw intelligentsia's confrontation with the Holocaust was often implicit or intertwined with events that impacted them directly, like Wyleżyńska's worry about her imprisoned friend, Śliwicki's concern for his patients, and Wojewódzki's fears for his printing equipment. Sustained contemporaneous intelligentsia engagement with Jewish persecution is not easy to find, which makes Jerzy Andrzejewski's 1943 novella *Holy Week* (Wielki Tydzień) crucial. Andrzejewski, born in Warsaw in 1909, studied philology at Warsaw University and was a prominent member of the interwar literary community, where his first novel was widely praised.[159]

---

[156] His section on the Ghetto Uprising is titled "My Family Tragedy." Wojewódzki, *W Tajnych Drukarniach*, 234–235.

[157] Zuckerman, *Surplus of Memory*, 236–238, 372; Grabowski, *Na posterunku*, 320.

[158] Zuckerman, *Surplus of Memory*, 239–240.

[159] Andrzejewski published in the interwar journal *ABC*, famous for virulent antisemitism. Carl Tighe, "Jerzy Andrzejewski: Life and Times" in *Journal of European Studies* 25, 1995, 341.

Andrzejewski distanced himself from youthful antisemitism and trundled leftward politically as he aged.[160]

During the war, "by unspoken accord, [Andrzejewski] became something of a leader of all the writers in our city," in terms of literary production and moral example, wrote Miłosz. When confronted with Jewish victimization, "Alpha [Andrzejewski] belonged to those inhabitants of our town [Warsaw] who reacted violently against this mass slaughter. He fought with his pen against the indifference of others, and personally helped Jews in hiding even though such aid was punishable by death.[161]" By the 1940s Andrzejewski's moralizing tendencies affected the subtlety of his prose. Composed as the ghetto uprising was suppressed, his novella *Holy Week* is set the week before Easter, when Christians prepare for the Triduum, the commemoration of the crucifixion and resurrection of Jesus Christ. The novella depicts intelligentsia response to Jewish victimhood: Andrzejewski's own experience is "fictionalized" in his prose. Miłosz explained Andrzejewski's whole corpus in this light. He "attempted to transpose actuality into fiction. This sensitivity to his immediate environment impelled him to touch upon the most drastic problems of [wartime] Poland" and recount them in his "fiction."[162]

Each character in *Holy Week* stands for a "type" in wartime Warsaw. There are two intelligentsia figures, one Jewish and one Polish, and neither is sympathetic. Jan Malecki, an architect living on the Warsaw outskirts, runs into an old girlfriend, Irena Lilien, by chance during the ghetto uprising.[163] Irena, a lovely Jewish woman from a wealthy family, is desperate. Jan invites her home to his pregnant wife, Anna, a peasant girl who compares badly to the sophisticated Irena. The Maleckis make room for Irena in their tiny apartment, though Jan's younger brother, Julian, an insurgent, is also living there. Neighbors instantly realize Irena is Jewish and low-class antisemites living downstairs report her to the landlord. Jan implores an old friend, whom Irena warns him travels in fascist circles, hoping she will take Irena in. Jan meets with this woman, stumbles into a plot, and is killed. His wife, meanwhile, is in church for Good Friday services and Irena alone in their apartment. The neighbor sneaks upstairs to rape Irena and his wife, jealous of the beautiful young woman, throws Irena out. Irena curses everyone and wanders off alone.

Jewish and Polish elites – Andrzejewski's peers – are represented by Jan and Irena. Both are given the chance to articulate their feelings, and each is myopic.

---

[160] Czesław Miłosz's *Captive Mind* focuses on "betrayal" of elites' cultural mission under totalitarian conditions: "Alpha," "Beta," and "Gamma." "Alpha" was Andrzejewski, who later made good with the communists. Miłosz, *The Captive Mind* (New York: Vintage International, 1990), 82–83; 85; Connelly, *From Peoples into Nations*, 639.

[161] Miłosz, *Captive Mind*, 89.

[162] Czesław Miłosz, *The History of Polish Literature* (Berkeley: U of C Press, 1983), 490; Miłosz, *Captive Mind*, 90.

[163] Bielany lies north of Żoliborz. Dunin-Wąsowicz, *Na Żoliborzu, 1939–1945*.

Jan Malecki's indecision captures intelligentsia paralysis in the face of the Holocaust. Andrzejewski tells us that "hardly anyone pitied the Jews," though the burning ghetto can be seen from the Maleckis' apartment.[164] When Jan runs into Irena, fighting in the ghetto has clogged traffic, filled the city with police, and produced crowds of gawkers. Irena is in terrible danger. Jan is not happy to see her:

> It made him uncomfortable, as never before in his entire acquaintance with Irena. He was terribly embarrassed and humiliated by her situation and by his own helplessness and privileged position ... More keenly than usual he felt the same onrush of emotion that inevitably took root of its own accord whenever he contemplated the increasingly frequent tragedies of the Jews. These feelings were different from those that arose within him for the suffering of his own compatriots and of the people of other nations ... At the moments of their greatest intensity, they became entangled in an especially painful and humiliating awareness of a hazy and indistinct sense of responsibility for the vastness of the atrocities and crimes to which the Jewish people [żydowski naród] had been subjected now for many years, while the rest of the world silently acquiesced ... There were times, as at the end of the previous summer, when the Germans had first begun the mass slaughter of the Jews and when for days and nights on end the Warsaw Ghetto had resounded with the sounds of shooting, that his feelings of complicity became exceptionally strongly aroused. He bore them then like a wound in which there seemed to fester all the evil of the world. He realized, however, that there was within him more unease and terror than actual love toward these defenseless people.[165]

That Jews of his prewar acquaintance have an entirely different fate from his own is something he knows, but tries to forget, and Irena disturbs his peace of mind and his ability to understand himself as a martyr. Andrzejewski's portrait of the Maleckis articulates the permanent rupture between Polish and Polish-Jewish elite experience.

What do these 1943 responses from Warsaw's intelligentsia mean? Andrzejewski gives a series of tropes, bracketing Nazi agency, which was uninteresting to him.[166] Wyleżyńska, Wojewódzki, and Śliwicki, Andrzejewski's peers, complicate matters, fleshing out inaction in the face of the burning ghetto into specific concerns. Together they help explain why

---

[164] Jerzy Andrzejewski and Oscar Swan, *Holy Week* (Athens: Ohio University Press, 2007), 8–9. Quotations from Swan's 2007 translation and Andrzejewski, *Wielki Tydzień* (Warsaw: Czytelnik, 1993).

[165] Andrzejewski and Swan, *Holy Week*, 13, 14.

[166] Like the forefront of Polish Holocaust scholarship presently, which assumes German agency and dissects that of Poles, which is less well known and often made a more striking impression on Polish-Jewish victims.

Varsovian elites – even those who helped Jews like Wyleżyńska, or who were involved in underground work that carried a Nazi death sentence as all were – were uninterested in taking up the ŻOB's call to arms, or answering Samsonowicz's plea for the Poles to fight alongside Jews "for your freedom and ours." Even Polish intelligentsia, Hitler's first Warsaw victims and the heart of underground conspiracy, did not see solidarity with the Jews fighting in 1943 as serving their interests – "Polish" interests. The Warsaw ghetto uprising was both too early and too late for surrounding Poles: too early for a citywide uprising, and too late to affect Nazi Jewish policy. For Wyleżyńska, too old to have been much use in an insurrection, the violence was horrifying, and a foretaste of what might be in store for Poles.[167] For Śliwicki, in the ghetto himself, he was already part of a struggle. Though he was touched by the bravery of ghetto fighters – and especially by their Polish patriotism – his fight was conspiracy in Pawiak. For Wojewódzki, Jewish fighters were "heroic," but their struggle was separate and in fact endangered his own. In 1943, for Warsaw's elite, Jewish suffering was suffering that was happening *in Poland* – and thus worthy of reporting out to the exiles to build international sympathy – but it was not suffering that was happening *to Poles.* For ghetto fighters who had hoped for support, this was a source of immense bitterness and a testament to the selfishness of the Polish national character.

4.7   Conclusion

When Stroop's men suppressed the 1943 uprising, they left a pile of rubble in the middle of the Polish capital: proof of Nazi willingness to enforce their racial agenda. In a space that had housed Jewish culture, religion, and politics for centuries, and had boasted some of the grandest synagogues in Europe, nothing remained. On May 16, 1943, Stroop mined the basements of the Tłomackie street synagogue, leaving a hole where it had stood since 1878.[168] The crushing of the uprising was not the end of Jewish life in Warsaw, as some of those hidden outside the ghetto or in its ruins survived until the citywide uprising the next August, and the "liberation" – or at least the arrival – of the Red Army in early 1945. Władysław Szpilman and Yitzhak Zuckerman outlived the final German withdrawal in this way.[169] But they, like the rest of the Jewish survivors, were alone: solitary individuals whose singularity threw into relief the destruction of the community of which they had been part.

The Holocaust of Warsaw's Jews, though it began in earnest after the anti-intelligentsia campaigns, proceeded faster than they did. The concentration of

---

[167] She may have fought in the 1944 uprising or was just an intelligentsia casualty: unclear.

[168] Stroop remembered the synagogue destruction with great relish. Moczarski, *Rozmowy z katem*, 94.

[169] Szpilman, *Pianista*, 83; Engelking and Leociak, *Getto warszawskie*, 816–819; 827–830.

Warsaw Jews in a ghetto – unlike the scattered intelligentsia during the September Campaign – made total exploitation and murder possible. For the Jewish elite, the period from mid-1942 to mid-1943 was a crisis, a "now" against which other persecution paled. Yitzhak Zuckerman, writing from postwar Israel, mulled the chasm that separated the Polish and Jewish communities, a chasm that had opened before the war, but widened unbridgeably thereafter: "when I began reading memoirs of members of the Polish government in London, I was stunned by the extent of their alienation from and indifference to the Jewish issue, which was about as important to them as a toothache."[170]

For Polish elites, the Holocaust was something that happened alongside and within their own wartime experiences, a subject of prurient interest rather than a provocation for sympathy. Antisemitic persecution occupied Polish attention and indicated what the occupation could do. Few reacted quickly or effectively even when they intended to help. Zofia Kossak, rare in the earliness of her protestations, was only able to save a few thousand people through Żegota – a fraction of those who survived liquidation. Jan Karski had more allies, safe from the horrors of occupied Warsaw, but they by and large did not believe what he told them. Karski and Kossak, uncommonly early in their reactions, were already too late. Those elites – most – who confronted the singularity of Jewish victimhood as the ghetto burned in 1943, were unable to help their Jewish neighbors even if they wished to do so. But these were already onlookers and no longer countrymen: the intelligentsia's consensus was that the ghetto's fight, in the heart of Warsaw, was not a Polish affair.

---

[170] Zuckerman, *Surplus of Memory*, 167.

5

Information Wars

The preceding chapters have fleshed out the military invasion and killing campaign visited on the Warsaw intelligentsia, and the German-directed institutions controlling and persecuting Warsaw: Pawiak prison and the Warsaw Ghetto. Awareness of this persecution framework, a façade of overlapping but occasionally contradictory restrictions, is essential to understanding what the capital's intelligentsia faced. Henceforward, the focus will shift to examining the most important intelligentsia endeavors, considering their origins, initiators, and operations.

The bedrock of intelligentsia response was the recording, collection, and sharing of information. Polish Warsaw, like the ghetto, was fed with three streams of information, which together formed what Barbara Engelking calls the "basic source of speculation about the future" and undergirded everyone's ability to plan: "official information, unofficial information, and rumours."[1] Accurate information undergirded everything else. Sourcing and disseminating this relied on publicists, journalists, and writers dispossessed by occupation and drew in scouts, students, and couriers, some of whom "double dipped" into other conspiracies. Paired with illegal underground publications, the best exemplar of which was Aleksander Kamiński's *Information Bulletin*, there were also people who got information out of Warsaw, keeping allies and exiles current. Information moved through networks rather than a hierarchical system. This meant couriers could be caught and tortured, printing equipment discovered, and publications shuttered without the city being starved of information. Information trafficking was effective in the judgement of both intelligentsia participants and occupation authorities. Nazi policy from the creation of the GG was premised on keeping Poles ignorant. Warsaw thwarted that goal by keeping their neighbors – and the world – informed. Any understanding of intelligentsia agency and response must begin with an examination of how information was created and moved around occupied Warsaw. Information production and trafficking initiated many conspirators and simultaneously

---

[1] The time horizons for ghetto inhabitants by 1942 were unquestionably shorter, and hence the importance of rumor escalated. Rumor was nevertheless also important and inflammatory outside the ghetto. Engelking, *Holocaust and Memory*, 140–141.

demonstrated how opposition relied upon and expanded existing intelligentsia networks.

In occupied Warsaw, knowledge was power. On the international stage, Warsaw's information kept Poland in the Grand Alliance. Knowing better than official propaganda kept up Varsovian spirits and was therefore some protection against tyranny. Figuring out how to weaponize it became the key to seizing power back from the Germans.

In a climate of misinformation, a "hunger for the printed word" stalked Warsaw.[2] Though much was uncertain and the difficulty of everyday life drained even the most introspective of their energies, the intelligentsia wrote feverishly. Chronicling was "emotional self-management," comfort, and some-times the beginning of opposition.[3] Varsovians were incorrigible diarists, though committing criticism to print put writers at risk of discovery – and required securing scarce paper.[4] The diary became a literary genre of its own during the war.[5] This was true for those who participated in significant events and those who observed occupation's quotidian horrors, though writers were disproportionately intelligentsia, the writing class. Ludwik Landau, the Polish-Jewish economist, mused in fall 1939 that he might be "too late" in taking up a diary, though he was sure what lay ahead was "still worth recording."[6] He was right. The teenage Zofia Kossakowska-Szanacja (1927–2010) began a memoir for her future grandchildren with the apology that,

> [though] whole tomes of memoirs, reminisces, different essays and inter-views by the people who witnessed those times have been written about the war and years of German occupation … through the whole war and uprising I never saw a rape, shooting, torture or other horror myself. However, I saw the horrible effects of these actions – the wounded, the dying, the beaten, the bloody patches left by those tortured after their executions.[7]

Her "ordinariness" was a matter of perspective in an intellectual family: Kossakowska-Szanacja joined the underground and served as a nurse during the 1944 uprising. Others turned their talents to memorialization, like Czesław Miłosz. He was in Warsaw for the siege and the anti-intelligentsia campaigns

---

[2] Szarota, *Okupowanej Warszawy*, 361.

[3] Carruthers, *Good Occupation*, 77.

[4] Aleksander Wat burned his library. Others were imprisoned for owning "dangerous" books. Watowa, *Wszystko co najważniejsze*, 33. Polish Jews and other occupied popula-tions kept diaries at higher rates than in peacetime. On Jewish diaries, including on Varsovian Chaim Kaplan, see: Amos Goldberg, *Trauma in First Person: Diary Writing during the Holocaust* (Bloomington: Indiana University Press, 2017).

[5] Dunin-Wąsowicz, *Warszawa w latach 1939-1945*, 169.

[6] Landau, *Kronika*, Tom I, 3.

[7] Kossakowska-Szanacja, *Zapiski dla wnuków*, 230–231. On Polish-Jewish diaries to future generations, see Leociak, *Text*, 102.

and observed Polish and Polish-Jewish suffering in verse.[8] He wrote through-out the occupation, publishing poems underground. Most wartime writing like Kossakowska-Szanacja's, Regulska's, and Landau's were begun for private use; Miłosz's wartime writing found an international public.[9]

Private writing was the nucleus of wartime information and postwar know-ledge, but many elites launched more substantial forbidden communication efforts. These initiatives became a world unto themselves, sustaining further opposition and building elite civil society among their readership. The power and reach of intelligentsia information projects was formidable, despite draco-nian punishments for participation in them and the ubiquity of Nazi propa-ganda and the regime's official newspaper, the *New Warsaw Courier*. The *Information Bulletin*, the cornerstone clandestine periodical, gave those who wrote and published it a mouthpiece for directing opposition. These clandestine periodicals undergirded a larger information project that involved radio and a local and international courier network. This library of forbidden information was put into play across Poland and even by exile propagandists, demonstrating the continental importance of information sourced in occupied Warsaw.

5.1   Nazi Information Control

Germans in Warsaw did not simply ban Poles from communicating, publishing, and broadcasting information: they provided their own.[10] In October 1939 Frank's GG outlawed publication and radio broadcasting, and seized printing equipment and radios in private hands.[11] In exchange, the Germans provided a paper, the *New Warsaw Courier* (*NKW*), hereafter the *Courier*, which appeared daily from October 11, 1939.[12] A badly translated German-language paper from Łódź, its news was "always late" and "contained no local contents."[13] The emerging underground told Poles to boycott it, but it was nevertheless ubiqui-tous, a baseline of information in a city denuded of its forest of prewar print.[14]

---

[8] Beinecke GEN MSS Box 89, Folder 1211, Czeslaw Milosz Papers, Series II: Writings, "Wstęp" (1940) and "Głosy biednych ludzi" (1943).

[9] Wyszyński, *Dzienniki*, 5–8.

[10] Dobroszycki, *Reptile Journalism*, 3.

[11] Similar measures were enforced in Prague and Athens, though Varsovians were unusual in that radio sets were comprehensively confiscated. Mazower, *Inside Hitler's Greece*, 85; Bryant, *Prague in Black*, 94.

[12] Printing bans were issued in October 1940, and three presses operated legally: Wydawnictwo Nowoczesne, Wydawnictwo Polskie, and Glob. They published regime-friendly news, smut or apolitical things. Szarota, *Okupowanej Warszawy*, 370–372; Korboński, *Fighting Warsaw*, 203.

[13] The Łódź original was the *Deutsche Lodzer Zeitung*. Landau, *Kronika*, Tom I, 42.

[14] Dobroszycki wrote one of the earliest document-based studies of the GG. He found a German publisher in 1977, and an English edition appeared in 1994. His claim was that the official "reptile" press was widely read and that Nazi propaganda vis-a-vis the Poles

The occupation supplemented the *Courier* with posters and a loudspeaker system of "squawk boxes" on main thoroughfares. Ubiquitous bilingual placards emblazoned "*Bekanntmachung-Obwieszczenie*" (Announcement) heralded fines, arrests, and executions.[15] German newsreels accompanied every film showing, though Poles disregarded the appeals of their own resistance when they bought tickets, a Wehrmacht revenue stream.[16] The Polish film industry was shuttered in 1941.[17] German-controlled Polish-language press or *gadzinówka* – the "reptile press" – was reviled, a testament to the ham-fistedness of its content. It was nevertheless necessary to daily life, as it communicated how the GG planned to treat Varsovians, and what would be demanded of them.[18] To say that Varsovians nevertheless distrusted the *Courier* was an understatement; many assumed the "lying little rag" printed the opposite of the truth.[19]

In *Courier* headlines the Wehrmacht was triumphant, the German "new order" sure to last a thousand years, and the anti-Axis alliance – let alone Polish military efforts abroad – nonexistent.[20] This rankled.[21] Half-truths gave way to fantasy as the Germans fought the Soviets, a conflict Warsaw followed avidly. In November 1941, when the Wehrmacht's eastern advance was grinding to a freezing halt outside Moscow, Varsovians were greeted with a triumphalist *Courier* spread and Hitler's boast of "3,600,000 prisoners, 15,000 airplanes, 22,000 tanks, 27,000 heavy guns": a collapsing Red Army.[22] Eastern Front expert David Stahel's assessment of the same week noted a "that the Wehrmacht "lack[ed] ... almost everything": a halt of the German armies.[23] While Varsovians lacked Stahel's detail, winter had arrived for them, too, and they knew the war was disappointing German hopes. The *Courier* was not to be

---

was more sophisticated than has been appreciated. Dobroszycki, *Reptile Journalism*; Korboński, *Fighting Warsaw*, 118.

[15] Dobroszycki, *Reptile Journalism*, 31.

[16] Boycotting movies was patriotic: "*tylko świnie siedzą w kinie.*" Polish Ministry of Information, *German New Order in Poland* (London: Hutchinson & Co., 1942), vii–xiv, 567; Szarota, *Okupowanej Warszawy*, 322–336.

[17] Benjamin G. Martin, *Nazi-Fascist New Order for European Culture* (Cambridge: Harvard University Press, 2016), 190; Dunin-Wąsowicz, *Warszawa w latach 1939–1945*, 181.

[18] Piątkowski, "Przestępczość w okupowanej Warszawie" in *Porządek publiczny i bezpieczeństwo*, 273.

[19] PISM London: MID: Dział Polski, A. 10. 4/1, "Odpis: List młodej dziewczyny z Warszawy do matki z dnia 2 lutego 1940 r.," [2 Feb. 1940], [1].

[20] *BI* called it "Hitler's irreversible strategic error." BN Mf. 45818, P.50 Konsp IIegz, *BI*, 4 lutego 1943 r., 3.

[21] As it rankled Germans. Victor Klemperer, a German-Jewish academic from Dresden, noted "Talks of success everywhere ... yet ... German troops have nowhere advanced far beyond our frontiers. How does it all fit together?" His Polish peers asked the same questions. Klemperer, *I Will Bear Witness*, 307.

[22] USHMM ARG 1281 Ring I 765, *NKW* 10 listopada 1941 r.

[23] Army Group Center, headed toward Moscow. Stahel, *Battle for Moscow*, 126–127.

trusted on this or other matters. The handsome two-color format and local classified advertisements did not ingratiate the paper to its skeptical readers.[24] Formally, though, criticism of German information was forbidden. As a consequence, those in the know distrusted "official" information as a matter of reflexive patriotism.

Press policy in occupied Warsaw was no surprise to those who had observed its development in Germany, where the Nazi Propaganda Ministry monopolized information.[25] "Intimidation was massive," and political opposition silenced.[26] Paul Joseph Goebbels' Propaganda Ministry was one of the Hitler regime's first creations and vetted "press, film, radio, propaganda, and theatre": total control over what Germans knew about their government and the outside world.[27] Goebbels and his deputy Otto Dietrich influenced Warsaw press policy after 1939, but so did the Wehrmacht and Frank's civilian administration.[28] Wilhelm Ohlenbusch (1899–1997) headed GG media for Frank's Department of Public Enlightenment and Propaganda. Ohlenbusch had none of Goebbels' legendary sophistication or cunning, and historian Lucjan Dobroszycki dismisses him "as a typical example of a German whose real life began only after 1933."[29]

Despite German infighting, Nazi publication controls in Warsaw were draconian and hit the native intelligentsia, who had printed, edited, written, and read this press, hard, putting many of them out of work. In parallel to the situation among civil servants, military personnel, and teachers, this meant a glut of under- and unemployed people ripe for exploitation – either for German labor conscription or by the emerging underground.[30] German-controlled Polish-language propaganda, however, simultaneously created a space for Polish cooperation with the regime, though the intelligentsia shunned it. Because Ohlenbusch – like Frank and most of the GG administration – did not speak

---

[24] Perhaps the reverse: as Jacek Leociak explains the contrast between Polish-Jewish intelligentsia diaries scrawled on scrap paper and the publication of Jürgen Stroop's report on the ghetto uprising's suppression: the "handwriting of victims and the handwriting of their executioners is different." Leociak, *Text*, 70–71.

[25] Elke Fröhlich, "Joseph Goebbels: The Propagandist" in *The Nazi Elite* (New York: New York University Press, 1993), 56–58.

[26] Kershaw, *Hitler*, 273.

[27] Anthony Read, *The Devil's Disciples: Hitler's Inner Circle* (New York: W. W. Norton & Co., 2003), 294–296; Nicholas O'Shaughnessy, *Marketing the Third Reich: Persuasion, Packaging and Propaganda* (London: Routledge, 2018).

[28] Józef Lipski, *Diplomat in Berlin, 1933–1939: Papers and Memoirs of Józef Lipski, Ambassador of Poland* (New York: Columbia University Press, 1968), 542; Peter Longerich, *Propagandisten im Krieg: Die Presseabteilung des Auswärtigen Amtes unter Ribbentrop* (Munich: R. Oldenbourg Verlag, 1987), 118–119.

[29] Longerich, *Goebbels*, 273–292; Dobroszycki, *Reptile Journalism*, 52–54.

[30] PISM London: MID: Dział Polski, A. 10. 4/3, Sprawozdania z Kraju, 1940: "Terytoria przyłączone do Rzeszy" ["Odpis raportu Poselstwa R.P. w Budapeszcie [K. [Ł]ochocki] z dnia 4 marca 1940 r., No. 39/W/3, charakteryzujący sytuacje godpodarcza ne terenie okupacji niemieckiej," 12].

Polish, his work depended on the labor of those who did. Volksdeutsche were a source of recruits for the *Courier*, but Ohlenbusch and his subordinates also found Poles to translate the GG line into fluent Polish. The elite of the city prewar media community demurred.[31]

5.2   Aleksander Kamiński and the *Bulletin*

A handful of Polish editors' and publicists' names remained on the mastheads of what had been their publications, providing a fig leaf for German takeover.[32] The vanguard of underground publishing were the journalists who wrote under siege, keeping the city informed after Starzyński's last radio broadcast faded from the airwaves. Like Jadwiga Krawczyńska who worked at the *United Gazette*, they kept journalism alive on a shoestring.[33] After capitulation they worked under pseudonyms but such anonymity was only outward facing: journalists knew who wrote what and why.[34] This underground of journalists, newsmen, and publicists spanned the political spectrum and included professionals and dabblers.[35]

If fighting Warsaw had *a* newsman, however, it was Aleksander Kamiński. His business – writing and publishing, while setting standards and policing behavior – was a quintessential intelligentsia one. Kamiński was the son of a pharmacist from a poor but educated Warsaw family. After spending his teens in the borderlands, he studied history at Warsaw University and then taught high school and was active in the scouting movement.[36] Kamiński moved to western Poland and started a family in Katowice, but returned to Warsaw during the September Campaign, riding to join the defenders on his bicycle. He led the "Grey Ranks," secret scouting units that put youth paramilitary skills at the disposal of resisters. In October 1939, Kamiński was running the Grey Ranks and later joined the Union of Armed Struggle (Związek Walki Zbrojnej, ZWZ).[37] His codename was "Hubert" but he also

---

[31] Dobroszycki names three *ideological* intelligentsia collaborators: Feliks Stefan Burdecki, Jan Emil Skiwski, and Jerzy de Nisau. They worked on the 1944 Krakow periodical *Przełom*. Dobroszycki, *Reptile Journalism*, 74–75; 137–139.

[32] "Franciszek Sowiński," supposedly editor in chief of *Courier*, was "a fictitious person." Dobroszycki, *Reptile Journalism*, 20.

[33] Krawczyńska, *Zapiski dziennikarki warszawskiej*, 54–67.

[34] Journalists had to register in 1939. Krawczyńska falsified her address. Krawczyńska, *Zapiski dziennikarki warszawskiej*, 70. Miłosz attended Sunday literary evenings with Jerzy Andrzejewski, Krzysztof Baczyński, and Witold Lutosławski, and they savaged gung-ho underground press patriotism. Franaszek, *Miłosz*, 192, 200–201.

[35] Krawczyńska, *Zapiski Dziennikarki Warszawskiej*; Zaremba, *Żeby chociaż świat wiedział*.

[36] Kamiński is a participant-historian. PAN III-423-47 Materiały Aleksandra Kamińskiego: Życiorysy, 3-44a (early life and education), 45–86 (interwar teaching); Ryszard Wasita, "Aleksander Kamiński on War and Education," in *Dialogue and Universalism* No. 7–9: 2004.

[37] BN Mf. 45818, *BI*, Nr. 5 (160), 4 lutego 1943 r.; Szarota, *Okupowanej*, 266.

had a literary alias, "Juliusz Górecki." His biggest underground project was the *Information Bulletin*, Warsaw's news lifeline.

From the businesslike title to the no-frills formatting, Kamiński's *Bulletin* kept Varsovians updated on information suppressed by the occupiers, and it had the longest uninterrupted publication record and largest readership of any underground title across occupied Europe.[38] Though his name did not appear (for obvious reasons) on the masthead, Kamiński created most of the content for the weekly (daily during the Warsaw Uprising). The first issue appeared on May 31, 1940 with the cryptic warning *"biuletyn zniszcz osobiście"* – destroy this bulletin personally – followed by four pages of dense type.[39] Later editions had nicer typesetting and a double-columned layout with the occasional illustration. The last issue, with a final sendoff from the still-anonymous editors and a prayer for fallen colleagues, was number 317, and dated January 19, 1945, after the "liberation" of Warsaw by the Red Army.[40] At peak circulation, the *Bulletin* printed 43,000–50,000 copies per issue, each of which had many readers, and some of which turned up far beyond Warsaw.[41] These print runs are one of the clearest indicators of the size of the intelligent-sia world and their audience of supporters, a formidable community.

The *Bulletin* billed itself as a neutral source of information in contrast to German propaganda but its political sympathies were never unclear to anyone paying attention.[42] "Information Bulletin" was a deliberately biparti-san phrase, and it appeared on other publications, distinguishing them from literary and creative efforts.[43] The *Bulletin* announced German policy devel-opments (including the 1940 anti-intelligentsia campaign), printed obituar-ies, and summarized military affairs, with gleeful delineation of German losses while highlighting Polish military efforts abroad.[44] It documented antisemitic persecution.[45] It also commented on patriotism, naming names when discussing Germans or traitors to (its definition of) the Polish cause.[46]

---

[38] The French communist daily *L'Humanité* issued 317 wartime editions. *La Vérité* was the first underground journal. Alfred Rieber, *Stalin and the French Communist Party* (New York: Columbia University Press, 1962), 106–107). Thanks to Rachel Johnston-White for the clarification.

[39] BN Mf. 45815, *BI*, 31 maja 1940 r.

[40] BN Mf. 45820, *BI*, 19 stycznia 1945 r.

[41] Gross, *Polish Society*, 254; KHPSGL, *Polskie Siły Zbrojne*, Tom III: *Armia Krajowa*, 277 (Highest figures: AK).

[42] Dunin-Wąsowicz, *Warszawa w latach 1939–1945*, 169; KHPSGL, *Polskie Siły Zbrojne*, Tom III: *Armia Krajowa*, 277.

[43] PONS (Polska Organizacja Narodowo-Syndykalistyczny) had a "biuletyn informacyjny" in 1941. USHMM ARG 1371 Ring I 718, nr. 29 12.1941, nr. 30 23.12.1941.

[44] BN Mf. 45815, *BI*, 6 lipca 1940 r., 5–7; *BI*, 19 lipca 1940 r., 5; *BI*, 2 sierpnia 1940 r.

[45] BN Mf. 45817, *BI*, 3 czerwca 1942 r., Rok IV, Nr. 22 (126), "Kraj: Obóz w Bełżcu," 6; 30 lipca 1942 r., Rok IV, Nr. 30 (134), "Warszawa: Początek Likwidacji Getta," 6–7.

[46] Gross, *Polish Society*, 165; Korboński, *Fighting Warsaw*, 137.

Kamiński's *Bulletin* outed Gestapo collaborators, those who squealed under torture in Pawiak, and the three men who organized the Easter 1940 pogrom before ghetto enclosure.[47] It suggested behavior, inviting readers to participate in activities – singing songs, boycotting businesses, shunning individuals, sabotaging German authority – in a way that made Kamiński an activist in his editorial capacities, to say nothing of his military ones.

Mały sabotaż – petty sabotage – the bread-and-butter of Warsaw's confrontational posture against occupation, was Kamiński's cause. His manifesto on November 1, 1940 demanded new behavior:

> There are certain forms of sabotage that are not just acceptable at the present moment, they are required. Each of us – men, women, children, members of organizations and people still unaffiliated – each of us must take part in the action of "petty" sabotage. This sabotage, which does not put anyone at risk, can still make everyday life exceptionally difficult for the occupier ... What is important is that this sabotage is implemented every day and everywhere.

In a city where most day-to-day intelligentsia activities were risky, this was a move to democratize opposition. Kamiński suggested six small ways Poles could obstruct occupation without endangering themselves, including dragging their feet at work and responding with "I don't understand" when queried by Germans.[48] The goal was to build opposition consensus, inconvenience Germans, and give conspirators a sense of whom to trust and recruit: the policy of an intelligentsia with democratic hopes. That such a manifesto appeared in the *Bulletin* is unsurprising: the capital read it for information and guidance. The petty sabotage article was Kamiński's statement about what the city *should* be doing and he introduced it as coming from "the military leadership and all the political groups of the country," an assertion of underground unity that did not yet exist, an aspiration at a moment of uncertainty in fall 1940. Kamiński was in the wartime information business, but it was a particular kind of business: here was a member of the intelligentsia as much shaping behavior as describing it. The two went hand in hand. As military conspiracies consolidated, Kamiński hitched the *Bulletin* to the Home Army, making it its central news organ and becoming chief of the underground Bureau of Information

---

[47] Leociak notes the three outed Polish fascists, Andrzej Świetlicki, Fr. Stanisław Trzeciak, and Jerzy Cybichowski, all died in the war, the first two at Nazi hands and the third during the uprising: they, too, were intelligentsia. Leociak, *Text*, 242.

[48] The six precepts: 1. Working [for Germans] as slowly as possible, 2. Making "mistakes" in work done for Germans, 3. Giving Germans wrong answers and bad information when asked, 4. Answering "I don't understand" to German questions, 5. Disrespect and foot-dragging in the implementation of German commands, 6. Anonymous denunciations of Volksdeutsch to the Gestapo. BN Mf. 45815, *BI*, 1 listopada 1940 r., 1.

and Propaganda (BIP) – Ohlenbusch's underground counterpart, but with more talent.[49]

Kamiński did not write the *Bulletin* alone. It printed and reprinted essays, feuilletons, poetry, prayers, songs, and art. It became one of the largest fora for disseminating the work of the city writing classes at war, despite dedicated literary publications and chapbooks.[50] The success of the *Bulletin* stimulated hunger for more writing and specialized periodicals, despite the risk.[51]

Kamiński had both colleagues and competitors who wrote what Warsaw read. Paramilitaries had newsletters like the *Dziennik Radiowy* (Radio Daily), for which Jadwiga Krawczyńska worked.[52] Other political factions, sympathetic and unsympathetic, had publications. The national syndicalists had *PONS Biuletyn Informacyjny*, the Polish Socialists their weekly *Barykada Wolności* (Barricade of Freedom) and monthly, *Gwardia* (Guard), the communists *Czerwony Sztandar* (Red Standard): every political club and faction had a newsletter and some several.[53] The desire to print did not have to be narrowly political: scouting organizations, Catholic sodalities, women's groups, regional associations, literary circles, theater groups, and professional associations had their own publications, snuck into print for a few issues.[54] The printing ban infused all publication with politics, even if that was not their authors' primary intent.

This information world was claustrophobic: a handful of intelligentsia figures edited one journal, wrote for a second, and took over a third when its staff ran afoul of the Gestapo – and read dozens more. Zofia Kossak, first introduced as the founder of Żegota, wrote as well. She remembered no fewer than fourteen distinct underground titles to which she had contributed, including the *Bulletin* and *Rzeczpospolita* (Republic).[55] There were underground publications across the GG, but Warsaw was the heart of operations and housed 200 hidden printing houses which produced around 700 unique

---

[49] The *Bulletin* was the initiative of an *inteligent* who brought it into the Home Army fold; its creation predated the Home Army by years. *Contra*: KHPSGL, *Polskie Siły Zbrojne*, Tom III: *Armia Krajowa* (Londyn: Instytut Historyczny im. Gen. Sikorskiego, 1950), 77.

[50] For example, the "September Warsaw" poems of poet Janiczek (*Antologia poezji współczesnej* ("Narcyz Kwiatek,") (Warsaw: Tajne Wojskowe Zakłady Wydawnicze, 1937 [1941])).

[51] Franaszek, *Miłosz*, 202–203.

[52] Krawczyńska, *Zapiski dziennikarki warszawskiej*, 75.

[53] They were printed in small format and read in the ghetto. USHMM ARG 1371 Ring I 718 PONS, 1941; USHMM P ARG 1354 Ring I 712 Barykada Wolności, 1940–1942; USHMM ARG 1360 Ring I 710 Gwardia, 1941–1942; USHMM P ARG 1302 Ring I 716 Czerwony Sztandar, 1940–1941.

[54] Franaszek, *Miłosz*, 203.

[55] *Bulletin, Rzeczpospolita, Opoka, Barykada Powiśla, Prawda, Prawda Młodych, Fałszerze, Orlęta, Pług i Miecz, Robotnik, Znak, Polska Żyje, Peżetka*, and *Dziś i Jutro. Rzeczpospolita* was a Christian-National Movement organ, created by Ignacy Paderewski and Wojciech Korfanty (AAN 2-1230-0 sygn. 76-III-57, "Uwagi Z. Kossak-Szczuckiej o prasie podziemnej Polski w czasie okupacji niemieckiej. Co wiem o prasie podziemnej," [1–2]).

titles.[56] "War," as Peter Fritzsche put it, "generated copy."[57] "There can be no doubt that there was too much," Kossak admitted.[58] "The underground press was the pride of the conspiracy, but it must be owned that we overdid it," Stefan Korboński agreed: "The publication of a newspaper was almost a certificate of importance to even the smallest organization, for it gave it a position in the underground world."[59] For Polish-Jewish intelligentsia, writing was "an irrestible imperative," immediately existential in its important: "the act of writing itself bec[a]me a heroic challenge thrown down to the Holocaust."[60] For non-Jewish Poles, national existence was thought to be at stake, even when individual survival was likelier. Publications served as a rebuttal to occupation and an assertion of the right to think and associate. They were a continuation of Polish discourse when the German administration was trying to destroy it, collectively "preventing the atomization of Polish society."[61] The extraordinary variety of publications was a demonstration that intelligentsia energies were not stifled: the project of defining and sustaining a Polish nation continued.

5.3 Practicalities

Printing required materials and equipment that were illegal to possess and difficult to transport. Michał Wojewódzki, first introduced as a commentator on the ghetto uprising, spent the occupation "in the trenches" of underground publishing.[62] Wojewódzki was a local boy; the war turned his world upside down.[63] He was called up as a reservist in 1939 and reported to his regiment, the 21st Warsaw Infantry, nicknamed the "Children of Warsaw." His regiment saw heavy fighting on Washington Boulevard, from which he watched his childhood home shelled into rubble.[64]

Wojewódzki became a POW and was released and returned home. His path to conspiracy took several steps, the most important of which was reconnecting with a high school teacher, Stefan Essmanowski (1898–1942).[65] A quasi-salon of

---

[56] Gross, *Polish Society*, 254: 650 titles; Szarota, *Okupowanej Warszawy*, 390: 690 titles. Stanisława Lewandowska, *Prasa okupowanej Warszawy, 1939–1945* (Warsaw: Instytut Historii PAN, 1992): 690 titles.

[57] Fritzsche, *Iron Wind*, xv.

[58] AAN 2-1230-0 sygn. 76-III-57, "Uwagi Z. Kossak-Szczuckiej o prasie podziemnej Polski w czasie okupacji niemieckiej. Co wiem o prasie podziemnej," [2].

[59] Korboński, *Fighting Warsaw*, 169.

[60] Leociak, *Text*, 28–29, 266, 263.

[61] Korboński, *Fighting Warsaw*, 256.

[62] Bartoszewski, *1859 dni Warszawy*, 551.

[63] Wojewódzki, *W tajnych drukarniach*, 15–16.

[64] Wojewódzki, *W tajnych drukarniach*, 52.

[65] Essmanowski died in 1942 at Palmiry or possibly Treblinka (Milan Lesiak, "Stefan Essmanowski," *Encyklopedia Teatru Polskiego*: www.encyklopediateatru.pl/osoby/70908/stefan-essmanowski).

friends and students gathered around Essmanowski, a consummate intellectual, and these soirees kept Wojewódzki up late, talking about politics, listening to illegal radio, and reading clandestine press: a clear demonstration of the inter-connectedness of the conspiratorial activities of educated Varsovians. The spring 1940 arrest of several members tore this circle apart and changed Wojewódzki's perspective. He wanted to do something concrete and by then there were already a dizzying variety of people *doing something*. He settled on joining the Polish Armed Organization (Polska Organizacja Zbrojna, POZ), which his friends were already in.[66]

In 1940 Wojewódzki began a multi-year career in the underground pub-lishing world. His first POZ job was monitoring Nazi press, looking for weaknesses.[67] To turn from press monitors to information creators, his spy team needed equipment. In fall 1941 they found a source: Germans. The bulky equipment meant that the "normal" route for conspiracies on the move, which involved the wives and sisters of conspirators hauling material piecemeal in handbags, baby carriages, and rickshaw taxis, was out of the question.[68] After a lot of planning, Wojewódzki, armed with a pistol, met his co-conspirators at the corner of Krakowskie Przedmieście and Bednarska Streets outside Warsaw's Old Town. A truck pulled up beside them driven by a man in SS uniform, complete with leather overcoat and swastikas – one of their buddies in disguise. The team loaded a roomful of stolen German equipment into the truck and, after a nervous night waiting for the end of curfew, drove the haul to their new printing "office."[69]

Wojewódzki's exploits drew the attention of the Secret Military Printing Works (Tajne Wojskowe Zakłady Wydawnicze; TWZW) and its manager, Jerzy Rutkowski ("Michał Kmita," 1914–89).[70] There were other such oper-ations, either the press wings of established conspiracies or printers serving multiple groups: recruits "shopped" for projects to commit to in a dizzying underground world. Rutkowski had been part of interwar national radical politics – Dmowski's people – and was an experienced conspirator. In 1942, the TWZW joined the new Home Army underground military umbrella group and became its central printer, churning out the *Bulletin* and other titles. Rutkowski brought Wojewódzki onboard.[71] Despite the greater prestige of

---

[66] His other option was PLAN, which was infiltrated. Wojewódzki, *W tajnych drukarniach*, 85, 89.

[67] Wojewódzki, *W tajnych drukarniach*, 99–100.

[68] USHMM RG-50.012.0046, AN: 1989.67.46, "Interview with Stefan and Sophia Korbonski," Part 2, 24:00–25:10.

[69] Wojewódzki, *W tajnych drukarniach*, 96–97.

[70] Rutkowski knew Wojewódzki from law school. He had helped Maksymilian Kolbe with *Mały Dziennik*.

[71] Wojewódzki emphasizes early TWZW independence. Wojewódzki, *W tajnych drukar-niach*, 130–131.

soldiering – "poets and literary people don't write about partisan presses and colportage" – Wojewódzki knew his work was essential.[72]

There were naturally some intelligentsia dissidents around underground publishing – including among literary figures. Miłosz "diverged from the mainstream of underground thinking," in the words of his biographer. The poet lacked enthusiasm for the secret printing press in the apartment above his on Independence Avenue, which he considered an insufferable nuisance, interrupting his sleep and work. Miłosz "was furious at the thought that he could have been killed by the Germans because someone else was producing a publication which was full of rubbish."[73] What the upstairs printer thought of the value of Miłosz's poetry is unknown, but the poet survived the war. Miłosz's irritation, however, was not misplaced: illegal printing operations were extremely dangerous and their large and noisy equipment made them hard to conceal from neighbors and passersby, requiring the (tacit) support of a community to survive. Wojewódzki lost colleagues and friends during raids and discoveries, and the TWZW constantly relocated and painfully secured new equipment and personnel to keep the city informed.

5.4   Rumor, Satire, and the Power of Images

Kamiński and Wojewódzki ran afoul of German regulations daily, and Miłosz's proximity to an illegal press was reason to worry, but no way of creating information was safe. A young woman writing to her mother from Warsaw described the situation in early 1940:

> We don't have any news here, because besides the lying little rag put out by the martinets (*pludry*) under the name 'Nowy Kurier Warszawski,' there are just other lying German papers. The Germans collected the radios and there is the death penalty for listening to one. Despite this some news reaches our ears by secret channels ... the most unlikely rumors are always swirling around the city.[74]

Radios were essential to military and civilian conspiracies, but risky: those discovered with radio equipment could be imprisoned, or, like the students whose set was found in 1940, shot.[75] Still, London broadcast details "became

---

[72] Wojewódzki, *W tajnych drukarniach*, 5.

[73] Franaszek, *Miłosz*, 205; 191.

[74] PISM London: MID: Dział Polski, A. 10. 4/1, "Odpis: List młodej dziewczyny z Warszawy do matki z dnia 2 lutego 1940 r.," [February 2, 1940], [1]. Mentioned in f. 7. Pludry, the term she uses, comes from the German Pluderhosen and refers to the short, baggy trousers worn by Renaissance soldiers – a jab at pretentious military men like the uniformed Germans who inundated Warsaw.

[75] Bór-Komorowski, *Armia Podziemna*, 189; PISM London: MID: Dział Polski, A. 10. 4/1, "Z raportu p. H. R. która opuściła Polskę," February 18, 1940, 2. They were betrayed by Polish police.

the property of the whole city by the end of the very same day."[76] Rumor was rampant, inside and outside the ghetto, and wild tales of Polish, German, and Soviet behavior – some entirely true – made their way around like lightning. The situation combined the most potent effects of rumor culture with those of a racialized occupation, "that mixture of danger and insecurity" and "the particularly rigid control of information" which sends "hearsay ... into over-drive," heightening the sense of danger.[77]

News and *grypsy* trickled out of Pawiak. Rumor got into and out of the ghetto, regardless of the walls. Information got out of Gestapo headquarters and Fischer's Brühl Palace, and it emerged from the Wawel complex in Krakow where Frank ran the GG and made its way to Warsaw. Jokes – usually at German expense – circulated, and were lovingly reprinted by the underground press. Joking was a non-violent means of reinforcing national community across east central Europe as it exploited the flexibility of the (often impenetrable) local language in a way Germans could not police, strengthening national community bonds.[78] Visual satire had an even larger audience and the additional audacity of being clearer to the occupier: caricatures and cartoons were scrawled on walls and defaced official announcement and propaganda placards (a crime, of course). Joking was a step toward petty sabotage and patriotic graffiti a step past it: nonviolent political acts that drew the public's attention to resistance in their midst and reminded the Germans that the city was not fully under their control.

The *kotwica*, a stylized anchor formed from an entwined "P" and "W" for "*polska walcząca*" (fighting Poland) or "*powstanie warszawskie*" (Warsaw uprising), appeared regularly – the Polish version of Churchill's "V for Victory."[79] Painting *kotwicy* was a scout favorite, but anyone could manage it: this was a form of publication the masses and elite could enjoy, and that worried the occupation.[80] Lest anyone miss the symbolism, the *Bulletin* described it in April 1942 as "drawn by a thousand unknown hands."[81] One even popped up on the stone column of the Airman's Monument on one of the city's main thoroughfares.[82] Like Kamiński's petty sabotage piece, the one on the *kotwica* updated those "out of the loop" – and encouraged them to join in.

---

[76] Korboński, *Fighting Warsaw*, 41.

[77] Hans-Joachim Neubauer, *The Rumour: A Cultural History* (London: Free Association of Books, 1999), 83, 91.

[78] Czechs also engaged in this. Chad Bryant, "The Language of Resistance? Czech Jokes and Joke-Telling under Nazi Occupation, 1943–45," *Journal of Contemporary History*, Vol. 41 No. 1 (January 2006), 134.

[79] Mazower, *Inside Hitler's Greece*, 91–93.

[80] Report of the Chief of Distrikt Warschau [Fischer to Frank] for the Month of March 1942, dated April 13, 1942. Fischer, *Raporty*, 491.

[81] BN Mf. 45817, *BI*, 16 kwietnia 1942 r., Rok IV, Nr. 15 (119), 7.

[82] A memorial of the 1942 graffiti is now on the Airman's Monument in Ochota.

The *Bulletin's* goal was to break the German informational monopoly. The news was text-based but limited means drove creativity, as mocking the occupier was an end in itself, boosting confidence for those "in" on the joke. The *Courier* was a perfect target, with its recognizable format, old news, and clumsy Polish. It was caricatured with serpents slithering from its pages or read by animals. Roman Tadeusz Wilkanowicz's woodblock print of a donkey reading the paper, emblazoned with the stylized caption "I always read the New Warsaw Courier" became one of the most enduring images of occupation cheek, ridiculing the passive wait-and-see crowd who obeyed the occupiers and had not – yet – fallen in behind the intelligentsia.[83] Faux *Courier* "issues" were lovingly concocted by underground printers, including Wojewódzki's TWZW, to the delight of Varsovians and rage of Germans who happened upon them (and understood enough Polish to realize the lampoon).[84] One mock issue sported the front-page headline "Spain enters the war" with an article on "Gibraltar attacked: first successes of the Spanish air force." Another faux *Courier* from May 6, 1944 announced that the Wehrmacht had invaded Sweden. A false copy of the parallel Krakow daily was recreated down to the classified ads, in December 1943, including an advertisement for Hitler's Berlin gynecological office and another posted by an Admiral Dönitz, commander of the *Kriegsmarine*: "lost: German fleet. I'm looking for my boats."[85]

The *Bulletin* offered occasional illustrations. On Holy Thursday 1942 a cross wearing a crown of thorns between two columns of victims' names adorned the front page, intertwining Polish patriotism with Catholic imagery (Figure 5.1).[86] The paper also made space for visual satire.[87] Wilkanowicz (1909–44), Stanisław Tomaszewski ("Miedza," 1913–2000,), and Henryk Chmielewski (1923–), who signed his drawings "YES," were the kings of this genre, turning the poverty of wartime printing opportunities into a high art.[88] The *Bulletin* and other publications immortalized their work.

The political cartoon freezes intelligentsia mood, a testament to scathing comments, jokes, and quietly exchanged glances otherwise lost. The depiction of the German – fat, sloppy, ridiculous, animalistic, effeminate – spoke to the failure of Nazi racial propaganda. In contrast to the Nazi self-image of the

[83] Janina Jaworska, *Polska sztuka walcząca* (Warsaw: Wydawnictwa Artystyczne i Filmowe, 1976), 69.

[84] Workshop W4, "Czwórka," was on Wawelska Street. Wojewódzki, *W tajnych drukarniach*, 162–167, 170.

[85] Reprinted in Załęski and Załęski, *Satyra w konspiracji*, 63–65.

[86] BN Mf. 45817, *BI*, 2 kwietnia 1942 r., Rok IV, Nr. 13 (117), [1]. Easter was April 5, 1942.

[87] Among others: BN Mf. 45817, *BI*, 14 maja 1942 r., Rok IV, Nr. 19 (123), [1]; BN Mf. 45817, *BI*, 18 czerwca 1942 r., Rok IV, Nr. 24 (128), 8; BN Mf. 45817, *BI*, 25 czerwca 1942 r., Rok IV, Nr. 25 (129), 8; BN Mf. 45817, *BI*, 9 lipca 1942 r., Rok IV, Nr. 27 (131), 8.

[88] Wilkanowicz died at Gestapo hands; Tomaszewski survived torture in Pawiak and became the godfather of Lech Kaczyński (1949–2010).

Figure 5.1 Front page of Aleksander Kamiński's underground *Bulletin* during Holy Week listing Varsovian victims of Nazism, April 1942.
Wikimedia Commons.

confident Aryan colonizer, the "bringer of culture" to uncivilized space, the Warsaw intelligentsia feared Germans but did not respect them.[89] To the Pole, the German was a destroyer of life, culture, education, and the arts, a wanton pillager whose behavior revealed his own primitiveness, not that of his victims.

Intelligentsia writing, from the private diary to the feuilleton, underscored occupier depravity. Ridiculing Germans was its own kind of sustenance: "laughter was the redeeming feature that saved us from going mad … as long as the Poles were able to laugh and joke they could not be vanquished."[90] In contrast to the veneer of German export propaganda, the Polish observer saw a different face of the Nazi regime: the ineptitude, wanton destruction, infighting, and competition between agencies, and the basic ignorance of Polish life, economy, language, and customs that scuttled German efforts and sent policy initiatives into a quagmire of ruin. Yes, the Germans threatened, stole, segregated, assaulted, and killed, but they did so with a reckless inconsistency that made the strangely immortal trope of the efficient Prussian bureaucrat with which Nazism remains associated outside of Eastern Europe completely unrecognizable in Poland. The German in Warsaw was threatening, but he was also ridiculous.

5.5   Local News

The city was wallpapered with announcements; vertical surfaces became bulletin boards. They provided death notices (*klepsydry*) and announced individuals were still alive, or arranged meetings between separated sweethearts. From the siege destruction to the Germanization of place names and the presence of soldiers, German agency changed the appearance of Warsaw. It also changed because of how the Poles laid claim to the physical space of the city, decorating it with patriotic graffiti and slogans, countering the "right" of the occupier to control their public space.

Most information, however, could not be posted publicly. Emerging elite conspiracies lived or died by what information they could move in secret, and how fast. They had to build sophisticated human networks and maintain complex radio, telegraph, and printing equipment in order to keep themselves afloat. Each also needed connections to others capable of securing funds or creating fake identity documents, which involved photographers, notaries, clerks, and secretaries in the German administration. Ideally, a viable conspiracy also had connections inside the ghetto and Pawiak and – most prized – in the Polish and Nazi police, for warning about upcoming raids and arrests.

---

[89] Isabel Heinemann, '*Rasse, Siedlung, deutsches Blut:' Das Rasse- und Siedlungshauptamt der SS und die rassenpolitische Neuordnung Europas* (Göttingen: Wallstein Verlag, 2003), 357–416; Lehnstaedt, *Occupation*, 125.

[90] Korboński, *Fighting Warsaw*, 198.

A single weak link could put an entire operation at risk and lose people and equipment. This was where the rarified world of underground publishing met another elite world: information trafficking.

Only German-controlled publications were sold openly – though destroying them became early sport for patriotic youth. The *Bulletin* was not sold at newsstands, though it could be obtained on the streets. This and other underground titles were distributed across Warsaw, including at bookshops or cafes where it could be bought from under the counter by a Pole asking the right question in a local accent.[91] Occupied Warsaw was full of contradictions: anonymous, confusing, and crowded to its foreign occupiers, it was intimate and local to its Polish residents, among whom "a stranger would immediately attract attention."[92]

Leaflets, newspapers, and correspondence were transported on foot and by tram, train, and rickshaw in satchels, handbags, and suitcases by an improvised courier network. Those who worked as couriers had no one master, and many also played other roles in underground and aboveground life. The key characteristics for a Warsaw courier were two: that the person was trusted, and that he or she was as inconspicuous as possible.[93] Because of the evacuation and then the targeting of men of military age, couriers were mainly women. Couriers doubled down on traditional gender stereotypes about female passivity, carrying groceries or pushing a stroller while they moved illegal material.[94] According to Jan Karski, "of all of the workers in the Underground, their [the female couriers'] lot was the most severe, their sacrifices the greatest, and their contribution the least rewarded."[95] Carrying information initiated many women into resistance, linking families and friends into conspiracy networks.[96] Liaisons (*łączniczki*) or "contact girls" were the only link between disparate cells of conspiratorial groups and among those in hiding. The necessity of their being known and trusted, combined with the intelligentsia origins of many conspiracies, meant that female relatives and friends of elite conspirators dominated. Moving information was a central way that women from intelligentsia families sustained resistance work.[97]

---

[91] The Piekarskis got theirs from a local shop: "in spring 1942 Miss Wanda Kamińska ... was arrested. It was a public secret that Miss Wanda was up to her ears in conspiracy, since she always had fresh copies of the secret press." Maciej Piekarski, *Tak zapamiętałem: wspomnienia z lat 1939–1945* (Warsaw: Państwowy Instytut Wydawniczy, 1979), 61.

[92] Korboński, *Fighting Warsaw*, 250.

[93] KHPSGL, *Polskie Siły Zbrojne*, Tom III: *Armia Krajowa*, 87–91; on women, see 87.

[94] Korbonski, *Fighting Warsaw*, 339.

[95] Karski, *Secret State*, 266.

[96] Korboński, *Fighting Warsaw*, 162, 317, 342.

[97] This bore similarities to later French resistance. Paula Schwartz, "Redefining Resistance: Women's Activism in Wartime France" in *Behind the Lines: Gender and the Two World Wars* (New Haven: Yale University Press, 1989), 141–153.

Couriering was not "innocent" in German eyes, even if young women were its main laborers.[98] Krystyna Idzikowska ("Krysia," 1921–44) was from a little town in central Poland. A delicately built country girl, she showed intellectual promise and was educated at significant cost to her family. She passed a clandestine *matura* – the national high school finishing exam – in 1942, and came to Warsaw to study philology at the underground university, heading into the intelligentsia ranks. Proud of her rural roots, she was recruited into the Peasant Battalions (Bataliony Chłopskie, BCh) military organization in early 1943. While studying, she worked as their Warsaw command staff's liaison, toting messages to regional cells.[99] In May 1944, aboard a train from Warsaw to Skierniwice, she was caught with a suitcase full of clandestine publications wrapped in grey paper. Hauled back to Pawiak, Idzikowska was grilled on her contacts for a month but did not betray them. She was shot in the prison courtyard in June 1944. Her body was burned with the sixteen other women who shared her dawn execution.[100]

A veritable army of ambitious young people shared Idzikowska's risks, some from Warsaw and others drawn there to study, fight, or intrigue. A team of contact girls, mechanics, assistants, and radio operators clustered around Stefan Korboński in one of the strangest wartime information manipulation schemes. In this case, those working against the Germans stumbled into one another without deliberate coordination as a "happy accident" of conspiracy.

Stefan Korboński, like Kamiński, wore a number of hats and was first introduced as the intermediary between Maciej Rataj and Mieczysław Niedziałkowski before their murder at Palmiry. Shaped by the Polish Socialist Party (PPS), Korboński was a soldier in the Polish-Bolshevik War, studied law in Poznań, moved to Warsaw to open a legal practice, and joined the Polish People's Party (PSL) as Rataj's protégé.[101] In 1938 Korboński married Zofia Ristau (1915–2010), a Warsaw journalist, and they worked as a team in the underground, a formidable intelligentsia duo.[102] Korboński was a lieutenant in the Polish Army in 1939 and imprisoned by the NKVD, from whom he escaped.[103] Returning to Warsaw, Rataj put him to work.[104]

[98] Anna Pawełczyńska toted *Pobudka* and *Orzeł Biały*. She was arrested on August 15, 1942 and spent nine months in Serbia before transfer to Auschwitz. Anna Pawełczyńska, *Dary losu* (Łomianki: Wydawnictwo LTW, 2013), 80–82.

[99] Kabzińska's *Sylwetki Kobiet-Żolnierzy (II)*, Służba Polek na frontach II Wojny Światowej – 10, 118–120.

[100] Domańska, *Pawiak więzienie gestapo*, 471, 478.

[101] Piotr Stanek, *Stefan Korboński (1901–1989): Działalność polityczna i społeczna* (Warsaw: IPN, 2014), 30–36.

[102] Korbońska said she was "his closest collaborator." Roman W. Rybicki, "*Piękna Zosia:*" *Pamięci Zofii Korobońskiej* (Warsaw: Wydawnictwo Rytm, 2011), 15.

[103] Kabzińska, *Sylwetki Kobiet-Żolnierzy (II)*, Służba Polek na frontach II Wojny Światowej – 10, 181.

[104] Stefan Korboński, "Rola 'Trójkąta' w Polsce Podziemnej" *in Maciej Rataj we wspomnieniach współczesnych* (Warsaw: Ludowa Spółdzielnia Wydawnicza, 1984), 234.

Korboński continued to build underground political life after Rataj's death. He focused on communication, and in 1941 became the head of the Directorate of Civilian Resistance (Kierownictwo Walki Cywilnej, KWC), linking conspiracies to information sources.[105]

Radio, which was his darling, obsessed him: how to get Poles back on the air? Varsovians had not heard their own radio since Starzyński's last broadcast. Korboński's wife Zofia – "Zosia" – Korbońska deciphered a 1942 message about a "secret underground radio station" broadcasting in Poland alongside the BBC.[106] This mysterious station used the name "Świt" (Dawn). German monitors pinpointed transmission sites and raided radio operations, so the station's continued broadcasts were puzzling. Świt's broadcasts delighted Poles and made "the Germans wild with rage" since they could not locate it.[107] Korboński and his team were enlisted to maintain what was in fact an illusion: Świt was broadcasting from London, not Warsaw. Nevertheless, they kept the deception authentic. Korboński, his wife, and their assistants furiously wired local news details to London, a ruse the Soviets realized quickly but the Germans did not.[108] The idea of Polish radio was heartening to those who heard its broadcasts, and it broke crucial news, including announcing the discovery of bodies at Katyń and the outbreak of resistance in the ghetto in 1943.[109] Korboński claimed its main victory was "terrorizing the Germans," who invested considerable resources to destroy it.[110] Though it cost the lives of multiple conspirators, the Świt scheme was a counterstroke against German information control *in* Warsaw from both inside *and* outside the city, confirming international support for its conspirators while masquerading as a local initiative.[111]

5.6   International Couriering

Serious political planning needed outside aid and that meant breaking the German information quarantine.[112] Warsaw's political future hinged on

---

[105] Stefan Korboński, *W imieniu Rzeczypospolitej* (Warsaw: Wydawnictwo Bellona, 1991), 56–99; Stanek, *Stefan Korboński*, 66–78.

[106] "Rzeczpospolita," 17.III.2010; Rybicki, *"Piękna Zosia,"* 39.

[107] Korboński, *Fighting Warsaw*, 204, 209.

[108] The Soviets had "Kościuszko" station. Korboński, *Fighting Warsaw*, 213; KHPSGL, *Polskie Siły Zbrojne*, Tom III: *Armia Krajowa*, 701–702.

[109] Kabzińska's *Sylwetki Kobiet-Żolnierzy (II)*, Służba Polek na frontach II Wojny Światowej – 10, 183; Stanek, *Stefan Korboński*, 73, 75.

[110] Korboński, *W imieniu Rzeczypospolitej*, 179; BABL R102/II/17, Gouverneur des Distrikts Warschau, Der Pressechef der Regierung des GG-Informations-Abteilung: "Vertrauliche Informationen," 25.11.1943, 7 of report.

[111] USHMM RG-50.012.0046, AN: 1989.67.46, "Interview with Stefan and Sophia Korbonski," Part 2, 24:00–25:50.

[112] Longerich, *Himmler*, 747–748. Paderewski countered Nazi propaganda (AAN 2/100/3064 Archiwum Ignacego Jana Paderewskiego: "Gdy pierwsze bomby . . . "; AAN 2/100/

keeping Polish suffering on the agendas of French, British, American, and perhaps even Soviet politicians. Information from Warsaw enabled the exile government to function, as it was meaningless disconnected from the situation "at home." Current detail on the occupation legitimated exile authority with still-invested belligerents.[113] Beyond these practicalities, sending information out of Warsaw was a political statement that Polish life continued despite German persecution.

The need to get information out of occupied Warsaw was pressing. The problem was that it was very difficult to do. German power policy depended on their information monopoly, both in the *Altreich* and in conquered territories, and this was enforced by an elaborate system of identification papers and guarded borders. Overcoming these hurdles required secrecy and guile.[114] A network of Polish agents and local handlers nevertheless couriered sensitive information around Europe. The number of people involved in this clandestine traffic is difficult to estimate, and their paper trail was deliberately obscured. For those captured by German, Soviet, or other hostile forces, that faint trail disappeared entirely.

The Polish international courier was a particular sort of person. The domestic courier, too, had a "typical" face – a woman's – but there was more diversity at home, as the trips were shorter, the terrain familiar, and the work mostly in Polish.[115] To leave Poland with information, let alone return, required specific attributes: a position within a conspiracy with the means for such a venture, robust physical health, a good memory, liquid assets, and foreign currency (supplied by the conspiracy, but private means were no impediment), the ability to "pass" in a number of different guises, and knowledge of foreign languages and customs. Other particulars might be required, like the ability to ski, unaccented Russian, or a plausible identity as, say, a chemical engineer or surgeon, if that was the cover. Well-connected, well-educated people who had traveled abroad and served in the military – intelligentsia – were the pool from which couriers were drawn.[116]

3072 Archiwum Ignacego Jana Paderewskiego: Situation in the GG . . . ; AAN 2/100/ 1030 Archiwum Ignacego Jana Paderewskiego: My Dear American Friends . . .).

[113] Jonathan Walker estimated Poles provided 80,000+ reports to British intelligence. Walker, *Poland Alone*, 86.

[114] Wireless communications and cryptography thrived; Warsaw University student Marian Rejewski broke the German "enigma" code. Max Hastings, *The Secret War: Spies, Ciphers, and Guerrillas* (New York: Harper Collins, 2016), 47, 12–13; Richard A. Woytak, *On the Border of War and Peace: Polish Intelligence and Diplomacy in 1937–1939 and the Origins of the Ultra Secret* (Boulder: East European Quarterly, 1979).

[115] Zawacka was the exception that proved the rule. Minczykowska, *Cichociemna Generał Elżbieta Zawacka "Zo,"* 125–129.

[116] Intelligentsia were impoverished: Karol Wojtyła, later Pope John Paul II, worked in the Zakrzówek mines. George Weigel, *Witness to Hope: The Biography of John Paul II, 1920–2005* (New York: Harper Perennial, 2005), 56; Jan Paweł II, *Autobiografia* (Krakow: Wydawnictwo Literackie, 2003), 24–25.

The Polish wartime international courier *par excellence* was a man we have already met: Jan Karski ("Witold"), who was born Jan Romuald Kozielewski in Łódź before the First World War and who leaked news of the Holocaust to the Western Allies.[117] Karski ended up by accident or design in some of the crucial theaters of wartime conflict. The youngest of four, Karski was a devout Catholic who grew up surrounded by Jewish friends.[118] His early life crisscrossed Poland in a way possible for a young man of his means and class. His elder brother, Marian Kozielewski, was police commandant and security chief in Starzyński's Warsaw, a valuable contact.[119] Though born in Łódź (which now and then functioned as a commuter city of Warsaw), he went to high school in Częstochowa and then to the Jan Kazimierz University in Lwów, where he studied law and diplomacy. He traveled extensively across Europe, completed his military service requirement, and trained in the consular staff.[120] He was mobilized in 1939, but missed most of the actual combat.[121] Captured by the Red Army, Karski disguised his officer status, got himself traded to the Germans, escaped from a Wehrmacht POW camp outside Radom, and headed straight to Warsaw.[122]

Though not a Varsovian by birth, the capital was Karski's home during the early occupation, and he had family and friends there who initiated him into conspiratorial work. In addition to Polish, Karski spoke French, German, and English, and he could understand or make himself understood in Russian, Czech, Slovak, and, when desperate, Hungarian.[123] He had lived, worked, or visited most of Europe's major cities and had a sprawling network of friends, colleagues, and acquaintances. He also had overwhelming personal motivation to resist Nazi Germany, sourced in his intelligentsia background: the Germans had invaded his country but Polish army retreat had denied him his fight,

---

[117] Karski's views are in his *Secret State* and his *Great Powers and Poland*.

[118] Marian Marek Drozdowski, *Jan Karski Kozielewski (1914–2000)* (Warsaw: Oficyna Wydawnicza Aspra, 2014), 32.

[119] E. Thomas Wood and Stanisław Jankowski, *Karski: How One Man Tried to Stop the Holocaust* (New York: John Wiley & Sons, 1994), 26; Grabowski, *Na posterunku*, 252–253.

[120] Karski worked with Starzyński and met Goering in 1935. Drozdowski, *Jan Karski Kozielewski*, 50; Maciej Sadowski, *Jan Karski: Photobiography* (Warsaw: Narodowy Bank Polski, 2014), 29–31.

[121] This "missed" war shaped those too young to fight. The best literature on a "war youth generation" as the foundation of later radicalism is on Germans who became Nazi extremists. Longerich, *Himmler*, 19–26, 738; Wildt, *Uncompromising Generation*, 11.

[122] Many underground leaders were escaped POWs. Wallace, *Life and Death in Captivity*, 7, 9. German and Romanian authorities turned a blind eye to escapes. Kenneth K. Koskodan, *No Greater Ally: The Untold Story of Poland's Forces in World War II* (Oxford: Osprey Publishing, 2009), 39; 43; Konrad Jarausch, *Reluctant Accomplice: A Wehrmacht Soldier's Letters from the Eastern Front* (Princeton: Princeton University Press, 2011), 94.

[123] Karski, *Secret State*, 1, 105–106, 158.

which frustrated him enormously and made him feel that he had contributed insufficiently to his country's defense; his social station made his family targets of Tannenberg and AB, but he returned to Warsaw in November 1939, "missing" the first arrests, but losing a brother, brother-in-law, and a number of friends in the process; his status as an escaped officer criminalized his existence, leaving him few options for aboveground life.[124] His two prewar activities, soldiering and studying, were forbidden. Karski was also twenty-five, unmarried, unmoored by the war, and eager for adventure.[125]

There are several stories about how Karski became a conspirator but his ending up there was overdetermined.[126] According to the tale he told in *Secret State* (published when friends might still be implicated), he was drawn in by a friend, Jerzy Dziepatowski, days after getting to Warsaw.[127] Dziepatowski – a violin-playing assassin – and Karski had become friends at university as self-conscious young intelligentsia eager to politicize the Lwów peasantry. Karski had toured the countryside giving "rousing" (his claim) lectures on "history, Polish literature, hygiene, or the co-operative movement." Dziepatowski had livened things up by playing the violin.[128] Their 1939 re-acquaintance continued this prewar project of Polish consciousness-building.

Karski did not really need friends to draw him into politics when family could.[129] His brother, Marian, was Polish police chief – like his boss, Stefan Starzyński, he remained at his post – and also trying to build an anti-Nazi conspiracy within the blue police.[130] The brothers met in fall 1939 in a pew

---

[124] His brother Marian was released from Auschwitz in 1941; his brother-in law Aleksander was shot by the Gestapo. Snyder, "Biographical Essay of Jan Karski" in *Secret State*, xxvii; USHMM RG-50.012.0044, AN: 1989.67.44, "Interview with Jan Karski," Part 2, 1:36–2:30.

[125] Bachelorhood made him eligible. Karski later married Pola Nireńska (1910–92), a Holocaust survivor, in 1965. Sadowski, *Jan Karski: Photobiography*, 36, 129; on spouses as leverage: Józef Garliński, *Survival of Love: Memoirs of a Resistance Officer* (Oxford: Basil Blackwell, 1991), ix.

[126] Karski and Korboński were friends. Korboński, *Fighting Warsaw*, 41; Drozdowski, *Jan Karski Kozielewski*, 66.

[127] Jerzy Dziepatowski was Jerzy Gintowt-Dziewałtowski, from a family of political activists His uncle, the lawyer Władysław Gintowt-Dziewałtowski, was shot at Palmiry in June 1940. File 11623 1, RG-68.112M Ghetto Fighters' House (Beit Lohamei Haghetaot), United States Holocaust Memorial Museum (USHMM), Washington, DC; Wardzyńska, *Był rok 1939*, 262.

[128] Karski was conscious of the gap between himself and others: "in Poland, unfortunately, many of the intelligentsia ... knew the peasants only from books and movies." He was touched by patriotic "commoners," since he associated patriotism with the elite (Karski, *Secret State*, 55–56). This conflation of class with patriotism is the mark of gentry status (Jakubowska, *Patrons of History*, 16).

[129] Drozdowski, *Jan Karski Kozielewski*, 65–68.

[130] Until May 1940 when he left his official post. Litwiński, "Policja Granatowa" in *Porządek publiczny i bezpieczeństwo*, 92, 111–115; Grabowski, *Na posterunku*, 23, 38, 252.

Figure 5.2 Jan Karski during his mission to the United States, July 1943.
United States Holocaust Memorial Museum, Photograph Number 90533.

of Holy Cross Church, a stone's throw from the old police headquarters. The elder brother updated the younger on Gestapo behavior, and likely secured him a new "official" identity.[131] A few months later Marian Kozielewski was arrested, tortured in Pawiak, and sent with a massive intelligentsia transport to Auschwitz in August 1940, from which he was released in 1941.[132]

The Polish Victory Service, the group that Dziepatowski and his brother pulled Karski into (about which he knew little except that it was patriotic, included those he trusted, and offered him work), would send him across Poland, into the Soviet Union, to France, and eventually to Great Britain and the United States (Figure 5.2). It would also sicken him, starve him, lock him in a barrel, get him imprisoned and nearly beaten to death, knock out his teeth, drive him to attempt suicide, and leave him as a permanent exile in the United States. A quick study with a fantastically good memory made Karski – his first pseudonym was Jan Kucharski – an obvious international courier.[133] His education often betrayed him to workmen and peasants, but he pulled off several disguises, including that of a teacher and a gentleman gardener.[134] After two 1940 test assignments during AB, Karski's big mission was in fall

[131] Wood and Jankowski, *Karski*, 28–30.
[132] Domańska, *Pawiak więzienie gestapo*, 58; 79–80.
[133] He worked for ZWZ after 1941 monitoring radio. Sadowski, *Jan Karski: Photobiography*, 66–68.
[134] Karski, *Secret State*, 61, 185.

1942. Tasked with getting to London through occupied Paris and contacting the exiles, his role was informational: to brief London Poles about all active political parties in Warsaw so they could appreciate the diversity of the anti-Nazi underground.[135] He also briefed the British government and then headed to the United States. Karski was courier and propagandist, a walking, talking endorsement for Western Allied intervention in Eastern Europe.

To prepare for this mission, Karski oriented himself in the opposition landscape. In summer 1942, that meant understanding underground Polish *and* Polish-Jewish life, which was crumbling as the ghetto was liquidated. The Polish story was complicated enough, requiring numerous meetings with leaders of major political factions. To learn the Jewish story, Karski embarked on the undertaking already discussed: like his compatriot Witold Pilecki, he snuck into the antisemitic persecution system. Conscious of the gulf between the Polish and Polish-Jewish elites, Karski queried two Jewish leaders in October 1942, one a Zionist, the other a Bundist, paralleling his representation of politics outside the ghetto.[136] These men made it possible for him to update the London Poles on Polish politics *and* Polish-Jewish politics, by then separated by an unbridgeable gulf of different persecutions.[137]

Carrying microfilm hidden in a key documenting Nazi atrocities, Karski relayed these details to Władysław Sikorski, exile prime minister, Władysław Raczkiewicz, exile president, British foreign secretary Anthony Eden, British military leaders, and later in the United States to President Franklin Roosevelt, Felix Frankfurter, justice of the Supreme Court, and Jewish community leaders.[138] Churchill ignored him and his British reception was "chilly," a fallout of increasing British dependence on the Soviet Union.[139] His 1942 mission did not secure Western Allied intervention but it did reinforce ties between Warsaw and the London Poles.

In the United States there were more possibilities since Americans were less dependent on the Soviets than Britons. American policies, as Karski characterized them, were fluidly "pragmatic" in late 1942 and early 1943, and had been worked on by the Polish-American community since 1939.[140] "Roosevelt,"

---

[135] His summary of the four parties – Socialists, Nationalists (ND), Peasant Party, and Christian Labor movement – is an exercise in restraint. Karski, *Secret State*, 121–126.

[136] The Bundist was Leon Feiner (1885–1945) who joined Żegota. Karski, *Secret State*, 302.

[137] Karski, *Secret State*, 314–315.

[138] Frankfurter disbelieved Karski but Roosevelt asked questions. Karski, *Secret State*, 358–366; Sadowski, *Jan Karski: Photobiography*, 82–83.

[139] Rafael Medoff, "The Man Who Told FDR About the Holocaust," *The Algemeiner*, July 17, 2013: www.algemeiner.com/2013/07/17/the-man-who-told-fdr-about-the-holocaust/#

[140] Pianist Artur Rubinstein and tenor Jan Kiepura performed at the New York Metropolitan Opera "for the cause of the Polish refugees." Artur Rubinstein, *Moje długie życie*, Tom 2 (Krakow: Polskie Wydawnictwo Muzyczne, 1988), 513.

Karski remembered, "received him with both interest and sympathy," though he made no commitments.[141] Ironically, the success of Karski's mission brought his couriering to an end, as his international reception made him too public a figure to risk another covert trip. Only around thirty men succeeded, and Karski retired with German rumors already swirling in Warsaw that he was "a Bolshevik agent in the pay of American Jews."[142]

While in London, Karski ran into another college friend, Jerzy Lerski ("Jur," 1917–92), whom he recruited into the same network going in the opposite direction: London to Warsaw.[143] They had similar biographies. Lerski was younger than Karski, a native of Lwów and the son of an army surgeon, a social democrat and a philosemite. Mobilized as a reserve officer in the anti-aircraft artillery, Lerski was captured by the Red Army in 1939, escaped, and returned to Lwów. With the NKVD on his trail, he fled Soviet-occupied Poland, followed the Polish armies through Hungary, and contacted friends in Budapest.[144] With their help, he made his way to England and began working for Władysław Sikorski and the London exiles. Lerski, a historian and legal scholar, knew decent German and French, and understood Ukrainian.[145] He was a part of the London Polish elite, "acting as the emissary of General Sikorski, Mikołajczyk, and Arciszewski."[146] Under Karski's tutelage, Lerski returned to Poland as one of the *cichociemni*, the "silent and unseen," a group of 316 men (and 1 woman) parachuted in to aid anti-Nazi resistance on Western Allied funding.[147]

Dropped outside Warsaw on February 21, 1943, Lerski got his bearings. The lawyer-turned-paratrooper holed up in his hostess's spare room, reading the *Bulletin* and *Rzeczpospolita*, before venturing out to attend Mass. Using the name Jerzy Gordziewicz (conspirators often retained Christian names in aliases), he tried to avoid being recognized. Despite his efforts, the Gestapo arrested his hostess and her family, and he ran into his old dentist (a Jewish

---

[141] London Poles kept track of American attitudes. Karski, *Great Powers and Poland*, 357, 365–366; PISM London: MID: Dział Polski, A. 10. 4/1, Robert Sherwood Memorandum, May 22, 1940, [1]-2.

[142] "He wrote memoirs, as did others: Karski's *Secret State*, Jerzy Lerski's *Emisariusz Jur* (Warsaw: Oficyna Wydawnicza Interim, 1989), 6, and fellow Warsaw *inteligent* Jan Jeziorański (1914–2005) or "Jan Nowak" and his *Courier from Warsaw* (Detroit: Wayne State University Press, 1982); USHMM RG-50.012.0044, AN: 1989.67.44, "Interview with Jan Karski," Part 2, 2:45–3:25.

[143] Karski, *Secret State*, 95, 112.

[144] Including Wanda Modlibowska. Kabzińska's *Sylwetki Kobiet-Żolnierzy (II)*, Służba Polek na frontach II Wojny Światowej – 10, 285.

[145] He had a borderlands accent. Lerski, *Emisariusz Jur*, 9–13; 23; 87.

[146] Karski, *Great Powers and Poland*, 447 n. 22.

[147] The woman was Elżbieta Zawacka. Jankowski, *Z fałszywym Ausweisem*, Tom 1, 400–422; *The Unseen and Silent: Adventures from the Underground Movement Narrated by Paratroops of the Polish Home Army* (London: Sheed and Ward, 1954).

man in hiding), his cousin, and his own father on the streets of Warsaw.[148] This was the drawback of intelligentsia connections: disguises didn't hold up well with one's own.

Lerski realized how quickly things changed in Warsaw. He brought recommendations for political positions the nominees for which had been arrested by the time he arrived. He was introduced to leaders in the emerging "secret state," meeting them in a café, or by a gravestone in the Powązki cemetery. He met Stefan Korboński on the steps of the National Museum in March 1943. Korboński used Lerski (as he had used Karski) to explain problems to London.[149] He also met with Zygmunt Zaremba, the hardened socialist who rallied the Polish Socialist Party in 1939. Afterwards he talked his way through the right wing, including Stefan Sacha and the underground Endecja – though they were not Lerski's political comrades. This was a lot of people, most a generation older than he, and almost all on the run. One connection came through Karski's brother: Kozielewski knew the still-active Pilsudskiites (indeed, he was one), and put Lerski in touch.[150] These men's politics diverged from Sikorski and the exiles but were vital in underground Warsaw.[151] The hard right, including the fascist National Armed Forces (Narodowe Siły Zbrojne; NSZ), ignored Lerski because they were unwilling to subordinate themselves to the exiles. Other pre-war radical nationalists were willing to bring Lerski up to speed on their accomplishments. Lerski returned to London to update the exiles, in a hurry to clarify the situation before it shifted. He left just before the outbreak of the Ghetto Uprising in April 1943 and returned to London as Karski sailed for the United States.

Karski and Lerski, prewar colleagues, represented the way that the social and political networks of the intelligentsia made wartime communication, and hence conspiracy, possible. Though their missions were secret, they had Polish and international publics. Karski published his reports in book form as *Story of a Secret State*. Lerski's information appeared in London publications and his postwar academic career promulgated it further. Though there was considerable sympathy for the Polish plight abroad, Karski's information on Jewish persecution was not believed.[152] Had it been, it would not have changed the fate of Warsaw's Jewish community: when Karski met with Roosevelt in July 1943 the last uprising in the ghetto had been crushed, and most Warsaw Jews were already dead. When Lerski brought his final report to London, careful compromises between the postwar visions of right-wing nationalists

---

[148] Lerski, *Emisariusz Jur*, 85–87.
[149] Korboński, *W imieniu Rzeczypospolitej*, 36.
[150] Wood and Jankowski, *Karski*, 26.
[151] Lerski, *Emisariusz Jur*, 95–97.
[152] Hanna Kozlowska, "How a Polish Courier Tried to Tell the World About the Holocaust," Passport, *Foreign Affairs*, April 24, 2014: http://foreignpolicy.com/2014/04/24/how-a-polish-courier-tried-to-tell-the-world-about-the-holocaust/.

and socialists were about to be steamrolled by the imposition of a Soviet-backed communist government in eastern Poland. In the laborious traffic of Warsaw secrets even the best information had its limits.

5.7 Polish Propaganda Abroad

The London exiles were Karski's 1942 destination, and they played a preeminent role in informing the world about Warsaw, leveraging Polish suffering to secure an independent state in the postwar world the Allies would surely design. (This project failed primarily because Stalin opposed it.[153]) As the war expanded, first with German conquests and then with Grand Alliance advances in 1943, the Polish story was drowned in an ocean of violence. The arrival of war at the doorsteps of the French and British in 1940 was a double-edged sword: it made the dangers of Nazism real to Poland's allies, but it also preoccupied them with their own travails. Making the case for material aid for Poland when so many were in distress was one of the Polish exiles' aims, and they agonized over how to portray occupied Poland to secure maximum help. For this they needed detail from Warsaw.

The London Poles were separated from Warsaw by more than 1000 miles, a distance lengthened by the German-friendly regimes between them. The initial government evacuation in 1939, and a second departure from Angers (in western France) during the fall of France in summer 1940 compounded difficulties. The early Paris Information and Documentation Center and the mature London Ministry of Information and Documentation (Ministerstwo Informacji i Dokumentacji, MID) worked with organizations in Warsaw and across Europe to obtain up-to-date information.[154] MID tabulated atrocities, decrees, thefts, and the names of the known dead.[155] The Polish Ministry of Information compiled two "black books" for Allied propaganda. They countered Ludwig Fischer's lavish volumes on the "revitalization" of Warsaw and the Baedeker guide to the GG. The first black book came out in 1940 and the second in 1942, almost 600 pages long, including photographs of executions and urban destruction.[156] These were the proof of Nazi barbarity that was

---

[153] Kochanski, *Eagle Unbowed*, 434–463.

[154] Stanisław Strzetelski (1895–1969) and Stanisław Stroński (1882–1955), nationalist politicians evacuated through Romania, led MID. MID received information through Paris, Stockholm, Trieste, Bucharest, Budapest, Rome, and the Vatican. PISM London: MID: Dział Polski, A.10. 4/4.

[155] In October 1940, MID received a 21-page list of German thefts. PISM London: MID: Dział Polski, A. 10. 4/4, "Sprawozdanie o Zniszczeniach Kulturalnych w Kraju," October 31, 1940.

[156] Polish Ministry of Information, *German Invasion of Poland: Polish Black Book Containing Documents, Authenticated Reports, and Photographs* (London: Hutchinson & Co., 1940).

supposed to draw Allied aid, and they were prepared in English and French (but not Russian) editions.

Showcasing the most provocative violence, the second Black Book opened with 100 pages on "massacres and tortures." "What the Germans did in Belgium [in 1914], terrible as it was, seems comparatively innocuous" when confronted with Nazi behavior a generation later, the ministry explained. It detailed ghettoization, and attacks on culture, language, and the Catholic Church.[157] The "Poland fights on" conclusion was tailor-made for the Allied audience: Poland was – *still* – a real ally. This was key: resistance became ubiquitous across Nazi Europe, but its efficacy was often limited. The Poles had to make an evidence-based case that their resisters were not merely isolated individuals but an army.[158] Despite hundreds of thousands of corpses, the Black Book pointed to a formidable movement worth supporting:

> The Germans hope . . . to murder one of the great European nations . . . In German plans, all that remains of the Polish nation after its intellectual classes have been crushed, its numbers have been greatly reduced, its arts and cultural treasures have been plundered, and the entire country devastated, is to be reduced to a German colony . . . The Poles are fighting so stubbornly and with such sacrifices that they occupy the leading place among those who though oppressed yet struggle . . .[159]

Maintaining this careful teeter-totter of Allied opinion, presenting a Poland that was heroic but not pathetic, kept MID busy. Its London offices were the last stop on Warsaw's information train, the result of painstaking efforts: coded messages, hidden letters, memorized passwords, paper-wrapped packages, and couriers snuck out of the city and across the continent at massive human cost.

5.8 Conclusion

This story of the Warsaw intelligentsia's information war is one of men and women who had traveled in the same circles prewar, shared formative experiences during the war, and who plunged – or slipped – into conspiratorial activities for similar reasons, often at one another's instigation. Their work against Nazi information control was essential because "legal" information was tailored to keep Warsaw passive and afraid. Conspirators often had dual underground and aboveground lives, or positions in multiple conspiratorial organizations. Securing and communicating good information within Warsaw and

---

[157] Polish Ministry of Information, *German New Order*, vii–xiv, 17–18.

[158] Their arguments earned them at least $12 million and American weapons and supplies. USHMM RG-50.012.0044, AN: 1989.67.44, "Interview with Jan Karski," Part 3, 17:13–18:07.

[159] Polish Ministry of Information, *German New Order*, 565, 571.

outside it was the foundation of all conspiracies, and a world of its own. Much of the intelligentsia, like Janina Regulska, Czesław Miłosz, Zofia Kossakowska-Szanacja, and Ludwik Landau, wrote: for themselves, their families, and posterity. Zofia Kossak wrote voluminously and doing so aided her Holocaust rescue work. Kamiński's *Bulletin* role intertwined with his scouting and Home Army projects. Illegal printing involved Michał Wojewódzki and Jerzy Rutkowski, who met at Warsaw University. College friends – or perhaps family – drew Karski into couriering, and he pulled in Jerzy Lerski, who Stefan Korboński briefed in 1943, who got intel from friends and from the *Bulletin*, which reported news from Kamiński's friends and colleagues, all of which was toted around the city at great risk by adventurous young people, predominately women, some of whom also studied, and many of whom died. Korboński sent information to London to sustain the Świt radio plot; he also used it to make decisions for the secret state. The story of their exploits was carried out of the city by friends and comrades to be utilized in London, Paris, and Washington, DC.

The network intelligentsia information traffickers built required enormous trust. Owning a radio, using printing equipment, reading or owning illegal publications, and criticizing the Nazis were all punishable by imprisonment or execution. Elites drew from prewar micro-communities, networks of familiarity built out of family, school, political, and class connections. These men and women were initiated into information trafficking people very close to them – sisters, spouses, school friends. They were then drawn into further, overlapping conspiracies led by those they knew.

In the underground publishing world, the intelligentsia wrote, edited, and published. They also read, discussed, and responded to underground publications – sometimes with more publications. And they and their students, spouses, and children toted them around town. What they wrote was read by the larger public. "The secret press," Kossak remembered, "was read by everyone . . . a continuous, living protest and proof of the unyielding stance" Varsovians took against occupation.[160] The vibrancy of the underground information war demonstrated the durable role of the intelligentsia in shaping Polish behavior, the foundation upon which all opposition depended.

---

[160] AAN 2–1230–0 sygn. 76-III-57, "Uwagi Z. Kossak-Szczuckiej o prasie podziemnej Polski w czasie okupacji niemieckiej. Co wiem o prasie podziemnej," [2]; Drozdowski, *Jan Karski Kozielewski*, 96–97.

School of Hard Knocks
Illegal Education

Polish information was essential to break the German monopoly on knowledge. More ambitious still than trafficking in illegal information was the project to sustain knowledge. That, too, was banned. Of all responses to occupation, Warsaw's secret schools most directly challenged anti-intelligentsia persecution, and in doing so united many of the educated elite. The Nazis forbade higher education for Poles in order to prevent the rebuilding of the intelligentsia targeted in 1939–40. Poland's – and especially Warsaw's – secret educational system was formidable, and among its graduates were some of the leading lights of eastern Europe's twentieth century. The future pope, Karol Wojtyła, studied theater in Krakow, Miłosz took philosophy, and Miron Białoszewski worked on a philology degree.[1]

During Tannenberg and AB, the Gestapo both targeted the living intelligentsia and the institutions associated with them, especially education.[2] In its very first report from Warsaw, Einsatzgruppe IV claimed it had arrested 21 people, with teachers topping the list.[3] On October 8, 1939, the Gestapo reported the arrest of 354 "priests and teachers" distinguished by their "Polish chauvinism" and therefore a "danger to the security of German troops and German officials."[4] By late October 1939, it was illegal to study, enter university buildings, or possess, loan, or sell books and periodicals.[5]

[1] Wojtyła began at Jagiellonian University underground. Weigel, *Witness to Hope*, 44–87; Jacek Chrobaczyński, *Tajna szkoła w okupowanym Krakowie (1939-1945)* (Krakow: Wydawn. Literackie, 2000); Franaszek, *Miłosz*, 207; Białoszewski, *Memoir*, 5.
[2] The connection between education and rebellion was longstanding in Poland; education bans were also common to the slaveholding American South because study made enslaved persons and freedmen "rebellious." Angela Y. Davis, *Women, Race & Class* (New York: Vintage Books, 1983), 100–102, 106, 124; Fields and Fields, *Racecraft*, 86–87, 179.
[3] BABL R58 7154 Meldungen der EG bis zum 1.10.1939, 1200 Uhr," 191/187/192.
[4] BABL R58 7154 Tätigkeitsbericht, SiPo EG IV, Warschau, 10.10.1939, Point 9, 215/216.
[5] Dunin-Wąsowicz, *Warszawa w latach 1939-1945*, 162–168.

Underground education developed in fall 1939 under military occupation, constituting the first systematic resistance.[6] The university system also emerged as a "feminine" response to Nazism. In contrast to military conspiracy, study increasingly became the purview of women. As underground education expanded, it entangled teachers and young people in illegal and increasingly violent conspiracies.

6.1   Education Closure

Dismantling Polish education served multiple Nazi purposes.[7] It shut down the pipeline of new intelligentsia, streamlined German labor requisitions, and silenced teachers. Nazi Germany believed that educators, like priests, had dangerous influence. Fischer's propaganda volume *Warsaw under German Mastery* celebrated triumphs over "chauvinistic" teachers who provided "instruction in hatred of Germandom."[8] By "chauvinism," Fischer meant teachers' desire to instill patriotic feeling in young people through teaching Polish history and literature, which thwarted German goals.

The attack on education began when the Gestapo seized the Polish Ministry of Education on Szuch Boulevard.[9] Himmler and Goebbels took a keen interest in the Polish "educational question" (*Schulfrage*). While Volksdeutsche schools reopened in October 1939, Himmler believed no Polish child needed mathematics more advanced than "basic sums to 500." Because Poles were to be used as Reich laborers, "schools that teach just fundamentals, basic math, writing, and reading would alone be permitted."[10] Foreign languages, literature, and history were forbidden.

On November 15, 1939, the GG closed some primary schools, most secondary schools (retaining vocational and trade schools), and all higher education (universities, polytechnics, seminaries, and conservatories)

---

[6] Christiane Eberhardt, *Geheimes Schulwesen und konspirative Bildungspolitik der polischen Gesellschaft im Generalgouvernement, 1939–1945* (Frankfurt am Main: Peter Lang, 2003), 48.

[7] It was also visited on Czech intelligentsia: Prague schools closed. Bryant, *Prague in Black*, 60, 87, 192.

[8] Friedrich Gollert, *Warschau unter deutscher Herrschaft: Deutsche Aufbauarbeit im Distrikt Warschau* (Krakow: Burgverlag, 1942), 256. Nazi policy understood teachers as agents of national indoctrination, sending German female teachers into eastern Europe as agents of empire to build Nazi feeling in Volksdeutsche communities. Wendy Lower, *Hitler's Furies: German Women in the Nazi Killing Fields* (Boston: Houghton Mifflin Harcourt, 2013), 84, 101, 113–114.

[9] Janina Kaźmierska, *Szkolnictwo warszawskie w latach 1939–1944* (Warsaw: Państwowe Wydawnictwo Naukowe, 1980), 27.

[10] Eberhardt, *Geheimes Schulwesen*, 51–53; BABL R58 7154, "Meldungen der EG bis zum 5.10.1939, 1200 Uhr," 207/203/208.

because of an alleged typhus epidemic. Disease became a weapon against still-open schools inside and outside the ghetto.[11] Opening new schools required German approval and was therefore impossible.[12] The Ministry of Education closed and its personnel scattered. Acting minister Kazimierz Szelągowski liquidated ministry assets before being sent to Sachsenhausen.[13] In March 1940, the GG issued a school administration order (*Schulverwaltungsordnung*) and created an education inspectorate.[14] The inspectorate brought a wave of German administrators to Krakow and Warsaw, most of whom spoke no Polish, leaving more unemployed Polish educators in their wake.

The situation was worst for Polish-Jewish students, teachers, and professors. The "typhus closure" was antisemitic, and Jewish schools closed even before ghetto creation in November 1940. Polish-Jewish intelligentsia continued their children's education with private tutoring and informal schools, utilizing unemployed teachers. Those with limited means created home study programs.[15] Ewa Gurfinkiel, a young Polish-Jewish woman about to start university study in psychology, spent the next year teaching English classes instead. She had pupils booked 4–6 hours a day and her pay doubled from prewar rates. Gurfinkiel's experience demonstrates how Polish – and especially Polish-Jewish – intelligentsia families found creative responses to German anti-intellectualism.[16]

After November 1939, the occupation despoiled Warsaw schools, universities, and libraries, retaining some materials for Volksdeutsche.[17] This was in explicit contrast to German occupation behavior during the First World War. In 1915, General Governor von Beseler re-opened the university as a gesture of good will toward the intelligentsia. In 1939, Fischer's closure was another clear sign that Poles were excluded from the Nazi future.[18]

School closures meant unsupervised children. Fears about wayward youth escalated, and hysterical reporting claimed "countless young waifs, half crazed by their experiences, are straying about amid the ruins of Warsaw." The British press worried that "approximately twenty per cent of Warsaw children have become mentally deranged" and "could only be made into normal human beings

---

[11] Bartoszewski, *1859 dni Warszawy*, 83.

[12] Kaźmierska, *Szkolnictwo warszawskie*, 33.

[13] Wojciech Świętosławski (1881–1968) was minister of education and evacuated.

[14] Eberhardt, *Geheimes Schulwesen*, 55.

[15] USHMM ARG 667 1 Ring 1 70, "O nauczaniu prywatnym, dokształcającym i pozaszkolnym w obszarze żydowskim w Warszawie," 10 grudnia 1940, 1–2.

[16] USHMM ARG 658 Ring I 40, Młodzież w Komitetach Domowych: Gurfinkiel, Ewa, ur. 1921 r., [1].

[17] Gollert and Fischer, *Warschau unter deutchen Herrschaft*, 76, 248–255.

[18] Kauffman, *Elusive Alliance*, 165–190.

[again] by very careful education."[19] Though reports about "derangement" were sensationalist, without school, youth pursued forbidden activites. The intelligentsia raised their children to attend university and replace them in the professions, universities, and government. The ban created an existential crisis: if the youth intelligentsia continued on this course, they would become criminals. Being a student during occupation was always political: those who "merely" studied were not playing it safe.[20] Between 1941 and 1944, there were over 4,000 arrests linked to illegal education. Considering underground university student enrollment numbered around 5,000, these rates were extraordinary.[21]

Closures provoked a two-pronged educational resistance. At the university level, it meant underground instruction. At the secondary level, there was a creative compromise: some junior high (*gimnazja*) and high schools (*licea*) remained open with approved official and secret supplementary curricula.[22] Others rebranded themselves as technical or vocational schools, and a few operated entirely underground.

Secondary schools and universities strove to maintain rigorous standards so their efforts would be recognized postwar. Even so, there was an attitude of seizing the moment to embrace Polish high culture, infusing the electricity of the forbidden into the humdrum of study. Private reading, musical evenings, modestly staged theatrical performances, and impromptu poetry recitals (Mickiewicz was a favorite) proliferated in intelligentsia circles.[23] A thousand crimes – traveling to class on forged identity papers or with a stolen transit pass, carrying books, staying out past curfew – entered student life and might provoke arrest, interrogation, or execution. Many students were also engaged in other conspiracies, entangling them further in a blurry underground intelligentsia world. Elżbieta Centkowska described this muddle:

> Danger was intensified by the fact that all, or nearly all the people involved in the circles of secret education also worked for other parts of the underground struggle. Lectures and university recitations, spirited discussions on interesting themes, literary evenings, organized by different conspiracy groups – they

---

[19] PISM London: MID: Dział Polski, A. 10. 4/4, "Germany's Death Space: Str. 146," 2.

[20] Attendance was as high as 80 percent. *Polskie Siły Zbrojne w drugiej wojnie światowej: Armia Krajowa*, 93; Gella, *Inteligencja polska*, 133–142.

[21] Manteuffel gives 3,500 for UW (Tadeusz Manteuffel, *Uniwersytet Warszawski w latach wojny i okupacji: Kronika 1939/40–1944/45* (Warsaw: UW Imprint, 1948), 14–17, 21). Centkowska gives 3,700 for UW and 1,200 for UZZ (Centkowska, *Na tajnych kompletach*, 7).

[22] The delegation created an education department in spring 1940. Eberhardt, *Geheimes Schulwesen*, 126–127.

[23] Ryszard Czugajewski remembered "patriotic evenings" of poetry and Chopin (Czugajewski, *Na Barykadach, w kanalach i gruzach Czerniakowa* (Warsaw: Instytut Wydawniczy Pax, 1970), 64). In late 1944, a revue with singing, dance, and drama was held at Syrena theater (Stanisława Mrozińska, *Teatr wśród ruin Warszawy* (Warsaw: Państwowy Instytut Wydawniczy, 1989), 33–39).

all provided for a certain kind of intellectual entertainment for both the lecturers and the students engaged in other forms of conspiratorial activity. Conspiracies met in the very same places where classes and social celebrations were held. The majority of female students dedicated a few hours each day to couriering or colportage, and male students finished secret officer training programs, worked in secret youth organizations, or in conspiratorial press.[24]

Students, like their parents and teachers, became multifaceted violators of Nazi anti-intelligentsia regulations.

6.2 Wartime Secondary Education

Junior high and high schools educated Warsaw youth, making various compromises along the way. Some held "secret study groups" in which "teachers would go from one private house to another, at the risk of dire punishment," hoping students could pass the *matura*, the comprehensive high school finishing exam.[25] Two secondary schools, one in the Żoliborz neighborhood and the other downtown, provide insight into this process. Prince Józef Poniatowski boys junior high and high school on Invalid Square (Państwowe Gimnazjum i Liceum Męskie im. Księcia Józefa Poniatowskiego w Warszawie) operated in two modes as an approved vocational school (*"jawny"*) and as a secret high school (*"tajny"*). The private Bolesław Prus boys' junior high school on Jasna Street in the city center (Prywatne Gimnazjum Męskie im. Bolesława Prusa w Warszawie) operated underground. Despite widespread wartime destruction, both have extant records.

Officially, the Poniatowski School was State Vocational School Number 5.[26] Tadeusz Dąbrowski (1888–1944) directed it from its September 1940 reopening through the uprising. Dąbrowski studied engineering at the Kiev Polytechnic before moving to Warsaw and spoke Polish, German, and Russian.[27] Officially, the Poniatowski School was a vocational school that happened to be using the old building.[28] To keep the Germans happy,

---

[24] Centkowska used Warsaw Teachers' Union archives to write the only illegal education study. Elżbieta Centkowska, *Na tajnych kompletach* (Warsaw: Wydawnictwo Szkolne i Pedagogiczne, 1974), 9, 68. On another military-education double conspirator, see Bronisław Pietraszewicz in Piotr Stachiewicz, *Akcja "Kutschera"* (Warsaw: Książka i Wiedza, 1982), 59.

[25] Zbigniew Czajkowski, *Warsaw 1944: An Insurgent's Journal of the Uprising* (Barnsley: Pen & Sword Military, 2012), x.

[26] Państwowe Kursy Przygotowywawcze do Szkół Zawodowych II Nr. 5/Staatlicher Vorbereitungsjahrgang für Fachschulen Nr. 5.

[27] He died in the uprising (https://www.1944.pl/ofiary-cywilne/tomasz-vel-tadeusz-dabrowski,6736.html); (APmstW-M, Państwowe Gimnazjum i Liceum Męskie im. Księcia Józefa Poniatowskiego w Warszawie (hereafter: Gimazjum/Liceum Poniatowski), z. 275/0, s. 628, Personel szkoły, "Nr. 74/41: Zaświadczenie," 40, 44).

[28] APmstW-M, Gimazjum/Liceum Poniatowski, z. 275/0, s. 630, "Sprawa: Korzystanie z lokalu i inwentarza Gimnazjum im. Ks. Józefa Poniatowskiego," 28.VIII.1940 1.

Dąbrowski and his teachers followed a minute system of bilingual reporting, specifying each course of study. While education is always bureaucratic, this level of documentation was especially cumbersome for the beleaguered faculty. It also meant the Gestapo had a detailed schedule with teachers' contact information, making it easier for police to conduct surprise inspections or make arrests.[29] In 1940, the Poniatowski school was cleared to teach religion, Polish, German, art, physics, chemistry, mathematics, geography, biology, and gymnastics (physical education), with approval to assign homework – a rigorous vocational school curriculum, but nonetheless.[30] It had 319 male students, 155 in the first class, and 164 in the second.[31] Vocational school bona fides consisted in reporting pupils' career plans, the German inspector's focus. In the intelligentsia Żoliborz neighborhood, the teenagers dutifully reported to the German board that they aspired to the following careers:

Boguski Jerzy (1925–): mechanic
Fogler Janusz (1925–): surveyor
Głąbkowski Sławomir (1923–): tradesman
Juszczak Jerzy (1925–): trade clerk
Kulik Adolf (1925–): tradesman
Makowski Jacek (1925–): mechanic

The list continued, indicating that Poniatowski School students were disproportionately hoping to become mechanics, tradesmen, foresters, farmers, gardeners, technicians, and builders.[32] Leaving aside where these city boys intended to farm, and whether they had volunteered these aspirations or they had been concocted by their teachers, this documentation passed muster with the German administration: the school was permitted to use the old building and employ a school nurse and a priest to teach religion.[33]

Dąbrowski had his hands full. The Germans constantly issued decrees and fees. Dąbrowski repeatedly verified his teachers' employment, since they could

---

[29] APmstW-M, Gimazjum/Liceum Poniatowski, z. 275/0, s. 630, Kursy przygotowawcze, "Stundenplan der Lehrer und Instruktoren," 24–36.

[30] The students did one hour of religion, four of Polish, four or six of German, two of drawing, two or four of physics, one or two of chemistry, four of math, one or two of geography, one or two of biology, and two hours of gym (APmstW-M, Gimazjum/Liceum Poniatowski, z. 275/0, s. 630, Kursy przygotowawcze, "Stundenverteilungsplan/Plan godzin," 23).

[31] APmstW-M, Gimazjum/Liceum Poniatowski, z. 275/0, s. 630, Kursy przygotowawcze, "Schüler im Schuljahre 1940/41," 22.

[32] APmstW-M, Państwowe Gimazjum/Liceum Poniatowski, z. 275/0, s. 660, Sprawy uczniów, "Sprawa: Wykaz uczniów kursów," 62–75; S. Juszczakiewicz is on 70 (8 of the original).

[33] The priest was confirmed by the school and archdiocese. The school nurse/dentist, Zofia Jachymczykowa, was a woman, as were some teachers and the secretary (APmstW-M, Gimazjum/Liceum Poniatowski, z. 275/0, s. 628, Personel szkoły, 10, 70–71, 128).

be seized for Reich labor without approved documentation. Students needed an avalanche of stamps and letters. Most carried a note on school letterhead signed by Dąbrowski in their knapsacks to allow them to buy tram tickets.[34] On September 19, 1940, only a few weeks after opening, teachers Kazimierz Baranowski, Kazimierz Lisowski, and Jan Dürr (who taught Polish and history) were arrested. Dąbrowski petitioned Fischer's School Administration at Brühl Palace for their release: "I am seeking by means of this letter the most helpful intercession of the appropriate authorities in order to free the specified persons, so that the normal operation of the school is not completely undermined."[35] School records contain no answer from Fischer, but they do contain supplemental personnel files and onboarding paperwork for a stream of replacement teachers.

Despite the complexities of maintaining German approval for a legal school, it was safer than operating completely underground like Bolesław Prus Junior High. Opened in 1922 as the first Warsaw junior high school, the Prus School educated city elites in a handsome building on Jasna Street. Whether it attempted a Poniatowski School-style rebranding is unclear, but its wartime records refer only to "tajne komplety" (secret courses) operating between 1940 and 1944.[36] Handwritten by a number of different authors, the secret records fill four student exercise notebooks bearing the school's prewar name. Blocked-out scheduling, lists of paid fees, teacher compensation, and columns and columns of grades were carefully documented. Though it had been a boys' school until 1939, some girls studied in wartime.[37]

Day-to-day operations are hard to discern from extant files. Many teachers and students participated for three full years. The Prus School had been a boys' three-year junior high school (*gimnazjum*) until 1939. In wartime it functioned as both a junior high and a high school (*liceum*), with the first class for the former and the second for the latter so that students could continue their studies even though they had technically graduated. Boys who finished junior high in spring 1939 and those who followed stayed at the school, keeping them within the fold.[38] Practically, securing space for lessons was a key task of the skeleton administration. Lists of apartments appear in

---

[34] APmstW-M, Gimazjum/Liceum Poniatowski, z. 275/0, s. 628, Personel szkoły, 24, 73, 83–84; APmstW-M, Gimazjum/Liceum Poniatowski, z. 275/0, s. 660, Sprawy uczniów, 1–14.

[35] Domańska's Pawiak files list Kazimierz Lisowski as a prisoner on September 19, 1940 and his transfer to Auschwitz on February 2, 1942 (Domańska, *Pawiak więzienie gestapo*, 107–108; 197); APmstW-M, Gimazjum/Liceum Poniatowski, z. 275/0, s. 628, Personel szkoły, n. 2/40 petition letter, 1; personnel records of arrested teachers: 85, 87, 91.

[36] Czesław Jędraszko (1892–1984) was its only wartime director.

[37] Notebook 2 mentions five girls in a class of thirteen (APmstW-M, Prywatne Gimnazjum Męskie im. Bolesława Prusa w Warszawie (hereafter: Gimnazjum Prus), z. 284/0, s. 170, Zeszyt II, 32–33).

[38] APmstW-M, Gimnazjum Prus, z. 284/0, s. 172, Zeszyt IV, [5b]-6.

several notebooks, crossed out as they were compromised or "burned."[39] Classes were held six days a week, and students selected morning or afternoon schedules.[40] In May 1941, the school had 48 registered students with 28 attending.[41] The account book for 1942/1943 listed 26 boys in junior high and 12 in high school, most of whom paid, though poor students received assistance.[42] Teachers earned 300 zloty per month, a piddling salary considering risks and occupation prices.[43]

Students were divided into a math and sciences or humanities curriculum, and history lectures – forbidden by Nazi policy – were detailed by topic.[44] Each student took eight to ten subjects annually in religion, Polish, German, French, Latin, history, biology, math, physics, philosophy, and civics.[45] Examination protocols were spelled out in detail, and each of four examiners had to sign off on student performances.[46] Grading was strict, and only half the students were promoted in all subjects. The highest mark of five was very rare, and in spring 1943 only the star student received all fives.[47] Teachers' notes indicate low grades came from poor writing, sporadic attendance, and one boy's departure to join the army.[48] There are other references to boys whose families relocated, and one student, Witold Tomalak, who lost his father.[49] Director Czesław Jędraszko was threatened – or perhaps warned – at least twice that the Gestapo was onto him and tailing his students.[50] Despite the risks, the Prus School stayed open until the uprising.[51]

Jędraszko survived and returned to teaching classics in the 1950s.[52] The Prus school scattered during the uprising, and many former students fought. After

[39] APmstW-M, Gimnazjum Prus, z. 284/0, s. 169, Zeszyt I, 16 (portions illegible).

[40] APmstW-M, Gimnazjum Prus, z. 284/0, s. 174, Dokumenty, 12.

[41] APmstW-M, Gimnazjum Prus, z. 284/0, s. 169, Zeszyt I, "Sprawozdanie na dzień 12. V. 1941," 30.

[42] There is a note for the RGO (APmstW-M, Gimnazjum Prus, z. 284/0, s. 170, Zeszyt II, [1a]-4).

[43] APmstW-M, Gimnazjum Prus, z. 284/0, s. 169, Zeszyt I, "1. Klasa 1941/1942," 56, 220, and unmarked page headed "lipiec 1942"; APmstW-M, Gimnazjum Prus, z. 284/0, s. 174, Dokumenty, 1.

[44] The history lectures page has the name "Błażejewski Jerzy" (Zeszyt II, s. 170). Błażejewski was likely the person who joined the Bałtyk battalion under the pseudonym "War" and fought in the uprising (APmstW-M, Gimnazjum Prus, z. 284/0, s. 169, Zeszyt I, 7).

[45] "Civics" for "zagadnienie życia wspólczesnego," now called "WOS" ("wiedza o społeczeństwie"). Thanks to Anna Krakus and family for the explanation.

[46] APmstW-M, Gimnazjum Prus, z. 284/0, s. 172, Zeszyt IV, protocols: 3, 5; examiners' remarks: 36–55, etc.

[47] Jerzy Piazewski (APmstW-M, Gimnazjum Prus, z. 284/0, s. 170, Zeszyt II, [12b]-13).

[48] APmstW-M, Gimnazjum Prus, z. 284/0, s. 170, Zeszyt II, 20–21.

[49] APmstW-M, Gimnazjum Prus, z. 284/0, s. 170, Zeszyt II, [16b].

[50] APmstW-M, Gimnazjum Prus, z. 284/0, s. 174, Dokumenty, 14–15. It was likely his relative, Gabriela Aleksandra Jędraszko, who died at Pawiak on April 26, 1944. Domańska, Pawiak więzienie gestapo, 452.

[51] APmstW-M, Gimnazjum Prus, z. 284/0, s. 170, Zeszyt II, 30, 32.

[52] He authored a Latin grammar, Łacina na co dzień, in 1968.

the war, Jędraszko surveyed students and their families. He asked about the rigor of their studies, how education had served them in their later lives and, of course, "who of their colleagues died in the struggle for independence and under what circumstances?"[53] No responses survive.

Students found underground schooling to be both chore and adventure.[54] For the Piekarski brothers, Antoni (1927–?) and Maciej (1932–99), education intertwined the legal and illegal. It required them to navigate a dynamic system of authority among their teachers, parents, and school administrators that kept them – by and large – safe. The boys were raised in an intelligentsia home in Sadyba, then on Warsaw's southern edge, and their father was an engineer and a Home Army soldier. Maciej turned seven as the GG formed, and he continued primary school while his brother Antek entered a secret junior high school. In fall 1941, Antek's junior high closed so he went off to a "trade" school downtown. Maciej remembered his father's fear as his brother boarded the tram to his illegal school, which "changed locations many times in the course of a year … from building to building."[55] Their father kept them studying because "when the war ended … they would need to be as well prepared as possible." Maciej remembered that,

> Our school was wonderful. Since the study of history and geography had been eliminated from the program [by German regulation], we did not take notes on them in our notebooks, but just in our heads … [then] an unexpected inspection fell on the school. While an inspector with a swastika on his lapel sat in the principal's office, talking with Miss Wanda and Auntie Genia, Miss Franciszkowa hid notebooks and books under her apron in a panic. Not any less frightened, we helped her stuff them into an unused oven. After the German inspector's visit the teachers organized secret courses [*tajne komplety*]. They always took place in different apartments. Outside the courses, I went to the geography classes of my first teacher, Miss Wanda Turowska. Antek … took classes on Polish literature, Latin, and English.[56]

Maciej's teachers had not expected the Germans to enforce regulations in sleepy Sadyba, and the inspector caught them off guard when he arrived in 1941.[57] His appearance in Sadyba means that the Poniatowski School in Żoliborz was certainly visited by an inspector. Thereafter a circle of Sadyba teachers offered forbidden supplementary subjects. Besides the school principal, all five teachers mentioned were women, including Maciej's beloved

---

[53] APmstW-M, Gimnazjum Prus, z. 284/0, s. 174, Dokumenty, 12.
[54] *Warszawa okupowana: relacje mieszkańców*, 44–48.
[55] Piekarski, *Tak zapamiętałem*, 60–61.
[56] Students as young as 9–10 were educated illegally. Piekarski, *Tak zapamiętałem*, 60–61.
[57] "Surprise" inspections were deliberate. Dobroszycki, *Reptile Journalism*, 110.

"Auntie Genia," Eugenia Łaukajtis-Sipayłło. Together, these women taught a large group of boys and at least one girl.[58]

Due to incomplete records, it is unclear how many secondary school students were educated. Extant records allow detailed consideration of two, the Poniatowski and Prus Schools, but no others. Many prewar institutions operated like these, and informal schooling bridged the gap between permitted rudimentary instruction and what parents wanted for their children.[59] Data from the postwar Verification Commission (Komisja Weryfikacyjna) about those who obtained recognition for wartime *matura* results give some sense of the scale of operations. Since the Germans had banned university study and redirected secondary education toward vocational training, wartime *matura* passage indicates illegal study, providing a minimum number of students.

A total of 6,715 students' *matura* examinations were accepted from wartime public secondary schools (1939–44): 1,324 girls and 1,289 boys from public schools; 2,373 girls and 1,279 boys from private schools, including Catholic ones; and 450 from coeducational schools. Of those that passed their *matura* during the war, 40 percent were boys and 60 percent were girls. Though the discrepancy is not huge at the secondary level, more girls than boys finished high school and passed their *matura*. The dramatic turn of teenage boys to underground soldiering explained the gender imbalance. Due to increased discrimination, Jewish children's education ended earlier. 120 Jewish girls and 72 boys obtained postwar recognition, but there were no *matura* results after the 1941–42 school year for any Polish-Jewish children.[60] Underground schooling educated about one-third of Warsaw students, with somewhere between 6,500 and 8,000 students completing high school under occupation.[61]

6.3   Warsaw University Underground

In 1939, Ludwig Fischer informed the rectors of Warsaw University and the polytechnic that higher education was forbidden.[62] Students who finished

[58] Maciej's Lithuanian "Auntie Genia" was a family friend with a fondness for caricature. For her sketch of Maciej's father see "Piekarscy – ich przodkowie, krewni i powinowaci:" http://piekarscy.com.pl/?p=1005.

[59] Mickiewicz Junior High and High School continued as a secret school but without records (APmstW, Państwowe Gimnazjum i Liceum Męskie im. Adama Mickiewicza w Warszawie, z. 72/273/0). Graduates – Mickiewiczacy – have erected a plaque marking the building next to Holy Cross Church where they held lessons (http://mickiewicz.edu.pl /stowarzyszeniev1/index.php/w-czasie-drugiej-wojny-swiatowej/).

[60] The 1,324 includes Hanna Czaki. Jewish students' fate is unknown. Kaźmierska, *Szkolnictwo warszawskie*, 290–299.

[61] Eberhardt gives 8,000 for wartime *matura* (*Abitur*) passage in Warsaw; Krakow had 1,679. Eberhardt, *Geheimes Schulwesen*, 260.

[62] USHMM RG 15.165M Proces Ludwika Fischera (IPN Sygn. GK 196), Reel 2, "Polski system oświatowy został zlikwidowany . . . ," Kraścicka, 19.

illegal high schools and passed the *matura*, however, could still study underground. The "flying" Warsaw University (UW) sustained a full, degree-granting curriculum in all prewar fields of study between 1939 and 1944.[63] Other Warsaw tertiary schools also continued operations.

The invasion caught Warsaw University students at the start of the academic year and they were at loose ends as Tannenberg ground to a halt. The first underground seminars were reassembled in November and December 1939 in law, with some in history.[64] This was a momentous task in the bombed-out city: university property was in ruins, students and professors imprisoned and scattered, and libraries and bookstores shuttered.[65] Funds to support education, students, and professors were scarce and scraped together, eventually a focus of multiple opposition groups that saw the value of supporting higher education. Placards around the city reminded everyone that participation in university study carried the death penalty. Reconstituting the university was thus explicitly political, an even more aggressive gesture of defiance than the half-secret secondary schools.

Underground higher education was not exclusive to the capital, though, like most conspiracies, the densest network existed in Warsaw. The city boasted two universities, Warsaw University (Figure 6.1) and the refugee University of Poznań evacuated from western Poland in 1939, operating under the nom de guerre "University of the Western Lands (Uniwersytet Ziem Zachodnich, UZZ)."[66] Secret classes (*komplety*) were held across GG cities, and students relocated to access them.[67] Students like Krystyna Idzikowska, the Peasant Battalion courier, came to Warsaw to study, enriching the educational landscape but entangling them in dangerous projects.

---

[63] Calling UW underground a "flying university" (*uniwersytet latający*) hearkened back to Jadwiga Dawidowa's secret and illegal higher education system for Warsaw women (and a few men) built in 1882, and pursued by Russian authorities. Classes relocated from place to place, hence "flying." Writer Zofia Nałkowska was a graduate. Connelly, *From Peoples into Nations*, 279. The term was resurrected under communism. Brandys, *Warsaw Diary*, 58.

[64] Kaźmierska claims that "in academic year 1939/40, outside a few exceptions ... there wasn't secret higher education happening in Warsaw." The few exceptions were crucial. Kaźmierska, *Szkolnictwo warszawskie w latach 1939–1944*, 204–205.

[65] UW underground information from BUW Gabinet Rękopisów, predominantly: Rpsy 2202, 2203, 2204, 2205, and 2208 (BUW Rps 2205 [Sprowadzanie z Apelu poległych w czasie wojny nauczycieli Warszawy wraz z wnioskiem Zarządu m.st. W-wy w sprawie opublikowanie Księgi Pamiątkowej, z dn. 31.X.1945 r.], 7–11 and [Manteuffel – Nauczyciele szkół wyższych i pracownicy naukowi z Warszawy], 2).

[66] Kaźmierska counts six in Warsaw: UW (including the UZZ), the Warsaw Polytechnic, SGGW, SGH, and the Free Polish University (Wolna Wszechnica), with some participation from the Pedagogical Institute, the Academy of Political Sciences, and the State Institute of Theater Arts. Kaźmierska, *Szkolnictwo warszawskie*, 205.

[67] Centkowska, *Na tajnych kompletach*.

Figure 6.1 Warsaw University's main gate on Krakowskie Przedmieście, 1931. Narodowe Archiwum Cyfrowe, 3/1/0/10/3270.

One of the participants in the underground or "flying" Warsaw University, Tadeusz Manteuffel (1902–70), a medievalist who had done his own doctoral study there, later wrote its history.[68] His *Warsaw University in the Years of War and Occupation* (1948) is the most substantial document on the clandestine university. Manteuffel also collected a paycheck from the German-requisitioned New Documents Archive (Archiwum Akt Nowych, AAN), taught history clandestinely, and edited *Wiadomości Polskie* (Polish News), an underground newsletter, during the war.[69]

The university was organized by departments, which included theology, law, medicine, philosophy, humanities (history, language, literature), mathematics and sciences, pharmacy, veterinary studies, and the library. Because of the university's history of political persecution, departments operated autonomously, selecting their own faculty, staff, and students. When the Germans closed the university, it collapsed into these independently run departments.

---

[68] Manteuffel was Dobroszycki's colleague at PAN when he worked on his reptile press book – this was a small world.

[69] Manteuffel joined the ZWZ-AK in 1940 while teaching. AAN was under German control. Szarota, *Okupowanej Warszawy*, 95; Bartoszewski, *1859 dni Warszawy*, 95.

Before the war, the university sprawled across Warsaw, and it owned considerable real estate and had scientific laboratory space in city hospitals. Prestigious departments were housed in the historic campus along Krakowskie Przedmieście. A Nazi police battalion commandeered the main buildings and "converted the cloakroom of the Great Auditorium into a stable and chopped up the ash wood reading room tables of the University Library to construct stalls for their horses."[70] Germans seized the Staszic Palace, one of the university's most elegant properties; scouts hastily hid its priceless collections in National Museum basements. The Wehrmacht used the museum itself as soldiers' barracks and also claimed the lecture halls, rector's office, and central campus kitchens.[71] The library was closed to Poles and its books pilfered for the Staatsbibliothek Warschau – though its reorganization offered paid work to a Polish staff. Czesław Miłosz and Stanisław Dygat (1914–78), a novelist, both secured paychecks for "help" with library reorganization, a process they dragged out endlessly, sitting among the books eating employer-provided lunches and, in Miłosz's case, reading a lot of French literature.[72]

Running a university secretly required flexibility. Without spaces for large lectures, classes were instead held in seminar-sized groups. This inefficient but intimate educational system forged lifelong bonds between students and professors. A young literature student remembered four hours of weekly classes in the Mokotów neighborhood. Her elderly professor, Leszek Adamczewski (1883–1952), was still revising a book manuscript but so poor he drafted it "on packing paper."[73]

Matriculation lists reveal the curiosities of wartime schooling. Every professor kept track of the real names of students who completed courses and research.[74] Facing discovery, a number of these lists were destroyed but those that remain are remarkably detailed. The total number of students dropped as the university went underground, though unevenly.[75] Compared

---

[70] Centkowska, *Na tajnych kompletach*, 67.

[71] Kaźmierska, *Szkolnictwo warszawskie*, 130–132.

[72] Marek Sroka, "Nations Will Not Survive Without Their Cultural Heritage: Karol Estreicher, Polish Cultural Restitution Plans and the Recovery of Polish Cultural Property from the American Zone of Occupation," *The Polish Review* 57, No. 3 (2012), 3–28; Franaszek, *Miłosz*, 192–193.

[73] Adamczewski also taught Krzysztof Kamil Baczyński. *Warszawa okupowana: relacje mieszkańców*, 49. Polish-Jewish intelligentsia were desperate for paper and wrote on "anything they could get ahold of." Leociak, *Text*, 68–69.

[74] *Uniwersytet Warszawski w latach 1915/16 – 1934/35: Kronika* (Warsaw: Nakładem Uniwersytetu Józefa Piłsudskiego, 1936) and *Uniwersytet Warszawski w latach wojny i okupacji: Kronika 1939/40 – 1944/45* (Warsaw: Nakładem Uniwersytetu Warszawskiego, 1948).

[75] Garliński gives a figure of 2,176 students enrolled at UW IN 1942 and 9,000 who "passed through" UW. Józef Garliński, "The Polish Underground State (1939–1945)" in *Journal of Contemporary History* 10 no. 2 (April 1975), 239.

to the last prewar academic year, the first year underground saw an *increase* in medicine and pharmacy diplomas: 390 students earned medical degrees in 1940, up from 202, and 54 students earned pharmacy degrees, up from 37.[76] Two things contributed to the surge: the first was the rising need for medical personnel to treat the wounded and ill, so Germans likely turned a blind eye to medical training. More important, though, was Professor Jan Zaorski's aboveground Nursing School. Zaorski (1887–1956) studied at the Universities of Lwów and Warsaw and worked as a field hospital surgeon in the Austrian Army in the First World War, from which he joined Piłsudski's Legions. He directed St. Elizabeth's Hospital in Mokotów in the 1930s and served as an army field surgeon again in 1939. He then turned to secret medical instruction. Zaorski successfully played German fears of disease against them, using epidemic-prevention as an excuse to train "nurses." His nursing school was a cover for in-depth medical research and taught around 2,000 wartime students.[77] He was nevertheless arrested and imprisoned in Pawiak in October 1943 for illegal teaching, and his subordinates carried on without him.

Though young Maciej Piekarski remembered his wartime school fondly, not all these stories ended well. For many, the cost of studying or teaching was imprisonment, torture, and execution. The transition from high school to university – taking the *matura* – was itself dangerous. Incoming UW law student Anna Pawełczyńska (1922–2014) was arrested on August 15, 1942, and ran into high school girlfriends in prison:

> I happily greeted my friends from the Queen Jadwiga School and other colleagues, including Danka Brzosko, Ala Dańska, Zosia Krasińska, and Jadzia Kamińska, in Pawiak. Danka and Ala were there for the second time. They belonged to a group the gestapo arrested while taking their *matura* for the secret courses. Their exam was scheduled in the morning, and mine in the afternoon. The gestapo arrived in the morning.[78]

The Gestapo had no proof Pawełczyńska was studying, but they arrested her after finding illegal periodicals on her. The intervention of parents and friends

---

[76] Kaźmierska, *Szkolnictwo warszawskie*, 127; Stachiewicz, *Akcja "Kutschera,"* 42.

[77] Zofia Rusecka, one of Zaorski's students, took osteology exams in a café. "Zofia Rusecka" in *Warszawa okupowana: relacje mieszkańców*, 48–49; Domańska, *Pawiak więzienie Gestapo*, 356. Some other tertiary school faculty had "aboveground" gigs: Warsaw Polytechnic architecture scholar Jan Zachwatowicz legally taught at the technical school. "Jan Zachwatowicz" in *Chronicles of Terror: Warsaw* (Warsaw: Witold Pilecki Center for Totalitarian Studies, 2017), 41. The ghetto also organized medical research and training. Engelking and Leociak, *Getto warszawskie*, 271–283; Charles G. Roland, *Courage under Siege: Starvation, Disease, and Death in the Warsaw Ghetto* (New York: Oxford University Press, 1992), 76–97.

[78] Pawełczyńska, *Dary losu*, 83–84.

obtained the girls' release, but several would be back in prison before the occupation ended.

The fate of Władysław Okiński's sociology seminar demonstrates the intermingling of intelligentsia conspiracies. Okiński (1906–44) taught a seminar of ten students in 1943/44, at least two of whom also worked for the Home Army. A few hours before their class was to meet on January 5, 1944, one of them, Hanna Czaki ("Helena," 1922–44), was arrested by German patrolmen. Czaki was carrying underground documents *and* her sociology notes. She had studied at the Aleksandra Piłsudska High School in its secret classes, passed her *matura*, and then started in sociology at UZZ – all with the approval of her parents, who were involved in underground publishing.[79] Not content merely to study, Czaki was active in the scouting movement and became secretary to the head of the Information Department (BIP) in the Home Army in 1942. The young woman was also a neighbor of Władysław Bartoszewski on Słowacki Street in Żoliborz, a hotbed of intelligentsia conspiracy. Bartoszewski fondly remembered late in life how he had befriended Czaki, who was the same age – both nineteen in 1941 – and how she had spent hours talking to him, sneaking him issues of the *Bulletin* to read in his sickbed after his release from Auschwitz.[80] With Czaki in custody, the Gestapo arrested her parents and Okiński's whole seminar.[81] After prolonged torture, Czaki passed a *gryps* out of Pawiak letting her co-conspirators know that a box of secret paperwork was still hidden in her apartment, which they carefully recovered.[82] On January 25, 1944, her other nine seminar classmates and their professor were sentenced to death. By the end of the month, the whole seminar, its professor, Czaki, and both her parents had been shot in public executions or in the ruins of the ghetto around Pawiak.[83] The Gestapo caught Czaki at random out longer than usual on the streets due to bad weather. Her possessions pointed toward multiple crimes: participation in underground information work, and in secret university circles as a sociology student. Studying – and everything that came with it – was a dangerous business.

---

[79] Państwowe Gimnazjum i Liceum Żeńskie im. Aleksandry Piłsudskiej w Warszawie where Czaki completed *komplety* as the Wipszycka Private Gardening School (APmstW 72/269/ 0 Państwowe Gimnazjum i Liceum Żeńskie im. Aleksandry Piłsudskiej w Warszawie).

[80] Thanks to the anonymous reader who noted that Bartoszewski remembered Czaki (Bartoszewski, *Życie trudne*, 81–82). According to prisoner intake records, Bartoszewski and Witold Pilecki, who was two decades older, arrived in Auschwitz on the same transport from Żoliborz (on September 22, 1940), and may have known each other in the camp.

[81] Domańska, *Pawiak więzienie gestapo*, 399.

[82] Bartoszewski, *Życie trudne*, 121.

[83] Centkowska, *Na tajnych kompletach*, 69–72; Domańska, *Pawiak więzienie gestapo*, 407–408; 419–420.

Czaki and her seminar was one of many sent to Pawiak, and she was not unique for engaging in multiple opposition efforts. A number of Pawiak survivors blamed their studies – or the combination of those studies with other illegal activities – as their ticket to prison. Wanda Tumidajska-Styrczula (1923–2007) remembered:

> We were arrested on the night of 15–16 November 1943 from our apartment at 25 Wileńska St. It was three of us. My brother Leszek Tumidajski [1921–43], an officer cadet in the AK, my friend Eliza Lamert, a scout ... and first year student at the SGGW [Warsaw University of Life Sciences], and me – Wanda Tumidajska – a part of the same scouting unit and studying in my first year of medical school at UW in secret courses. Eliza lived with me for two years while in high school, and that day she was visiting us and spending the night. There had been cadet classes, AK meetings, Union of Polish Scouts meetings, secret education courses, and we kept weapons and underground press in our apartment, and my brother and his friends had left for *akcje* [armed actions] from there, and we had even hidden someone a few times. About my brother's work I knew little ...[84]

Their Wileńska Street apartment in Praga on the eastern side of the Vistula was a nexus of underground activity. A Gestapo search condemned them on multiple counts, including the anatomy textbook open on the kitchen table. Wanda's and Leszek's enthusiastic leap into conspiracy was not a surprise to their families: their father, Kazimierz Tumidajski (1897–1947), was serving as an underground military officer in Lublin when his children were arrested.[85] The Gestapo hauled them to Pawiak, where they were tortured and accused of participating in a communist conspiracy – ironically, since their politics were to the right. They executed Leszek on December 3, 1943 but released Eliza on January 6, 1944 because she was not registered at that apartment. Wanda was transferred to Ravensbrück in March 1944.

Wanda Tumidajska-Styrczula's story was similar to her cellmates at Pawiak, Ravensbrück, Auschwitz, and Dachau, where many participants in underground education ended up. Though she and her brother were in their twenties, younger students were targeted.[86] Sixteen-year-old Grzegorz Wieczorkiewicz was at home at no. 6 Jasna Street, down the street from the Prus School, when policemen arrived on January 7, 1944:

> I was arrested at sixteen together with my father Józef and my aunt Barbara Wieczorkiewicz ... I was a student of the secret courses organized

---

[84] Wanda Tumidajska-Styrczula, *Pawiak był etapem*, 366–371; on cadet classes see Stachiewicz, *Akcja "Kutschera,"* 24–32.

[85] *Polskie Siły Zbrojne w Drugiej Wojnie Światowej*, Tom III: *Armia Krajowa*, 623.

[86] Zbigniew Dębczyński (Czajkowski) was 15–16 while at the Lelewel School and in the Grey Ranks. Czajkowski, *Warsaw 1944*.

by the Mikołaj Rej High School.[87] My father and his sister Barbara were connected with a conspiracy organization, but I don't know which one. During breaks between classes, I often visited the apartment . . .[88]

Though he was tortured on Szuch Boulevard in the infamous "streetcars," Wieczorkiewicz claimed he was uninvolved in what was going on in the apartment. His father could not make that argument and was publicly executed on January 28, 1944.[89] Nevertheless, Grzegorz's illegal studies kept him in custody, and he was transferred to Gross-Rosen camp on April 26, 1944. His cousin, mother, and aunt were sent to Ravensbrück.[90]

Students' multiple conspiratorial activities and the inconsistency of Nazi behavior make it difficult to evaluate the danger of underground education for both students and faculty: the way participation in one conspiracy fed into others characterized the intelligentsia experience during the occupation. Professors had been targeted since Tannenberg and the consequences for secretly teaching were harsher than what students endured. People engaged in both underground schooling and military conspiracies were treated more seriously than those who were "only" studying, but the lines were blurry. German punishments did vary somewhat based on the accused's age and sex. Anna Pawełczyńska's female friends were imprisoned but released. Hanna Czaki, involved in underground study and information trafficking, was extensively tortured and executed even though she was female – along with her classmates and professor, some of whom were not engaged in any other illegal activities. Leszek Tumidajski, who was male, in his twenties, and involved in both illegal schooling and in sabotage and diversion work, was executed. His sister was sent to a concentration camp, receiving a lighter sentence. Perhaps the Germans took her illegal activities less seriously since she was female, but more likely her brother took the blame for them both. The fate of Grzegorz Wieczorkiewicz, younger than the Tumidajski siblings, indicates that underground high school study alone could carry a concentration camp sentence for a teenage boy, even with no other charges.[91]

6.4 Scale of Operations

Warsaw University was the largest tertiary school in the city, and it educated most of the students and employed most of the faculty, and granted some – but not most – degrees, since its sister institutions proved more efficient.

[87] Like the girls' schools, the Rej Boys' School records did not survive. APmstW-M Gimnazjum i Liceum Męskie im. Mikołaja Reja w Warszawie, z. 305/0.

[88] Wieczorkiewicz, *Pawiak był etapem*, 379.

[89] Domańska, *Pawiak więzienie gestapo*, 409, 411.

[90] Wieczorkiewicz, *Pawiak był etapem*, 381.

[91] Women disproportionately survived, since men were punished more harshly. Domańska, *Pawiak był etapem*, 24–25; 57–63.

Compared to the last prewar school year (1938–39), when UW granted 1169 degrees, it issued only 529 in 1939–40 and a total of 118 between 1940 and 1944. In total, 118 students devoted themselves to study, though a much larger number studied without finishing a degree. Miron Białoszewski, for instance, was studying Polish literature with friends in an apartment on the corner of Swiętokrzyska and Jasna streets, but did not graduate.[92] Numbers increased in law, which UW and UZZ taught jointly. During the 1940–41 academic year, there were 35 students and 13 lecturers; the next year 180 students and 18 lecturers, then 350 students and 26 lecturers, and, for the final year of occupation, 580 students and 28 lecturers. Other degree-issuing schools include the Polytechnic (198 wartime degrees), UZZ (97), the Warsaw School of Economics (SGH, 85 degrees), and the Warsaw University of Life Sciences (SGGW, 130 degrees).[93] These numbers do not reflect students who were not degree-seeking, like Białoszewski and Miłosz, who attended philosophy seminars with Professor Władysław Tatarkiewicz (1886–1980), a specialist in aesthetics.[94] The total number of those who violated Nazi regulations by studying remains unknown.

6.5   Gendered Aspects

Wartime changed the gender composition of students and faculty. As the war continued, a rising percentage of students and faculty were women. This reflects the broader gender dynamics of occupation, in which the majority of the Polish victims of Nazi persecution were men.[95] Combat deaths were overwhelmingly male. The first Nazi attacks on the intelligentsia involved target lists and the majority of those named were men.[96] Men comprised the majority of the 10,000–15,000 killed during AB. When the Wehrmacht invaded the Soviet Union in 1941, huge numbers of Poles were conscripted for Reich labor; more than three-quarters of those taken were men.[97] The majority of those imprisoned in street roundups were men. The Germans held men in prison for longer and sentenced them more harshly. Men were the majority of victims in retaliation shootings, hostage-takings, "disappearances," and late-night raids. As Zofia Korbońska remembered years later, the legendarily "systematic" Germans "were not interested in anything but men . . . men,

---

[92] Białoszewski, *Memoir*, 5.
[93] Kaźmierska, *Szkolnictwo warszawskie*, 217, 239.
[94] Franaszek, *Miłosz*, 207.
[95] Białoszewski, *Memoir*, 61, 89, 135.
[96] Of these names, 68–70 percent are male – including mentions of a particular person "and wife," or "and family." *Sonderfahndungsbuch Polen* (Berlin: Reichskriminalpolizeiamt, 1939).
[97] Adam Winiarz, *Gender and Secondary Education in Poland and Sweden in the Twentieth Century* (Lublin: Marie Curie-Składowska University Press, 2002), 50.

men, men," ignoring the political work of Polish women.[98] The male population of Warsaw bore the brunt of Nazi terror, and the male intelligentsia
population, which was subject to targeted extermination efforts, suffered
disproportionately.

Day-to-day interaction with the German administration, however, was
performed by women. Women came to dominate wartime education for
parallel reasons. Women waited in lines for food and ration cards, and went
to offices to register their families' residences and obtain death certificates and
identification cards.[99] The city of Warsaw, insofar as it existed between 1940
and 1945, was sustained heavily by the efforts of Polish women, who maintained "aboveground" life.[100] Gaps in the ranks of teachers, professors, and
students were filled by women. Primary school teachers were mostly female
before the war, though the proportion of female secondary school teachers still
increased.[101] Maciej Piekarski and his brother were taught by women. Even in
the Poniatowski and Prus boys' schools, there were some female teachers.
Records from girls' schools would broaden this story if they were extant.[102]
Nevertheless, postwar *matura* recognitions reveal that even at the secondary
level, the proportion of female students increased, especially after 1943.

Women were in the minority among students during the interwar years
when they were first admitted to Polish universities. They reached 27 percent
of students by 1939, heavily concentrated in nursing and teacher training.
Women never broke 14 percent of enrollments in the hard sciences, law, or,
unsurprisingly, theology, which primarily trained priests.[103] These women
were drawn from the ranks of urban intelligentsia able to pay fees, send their
children to elite high schools, and afford accommodations in the capital –
a group that favored native Varsovians. Professors, administrators, and rectors

---

[98] USHMM RG-50.012.0046, AN: 1989.67.46, "Interview with Stefan and Sophia Korbonski," Part 2, 19:08–20:39.

[99] Take Zofia Nałkowska, who spent January 1941 in queues outside various ministries obtaining forms and stamps. Her comrades in this activity were women, and she returned home to her mother. Male names appear rarely in her diary. Zofia Nałkowska, *Dzienniki*, 157–158, 169.

[100] "The saving grace [for Jews securing identity papers] was that because many people in Warsaw were living underground, living unregistered did not by itself betray someone as a Jew." Paulsson, *Secret City*, 101.

[101] Aneta Ignatowicz, *Tajna oświata i wychowanie w okupowanej Warszawie: Warszawskie Termopile, 1939–1945* (Warsaw: Fundacja Warszawa Walczy 1939–1945, 2009); Kaźmierska's *Szkolnictwo warszawskie*, 25–119.

[102] Pawełczyńska attended the Queen Jadwiga School (APmstW-M, Państwowe Gimnazjum i Liceum Żeńskie im. Królowej Jadwigi w Warszawie, z. 270/0). Danuta Krystyna Domańska, a Piłsudska School graduate, passed her matura in 1943, fought with the "Baszta" group, and was held in Pawiak and Ravensbrück (*Przetrwałam*, 207).

[103] Hanna Solarczyk, *Doświadczenia edukacyjne kobiet w Polsce i w Niemczech: Raport z badań biograficznych* (Toruń: Biblioteka Edukacji Dorosłych, 2002) and Manteuffel, *Uniwersytet Warszawski w latach 1915/16–1934/35*.

were all male. Thus, when the war broke out, women were part of Polish higher education, but only a small part.

Underground enrollment figures kept by the dwindling male professoriate tell a larger story. By 1943, law and biology had 80 percent female enrollment. Medicine was nearing 65 percent.[104] Only the theology seminars remained all male.[105] Ewa Krasnowalska, Professor Adamczewski's literature student, remembered that "everywhere [in all the courses] there were more girls, but in ours there were seven guys and just three [young women]—atypical."[106] Marian Gieysztor ("Krajewski" 1901–61), a biologist who taught at UW and the Warsaw University of Life Sciences (SGGW), kept student data for physics, chemistry, math, biology, geography, dentistry, and pharmacy.[107] According to him, 234 of the 288 students who began in the fall of 1943 completed the year. Only 28 percent were male. The fifty-four losses included two who were shot, four arrested, and two caught in *łapanki*. The gender breakdown was:

Department of Physics: 15 students (7 men, 8 women)
Chemistry: 64 (29 men, 35 women)
Math: 14 (9 men, 5 women)
Biology: 8 (1 man, 7 women)
Geography: 12 (2 men, 10 women)
Dentistry: 50 (1 man, 49 women)
Pharmacy: 83 (17 men, 66 women)

Only the math department retained a male majority in 1943. That was gone by 1944, the last class to complete studies before the uprising, which closed the university.[108] These figures do not tell the whole truth, however, as "absent" male students departed for the military underground remained on the books until reported dead.

Several engineering professors began to discuss the consequences of the academy's feminization. In one exchange, a professor confessed to his male research assistant that he continued teaching because he was too old to fight and he felt that this was the most opposition he could muster. The correspondence of

---

[104] Hospitals operated "aboveground" giving cover to their personnel. A medical curriculum was offered as "nursing." J. K. Zawodny, *Nothing but Honour: The Story of the Warsaw Uprising, 1944* (Stanford: Hoover Institution Press, 1978), 165. Nurses (*sanitariuszki*) celebrated in the "Pałacyk Michla" song were likelier medical residents. *Warszawa okupowana: relacje mieszkańców*, 48.

[105] Among the medical and science faculties, four of forty-five instructors were women and none full (habilitated) professors. Manteuffel, *UW w latach wojny i okupacji*, 29–33.

[106] "Ewa Krasnowolska," *Warszawa okupowana: relacje mieszkańców*, 49.

[107] Gieysztor worked as Stefan Korboński's deputy in the Directorate of Civil Resistance (*Kierownictwo Walki Cywilnej*, KWC).

[108] The 54 dropouts were men. BUW Rps 2203 (akc. 2466a): Letter from Marian Gieysztor to Tadeusz Manteuffel dated November 6, 1946.

administrators betrayed the same fear: all their work in putting the Warsaw educational system together might be for naught, as higher education became a "lady's project."[109] This was not simply a matter of the gendered nature of Nazi persecution, which weighed more heavily on men than women: this was also about the rise of the armed underground. Armed resistance and the Warsaw Uprising, which killed as much as half the graduating classes before fall 1945, drained the university of students.[110] The young Warsaw intelligentsia studied and worked in myriad clandestine projects. Unfortunately for the "flying" university, insurgency in the late occupation made overlapping opposition projects distinct. Participating in one came at the exclusion of others: as the front moved back toward Warsaw, contesting the occupation became a zero-sum game, and the university lost male students to the militaries.

The academy took heavy wartime losses. As in all conspiracies, there may be overlap in counting, as teachers, professors, and students were often engaged in other illegal projects, or caught up in the labor roundups and mass executions that stalked Warsaw.[111] Jan Gross estimates that by 1945 "more than half of [Poland's] lawyers were no more, along with two fifths of its medical doctors and one third of its university professors and Roman Catholic clergy."[112] A GG total of 16,936 (or 15.5 per cent) casualties among primary and secondary school teachers meant thousands of deaths in Warsaw.[113]

It might appear at first glance that the Warsaw professoriate suffered less than Poznań's – whose whole university fled to Warsaw – or Krakow, where 185 professors of the Jagiellonian University (UJ) faculty were arrested in November 1939 in *Sonderaktion Krakau* (Special Action: Krakow). The Krakow Gestapo sent them to Oranienburg and Sachsenhausen and killed seventeen.[114] International outcry stymied the *Sonderaktion*, as the Vatican and even Mussolini protested.[115] The roundup happened as Hans Frank was assuming office, and he backpedaled furiously.[116] Krakow was in better order than Warsaw in

---

[109] BUW Gabinet Rękopisów, Rps. 2203, Gadzikiewicz; Opoczynski.

[110] BUW Gabinet Rękopisów, Rps. 2203; Zaorski, Manteuffel, and law student responses.

[111] Some academics, like legal historian Adam Vetulani, were also reservists. Adam Vetulani, *Poza płomieniami wojny: internowani w Szwajcarii 1940-1945* (Warsaw: Wydawnictwo Ministerstwa Obrony Narodowej, 1976).

[112] Gross, *Fear*, 4.

[113] Eberhardt, *Geheimes Schulwesen*, 257.

[114] Zygmunt Starachowicz, *Sonderaktion Krakau: Wspomnienie z akcji przeciwko profesorm uniwersyteckim w Krakowie (6–10 listopada 1939 roku)* (Gdańsk: Muzeum II Wojny Światowej, 2012), 8–9; Stanisław Urbańczyk, *Uniwersytet za kolczastym drutem: Sachsenhausen-Dachau* (Krakow: Wydawnictwo Literackie, 2014); Kubalski, *Niemcy w Krakowie*, 40, 53.

[115] Mussolini requested "some realism on Poland" (R. J. B. Bosworth, *Mussolini* (London: Oxford University Press, 2002), 363). Prince Janusz Radziwiłł petitioned Goering for professors' release (Jakubowska, *Patrons of History*, 69).

[116] Winstone, *Dark Heart*, 58–59.

November 1939, and Bruno Müller, head of its Gestapo, had a simpler job than the men at Szuch Boulevard. Since Krakow was less violent, the arrest of its university faculty was striking.[117] In Warsaw where arrests and executions were commonplace, the targeting of educators was disguised by wider anti-intelligentsia campaigning and never triggered international protest.[118]

Warsaw's educators appeared on the initial Tannenberg lists. Even when otherwise unmolested, teachers and professors lost their jobs as Polish higher education closed and became vulnerable to labor requisitions. Before Sonderaktion Krakau, the Warsaw Gestapo arrested 354 people on October 8, 1939. Predominantly priests, teachers, and academics, they became hostages during Hitler's victory parade. In preparation for Polish Independence Day on November 11, 1939, the Gestapo arrested a few dozen elites, including Konstanty Krzeczkowski, professor at the Higher School of Economics and director of the Parliamentary Library. In spring 1940, they arrested people in cafes and restaurants, claiming at least one UW professor and a slew of politicians, lawyers, and publicists. In the first Palmiry murders, two educators and a junior high school principal were among the victims.[119] Teachers and professors were targeted during Tannenberg and AB, filled Pawiak cells, were transferred to Auschwitz and Sachsenhausen, and executed. Okiński was executed after Hanna Czaki's arrest, and he was not the only professor to die for his students. Manteuffel compiled a list of wartime university damages and came up with a figure of 159,778,564 zl in material losses. He approximated 3,500 arrested students and faculty. With more hesitation, he calculated 513 deaths of faculty and teaching staff, including a handful of suicides.[120]

In the material collected for Ludwig Fischer's postwar trial, the prosecution estimated that "35% of secondary school teachers and 30% of professors of higher education" were murdered or died prematurely and tallied "16 pre-school teachers, 75 primary school teachers, 233 secondary school teachers, 131 professors . . . and 29 people in education administration" killed under occupation.[121] Despite the outcry in Krakow over the 185 arrested and 17

---

[117] Sonderaktion Krakau is mentioned in histories of Nazi atrocity because it stands out; Warsaw drowned in arrests and faculty targeting was hard to distinguish. Mazower, *Hitler's Empire*, 75, 90.

[118] Szarota, *Okupowanej Warszawy*, 89.

[119] Bartoszewski, *1859 dni Warszawy*, 70, 81, 90, 103, 118, 120, 126, 136.

[120] BUW Rps 2205 [Sprowadzanie z Apelu poległych w czasie wojny nauczycieli Warszawy wraz z wnioskiem Zarządu m.st. W-wy w sprawie opublikowanie Księgi Pamiątkowej, z dn. 31.X.1945 r.], 7–11 and [Manteuffel – Nauczyciele szkół wyższych i pracownicy naukowi z Warszawy], 2; Manteuffel, *Uniwersytet Warszawski w latach wojny i okupacji*, 14–17, 21.

[121] USHMM RG 15.165M Proces Ludwika Fischera (IPN Sygn. GK 196), Reel 2, "Polski system oświatowy został zlikwidowany . . .," Kraścicka, 22.

killed, Fischer's trial material indicates that faculty losses in Warsaw were eight times higher. Though the precise tabulation of arrests, imprisonments, and murders vary, educators were deliberately targeted, with grave consequences for Polish society.

6.6   Conclusion

In combination with killing the intelligentsia, targeting Polish higher education was the most direct way the Nazi occupation decapitated Polish society. These barbaric tactics harmed the Warsaw intelligentsia, especially teachers and professors, and writers, publicists, librarians, and young people. Destruction and theft depleted school resources, in some cases closing them forever. Occupation ended academic careers, and only some could continue through risky underground classes. Participation in underground schooling, for boys as young as Maciej Piekarski and adults as old as the emeritus faculty of UW, changed the course of their lives. High numbers of women participated. Despite the harrowing risks of Gestapo arrest, torture, imprisonment, and execution, survivors of underground education remembered it with fondness. The high rates of graduation despite the circumstances demonstrate the perseverance and creativity of school directors like Dabrowski and Jędraszko. Home Army records and student and professor memoirs point to a contrarian success for education, which thrived as persecution imbued study with a spirit of patriotic danger and adventure.[122] The Germans turned study into a bloody fight for the education of a new generation of national leaders – one the Poles could win.

---

[122] Franaszek, *Miłosz*, 196.

Matters of Faith

Catholic Intelligentsia and the Church

Warsaw's Roman Catholic Church was much, much older than the conspiracies that mushroomed under occupation. Catholics acted variously, and Nazi persecution of Catholics and the Catholic Church was uneven. How Nazis treated Catholics underscores the inconsistencies of anti-intelligentsia policy as a whole. How Catholic leaders, priests, and lay people responded to Nazi persecution within the contours of their religious faith reveals not only much about the power of Catholicism in Poland, but also how religion was interpreted differently by its most devout adherents.

Catholicism predated Nazi occupation by a thousand years, and the majority of the city's population – especially its elite – belonged at least formally to the Church during the Second World War.[1] Warsaw boasted a higher percentage of Catholics than the rest of Poland. In 1939, Catholics composed 77.3 percent of the population in the Archdiocese of Warsaw. After the Nazis murdered Warsaw's Jewish community in 1942–43, the percentage of Catholics increased to more than 90 percent.[2] The Church, however, was not monolithic in its power. The diversity of parishes, religious orders, and episcopal personalities and the sprawl of lay faithful make it tricky but not impossible to describe specifically "Catholic" behavior. The faithfulness of its faithful, too, is up for debate, and Catholics emphasized very different religious teachings or flouted them entirely in opposing the occupation.

The historical position and power of the Church had always fluctuated, and it enjoyed uncertain prominence during the Second Polish Republic. This fluctuation was not particular to Poland: Catholics globally spent the twentieth

---

[1] In 1931, Catholics were 64.8 percent of the population, in 1970, 92.9 percent. In 1939, Poland was 64.8 percent Catholic; Warsaw archdiocese was 77.3 percent Catholic. Percentages in the *kresy* (eastern borderlands) were lower: Lwów Archdiocese 29.7 percent and Wilno Archdiocese 58.9 percent. Minorities included Protestants and Greek Catholics (Uniates). Główny Urząd Statystyczny Rzeczypospolitej Polskiej, *Mały Rocznik Statystyczny 1939* (Warsaw: Nakładem Głównego Urzędu Statystycznego, 1939), 354.

[2] Elżbieta Bilska-Wodecka, "From Multi-Confessional to Mono-Confessional State: State–Church Relations in Poland following World War II," *GeoJournal*, Vol. 67, No. 4, (2006), 341–355, 345.

century seeking a "proper form of Catholic modernity."[3] In his examination of the tensions in modern Polish Catholicism, historian Brian Porter-Szücs portrays a Church negotiating for influence in volatile interwar politics, not always successfully. He claims the Church secured the strongest spiritual and cultural influence precisely when Poland was partitioned, occupied, or controlled by foreigners.[4] In the old Russian partition, the sovereign was anti-Catholic; in the new Second Polish Republic, Catholicism was the majority religion.[5] After 1939, the Church had a new anti-Catholic master in Nazi Germany, but it preserved the loyalty of most Varsovians.

Catholic tradition influenced the intelligentsia's response but not because of consistent leadership from Church hierarchy. Instead, opposition emerged out of a culture infused with Catholicism. Polish antisemitism, anti-communism, and anti-Nazism were all deeply intertwined with Catholic culture. The Catholic elite response was a patchwork of initiatives encouraged, embraced, or dismissed by the Church.[6] The bishops were severed from the Vatican hierarchy, and Polish clergy were targeted, thinning the ranks of "professional" Catholic leaders. Facing these losses, the "lay" Catholic elite – churchgoers employed in secular professions – filled the gaps, diversifying "Catholic" response to Nazism. Both lay and religious Catholic opposition to occupation emerged from the intelligentsia, but not from the top of the ordained hierarchy, which was more willing to accommodate the occupation. Instead, most opposition came from local leaders, and sometimes from Catholic youth. Although this was an elite movement involving people of established social and cultural significance, it was not an institutional one. Most bishops did not publicly protest occupation, but pastors of major parishes and other priests did.[7] In Warsaw, the cardinal's absence was at least as important as the pope's silence. Nevertheless, despite little encouragement from Church hierarchy, robust lay and clerical Catholic initiatives blossomed.[8]

---

[3] James Chappel, *Catholic Modern: The Challenge of Totalitarianism and the Remaking of the Church* (Cambridge, MA: Harvard University Press, 2018), 255.

[4] Porter-Szücs, *Faith and Fatherland*, 208, 232.

[5] And was therefore able to seize Orthodox Church property – and occasionally its believers' loyalty. See "Revindications of Souls" in Snyder, *Sketches from a Secret War*, 147–167.

[6] Dean, "Where Did All the Collaborators Go," 796; Dunin-Wąsowicz, *Warszawa w latach 1939–1945*, 189.

[7] Michael Phayer considers the hierarchical nature of the Church a potential asset, in contrast to Protestantism. In Warsaw, it is clear the Church did *not* "realize its potential" as a resistance "vehicle." Phayer, *The Catholic Church and the Holocaust* (Bloomington: Indiana University Press, 2000), 114.

[8] This argument follows Michael Phayer's *Catholic Church and the Holocaust*, in which he asserts that "Pope Pius XII did relatively little ... and ... ordinary Catholics did a great deal more" during the war to undermine Nazism. Phayer's focus is on the Holocaust, but this holds true of anti-Nazi resistance broadly. Phayer, *Catholic Church and the Holocaust*, xi.

To explain how elite Catholic opposition emerged, the Vatican's posture and that of the Warsaw archbishops needs elucidating first. Since most of Warsaw's population was Catholic (though religious practice and belief varied), many of those we have already met fit under the umbrella of Catholic response.[9] Though there is continuity in Catholic theology and ritual, the precise beliefs of individual Catholics are slippery. Kossak, Pilecki, and Karski were religious; Karski's Jesuitical piety was renowned and encouraged co-conspirators to trust him.[10] Notably, these three lay Catholics were motivated by faith to very different actions, and this was also true of priests and religious ("religious" being the standard way to designate monks, nuns, and brothers in Catholic orders).

In defining a "Catholic response," some restraint must be exercised, acknowledging that the division between religious and political motivations was blurry. Nevertheless, for the purposes of trying to answer the tangled question of what the Church was doing during the occupation and the Holocaust, "Catholic response" will be limited to that undertaken by priests, monks, and nuns, and by lay men and women motivated by faith. In other words, those who defined their response to occupation *as Catholics*, functioning as a Catholic intelligentsia, are the emphasis here.

7.1 Nazi Treatment of Non-Polish Catholics

Nazi Germany first formulated Catholic policies at home.[11] Nazism arose in Bavaria, the heartland of German Catholicism. Although Germany's Catholics

---

[9] In June 1940 the GG was 81.1 percent Catholic and 64.5 percent after the 1941 expansion (Zenon Fijałkowski, *Kościół katolicki na ziemiach polskich w latach okupacji hitlerowskiej* (Warsaw: Książka i Wiedza, 1983), 62. G. K. Chesterton, the contemporary British publicist cum lay theologian, pointed to this messy reality, noting wryly that the "Church is larger inside than it is outside." Chesterton, "Why I Am a Catholic," in *The Collected Works of G. K. Chesterton*, Vol. III (San Francisco: Ignatius Press, 1990), 125–132.

[10] Karski was part of Kossak's Front for the Rebirth of Poland (Drozdowski, *Jan Karski Kozielewski*, 95–97). Marian Borzęcki, former minister of the interior, recruited Karski in 1939 on his brother's recommendation, trusting him as a member of the *Sodalicja Mariańska* (Wood and Jankowski, *Karski*, 32; USHMM RG-50.012.0044, AN: 1989.67.44, "Interview with Jan Karski," Part 1, 19:56–21:01). Notably, the intelligentsia was not straightforwardly Catholic: Miłosz was not an orthodox believer (Franaszek, *Miłosz*, 172, 220–222) and Karaszewicz-Tokarzewski became a bishop in a renegade offshoot church (Müller, *If the Walls Could Speak*, 87). Kulski was a Freemason of Jewish origin; he raised his son secular (USHMM RG-50.030.0769, AN: 2014.238.1, "Interview with Julian Kulski [Jr.]," 22:00–22:12).

[11] The treatment of Austrian Catholics – and Austrian Catholics' role in the Nazi empire – forms a tangent after the 1938 *Anschluss*. Austrians were prominent in the T4 euthanasia program and eastern European imperial projects. Sheffer, *Asperger's Children*, 21–22, 208–210.

survived Bismarck's nineteenth-century *Kulturkampf*, their social position was still vulnerable.[12] German bishops negotiated with Hitler while he consolidated power. During the *Gleichschaltung* (coordination) of German society in 1933, Hitler signed a Concordat with the Vatican, making clergy independent in matters of faith. The Concordat meant the Catholic Church's recognition of Hitler's state and was a key moment in its normalization in European politics.[13] Nevertheless, it was the gesture of a still-weak regime, not a sign of durable good will. After several years' cooperation, the Nazi regime attacked churches in 1935 and imprisoned a dozen priests in concentration camps, primarily Dachau.[14]

In response to clergy mistreatment, Pope Pius XI circulated "With Burning Hearts," an encyclical "On the Church and the German Reich," which priests read to their congregations in 1937. Pius XI acknowledged the Concordat's failure and warned against a coming "religious war."[15] In general, however, "the church ... carefully limited its struggle to the defense of Catholic interests and individuals."[16] Except for the so-called German Christians collaborating with Hitler's regime, the Nazi state curtailed religious freedom as it consolidated and rearmed.[17] No systematic Christian resistance developed in Germany.[18] The Nazis inconsistently persecuted German Catholics. The annexation of Austria, the citizens of whom were more than 90 percent Catholic, indicated how pronounced anti-Church sentiment had become by spring 1938: historian Evan Burr Bukey claims that Hitler considered "the Roman Catholic Church as his principal ideological opponent" there, restricting the Church's financial, political, and social power, and arresting and killing priests. This gross mistreatment resulted in spontaneous protests by Viennese Catholic youth, but the disorganization of Austrian bishops

---

[12] Christopher Clark, *Iron Kingdom: The Rise and Downfall of Prussia, 1600–1947*. (Cambridge: Belknap Press, 2006), 568–571; Smith, *Germany*, 279–280.

[13] Gerhart Binder, *Geschichte im Zeitalter der Weltkriege: Unsere Epoche von Bismarck bis heute. Erster Band: 1870 bis 1945* (Stuttgart: Seewald Verlag, 1977), 472; Gellately, *Backing Hitler*, 14; Phayer, *Catholic Church and the Holocaust*, 6.

[14] Religious victims were primarily Jehovah's Witnesses. Wachsmann, *KL*, 126; Guillaume Zeller, *The Priest Barracks: Dachau, 1938–1945* (San Francisco: Ignatius Press, 2017).

[15] The Holy See, Pope Pius XI, "*Mit Brennender Sorge*: Encyclical of Pope Pius XI," March 14, 1937: http://w2.vatican.va/content/pius-xi/en/encyclicals/documents/hf_p-xi_enc_14031937_mit-brennender-sorge.html.

[16] David Clay Large, *Berlin* (New York: Basic Books, 2000), 308–309; Zofia Waszkiewicz in *Na przełomie stuleci: Naród – kościół – państwo w XIX I XX wieku* (Lublin: Klub Inteligencji Katolickiej, 1997), 429–443.

[17] See Doris L. Bergen, *Twisted Cross: The German Christian Movement in the Third Reich* (Chapel Hill, NC: The University of North Carolina Press, 1996).

[18] Michael Burleigh, *Sacred Causes: The Clash of Religion and Politics, from the Great War to the War on Terror* (New York: HarperCollins, 2007), 176, 204; Jill Stephenson, *Hitler's Home Front: Württemberg under the Nazis* (London: Hambledon Continuum, 2006), 229.

stymied institutional opposition to Nazism.[19] Across the expanding Nazi empire, treatment of non-German Catholics depended on state relations.[20]

Heinrich Himmler became Nazi Germany's preeminent anti-Catholic, an "anti-Church hardliner" in Nazi circles where antipathy to religion varied. Himmler, as biographer Peter Longerich elaborates, harbored deep-seated resentments against the Catholic Church in which he was raised and was "bent on the destruction of Christianity."[21] He led anti-religious press campaigns and targeted priests, but his efforts were mollified by Hitler and others wary of international scandal. Himmler never had free rein to persecute German Catholics but experienced fewer restrictions in Poland.[22] German clergy occasionally protested the mistreatment of Polish coreligionists, but their influence was limited.[23] Polish Catholics also did not benefit from an early period of church–state cooperation; the Polish situation was dramatically more hostile. Nevertheless, the cautious role the Vatican took in Germany was the model for its approach in Poland.

Multiple strains of Nazi policy exacerbated the persecution of Warsaw Catholics, including the dismantling of Polish state structures, initial intelligentsia persecution, an association of Catholicism with Polish patriotism, attacks on education and cultural advancement, the use of priests as hostages for good behavior, and reprisals for resistance (real and imagined). Economic exploitation separated families, shattered parishes, and interrupted the liturgical calendar, turning centuries of feasting and fasting, thanksgiving, and penitence, into a stretch of secular exploitation. Pious Catholics – especially women – preserved holiday traditions and catechized children.[24] Certainly Catholics were persecuted and resisted in other Axis-controlled territory, but the combination of Nazi persecutions meant that the Church and its faithful were more viciously attacked in Poland than elsewhere.

Examining the experiences of Catholics living in states with intact Vatican relationships provides a useful contrast to Warsaw.[25] The Vatican prioritized

[19] Evan Burr Bukey, *Hitler's Austria: Popular Sentiment in the Nazi Era, 1938–1945* (Chapel Hill, NC: The University of North Carolina Press, 2000), 95, 110, 99–101.

[20] Pieter Lagrou criticizes the "Catholic resistance myth" among French priests in *The Legacy of Nazi Occupation: Patriotic Memory and National Recovery in Western Europe, 1945–1965* (Cambridge, UK: Cambridge University Press, 2000), 148–149. Austria was an interesting exception because of the Anschluss; see "Austrian Catholicism" in Bukey, *Hitler's Austria*, 93–111.

[21] Longerich, *Heinrich Himmler*, 220.

[22] Longerich, *Heinrich Himmler*, 104–109, 197, 218–225, 376, 677; Phayer, *Catholic Church and the Holocaust*, 111.

[23] John J. Delaney, "Racial Values vs. Religious Values: Clerical Opposition to Nazi Anti-Polish Racial Policy," *Church History* 70, No. 2 (2001), 271–294, 273.

[24] Zaprutko-Janicka, *Okupacja od kuchni*, 187–203.

[25] Wayne H. Bowen, "Spain and the Nazi Occupation of Poland, 1939–44," *International Social Science Review* 82, No. 3/4 (2007): 135–148.

official state relationships, but this was at the expense of articulating bolder anti-Nazi positions and advocating for non-Catholics.[26] Polish Catholics – let alone Polish Jews – were left in the cold: since the Vatican did not recognize the Nazi or Soviet occupations, it had no Warsaw government with which to work. Slovakia, France, and Germany all had significant Catholic populations and maintained Vatican relationships, and this was why their Catholics never faced the dangers Poland's did.

In Slovakia and Vichy France, bishops supported Nazi-allied regimes.[27] Slovakia was an overwhelmingly Catholic nation. It collaborated willingly with the Third Reich as a satellite. In Bratislava, unlike in Warsaw, there was no anti-intelligentsia campaign targeting priests, no despoiling of Church property, no closure of Catholic schools, and no Slovak contingent in the priest barracks at Dachau. There was also not much Slovak Catholic resistance. Not only did Slovak bishops cooperate in the new Slovak Republic puppet state, the president, Msgr. Jozef Tiso (1887–1947), was a Catholic priest. Unlike in Poland, the presence of a Catholic priest as head of state protected Catholic clergy, property, and the faithful. Tiso used the war to promote "political Catholicism," advance charities, and open schools.[28] He also helped deport the Bratislava Jewish community to the death camps during the Holocaust. Despite his participation in Nazi crimes, the Vatican never formally broke with Tiso and he was not excommunicated: "he was still dressed as a priest while in prison awaiting execution for treason in April 1947."[29]

Unlike Slovakia, the French Catholic Church did not have a monopoly on religious life. France was divided after its 1940 defeat, but rump Vichy France collaborated with Nazi Germany. Its head, the aging marshal Philippe Pétain (1856–1951), was popular with Catholic bishops. "Vichy's themes of contrition, sacrifice, and suffering resonated with Catholics" and strengthened the Church's role in education and politics, reversing the secularizing tendencies of interwar France.[30] Some – like Paris Cardinal Emmanuel Célestin Suhard (1874–1949) – were devoted to Pétain. Others criticized Vichy dependence on Germany, encroachments on Church authority, and the treatment of French Jews, but criticisms were not loud.[31] As the war turned against the Axis,

---

[26] John S. Conway, "The Silence of Pope Pius XII," *The Review of Politics* 27, No. 1 (Jan. 1965): 105–131; Robert S. Wistrich's "The Vatican and the Shoah," *Modern Judaism* 21, No. 2 (2001): 83–107.

[27] Ditto for Catholic Croats in the Independent State of Croatia (NIH). Greble, *Sarajevo*, 81–84.

[28] Ward, *Priest, Politician, Collaborator*, 202–245.

[29] Msgr. Domenico Tardini, Pius XII's aide, wanted harsher sanctions. Rees, *Holocaust*, 286–288.

[30] Jackson, *France: The Dark Years*, 269; John F. Sweets, *Choices in Vichy France: The French under Nazi Occupation* (New York: Oxford University Press, 1986), 54–60.

[31] Paxton gives French Catholics more credit for opposing Jewish persecution. Paxton, *Vichy France*, 153.

Catholic and other resistance increased. Still, no realistic portrait of the French Catholic Church could call it an opposition institution. The day-to-day persecution of Catholic priests that Warsaw endured was nonexistent, and the behavior of the Church contributed to that passivity. Apologists for the French posture asked, "Did not the Vichy regime save France from 'Polandization'?"[32] New Nazi colonies feared Warsaw's fate with good reason.

Though priests, bishops, and lay Catholics in Germany, Austria, Slovakia, and France took a variety of positions on Nazism, their freedom in navigating this was greater than that possessed by Polish Catholics. In much of Axis-dominated Europe, "Catholic policy" was negotiated between the Third Reich and the Vatican. The absence of the top of the Polish Catholic Church, after its September 1939 evacuation, prevented such negotiation, with enormous consequences for the lives of Warsaw Catholics. Their bishops did not mount a vigorous response, leaving the door open for a host of creative – but often conflicting – initiatives against the regime in the name of religion. The deep connection between Polishness and Catholicism meant that, since Nazi Germany wanted to "decapitate" Polish society and control its population, it placed itself in opposition to the Roman Catholic Church and its faithful.

7.2 The Vatican and the Church Hierarchy

While Germany planned its invasion of Poland in spring 1939, Eugenio Pacelli (1876–1958) became Pope Pius XII.[33] Pius XII upheld the Concordat he had arranged earlier with Germany, roundly denounced communism, and was quiet about Nazi antisemitism.[34] Privately, however, he nurtured ties to German anti-Nazi resistance.[35] His contradictory actions led people to characterize him as everything from "Hitler's pope" to a saint; in 2009, Pope Benedict XVI made him a "venerable," the last step before canonization.[36] A conservative institution, Pius XII's Catholic Church gravitated toward the right of the political spectrum and was suspicious of the left.[37] Certainly, the Church preferred traditionalist authoritarianism *a la* Franco's Spain over atheist communism, but it was also loath to embrace

---

[32] Paxton, *Vichy France*, 357.

[33] Pacelli was papal nuncio to Germany and then Cardinal Secretary of State.

[34] Pius XII (Eugenio Pacelli) was Vatican secretary of state during the Concordat. Pacelli proceeded with a conservative diplomacy. Binder, *Geschichte im Zeitalter der Weltkriege*, 473; Mark Riebling, *Church of Spies: The Pope's Secret War against Hitler* (New York: Basic Books, 2015). 58, 42.

[35] Riebling, *Church of Spies*.

[36] John Cornwell, *Hitler's Pope: The Secret History of Pius XII* (New York: Viking Press, 1999).

[37] Kosicki traces French-influenced left-leaning Polish Catholicism. Piotr H. Kosicki, *Catholics on the Barricades: Poland, France, and the "Revolution," 1891–1956.* (New Haven: Yale University Press, 2018), 66, 70, 92.

atheistic fascisms.[38] It rejected fascism and communism, "regard[ing] both [Soviet and Nazi] regimes as alien totalitarian ideologies."[39] Managing this double rejection while inside fascist Italy during the war became increasingly difficult. Poland, caught between the Soviet Union and Nazi Germany, was attacked from both sides. The Catholic Church officially opposed the ideologies of both occupying states as well as the persecution of its faithful. Poles believed this would mean substantive Church support. The Vatican nevertheless had few wartime directives for Varsovians. Individual Catholics, both priests and laymen, turned to Church teaching. Recognizing this need and opportunity, many lay elites rose to the challenge.[40]

Primate Cardinal August Hlond (1881–1948), in exile at the Vatican after his evacuation, pleaded Polish Catholics' wartime case to the pope.[41] He was vociferously anti-communist, anti-secular, and antisemitic, viewing Polishness as explicitly and exclusively Catholic.[42] Hlond's exile spared him the worst fate of Polish priests, but he did not entirely escape persecution. The German westward invasion in spring 1940 overtook his inauspiciously timed pilgrimage to the Marian shrine of Lourdes in France and made him a quasi-prisoner of the French Vichy collaborationist regime. Housed in a Benedictine abbey at Hautecombe, Hlond nevertheless broadcasted information about occupied Poland until he vanished in 1944.[43] As it turned out, the Gestapo had arrested him. The papal nuncio at Vichy, the pope, and Anthony Eden intervened at "this new act of unjustifiable violence by the Nazi regime," though Hlond was "reasonably well treated" by his captors.[44] He continued agitating on behalf of

---

[38] And it tried to balance between them. Stanley G. Payne and Jesús Palacios *Franco: A Personal and Political Biography* (Madison: University of Wisconsin Press, 2014); Applebaum, *Red Famine*, 303–304.

[39] Burleigh, *Sacred Causes*, 160.

[40] Kosicki, *Catholics on the Barricades*, 64.

[41] He evacuated with the government and reported to Rome. Hlond was in communication with Paderewski, media darling. AAN 2/100/1376 Archiwum Ignacego Jana Paderewskiego: Listy Augusta Hlonda.

[42] The intellectually formidable Hlond had doctorates in philosophy and theology and dominated the interwar church. His 1936 pastoral letter asserted Poland had a "Jewish problem" and associated Jews with prostitution, sedition, and Bolshevism. He called for a Jewish business boycott, but drew the line at violence or property destruction: "one may love one's own nation more; one may not hate anyone. Even Jews." The influence of Hlond's letter lingered. What his behavior might have been under occupation – and whether it would have changed Polish Holocaust responses – is unknowable. August Hlond, List Pasterski: "O Katolickie zasady moralne," Poznań February 29, 1936; Kunicki, *Between*, 39.

[43] TNA HW 12/299 Decrypts of Intercepted Diplomatic Communications, Decrypts 130016 (3 April 1944) – "he has not been heard of again" – and 130479 (April 4, 1944).

[44] AAN 2/493/0 Konsulat Generalny RP w Nowym Jorku: "Wizyta w USA kardynała Augusta Hlonda"; TNA FO 371/39513, Arrest by Germans of Cdl. Hlond (unpaginated). Quotations from: Polish Embassy (London) to Anthony Eden, March 25, 1944; O. O'Malley, British Embassy to Poland, March 9, 1944.

Polish Catholics. Hlond was eventually liberated by American troops and returned to Poland in summer 1945.[45]

Hlond kept the Polish-Catholic – but not the Polish-Jewish – plight a subject of international attention during the war. Western European Catholic press covered Poland sympathetically.[46] There were two Vatican broadcasts, on January 21 and mid-November 1940, which discussed the "martyr's fate" of Poland. The broadcasts conflated the ghettoization of Polish Jews with the persecution of Catholic Poles, like many wartime announcements.[47] They received a wide American Catholic audience and were translated into multiple languages.[48] The coverage did not ingratiate the Church to the Third Reich, but many Varsovians still believed the Vatican should provide more robust condemnation and concrete aid.[49]

Hlond's 1939 evacuation meant that the Polish Church was acephalous and Warsaw lacked Catholic leadership. Even had there been a complete hierarchy, relations between Warsaw and the Vatican would have been complex. The divide between Polish bishops and the "distant Vatican" had widened during the interwar, exacerbated by episcopal distrust of the late pope's pro-Piłsudski stance. The bishops believed Rome misunderstood the fraught relationship between Catholicism and Polish nationalism, and most sided with the Endecja.[50] In Michael Phayer's words, the young Poland "vibrated with a national Catholic identity that excluded Jews," and bishops encouraged these sentiments.[51] The pope who dominated the interwar, Pope Pius XI, spent three years as papal nuncio in Warsaw before his election to the papacy and comprehended Polish Catholicism.[52] His successor, Pope Pius XII, did not share the same concern for Warsaw.

---

[45] From a 1947 report, Adam Dziurok, *Instrukcje, wytyczne, okólniki dyrektor Departmentu V MBP dotyczące działań przeciwko Kościołowi katolickiemu w latach 1945-1953* (Krakow: Wydawnictwo Avalon, 2012), 286–287.

[46] Nowak, *Courier from Warsaw*, 238.

[47] From the "Vatican Broadcasts on Persecutions in German-Occupied Poland" in *The Persecution of the Catholic Church in German-Occupied Poland: Reports Presented by H. E. Cardinal Hlond, Primate of Poland, to Pope Pius XII, Vatican Broadcasts and Other Reliable Evidence* (London: Burns Oates, 1941), 115–123.

[48] And a December 1940 article in *L'Osservatore Romano*. The Chicago Catholic League sent assistance; Polish-American behavior was clergy-driven. Alfred L. Abramowicz, "The Catholic League for Religious Assistance to Poland," *Polish American Studies* 20, No. 1 (Jan.–Jun., 1963): 28–33, 32–33 and also A. J. Wycislo's "American Catholic Relief for Poland," *Polish American Studies* 19, No. 2 (Jul. – Dec., 1962), 100–107.

[49] Rees, *Holocaust*, 286; Phayer, *Catholic Church and the Holocaust*, 20–30.

[50] A fully-staffed Church would have approximated 1937 figures: 2 cardinals (1 primate), 3 archbishops, 41 bishops, 9,685 diocesan priests (with 97 military chaplains), and 16,820 male and female religious (monks, nuns, religious brothers and sisters). *Mały Rocznik Statystyczny 1939*, 23.

[51] Phayer, *Catholic Church and the Holocaust*, 7.

[52] Pius XI was opposed to a Church party (the Endecja), and dismissive of antisemitic violence. David I. Kertzer, *The Popes against the Jews: The Vatican's Role in the Rise of Modern Anti-Semitism* (New York: Vintage Books, 2001), 244, 250–252.

Figure 7.1 Warsaw's Catholic leadership before the war: Aleksander Kakowski (center), Antoni Szlagowski (second from right), and Stanisław Gall (third from right), 1938. Narodowe Archiwum Cyfrowe, 3/1/0/15/823.

Occupied Warsaw lacked both its primate and its archbishop. The old Cardinal Archbishop Aleksander Kakowski (1862–1938) died in late 1938 and the Germans obstructed his successor's appointment (Figure 7.1).[53] In lieu of an archbishop, Bishop Stanisław Gall (1865–1942) served as apostolic administrator. He opposed the Nazi occupation but advanced age and ill health constrained his actions.[54] When Gall died in September 1942, he was replaced by Bishop Antoni Szlagowski (1864–1956), a biblical scholar with a chair in homiletics at Warsaw University.[55] Szlagowski ran the archdiocese and handed power back to Hlond in 1945, happily returning to his studies. He supported his priests' political activities, though he

[53] Pierre Blet, *Pius XII and the Second World War: According to the Archives of the Vatican* (New York: Paulist Press, 1999), 72.

[54] Gall was a Varsovian. He studied in Warsaw and Rome, was promoted to archbishop in 1918 and served as field bishop in the Polish Army. His relations with Piłsudski were rocky and he retired in 1933 to be reinstated by the Vatican in 1940. Jerzy Prochwicz, *Arcybiskup Stanisław Gall (1865–1942): Biskup polowy Wojsk Polskich* (Warsaw: Ordynariat Polowy, 2018), 46, 6–9, 12, 24–25, 38–39. Warsaw mourned his death (BN Mf. 43293, *Prawda*, Wrzesień 1942 r., 8).

[55] Szlagowski was a theologian, educated in Warsaw and St. Petersburg. Waldemar Wojdecki, *Arcybiskup Antoni Szlagowski: Kaznodzieja Warszawy* (Warsaw: Wydawnictwo Archidiecezji Warszawskiej, 1997), 11, 31–32, 29.

condemned violence and insurgency, believing it would spark Nazi retaliation.[56] Still, Szlagowski was nearly eighty when he took up the post, a year older than his predecessor – archbishops were not young men.[57] Though Warsaw bishops had undeniable influence, many were elderly and preoccupied with protecting the Church. Most were silent on matters of Jewish persecution, defining their purview as the defense of Catholic interests.[58] Bishops in the GG maneuvered around the broken chain of command and "began to address themselves to the [papal] nuncio in Berlin, since this was the only recourse against the arbitrary actions of the German authorities."[59] The move further undermined the hierarchy and was another way Poles were ruled from Berlin, not Warsaw.

The senior GG clergyman, Cardinal Prince Adam Sapieha, attempted to rally Polish bishops from Krakow. Karol Wojtyła (1920–2005), later Pope John Paul II, studied under him as a seminarian. Wojtyła called the cardinal "the uncrowned king of Poland" and a center of moral authority, and he certainly was in the young priest's life.[60] Sapieha's presence was in sharp contrast to the absent Hlond, but Krakow, not chaotic Warsaw, was the center of his authority.[61] Sapieha gathered bishops in November 1940 for a conference, but Gall stayed away, afraid an ecclesiastical convention would be seen as political and provoke Nazi attack.[62] Sapieha also supported the Main Welfare Council (Rada Główna Opiekuńcza, RGO), intervened with Hans Frank on arrestees' behalf, and may have aided the Catholic underground movement, Unia (Unity).[63] In Warsaw, Szlagowski was more aggressive than Gall. In particular, he protested street executions and obtained some Pawiak prisoner releases from Fischer.[64]

Church hierarchy worked more closely with the German administration than most other Polish institutions and accommodated itself to occupation in ways intended to protect the Catholic faithful and keep the peace. This posture was

---

[56] Wojdecki, *Arcybiskup Antoni Szlagowski*, 8, 29.

[57] Fijałkowski, *Kościół katolicki*, 63. As Austrian bishops were, Bukey, *Hitler's Austria*, 106, 110.

[58] Henryk Muszyński, "Kardynał August Hlond (1926–1948) wobec Żydów," *Collectanea Theologica* 61/3, 1991: 81–87; Weigel, *Witness to Hope*, 47; Mordecai Paldiel, *The Path of the Righteous: Gentile Rescuers of Jews during the Holocaust* (Hoboken: KTAV Publishing House, 1993), 178.

[59] Blet, *Pius XII and the Second World War*, 72.

[60] Jan Paweł II, *Autobiografia* (Krakow: Wydawnictwo Literackie, 2003), 16–17.

[61] Sapieha's resignation was sitting – unsigned – on Pius XII's desk. Blet, *Pius XII and the Second World War*, 71; Weigel, *Witness to Hope*, 46, 73; Phayer, *Catholic Church and the Holocaust*, 28–29.

[62] Prochwicz, *Arcybiskup Stanisław Gall (1865–1942)*, 46–48. He did, however, refuse to join the Nazi occupation in an anti-communist crusade. Tomasz Szarota, "A Church Report from Poland for June and Half of July 1941," *Polin Studies in Polish Jewry, Vol. 30: Jewish Education in Eastern Europe*, ed. E. R. Adler and A. Polonsky (Liverpool: Liverpool University Press, 2018), 443.

[63] Fijałkowski, *Kościół katolicki*, 105–109; Ronikier, *Pamiętniki*, 35–36; Weigel, *Witness to Hope*, 73.

[64] Wojdecki, *Arcybiskup Antoni Szlagowski*, 30.

clearest in the cold relationship Sapieha had with Frank in Krakow, and the even colder one Szlagowski maintained with Fischer.[65] Bishops remained at their posts and were among the few Poles who obtained audiences with Nazi higher-ups. This likely borrowed from the Nazi obsequiousness toward the similarly internationally connected gentry, whom they treated gingerly. "Aristocratic titles, recognizable names, and grand estates," anthropologist Longina Jakubowska argues, "were an advantage when dealing with authorities, especially with high-ranking German officers."[66] Sapieha was, after all, a prince. German Catholics also deferred to men who led *their* Church, as they had from 1938 in Austria: when the Nazis arrived in Austria their supporters (fiercely anticlerical like most fascists) arrested a bishop and an archbishop but lacked the nerve to arrest the cardinal, who remained unmolested.[67] In a bizarre gesture indicative of this intermittent deference, Fischer and SS commander Erich von dem Bach-Żelewski gave Szlagowski an urn with Friedrich Chopin's heart for safekeeping during the 1944 uprising.[68] Szlagowski, a devotee of Chopin's music, was skeptical about the gift: he had received disturbingly inconsistent occupation treatment. Still, he remained at his post, and he accepted the urn.

Church hierarchy, though, did not always speak for the faithful: bishops, from the ambitious like Sapieha to the cautious like Gall, were conservative and their task was keeping the faith – not modifying or abandoning it. They clustered haphazardly on the political right, keen to condemn what they saw as "Jewish influence" in Poland, skeptical of democracy but most wary of atheist Marxism: they were authoritarians and traditionalists but not fascists.[69] The lay faithful, however, were more diverse: there were pious Catholics who embraced fascism and communism, or whose political and religious sensibilities changed under wartime pressures.[70] Church hierarchy spoke *to* the faithful in sermons, letters, and confessional boxes, but it did not control the Catholic intelligentsia. Nazi pronouncements demanded the Church stay outside politics.[71] As occupation unfolded, Catholic leaders – lay and religious – developed their own ideas about how they should behave.

[65] Some priests released parishioner records. Sapieha was asked to witness the Katyń exhumations in 1943, and refused, telling Frank he should improve treatment of Poles. Winstone, *Dark Heart*, 203.

[66] Jakubowska, *Patrons of History*, 67; Lehnstaedt, *Occupation*, 62.

[67] Bukey, *Hitler's Austria*, 97.

[68] In 1926 Szlagowski blessed Holy Cross Church's Chopin memorial. The bishop evacuated to Milanówek before the uprising and the Nazi governor gave him the urn to take with him. Wojdecki, *Arcybiskup Antoni Szlagowski*, 30, 208.

[69] In Austria the leaders of the Church were by and large monarchists; in Poland they had generally embraced the Second Polish Republic. Bukey, *Hitler's Austria*, 93.

[70] The best example is Bolesław Piasecki (1915–79). Kunicki, *Between*, xiii, 3.

[71] Zygmunt Zieliński, "Christian Churches in Poland under Nazi and Soviet Occupation," *Polish Review* 40, No. 3 (1995), 336, 340.

7.3   Cassocks, Confessionals, and Convents

A hierarchy of male religious structured Polish Catholic communities. The Church was also a real estate empire: churches, shrines, schools, convents, abbeys, monasteries, monuments, statues, cemeteries, hospitals, crypts, tombs, relics, and sundry devotional objects.[72] The Catholic Church is both its congregation and its possessions, impossible to thoroughly police. Attacking the Church and its faithful involved a politicization of objects and spaces that had resisted state encroachment for a millennium: the practicalities of Catholic life aided conspirators. The churches from which virtue and patriotism were preached on Sunday could provide meeting and hiding places for conspirators and storage for their equipment, personnel, and periodicals.

Churches were never above the fray, but intertwined with the population's fate.[73] Ola Watowa, poet Aleksander Wat's wife, took shelter in St. Alexander's on Three Crosses' Square in 1939.[74] Holy Cross Church (Figure 7.2) housed a field hospital during the invasion, and Karski met his brother there to discuss emerging opposition a few months later. Ryszard Czugajewski ("Orzeł," 1928–97), a devout Catholic teenager who joined the armed underground, was an altar boy at the Carmelite Church on the Vistula. He served at the Sunday lunchtime Mass when Fr. Tadeusz Jachimowski preached patriotic sermons and gave spiritual advice to conspiracy-minded youth.[75] Holy Savior's parishioners heard the sermons of Fr. Marceli Nowakowski (1882–1940), pastor of Holy Savior Church. They were not calls for pacifism. City convents and monasteries took in the homeless and those in hiding. Priests and nuns hid Gestapo targets, endangering entire religious communities.[76] People hid in churches during inclement weather, łapanki, aerial bombardment, and shelling. They prayed, ate, slept, and were reunited with families and friends in churches. The dead were buried in churchyards or memorialized on plaques tiling the entrances to sanctuaries, and commemorated in Masses or with lit candles in side altars flickering long after 1945. Sometimes this public use of city churches was the explicit initiative of priests; at others, people arrived and demanded help where they had been taught it would be given.

---

[72]   Phayer, *Catholic Church and the Holocaust*, 113.

[73]   The Nazis, too, attempted to seize church space for their own purposes: After the murder of its pastor, St. Anne's Church in Wilanów was used as an internment camp during the anti-intelligentsia actions and the uprising. Karol Mórawski and Wiesław Głębocki, *Warsawa: przewdonik turtystyczny* (Warsaw: Krajowa Agencja Wydawnicza, 1982), 307.

[74]   Watowa, *Wszystko co najważniejsze*, 30–33; Shore, *Caviar and Ashes*, 154.

[75]   Czugajewski, *Na Barykadach*, 9.

[76]   Zawacka was hidden by sisters of the Immaculate Conception of the Blessed Virgin Mary in Szymanów. Minczykowska, *Cichociemna Generał Elżbieta Zawacka*, 149–150, 156–157.

Figure 7.2 View from the Staszic Palace looking north up Krakowskie Przedmieście. Visible in the foreground is a statue of Copernicus and behind it the double towers of Holy Cross Church, ca. 1937.
Narodowe Archiwum Cyfrowe, 3/1/0/9/6705a.

The Gestapo understood city churches as nexuses of rebellion. Convents and monasteries, with their intricate layouts, subterranean crypts, and numerous exits, made them fabulous places to hide people, weapons, and equipment. The Gestapo shuttered churches and monitored Masses, seizing paintings, tapestries, and fixtures to "insure their safety."[77] German misuse desecrated Church property.[78] The Gestapo raided the Capuchin convent on

---

[77] PISM London: MID: Dział Polski, A. 10. 4/4, "Nazi love of art ...," press clipping, 21 December 1939.

[78] PISM London: MID: Dział Polski, A. 10. 4/1, "Kościoły bombardowane, niszczone i profanowane przez Niemców w Polsce," [n.d.], pp. 2–3; PISM London: MID: Dział Polski, A. 10. 4/1, "Ściśle tajne," [n.t.] [January 29, 1940], 4.

Miodowa Street in June 1941, looking for printing and radio equipment. Before 1939, Catholics produced an avalanche of journals, newspapers, and devotional tracts, and religious samizdat was a formidable branch of Warsaw's clandestine publishing.[79] During the Capuchin raid, policemen arrested thirty-eight, including the Capuchin provincial, Fr. Marian Brzeziński, and sent them to Pawiak, and then to Auschwitz.[80] In October 1941, the Niepokolany (Immaculata) met the same fate. The Gestapo arrested five Franciscan monks, including Br. Piotr Żukowski, for illegal printing, and sent them to Auschwitz.[81] The Allies liberated the only survivor in April 1945. In early 1944, the Salesian fathers heard the Gestapo's knock, and all twenty-six priests and brothers were taken to Pawiak, along with the fifteen priests left at Holy Cross Church. A few were publically hanged on Leszno Street, still in their cassocks. Bishop Szlagowski protested to Governor Fischer, who released some of them, indicating the bishop's influence at Brühl Palace when he employed it.[82]

Even when they rejected violent opposition, priests provided spiritual counsel to those who opposed the Nazi regime. Underground paramilitaries – save for committed atheists – wanted chaplains and found enthusiastic volunteers. Hearing confessions and distributing blessings and administering last rites for assassins and saboteurs, saying Masses of thanksgiving, and offering funerals – which the Gestapo patrolled, looking for suspects – kept priests busy.[83] Even the communist People's Army secured a Jesuit, Fr. Stefan Śliwiński, during the 1944 uprising.[84] Though the archbishop never joined any conspiracy, a refugee western bishop, Stanisław Adamski of Katowice (1875–1967), did. Using St. Anne's University Church on Krakowskie Przedmieście as his base, Adamski supervised Home Army spirituality.[85] Home Army and National Armed Forces (Narodowe Siły Zbrojne, NSZ) units had chaplains, some in high places. Zbigniew Kraszewski (1922–2004) was the officer-chaplain of an NSZ unit while a seminarian, and later became a bishop. Other NSZ officers had links to Church hierarchy, including a women's auxiliary group led by Hlond's niece and a platoon leader who was (postwar) primate Stefan

---

[79] The Church had some printing permissions. Dobroszycki, *Reptile Journalism*, 58–61.

[80] Twenty-two were imprisoned (16 released) and transported to Auschwitz in September 1941. Fijałkowski, *Kościół katolicki*, 77–78; Domańska, *Pawiak więzienie gestapo*, 159, 168.

[81] Not Kolbe's convent. Kolbe's brothers arrived at Auschwitz after his death.

[82] Domańska lists 26 Salesians; Fijałkowski 22. Domańska, *Pawiak więzienie gestapo*, 175, 417; Fijałkowski, *Kościół katolicki*, 78.

[83] Another example of differentiated Polish and Polish-Jewish persecution: funerals became occasions for further Polish political persecution; ghetto Jews were effectively denied funerals, or even decent burial of their dead. Bór-Komorowski, *Armia Podziemna*, 188; Leociak, *Text*, 183.

[84] Myszor, "Die katholische Kirche" in *Polnische Heimatarmee*, 383.

[85] Myszor, "Die katholische Kirche," 375.

Wyszyński's half-brother.[86] Clergy were vital to anti-Nazi activity, despite episcopal reticence.

7.4 Moral and Spiritual Crises

Ordained priests and lay people leapt into the struggle to combat the degradation of cultural, social, and moral life under occupation, behavior that does not fall neatly into collaboration and resistance dichotomies. According to one pessimistic diarist, Adam Chętnik, "a complete anarchy and lawlessness dominated Warsaw."[87] There were calls for patriotic prayer, upright behavior, and attention to dress, manners, and morals within families – or what was left of them.[88] Catholic periodicals and devotional literature attempted to keep faith alive, especially among youth.[89]

Fischer's administration also observed collapsing public morale. School closures and religious instruction bans left the young idle, alongside spikes in drinking and gambling.[90] Drunkenness as a moral and social blight was a shared obsession of both the underground and occupation, each of which blamed the other for its omnipresence.[91] Alcohol abuse was so prevalent that the Home Army condemned drunkenness in 1943.[92] Crime rose, especially

---

[86] Leszek Żebrowski, "Duszpasterstwo Narodowych Sił Zbrojnych" in *Na przełomie stuleci*, 458. With thanks to Brian Porter-Szücs for drawing my attention to this.

[87] BN Mf. 58174/Sygn. III. 7925, Adam Chętnik, "Pod niemiecko-hitlerowskim obuchem," 16.

[88] Witold Gombrowicz used the moral chaos of wartime Warsaw as the setting of his *Pornografia* (1960), a tale of exploitation and intergenerational conflict. Witold Gombrowicz, *Ferdydurke, Pornografia, Cosmos: Three Novels* (New York: Grove Press, Inc., 1978).

[89] Ronald Modras, "Interwar Polish Catholic Press on the Jewish Question," *Annals of the American Academy of Political and Social Science* 548, No. 1 (Nov., 1996), 169–190.

[90] This exacerbated the plight of poor children whose parents drank and gambled, and young intelligentsia women led efforts to care for them. Anna Zawadzka and Zofia Zawadzka, *Pełnić służbę: Z pamiętników harcerek Warszawy, 1939–1945* (Warsaw: Państwowy Instytut Wydawniczy, 1983), 57–61. (Authors were relatives of Tadeusz Zawadzki: another participant-analyst family).

[91] Chętnik attributed drunkenness to German requisitions, which rural Poles dodged by distilling *bimber* (moonshine) and selling it in cities. BN Mf. 58174/Sygn. III. 7925, Adam Chętnik, "Pod niemiecko-hitlerowskim obuchem," 60. According to London Poles, Germans monopolized distilling and selling liquor after November 1939 and encouraged drunkenness as a form of cultural debasement. PISM London: MID: Dział Polski, A. 10. 4/4, "Różne opracowania dotyczące sytuacja w Kraju: 1940–1941:" "Niszczenie Kultury Polskiej:" "Celowe Ogłupianie i Demoralizowanie Społeczeństwa Polskiego"; A. 10. 4/3, Sprawozdania z Kraju, 1940: "Sprawozdanie Gospodarcze z obszaru Polski zajętego przez Niemców," 10. Germans complained about drunkenness. BABL NS 19 2664, Partei und Wehrmacht im GG und ihre Führungsaufgaben, 24 August 1944, Point 2, "Dem Missbrauch von Alkohol muss energisch gesteuert werden," 199–200; Lehnstaedt, *Occupation*, 146–148.

[92] Order 123 issued December 15 1943. Pawlina, *Praca w dywersji*, 80–81; Engelking, "*Szanowny panie gistapo*," 35.

theft, and troubled Poles. Crimes committed under a violent regime – like loitering, theft, assault, arson, or murder – are more complex in their motivation than those committed outside a brutal occupation and their victims starkly politicized: to rob some people was patriotic, others treasonous.[93] The property and persons of Polish Jews could easily be targeted, and demands by the London Poles that denouncing Jews to the Gestapo or exploiting them was forbidden were repeated, and repeatedly ignored. Denunciation in general was ubiquitous and often anonymous; Poles felt themselves under surveillance by not only their occupiers but their own neighbors. The wartime environment reversed prewar moral and legal norms and flouting occupation policy became a form of political virtue.[94] Poles applauded people operating illegal businesses or smuggling food, as they depended on such "crimes" to live.[95] During Barbarossa in 1941, the "public mood" became especially tense, with a steep rise in Polish violence against Germans – civilians, police, military – from 1942 until the end of occupation.[96] Killing Germans was sometimes applauded, sometimes condemned, but always news.

To combat the collapse in public morality and calm the panicked, priests preached virtue and steadfastness from the pulpit. They called parishioners to avoid occasions of sin like the bottle, the cinema, and the casino.[97] They reached a broad audience, as Church attendance climbed under occupation (unsurprising considering other institutions' closure and widespread suffering).[98] Others utilized existing Church structures to protect young people.[99] Scouting and student organizations were prominent, and themselves became schools of opposition activity in Warsaw.[100]

"Tender" youth – ever the subject of their elders' worries – understood the situation differently. They saw themselves as actors in their own right, rather

---

[93] For recidivists, "Poland was a special case" and current Reich law, pre-1939 Polish law, and Polish and Soviet sentencing from the *kresy* were all used, with harshest punishments preferred. Majer, *"Non-Germans" under the Third Reich,"* 414–415; Piątkowski, "Przestępczość w okupowanej Warszawie" in *Porządek publiczny i bezpieczeństwo,* 271–275.

[94] On moral reversals under other occupations: Mazower, *Inside Hitler's Greece,* xv, 91–96; Bryant, *Prague in Black,* 258. See also: Engelking, *"Szanowny panie gistapo,"* 14, 23.

[95] "Warsaw was the only city in Europe in which it was possible to buy almost anything." Zaprutko-Janicka, *Okupacja od kuchni,* 79.

[96] From the Report of the Chief of Distrikt Warschau [Fischer to Frank] for the month of June 1941, dated July 12, 1941. Fischer, *Raporty,* 339–340.

[97] BN Mf. 43293, *Prawda,* Październik 1942 r., 13.

[98] Zieliński, "Christian Churches in Poland," 340. Also in Austria. Bukey, *Hitler's Austria,* 104.

[99] Wacław Auleytner, "Organizacje akademickie w okresie okupacji," *Sesja Historyczna, 50-lecia Duszpasterstwo Akademickiego* (Warsaw: Rektorat Kościoła Akademickiego św. Anny, 1981), 119.

[100] Scouting founder Kazimierz Lutosławski was priest and physician. Porter-Szücs, *Faith and Fatherland,* 253.

than impressionable Nazi victims. Pious teenagers made pledges of sober living and "vowed not to dance and stopped going to parties and movies."[101] Others were ready consumers of illegal liquor and profiteers of slackened wartime social and moral strictures, moving around Catholic norms with varying commitment to their reestablishment. For some, this was a crisis, the worst of the occupation, for others, an opportunity.

7.5   Persecution of Priests

Occupation interest in Varsovian virtue was primarily about passivity and extracting labor; the Church was both Nazi ally and enemy from day to day. International clout protected the top of the Church from the worst persecution, though the 1939 siege destroyed churches and wounded priests and faithful.[102] In power, Fischer's administration and the Gestapo inconsistently mistreated Warsaw Catholics. During the anti-intelligentsia campaigns, the Gestapo arrested and killed priests, restricted seminary training, and robbed Church assets.[103] The occupiers took clergy hostage, arresting around 300 priests in fall 1939.[104] By Tomasz Szarota's calculations, "one in eight priests and one in twelve religious brothers gave his life for Poland."[105]

Church persecution was not concentrated on Warsaw, however: western Poland, incorporated into the Reich and de-Polonized, saw the harshest religious oppression.[106] De-Polonization was linked with de-Catholicization because Germans perceived that Catholicism was part and parcel of Polish identity.[107]

---

[101] Rowinski, *That the Nightingale Return*, 140.

[102] Jakub Dąbrowski, Pastor of St. James the Apostle in Ochota, was killed during bombardment: http://parafiajakuba.pl/historia-parafii/.

[103] 800 priests were arrested from 1939 to 1940. Winstone, *Dark Heart*, 69; Phayer, *Church and the Holocaust*, 22.

[104] More violent than anywere else: 15 Austrian priests were killed in 1938, though more were arrested. Bukey, *Hitler's Austria*, 99. Holy Cross priests were released, though they would end up in Gross-Rosen in February 1944. See: "Historia: najważniejsze daty:" http://www.swkrzyz.pl/index.php/historia/najwazniejsze-daty [accessed March 14, 2018]. Chopin's heart is buried inside Holy Cross Church. Mórawski and Głębocki, *Warsawa: przewodnik turtystyczny*, 104–106.

[105] Szarota, *Okupowanej Warszawy*, 92.

[106] Most closures were in western Poland in Arthur Greiser's Warthegau, which killed 133 priests; arrested bishops; shut down Catholic presses, schools, relief organizations, and banned singing "Boże coś Polskę" and the use of Polish in the confessional. Rees, *Holocaust*, 152; Epstein, *Model Nazi*, 102, 222–230; Rutherford, *Prelude to the Final Solution*, 82; Czesław Łuczak, "Polityka Arthura Greisera wobec wspólnot wyznaniowych w Kraju Warty (1939-1945)," in *Na przełomie stuleci:*, 445–449. Diemut Majer's assertion that "Church life was not affected ... because the church was required as a steadying and disciplinary factor" in the GG is false. Majer, *"Non-Germans" under the Third Reich*, 223, 291.

[107] Porter-Szücs, *Faith and Fatherland*, 328–359; Lehnstaedt, *Occupation*, 140–141.

Priests expelled from western Poland fled into the GG.[108] Despite clergy murders, Warsaw therefore had "extra" priests. Nevertheless, religious communities were discombobulated and newcomers badly positioned to replace arrested locals in the paranoid circumstances of occupation, as they lacked established relationships to parishioners. German occupation personnel were sometimes also Catholics, but potential solidarity between German Catholic occupiers and Catholic Poles was thwarted by careful provision of separate German-language services and clergy.[109]

Seminary training was a crucial matter, as it ran afoul of Nazi plans: a higher education project with a Catholic bent.[110] Wincenty Kwiatkowski, an academic priest in Warsaw University's theology department, directed underground instruction when seminaries shuttered. Kwiatkowski taught forty-five seminarians and oversaw nine research projects under occupation. His "flying" seminars met at the Church of St. Teresa in Powiśle, the Felician sisters' convent (in Wiśniew), and the rectories of the Church of Our Lady in the Old Town and St. Anthony's on Senatorska Street. Kwiatkowski survived, but he lost two priest colleagues and one seminarian to the Gestapo.[111]

Pastor of All Saints' Church Fr. Marceli Godlewski (1865–1945) also found himself in opposition to Nazi occupation. Though his antisemitic reputation would not have inclined anyone to expect it, he rescued Jewish children.[112] Godlewski's prewar politics followed the Endecja, and he preached on German, Jewish, and socialist hostility to Poland.[113] His massive church – another Marconi architectural project – sat on Grzybowski Square and counted 50,000 parishioners.[114] Not far from Pawiak, it was enclosed in the ghetto in 1940. Officially in charge of the souls of ghetto Catholics (the 2,000 Varsovians of Jewish origin who had converted to Catholicism) the priest became a human link between the ghetto and the city after 1940.[115] His

---

[108] "First Report of Cardinal Hlond, Primate of Poland, to Pope Pius XII: Religious Situation in the Archdioceses of Gniezno and Poznan" in *Persecution of the Catholic Church in German-Occupied Poland,* 5 and "supplementary reports," March 1941, 109.

[109] Lehnstaedt, *Occupation,* 142–143. They were just as likely Austrian as German Catholics because of the overrepresentation of Austrians in Nazi imperial administration and especially the SS. Bukey, *Hitler's Austria,* 43.

[110] Gollert and Fischer, "Das polnische Schulwesen und das Minderheitenschulwesen" in *Warschau unter deutchen Herrschaft,* 256; Chrobaczyński, *Tajna szkoła w okupowanym Krakowie (1939–1945),* 49, 91; Zieliński, "Christian Churches in Poland," 340.

[111] BUW Rps 2203 [Kwestionariusz w sprawie tajnego nauczania], 15 October 1945, Ks. prof. dr Wincenty Kwiatkowski, 1–2.

[112] Prochwicz, *Arcybiskup Stanisław Gall (1865–1942),* 49; Karol Madaj and Małgorzata Żuławnik, *Proboszcz Getta* (Warsaw: IPN, 2010), 31.

[113] APmstW 72-201-0-25-674, Mf. 21162–21227, Zbiór Korotyńskich: Godlewski Marceli; Madaj and Żuławnik, *Proboszcz Getta,* 34–36.

[114] Mórawski and Głębocki, *Warsawa: przewdonik turtystyczny,* 246–247.

[115] There were 1,718 "official" converts but 4,000 at some Masses. Dembowski, *Christians in the Warsaw Ghetto,* 66.

presbytery housed and protected several converts, most notably the family of Ludwik Hirszfeld (1885–1954), a leading European microbiologist and the discoverer of human blood types. Hirszfeld was a devout Catholic of Jewish origin and organized public health measures in the ghetto. The Hirszfelds escaped into Polish Warsaw in 1943 though their daughter, Marysia, died of tuberculosis and was buried by the family priest in a Polish "country churchyard."[116] Their protector, Godlewski, was an antisemite moved, in Peter Dembowski's judgment, "by the mysterious quality of human decency."[117] He smuggled twenty Jewish boys and then hundreds more children out of the ghetto into two Franciscan orphanages, where the sisters disguised them as Catholic orphans.[118] The Jewish community, however, had little reason to trust a famous antisemite like Godlewski. Emanuel Ringelblum looked askance at converts and accused the priest of "soul snatching," worrying Jewish children would be converted to Catholicism, which they by and large were – though they survived the war when their families did not.[119]

Godlewski also "adjusted" baptismal certificates, vital documents for verifying identity and allowing Varsovians to obtain work and residence cards. Though he (and other clergy) were loath to impugn sacraments by issuing false certificates of baptism, he eagerly protected converts. Catholics of Jewish origin brought documents to All Saints' rectory for "aryanization," changing family first names to erase traces of Jewish identity.[120] This multifaceted aid scheme was vulnerable: Godlewski's transit pass was cancelled in 1942, shutting him out of his parish, a slap on the wrist compared to many of his co-religionists in clerics.[121] Though Godlewski was a confirmed antisemite, he took pity on ghetto children and used Catholic religious networks to save a number of them. His focus, however, remained on baptized Catholics.

---

[116] Leociak, *Text*, 115, 169; Engelking and Leociak, *Getto warszawskie*, 678.

[117] Dembowski, *Christians in the Warsaw Ghetto*, 65.

[118] Six by Godlewski himself, another infant whose mother died in 1943, and the rest through the system he established. Madaj and Żuławnik, *Proboszcz Getta*, 107–108; Bikont, *Sendlerowa w ukryciu*, XX.

[119] Ringelblum came down in favor of Catholic rescue of children. Ringelblum, *Kronika getta warszawskiego*, 434–436; Dembowski, *Christians in the Warsaw Ghetto*, 80–82. Catholics caring for Jewish children often raised them Catholic: Edward Reicher, a Polish-Jewish doctor, left his five-year-old with a Pole. The girl's prayers to the Blessed Virgin later thwarted several Poles attacking the family, since they believed the child was Catholic. Edward Reicher, *Country of Ash: A Jewish Doctor in Poland, 1939–1945* (New York: Bellevue Press, 2013), 156. See also: Grabowski, *Na posterunku*, 183.

[120] Warsaw clergy were stingy with baptismal certificates. Madaj and Żuławnik, *Proboszcz Getta*, 113–114. In occupied Sarajevo, non-Jewish religious leaders freely approved "conversions." Greble, *Sarajaevo, 1941–1945*, 93–94. In Vienna, Georg Bichlmair of the Pauline Missionary Society supported Catholics of Jewish origin and helped some emigrate. Bukey, *Hitler's Austria*, 106.

[121] Dembowski, *Christians in the Warsaw Ghetto*, 130–131.

Monsignor Zygmunt Kaczyński (1894–1953), Polish Catholic Press Agency director, kept Hlond and the pope informed of how priests were treated and how the situation was developing. Kaczyński began a 1940 report to Hlond with the telling caveat that, "I have had to bear relatively less ill-treatment and injury from the Hitlerian regime than others of my fellow-clerics, having been arrested only once and having been interrogated by the Gestapo eight times, without having been beaten or otherwise injured as others were." (Focusing on Church persecution, reports omitted Jewish victimization – even that of Polish-Jewish converts.[122]) Arrest, interrogation, and torture was standard fare for Warsaw priests. Kaczyński came off lightly compared to Holy Savior's Fr. Nowakowski, who "was sentenced to death merely because he was found in his church praying for the independence of Poland."[123] To be clear, Nowakowski was no humble cleric, but the pastor of one of Warsaw's biggest parishes and a leading figure in the Endecja.[124] His pulpit shaped Varsovian opinion. His fire and brimstone homilies infuriated the Gestapo and sent him to Pawiak in December 1939.[125] Nowakowski was shot at Palmiry with eighty others in January 1940; he was not the only Warsaw priest buried there.[126]

Kaczyński conservatively estimated thirty priests imprisoned in Warsaw when he wrote to Hlond. The clergy were well aware their mistreatment formed part of the "annihilation of the intellectual classes."[127] Arrests intimidated priests and their congregations; cassocks were scarce on Warsaw streets because priests dressed "as civilians" to avoid police harassment.[128] The priests of St. Anne's university church on Krakowskie Przedmieście were in and out of Pawiak.[129] The Gestapo shot those who disobeyed publically, like Nowakowski.

Because of the Church's international influence and because execution risked making martyrs of them, the Nazis preferred to imprison clergy rather than kill them.[130] Hundreds moved through Pawiak into concentration camps.

---

[122] Rees, *Holocaust*, 285–286.

[123] His church was one of Warsaw's landmark parishes. See "Historia," "Sanktuarium Matki Parafia Zbawiciela" http://parafiazbawiciela.org/historia/ [accessed March 14, 2018]; "Report of Monsignor Kaczynski," *Persecution of the Catholic Church in German-Occupied Poland*, 89, 92–93.

[124] PISM London: MID: Dział Polski, A. 10. 4/1, "Notatka z rozmowy z panem N. R. który wyjechał z Warszawy 26 stycznia 1940," Rome, [1].

[125] Also Fr. Bronisław Wróblewski, executed in 1940. Bartoszewski, *1859 dni Warszawy*, 89.

[126] According to Bartoszewski, Nowakowski was executed with "Jewish intelligentsia" (Bartoszewski, *1859 dni Warszawy*, 105); Fr. Zygmunt Sajna and the pastor of St. Anne's in Wilanów, Jan Krawczyk, were killed at Palmiry (Wardzyńska, *Był rok 1939*, 244, 263; Fijałkowski, *Kościół katolicki*, 76).

[127] Fijałkowski, *Kościół katolicki*, 95.

[128] PISM London: MID: Dział Polski, A. 10. 4/2(II), "Notatka z rozmowy z panią, P.D.W." Rome, April 1,1940, x.

[129] Auleytner, "Organizacje akademickie w okresie okupacji," 120.

[130] Riebling, *Church of Spies*, 61.

In 1939 and 1940, priests went to Buchenwald, Oranienburg-Sachsenhausen, Mauthausen-Gusen, and, after 1940, Auschwitz, while military chaplains went to POW camps.[131] Nuns went to Ravensbrück or Auschwitz.[132] In most camps, priests intermingled with other Polish political prisoners. Here, too, the Nazis used them as hostages to ensure prisoners' good behavior.[133] Due to the intervention of the apostolic nuncio in Berlin, Nazi Germany streamlined its treatment of priests at the beginning of 1941 and collected them in Dachau.[134] There a kind of mini-Vatican formed of priests from Czechoslovakia, Austria, Germany, France, Belgium, and Poland. The SS housed them in designated barracks and offered privileges, like access to communion wafers and the chance to say Mass. These privileges were used against them, however, as "SS and Kapos repeatedly turned religious ceremonies into occasions for torture . . . and dished out special abuse during holy days."

Poles were the majority of Dachau priests and occupied the bottom of camp hierarchies. According to Guillaume Zeller, the author of the first study on Dachau priests, "sixty-five percent of the priests interned in Dachau, and eighty-four percent of those who died there, were Polish." Of the 1,870 Polish Catholic priests in the camp, 900 died at SS hands.[135] Polish priests had a higher mortality rate than other clergy, were housed separately, given lower rations, beaten by fellow prisoners, and selected for medical experimentation. During a virulent typhus epidemic in 1944, Polish priests volunteered to care for the sick. Half survived until liberation by the American army in April 1945.[136]

Dachau survivors remembered the Polish priests well. Bernard Nissenbaum, a French-Jewish intellectual, spent time in fourteen different camps. He encountered Varsovian priests in summer 1944. Ill disposed toward Poles,

---

[131] Oranienburg-Sachsenhausen was the destination of the UJ faculty in November 1939, including two priests. PISM London: MID: Dział Polski, A. 10. 4/2(I), „Listy uczony krakowskich," [2].

[132] Warsaw nuns arrived in Ravensbrück in late 1944 after having been raped. A dozen were executed before the evacuation. Helm, *Ravensbrück*, 406–408; 579–580.

[133] The most famous is Franciscan Maksymilian Kolbe (1894–1941). Kolbe was prominent in the Catholic press and founded a Marian monastery (Niepokolanów). He was imprisoned in Sachsenhausen and released. In 1940, he revived his prewar journal, *Rycerz*, with German approval, for which he was vilified as a collaborator by other Poles. In early 1941, *Rycerz* and the monastery were closed and Kolbe sent to Pawiak and then Auschwitz. In Auschwitz, Kolbe volunteered to replace another Pole selected to die. He was canonized by John Paul II in 1982. Danuta Czech, "The Auschwitz Prisoner Administration" in *Anatomy of the Auschwitz Death Camp*, 377; Dobroszycki, *Reptile Journalism*, 62.

[134] Zeller, *Priest Barracks*, 31.

[135] Wachsmann, *KL*, 505.

[136] Their 48 percent mortality rate was "ten points more than the average." Zeller, *Priest Barracks*, 27, 85–86, 110, 114, 130–132, 148, 154–157.

whom he considered "strongly antisemitic, more than any other population in the world," he remembered the Polish priests, writing, "We soon came in contact with the inmates of Dachau ... They behaved towards us very comradely. Still more impressed we were by the behavior of the Polish priests (prisoners, of course), who registered us. These Polish priests deserved all praise!" The solicitous conduct of the priests made Dachau "the best [camp] I have been interned in," though half, unlike Nissenbaum, perished.[137]

Priests' exploitation was no secret. Exiles called Church persecution "a campaign of barbarous extermination ... [that] can find no parallel other than the anti-religious terror of the Bolshevists" and estimated "over seven hundred" priests had been killed and 3,000 more imprisoned.[138] Imprisoning priests was designed to intimidate Catholics.[139] Arrests nevertheless did not end Catholic opposition. In fact, the murder of priests, understood by many Catholics as martyrdom on the model of Christ, brought some faithful closer to the Church. It narrowed the gap between the "common" parishioner and the "elite" priest in wartime Warsaw.[140] As the war spread, London Poles sought to keep Polish suffering the subject of international attention; they hoped Catholics in France, Great Britain, and the United States might sympathize with their co-religionists and respond. Despite the greater persecution in western Poland, Nazi anti-Catholic persecution affected Warsaw deeply, expelled a number of her priests to distant prisons and camps, and raised fears about the Church's future.

7.6   Unionism and Future Catholic Polands

Nazi persecution of clergy paved the way for lay Catholic intelligentsia projects and lay-clergy cooperation. A lay-clergy initiative arose around Iuventus Christiana (Christian Youth) at St. Anne's University Church, an opposition hub. The church was damaged in 1939, its priests repeatedly arrested, and Bishop Adamski used its convent as his offices. In November 1939, while anti-intelligentsia campaigning unfolded, Iuventus members reformed their group underground in a network of five-person communities. Perhaps twenty of these existed in 1939, doing charity work with refugees and prisoners alongside Śliwiński's ROM. Polish education closures affected Iuventus's student participants. Organizers were arrested in March 1940, including the previously-mentioned Fr. Peplau, one of their spiritual advisers. This decimated Iuventus and other charities, which only resurfaced as anti-intelligentsia campaigning

---

[137] USHMM RG 02.005.01, "My Deportation," Bernard Nissenbaum, 1; 26; 34–35.

[138] Polish Ministry of Information, *German New Order*, 317, 310.

[139] Fijałkowski, *Kościół katolicki*, 65, 68.

[140] Priests earned "about twice what state civil servants earned." Occupation reduced clergy finances but enhanced moral authority. Porter-Szücs, *Faith and Fatherland*, 135; Fijałkowski, *Kościół katolicki*, 71.

quieted.[141] Catholic opposition, like other initiatives, had numerous false starts in 1939 and 1940.

One Catholic intelligentsia project weathered early occupation: Unia (Unity), named for the first of the "four marks" of Roman Catholicism.[142] Unity became the largest wartime Catholic underground organization and through it, priests, lay elites, and youth shaped occupation life. Its creator, Jerzy Braun (1901–75), was a prominent Krakovian literary figure. Braun's grandfather fought in the 1863 uprising, his mother joined the women's auxiliary to Piłsudski's Legions, and the whole family participated in scouting, one of his lifelong passions.[143] Braun fought in the Polish-Bolshevik War and held a degree from the Jagiellonian. He wrote prolifically – novels, poetry, political treatises. He published *Nowa Polska* (New Poland) and *Kultura Jutra* (Tomorrow's Culture) under occupation.[144] A fervent Catholic, he criticized what he saw as insufficient religiosity and fractious politics during the Second Polish Republic.[145] He saw the war as an opportunity – though a brutal one – to rebuild a more Catholic Poland in the postwar. He called this movement to rebuild Poland "Unionism" and the organization that promoted it, "Unity."

Braun founded Unity in Warsaw in spring 1940, merging Catholic groups into a multifaceted religious conspiracy. The movement meant different things to different people: in mature form, it encompassed five subdivisions: a social union, a cultural union, a labor union, a women's union, and a youth union.[146] Seminarians like Karol Wojtyła participated in Unity rosary sodalities.[147] Violence was not outside its purview: Colonel Stanisław "Edward" Grodzki (1895–1946), an army staff officer, commanded its military branch (Organizacja Wojskowa "Unia"). In 1941–42, Unity forces numbered 20,000 men and had their own grenade factory, but merged with the Home Army in summer 1942.[148] Unity existed autonomously for three years before fusing with the Labor Party (Stronnictwo Pracy, SP) in March 1943, part of the

---

[141] Auleytner, "Organizacje akademickie w okresie okupacji," 119–123.

[142] The Four Marks of Catholicism – unity, holiness, universality, apostolicity – date to early Christianity. Braun saw them as a touchstone for connection outside party and class divisions.

[143] Maria Żychowska, *Jerzy Braun (1901–1975): Harcerz, poeta, filozof, publicysta,* Nr. 4 (Warsaw: Zespół Historyczny GK ZHP, 1983), 5–7.

[144] Bartoszewski, *1859 dni Warszawy,* 343.

[145] Endecja captured the clergy, though with difficulty. Porter-Szücs, *Faith and Fatherland,* 254.

[146] Maria Żychowska, *Jerzy Braun (1901–1975): twórca kultury harcerskiej i 'Unionizmu,'* (Tarnów: Harcerska Pracownia Archiwalno-Naukowa, 2003), 41.

[147] It brought together Catholic intellectuals like Jerzy Braun and Jerzy Turowicz, who created *Tygodnik Powszechny,* the biggest Polish Catholic periodical. Kosicki, *Catholics on the Barricades,* 89–91; Weigel, *Witness to Hope,* 66–67.

[148] KHPSGL, Polskie Siły Zbrojne, Tom III: Armia Krajowa, 163; Żychowska, *Jerzy Braun,* 43.

alphabet soup of overlapping organizations across the underground. After the merger, Unity retained considerable independence. Braun served in the underground parliamentary body alongside Stefan Korboński and became the last government delegate (*delegat rządu na kraj*) to the London exiles, demonstrating his influence under occupation.[149]

Unity had a distinct vision. Though it had its origins in Polish Christian Democracy and Catholic subsidiarity, it rejected the Second Polish Republic entirely.[150] When he assumed "the Second World War was drawing to a close" in 1942, Braun specified its program.[151] Blaming both world wars on imperialism externally and on internal political confusion between left-wing atheists and right-wing reactionaries, unionism saw itself as a middle course promoting long-term peace in Poland and Europe. Diagnosing European civilization as caught between two worldviews whose conflict played out in a three-phase cycle – first liberal-democratic, then totalitarian-nationalist, then social-communist – Braun believed unionism, the "Polish moral-political system" would break the cycle. He also thought that, through a central European Union of Nations led by Poles, they could bring (western) Christianity to Russia. Contemporaries might have noticed a whiff of Hegelian synthesis in this, but metaphysician Braun preferred to categorize knowledge in paired antinomies. He wanted international law re-grounded in natural law. He despised Woodrow Wilson's League of Nations, which perpetuated imperialism by allowing great power domination. Within Poland, he called for a "moral renewal of democracy," a revolution. Unionism held that the "majority is not always right" and a just society would balance majority rule against objective truth, as "the mechanical precept of majority rule must be perfected by the addition of the right moral precept."[152] The right moral precept came from Catholic teaching.

Unionism promised a society "better in accord with human nature" and an end to conflicts based on class, racial, and national difference. Although Braun believed in nations, he discounted class and race as materialist illusions. Unionists wanted a society based on the family, with each nation grounded in the family as a "unity of common descent" and "school of love for the Fatherland," all based on the Church, a "spiritual unity," a collective built on love. Decrying the excesses of liberal democracy which allowed the few to enrich themselves "without limits" to the detriment of the many, he wanted economic

---

149 *Stronnictwo Pracy* was Wojciech Korfanty's Christian Democratic Party. Żychowska, *Jerzy Braun*, 44–45.

150 Nicholas Aroney, "Subsidiarity, Federalism and the Best Constitution: Thomas Aquinas on City, Province and Empire," *Law and Philosophy* 26, No. 2 (2007), 161–228.

151 AAN 2-1440-0 sygn. 344/1, Unia [Organizacja podziemna z siedzibą w Warszawie], "Unionizm: podstawowe zasady doktryny," [1942–1943], [2]. His 1942 "Unionizm: podstawowe zasady doktryny" was printed in 2,000 copies (Żychowska, *Jerzy Braun*, 41).

152 AAN 2-1440-0 sygn. 344/1, Unia, "Unionizm," [1942–1943], [7], [4], [12], [4].

interdependence to replace capitalist competition.[153] Though governance was not detailed, Unionists rejected a clerical party state. Instead, they promised an end to the party squabbling that overwhelmed the Second Polish Republic.

Admittedly, lay Catholics under occupation were more concerned with survival than Braun's Catholic solidarity program. His central idea – a union of political and ethical principles, with no division between public and private life – was nevertheless promulgated widely. Scouts regarded Braun as their hero and worked tirelessly to further his causes; Braun was hardly a fringe figure in the underground.[154]

Braun and his Unionist compatriots focused on the Polish nation (*naród*) in a unionist future. Non-Catholic religions, and particularly Warsaw's large Jewish community, presented a problem. Influenced by interwar ideas of Jewish removal supported by Bolesław Piasecki's National Radicals and Wojciech Korfanty's Christian Democrats, Braun sketched a "solution" to the Jewish question as a "project for discussion" among Unionists. It drew on a tradition of radical answers to the "Jewish question" entertained in free Poland, not just antisemitism imported from Nazi Germany.[155] Beginning with citations from Luke's and Matthew's Gospels, Braun considered Judaism antithetical to a future unionist Poland.[156] He clarified that his objection was not on racial grounds (condemned by Church teaching), but instead on "religious and national" ones. Braun believed the Jewish community unassimilable into the Catholic majority.[157] Acknowledging the complexity of Polish-Jewishness, he nevertheless believed in a Jewish "international mafia organization" opposed to Christian interests:

> The most effective defense against Jews is a high moral standard in society . . . Jews have recognized the Catholic Church as their greatest enemy . . . a struggle with the Catholic Church and Catholic nations is the main goal of Jewishness [*żydostwo*] . . . In this activity the Jews make use of Masonic

---

[153] AAN 2-1440-0 sygn. 344/1, Unia, "Unionizm," [1942–1943], [4a], [5], [5a].

[154] Braun was arrested in 1948 and tortured. Released in 1965, he spent the rest of his life in exile and participated in the Second Vatican Council. Żychowska's studies were created as devotional material for scouts. Żychowska, *Jerzy Braun* [it.], 43.

[155] Piasecki's 1937 "green program" advocated banning national minorities – especially Jews – from politics and their expulsion. Catholics disparaged its totalitarianism. Kunicki, *Between*, 38–39. Korfanty advocated a 1937 Madagascar Plan for removing Jews from Poland. Kosicki, *Catholics on the Barricades*, 88; AAN 2-1440-0 sygn. 344/1, Unia, "Zagadnienie Żydowskie," 127.

[156] Luke 11:47–51 and Matthew 24:15–35.

[157] Pope Pius XI's "With Burning Hearts" rejected racism as unchristian. Pope Paul VI's 1967 "Populorum Progressio, Encyclical of Pope Paul VI on the Development of Peoples" indicated Catholics had *not* heeded earlier exhortations. As a Catholic, Braun was not free to exclude Jews on racial grounds, hence his "religious-national" objections. See: Bryan N. Massingale, *Racial Justice and the Catholic Church* (Maryknoll: Orbis Books, 2010), 46, 55.

> organizations . . . Without the influences of Masonry we would not have seen the recent extreme growth of materialism and the collapse in faith and morals that we have. Hitlerism is totally a product of this Jewish spirit.[158]

In light of what he saw as irreconcilable differences between Christians and Jews, Braun set out a twenty-four-point program. The first point required Jewish emigration from Poland, beginning with those ages 18 to 40 (and also from neighboring countries, with which Poles would cooperate – a first use for the Central European Union of Nations).[159] Such emigration would be financed (point 3) by the sale of Jewish property. Awaiting mass emigration, Jewish communities would self govern with Polish oversight (points 6–14). Self-governance would disentangle Polish from Jewish economic interests (point 15). While this was ongoing, Jews would be banned from Polish culture, using Polish names (they would return to "Jewish names"), acting as public servants – particularly as lawyers representing non-Jewish clients – and military service (points 16–19). For Polish Jews baptized after November 11, 1918, exceptions would be made on a case-by-case basis. A "special citizen committee" would be created to make determinations, and those with two or more Jewish grandparents would be considered Jewish (points 21–22). For Poles unmoved by Braun's arguments, the program warned that "Poles consorting with Jews after the dissemination of these regulations will be automatically treated the same as the Jews."[160]

This memo on the "Jewish question" was for internal discussion among Unionist leadership. Discussion must have ended in consensus on the main points, however, because the 1942 Unionist manifesto, "A Declaration of Union Ideas," mentioned it. At the bottom of its thirteenth page, under "A New Minority Policy," the reader learned:

> . . . The owner and creator of the state [państwo] is the Polish nation. Minorities who recognize its historical mission and will cooperate with it will receive full political rights. Those [minorities] however that have demonstrated ruthless hostility and opposition to Polish ideals must be removed from our borders. This pertains in particular to the German population and also to the Jewish one, which must be separated from a common life with the Polish nation and be directed to emigrate to regions specially designated for this purpose by international decision.[161]

The two "hostile" minorities were Germans and Jews, conflating the Nazi occupation with longstanding Jewish life in eastern Europe. Notably, neither

---

[158] AAN 2–1440–0 sygn. 344/1, Unia, "Zagadnienie Żydowskie," [127]-[128].

[159] Braun was not the only Catholic to advocate this, as mass Polish-Jewish emigration was advocated in the anonymous "Sprawozdanie kościelne z Polski za czerwiec i połowe lipca 1941 roku" for the exiles, likely written by a friend of Braun's or even Braun himself. See: Szarota, "A Church Report," 442, 445–446.

[160] AAN 2–1440–0 sygn. 344/1, Unia, "Zagadnienie Żydowskie," [128–130].

[161] AAN 2–1440–0 sygn. 344/1, Unia, "Deklaracja Ideowa 'Unii,'" 13–14.

Russians nor Soviets were considered hostile. Similarities between Nazism and Unionism are glaring.[162] Braun's plan dovetailed with aspects of early Nazi policy, including designations of Jewishness from the Nuremberg Laws, bans on Jewish participation in public life, and renaming of persons for racial "clarity."[163]

Braun sketched the Polish future – with plans for the emigration of the Jewish community – during the Holocaust's greatest lethality. When Unity's declaration was printed, much of Warsaw's Jewish community – the people Braun would resettle – was being murdered. Their property – which he would have liquidated to finance this scheme – had already been expropriated. That his country's atheist Nazi occupiers had anticipated much of his "Jewish policy" seems to have escaped Braun. Like many Polish Catholics, and some of his intelligentsia peers, Braun saw Poland – both nation and state – as inherently Catholic. Braun argued that non-Catholics, be they Jewish, German, or Ukrainian, were outsiders to be converted or removed upon the resumption of sovereignty. Braun's detailed planning indicates that the overlapping Nazi persecutions of Polish Jews and Catholics did not mean solidarity among them and could mean entirely the opposite: common ground between Poles and their occupiers.

Jerzy Braun was not the only layman organizing co-religionists, nor was he alone in seeing the crisis as an opportunity to build a different future. Zofia Kossak (Figure 7.3) travelled in the same circles and was one of the few who out-published Braun. Her "Protest" over ghetto liquidation has already been introduced. While Braun spent the war contemplating a future Poland, Kossak was grounded in the present. Her work with Żegota indicates she was clear about the genocidal nature of Jewish persecution and alarmed by it; Braun's treatises do not. She wrote for clandestine publications including: *Polska Żyje* (Poland Lives), *Miecz i Pług* (Sword and Plow), and *Prawda* (Truth).[164] Witold "Grzegorz" Hulewicz (1895–1941), *Polska Żyje*'s editor, brought Kossak on board in in October 1939 when the paper launched. The Gestapo arrested Hulewicz in September 1940 and she inherited his paper.[165] She also wrote for

---

[162] Klemperer had experienced the Jewish lawyers ban in March 1933, the firing of Jewish civil servants in May 1936, and the imposition of "Jewish" names (Israel, Sarah) in August 1938. Klemperer, *I Will Bear Witness*, 8, 165, 264.

[163] The 'Law for the Protection of German Blood and German Honor' and the 'Reich Citizenship Law' defined Jewishness. For Nazis, a "full Jew" had three Jewish grandparents and someone with two was a "Mischlinge," first degree. Braun's system – points 21 and 22 – posited anyone with *two* Jewish grandparents as Jewish. His plans for the restriction of Jewish participation in public life paralleled Nazi policies between 1933 and 1935 removing German Jews from civil service. Whether he was borrowing from Korfanty or aping Nazi policies is unclear. Kershaw, *Hitler*, 344–349.

[164] Not to be confused with the Russian/Soviet *Pravda*.

[165] Witold Hulewicz was shot at Palmiry on June 12, 1941. He handed *Polska Żyje* off to his brother Jerzy, who was arrested. Witold's wife, Stefania née Ossowska, was arrested and

Figure 7.3 Zofia Kossak, date unknown.
Narodowe Archiwum Cyfrowe, 3/1/0/11/1565/1.

Miecz i Pług and ran it after the Gestapo killed its founders, Fr. Peplau and Krystyna Karjer, at Auschwitz and Ravensbrück, for their role in Iuventus Christiana.[166] Her *Prawda* engaged Catholic Varsovians with spiritual direction and it continued on after her own arrest.

Besides writing, Kossak had been a founding member of Unity's women's section. She also created the Front for the Rebirth of Poland (Front Odrodzenia Polski, FOP) in early 1941 in Warsaw with friends, including a Holy Cross priest, Fr. Dr. Edmund Krauze. In line with Braun's Unionism, her organization wanted a substantively Catholic Polish state, but with her own stamp.[167] *Prawda* was the Front's press organ, and Kossak launched it in April 1942 with a declaration of their goals:

> The Front for the Rebirth of Poland [FOP] unites an honest and creative understanding of the love of the Fatherland with a Christian moral rebirth. The Christian worldview is tightly connected with the psyche of the Polish nation. Only a deep, conscious, and consistent religiosity can

sent to Ravensbrück. Witold and Jerzy's sister, Regina Domańska (née Hulewiczowa), dedicated her life to documenting Pawiak, where her brothers were imprisoned. Kossak knew them.

[166] AAN 2–1230–0 sygn. 76-III-57, "Uwagi Z. Kossak-Szczuckiej o prasie podziemnej Polski w czasie okupacji niemieckiej. Co wiem o prasie podziemnej," [1].

[167] Fijałkowski, *Kościół katolicki*, 139, 143.

secure the great historic role destined for Poland by God. Based on this conviction and grounded in Catholic ideology, FOP is taking up the moral rebirth of Poland as the aim of its activities and, through this rebirth of Poland, aims for the rebirth of the whole world.[168]

The Front advocated concrete action, pledged loyalty to the London Poles and local underground, and claimed that "military service" for the "independence and borders of the republic [Rzeczpospolita]" was the "absolute obligation of every Pole."[169] Their diagnosis of the Second Polish Republic's weakness lay in its distance from the Church. They called for religious revolution and wanted a strictly Catholic Poland that left "democratic-liberal-capitalist, communist, fascist systems" behind – something with which Unionists found common ground. The Front wanted renewed Catholic Action with a "Polish Christian social program" and politics "grounded in the Christian worldview."[170]

Prawda considered theological-philosophical and practical matters, with an emphasis on Polish Catholic behavior. It ran as a Warsaw monthly from April 1942 through May 1944, despite Kossak's arrest in September 1943. Articles paired with death notices (*klepsydry*), prayers, poems, and even the occasional joke. It printed her "protest" in fall 1942. *Prawda* was aware of itself as part of an underground conversation, and referred to current events and other periodicals, especially the *Bulletin*.[171] Lest the faithful lose track, a brief article in February 1943, "How Does the Catholic Church Evaluate War?" reminded that "Catholic ethics contain the commandment 'thou shalt not kill'" but that Pius XII's 1939 encyclical praised Polish self-defense against Nazism.[172]

Kossak's brand of conservative, traditionalist Polish patriotism was evident in every article, including the op ed in the second issue, "Catholic-national or national-Catholic," debating the proper balance between patriotic and religious obligations. Coming down on the "Catholic-national" side of the matter, Kossak asserted that "faith is the soul of the nation" and that religious and patriotic impulses joined in the Pole like the body and soul joined to make a human person – but with religious obligations properly shaping patriotic

---

[168] BN Mf. 43293, Prawda, "Deklaracja Frontu Odrodzenia Polski" Kwiecień 1942 r., 2–3.

[169] And what became the Council of National Unity (RJN) in 1944. BN Mf. 43293, Prawda, "Deklaracja Frontu Odrodzenia Polski" Kwiecień 1942 r., 2–3.

[170] Catholic Action was born in France to reclaim workers from Marxism through evangelization. Lagrou, *Legacy of Nazi Occupation*, 146–147. "Katholische Aktion" was one of the "enemy organizations" stipulated by the SS in January 1940 during AB whose members were targeted, along with the Endecja and POW (BABL R102/II/21, Gouverneur des Distrikts Warschau, "Zusammenstellung der deutschfeindlichen polnischen Organisationen," 3.1.1940, [1]). FOP was anti-Marxist and rejected class politics. BN Mf. 43293, Prawda, "Deklaracja Frontu Odrodzenia Polski" Kwiecień 1942 r., 2–3; BN Mf. 43293, *Prawda*, Dodatek Prawdy, "Odrodzenie rodziny podstawowym warunkiem potęgi państwa" Grudzień 1942 r., [1]-6.

[171] BN Mf. 43293, *Prawda*, "Kronika Warszawy" Kwiecień 1943 r., 22.

[172] BN Mf. 43293, *Prawda*, "Jak Kościół Katolicki ocenia wojnę?" Luty 1943 r., 5–6.

ones and not vice versa. She contrasted this with the Nazi error of failing to limit national feeling with religion, resulting in bigotry and racism.[173]

The Front had an educational mission and encouraged youth activity. A July 1942 article, "Rights and Responsibilities of Youth," reminded its readers of the stories of David and Goliath, Joan of Arc, and the fourteenth-century marriage of Queen Jadwiga to Grand Duke Jagiełło, and then called for thoughtful self-sacrifice that did not squander young life.[174] Cautioning the mother who forbade her child from joining a conspiracy but also the "thought-less youth" who wandered into the cinema, the paper told teenagers they had patriotic obligations but cautioned them against "unnecessary risk."[175] The timing of the article was important, since summer 1942 saw ghetto liquidation against the backdrop of a triumphant Wehrmacht campaigning toward Stalingrad. It was a heady moment when conspirators faced an undefeated – and clearly genocidal – opponent.

Władysław Bartoszewski, Hanna Czaki's friend in Żoliborz and later witness to the postwar Pamiry exhumations, joined the Front.[176] After reading a 1942 Front pamphlet, "In Hell," which inspired his own Auschwitz memoir, he tracked down its author in a used book store on Marszałkowska Street, a haunt of various conspiracies (Figure 7.4). Kossak agreed to meet him at a Noakowski Street café near the Polytechnic to get acquainted. Impressed with her modest demeanor, wisdom, and tirelessness, Bartoszewski recalled that:

> Her individual efforts in saving people of Jewish origin threatened with death preceded all later efforts in this regard. She served people at every moment and in every possible way. For her no matter was too small or too unimportant. While the Gestapo was looking for her, she went deliber-ately to Krakow to pick up an orphaned Jewish child ... [In her efforts] she did not even spare her own family or her beloved children, Anna and Witold, who were in junior high school.[177]

Kossak recruited Bartoszewski, already engaged in various opposition projects, to tote pamphlets across the city and visit convents where she hid children and stored material. Kossak was an auspicious mentor for Bartoszewski, whose life as a Catholic intellectual and advocate of Polish-Jewish rapprochment was just beginning.

---

[173] BN Mf. 43293, *Prawda*, "Katolicka-narodowa, czy narodowa-katolicka" Maj 1942 r., 1.

[174] Jadwiga of Poland was crowned in 1384 and married to Jogaila (Jagiełło), Grand Duke of Lithuania in 1386 at twelve with the stipulation that Lithuania accept western Christianity.

[175] BN Mf. 43293, *Prawda*, "Prawa i obowiązki młodzieży" Lipiec 1942 r., 5–6.

[176] Kosicki, *Catholics on the Barricades*, 62–63.

[177] Her children were of course studying illegally. AAN 2/2514/0 sygn. 1/1644: Telewizja Polska SA: Zbiór wycinków prasowych: Kossak-Szczucka Zofia, "Z Zofią Kossak w Podziemiu" by Władysław Bartoszewski, clippings from *Tygodnik Powszechny*, 16. VI.1968.

Figure 7.4 Auschwitz prisoner intake photographs for Władysław Bartoszewski, prisoner 4427, September 1940.
Archive of the Auschwitz-Birkenau State Museum.

Kossak was inundated with projects: emergencies and opportunities seemed to find her. The Gestapo never uncovered her myriad activities, and this – combined with the fact that she was a mother in her fifties – spared her immediate execution. The Gestapo nevertheless caught up with her on September 25, 1943, living under the name of Zofia Śliwińska. They had incomplete information: they knew her prewar literary reputation (they had interrogated her brother-in-law Alfred Szatkowski, who may have betrayed her under torture) but also suspected she was Jewish and hiding in "Aryan" Warsaw. They never uncovered her connections to *Prawda*, Żegota, or the Front.[178]

In October 1943, Kossak went from Pawiak to Auschwitz-Birkenau.[179] She survived the camp surrounded by women to whom she developed a sense of familial obligation. Her transport was a mixture of 250 female conspirators: philology students, a gymnastics teacher, the social activist Wanda Lewandowska, Catholics, and Jews. On her arrival at Auschwitz, she was cheered to find a chapel – and what she later learned were the chimneys of the crematoria. Her writing about Auschwitz is saturated with religious import and meditations on human solidarity, especially solidarity among women.[180]

Kossak's imprisonment was a huge loss for the Warsaw underground, and as a female prisoner she was outside Pilecki's male camp conspiracy. Friends well-connected to the exile government bribed someone to transfer Kossak

---

[178] Domańska, *Pawiak więzienie gestapo*, 354, 389.
[179] Zofia Kossak-Szczucka, *Z otchłani: Wspomnienia z lagru* (Częstochowa: Wyd. Księgarni Wł. Nagłowskiego Nakładem Drukarni Św. Wojciecha, 1946), 2, 5, 7.
[180] Kossak-Szczucka, *Z otchłani*, 4, 8–13,17, 28.

and twenty other political prisoners back to Pawiak. That summer, German personnel, including prison and camp administrators, were evacuating sensitive material westward before the Red Army. They bargained with Polish conspirators able to pay – or fight – to spring comrades. Kossak was released from Pawiak on July 29, 1944, a near-miraculous outcome days before the citywide uprising. She made straight for St. Anthony's Church on Senatorska Street "to thank God for her release."[181] She returned to her previous work, issuing a call in Kamiński's *Bulletin* for Catholics "not [to] turn their backs on God" and help "the poorest of the poor."[182] During the uprising she escaped Warsaw and made her way to Częstochowa, the home of Poland's oldest Marian shrine and there wrote a memoir, *Z otchłani* (Out of the Abyss).[183] Despite her lifelong emphasis on the essentially Catholic nature of Polishness, Kossak was distinguished posthumously by Yad Vashem as one of the "righteous among nations" for her aid to Warsaw Jews.[184] Her consciousness-raising and charitable work among Varsovians were driven by her religious faith and her conviction that obedience to Catholicism was crucial for the Polish future.

7.7 Conclusion

It would be hard to overestimate the importance of Catholicism to Polish life, so any examination of intelligentsia behavior during the occupation must explain what posture the Church took, and what agency Catholics had. Though the Church's hierarchical structure might have led to a unified response to Nazi occupation, the exile of its primate, Hlond, undermined Catholic elites' ability – religious and lay – to respond to Nazism collectively.[185] More importantly, Nazi persecution of the clergy and destruction of churches and convents hurt priests and frightened the faithful, subduing opposition. The GG saw priests and religious as national elites, and executed, imprisoned, and interned them in concentration camps – primarily Dachau – during the anti-intelligentsia campaigns. Nevertheless, there was a rich, wide variety of Catholic elite opposition. There was never *a* Catholic response, but numerous people responded to occupation *as Catholics* in accord with their understanding of Church teachings.

---

[181] AAN 2/2514/0 sygn. 1/1644: Telewizja Polska SA: Zbiór wycinków prasowych: Kossak-Szczucka Zofia, "Powstańczy epizod ..., " press clipping from *Dziennik Katolicki*, 17.09.96.

[182] Bartoszewski, *1859 dni Warszawy*, 642–643.

[183] Kossak-Szczucka, *Z otchłani: Wspomnienia z lagru*.

[184] Yad Vashem: Righteous Among Nations: File 2377a: Szczucka Zofia (1889–1968). Miłosz was also distinguished by Yad Vashem: FileM.31.2/4118: Miłosz Czesław (1911–2004); Franaszek, *Miłosz*, 185–186.

[185] Not unlike Vienna. Bukey, *Hitler's Austria*, 106, 110.

Though elderly archbishops opposed occupation and intervened with the German regime to save Polish Catholics, they were not the vanguard of opposition. They did not defend Jewish Poles, and rarely defended Jewish converts. Underground organizations, however, were confident of the bishops' patriotic sympathies and considered them allies, if quiet ones.[186] Many priests participated in anti-Nazi activities, from Nowakowski's sermons to Kaczyński's reports, Pepler's periodicals, and Godlewski's rescue of Jewish children, and were punished for them. Catholic clergy, nuns, and religious were imprisoned in large numbers and were tortured and died at Pawiak, Palmiry, Ravensbrück, Auschwitz, and Dachau.[187]

For some lay Catholics, including Jerzy Braun and Zofia Kossak, the postwar future beckoned to them as a time when the fractiousness of the Second Polish Republic and the horrors of war could be replaced with a robustly Catholic state. In both that Polish future and the grim Polish present, the "Jewish question" loomed large. This carried over from a long history of Polish Catholicism in which the relationship between Polishness and religious confession was fiercely contested. The presence of Jews in Poland belied the Catholic monopoly on Polish souls. The genocidal persecution of the Jews threw such debates into new discord. For some, like Braun, the war proved that there was no Jewish future in Poland. For others, like Kossak and Godlewski, the persecution of Jews demanded Christian charity, and they risked their lives providing aid despite their own antisemitism. Though all three would have rejected the notion, the "acid test" of the morality of Polish Catholic behavior under Nazi occupation has increasingly become how they responded to the Holocaust.

Despite regime restrictions, the Church and its intelligentsia faithful continued religious instruction, administered sacraments, served as spiritual advisors to military formations, and contributed personnel and resources to conspiracies. They did so without coming to any consensus on the nature of Polish Catholicism, the role of Jews in Polish life, or their exact moral obligations in the face of the occupation and the Holocaust.[188] Catholicism – the faith and the community of believers – drove some elites, both lay and ordained, to intense and effective opposition. Considering its hierarchy's stymied response to Nazism, it would nevertheless be a gross overstatement to associate this posture with the Church as a whole.

[186] Stefan Rowecki considered clergy support reliable. Myszor, "Die katholische Kirche" in *Polnische Heimatarmee*, 374–375.

[187] Madajczyk, *Polityka III Rzeszy*, Tom II, 209–212.

[188] Soviets were harsher: Zygmunt Kaczyński had *not* been tortured by the Gestapo but was killed under communism. Zieliński "Christian Churches in Poland," 335–348.

Spoiling for a Fight

Armed Opposition

Information trafficking, religious initiatives, and illegal education undermined Nazi goals and got the intelligentsia arrested and killed, but many Varsovians longed for violent confrontation with their German enemy. Mature elite opposition to the occupation was a cornucopia, what Piotr Kosicki calls "a complex latticework of conspiratorial activities – some violent, some non-violent."[1] Elites involved themselves in numerous projects, but as occupation dragged on, frustrations mounted.[2] The founding impulse of the first officers' conspiracy, the Polish Victory Service (SZP), was to re-secure Polish statehood by force. The London Poles commandeered the SZP in order to control violence and drew many into their orbit, forming an underground coalition. The SZP was not the only group spoiling for a fight, however. The larger strategic situation initially kept militaries and paramilitaries isolated and mitigated against successful insurgency. The fractiousness of prewar politics and the evacuation of the Second Polish Republic also meant that no single group claimed the loyalty of all Varsovians willing to fight – far from it. Consolidating the military underground was a protracted struggle, and draconian persecution during the anti-intelligentsia years killed many potential recruits.

Much of the literature on Poland during the Second World War focuses on military resistance and the capacities of the Home Army, the SZP's main surviving heir, from late 1943.[3] The Home Army did become the largest underground military organization by far, but this was not immediate. That emphasis forgets the exclusive, elite nature of early work and emphasizes a democratic mass movement bent on violence that only emerged late. It obscures the Home Army's slow birth, its robust competitors, and the way it

---

[1] Kosicki, *Catholics on the Barricades*, 75.

[2] Piotr Majewski, "Konzept und Organisation des 'zivilen Kampfes'" in *Polnische Heimatarmee*, 303.

[3] Dunin-Wąsowicz, *Warszawa w latach 1939–1945*, 244–280; Jacek Czaputowicz, *Administracja cywilna Polskiego Państwa Podziemnego i jej funkcje w okresie powstania warszawskiego* (Warsaw: KSAP, 2011) and Krzysztof Komorowski, *Armia Krajowa: rozwój organizacyjny* (Warsaw: Wyd. Bellona, 1996). Norman Davies' *Rising '44: Battle for Warsaw* (New York: Viking, 2003), 169–240; Gross, *Polish Society*, 213–291.

absorbed groups with different characters and ambitions: it implies that the mature Home Army was unified and its politics – those of the London Poles – represented Warsaw straightforwardly. Military resistance and its turn to insurgency was more convoluted and existed alongside and in competition with other projects. Notably, there were always intelligentsia who opted for non-violent opposition and feared reprisals: Władysław Studnicki, the would-be collaborator, was only the most dramatic example, certain that calls for insurgency cloaked a communist plot.[4] Advocates of non-violence followed the model of Warsaw positivists, and had the sound argument that Nazi reprisals invoked collective responsibility and were always murderous.[5]

In order to understand the increasing importance of violence as an opposition strategy, it needs to be considered in its circuitous development. There were early intelligentsia military projects, including the Polish Victory Service, most of which were fleeting. Then, military opposition slowly democratized between mid-1941 and mid-1943. During this period, the Home Army became the largest underground military through the incorporation of competitors and the aggressive turn of the urban population, moving violence from elite initiative to mass movement.[6] Nevertheless, organized violence was an elite-developed project, and it shared the vulnerability of other intelligentsia efforts in addition to problems particular to its nature.

8.1   Insurgency Terrain

Intelligentsia who embraced violence under occupation had a rich local history on which to draw. Like the inmates of Pawiak who saw themselves following in the footsteps of fathers and grandfathers (or mothers and grandmothers), Varsovians knew their own insurrectionary legends from childhood. Uprisings against the partitioning powers – primarily the Russian Empire, but also the Germans – had ended in bloody failure. They were often credited with inspiring the patriotism of new generations, though, even when their military value was nil. The *powstańcy* of the Second World War self-consciously followed the examples of the November and January Insurrections of 1830 and 1863, but historical models cannot explain what they faced. For that a comparison with other insurgents in the same conflict

---

[4] JPI Archiwum Władysława Studnickiego 96: 3 "Do rozdziału 'Aneksja i wojna z Sowietami,'" 3 (246 of file).

[5] Miłosz was one skeptic; Studnicki another. Miłosz was on the left and thought violence impractical; Studnicki was on the right and thought it Soviet provocation. JPI Archiwum Władysława Studnickiego 96: 3 "Do rozdziału 'Aneksja i wojna z Sowietami,'" 3 (246 of file).

[6] Chodakiewicz confirms early conspiracy as an elite "cadre organization." Marek Jan Chodakiewicz, *Between Nazis and Soviets: Occupation Politics in Poland, 1939–1947* (Lanham, MD: Lexington Books, 2004), 185.

contesting the same enemy – a large force of German civilian personnel, policemen, and soldiers with heavy equipment and auxiliary support – is necessary. Luckily, the Second World War had other such movements.

Surveying the insurgencies of the Second World War reveals a swathe of tragic failures and two notable successes: Soviet Red Army partisans, primarily those who worked from the forests of Belarus, and Josip Broz Tito's communist partisans in Axis-occupied Yugoslavia.[7] Both the Soviet partisans and Tito's forces experienced significant setbacks, but each eventually succeeded because they possessed two attributes Warsaw insurgents lacked: a base on difficult terrain that their enemy, a conventional force, could not easily traverse and on which it could not use its most effective heavy equipment, and the support of a military ally in close enough proximity to provide tangible support.[8] In the case of the Red partisans, this ally was the field army of their own state, the Soviet Union, but the dense forests stretching across Belarus were also essential.[9] Their peers in the open country of Ukraine, which was easier for the Germans to navigate with tank and air support, were nearly destroyed. Tito's partisans withdrew to mountainous Montenegro, thwarting German encirclement.[10] They received aid from the British and the Soviet Union.

These two successful insurgencies relied on difficult rural terrain to protect themselves, train, and stockpile weapons.[11] Without this their enemy had the advantage even though German forces were usually reacting – or wildly overreacting – to resistance behavior.[12] Low population density in Yugoslav and Belarussian retreat areas also reduced reprisals against local civilians (since there were fewer people around to punish) and lessened the danger of locals turning against insurgents out of fear of German retaliation.

[7] Kenneth Slepyan argues Soviet partisans were fractious and had a complex relationship with Moscow; the point about terrain stands. Kenneth Slepyan, *Stalin's Guerrillas: Soviet Partisans in World War II* (Lawrence, University Press of Kansas, 2006), 3, 25 122, 158, 162, 184. Tito's partisans were careful not to "incite a general uprising" and made use of mountains. Milovan Djilas, *Wartime* (New York: Harcourt Brace Jovanovich, 1977), 8, 75, 216. On Yugoslav occupation: Tomasevich, *War and Revolution in Yugoslavia*. The Greeks, too, built formidable resistance but their postwar civil war eclipsed this (Mazower, *Inside Hitler's Greece*, 87–89, 123–13). On whether the French should be considered resisters see Max Boot, *Invisible Armies: An Epic History of Guerrilla Warfare from Ancient Times to the Present* (New York: Norton & Company, 2013), 307.

[8] Stephen Fritz, *Ostkrieg: Hitler's War of Extermination in the East* (Lexington: University of Kentucky Press, 2011), 333, 340.

[9] Bogdan Musiał, *Sowieccy partyzanci, 1941–1944: Mity i rzeczywistość* (Poznań: Zysk i S-ka Wydawnictwo, 2011), 164–170.

[10] Matthew Bennett, "The German Experience" in *Roots of Counter-Insurgency: Armies and Guerrilla Warfare, 1900–1945*, ed. Ian F. W. Beckett (London: Blandford Press, 1988), 76–77; Boot, *Invisible Armies*, 310; Prusin, *Serbia under the Swastika*, 77, 92.

[11] Some Poles resisted from eastern forests. Varsovians faced an entirely different insurgency calculus. Kunicki, *Between*, 70–75; Zimmerman, *Polish Underground*, 268–282.

[12] Ian F. W. Beckett, *Roots of Counter-Insurgency*, 13.

The Second World War saw some of the most repulsive instances of urban killing in human history, as new technologies were turned against concentrated and relatively defenseless populations: in Belgrade in spring 1941, in German-besieged Leningrad, during the Battle of Stalingrad, across the urban ghettoes of eastern Europe during the Holocaust, and specifically in Warsaw in 1939, 1943, and 1944.[13] Varsovians were surrounded by forests – primarily Kampinos and Kabacki – that potential soldiers used for training, storage, and hiding out, but their biggest fights were in the city itself. That space was precisely what they were contesting, so retreating to better ground was not politically or psychologically feasible. This was both their strength and, practically speaking, their undoing. Bard O'Neill, whose analysis functions as a kind of contemporary insurgency manual, explains why their chances were bleak:

> Small, urbanized countries ... are unsuitable for strategies that call for substantial guerrilla warfare ... the reality is that any thought of adopting either a protracted-popular-war or a military-focus strategy stressing guerrilla warfare would be a mistake because armed insurgent units could easily be detected and attacked during the beginning stages of the conflict ... It has yet to be determined whether a prolonged military-focus strategy that involves considerable terrorism in urban centers across the world ... can succeed.[14]

Varsovians were operating in catastrophically bad insurgent territory: an overcrowded city with the highest population density in Poland on terrain – an urban area split by a river – on which their enemy could use its best weaponry while their own limited supplies were frequently discovered and destroyed. Warsaw was not a remote space in which Polish insurgents might leverage their strengths and weaken their enemy; it was the place in which Nazi German police and military personnel were most concentrated. It was also a space in which reprisals against local civilians reached catastrophic proportions, weakening popular support for insurgency, dividing potential recruits among quarreling conspiracies, and destabilizing Polish society. Varsovian allies were remote and unreliable: the British and the French were friends, but far from Poland (and had not honored 1939 commitments), and the Soviets, technically allies from 1941 onward, showed themselves hostile to

---

[13] Kristián Ungváry, *The Siege of Budapest: 100 Days in World War II* (New Haven: Yale University Press, 2005), 428–429; Tomasevich, *War and Revolution in Yugoslavia*, 48–50; Peri, *War Within*, 4; Prusin, *Serbia under the Swastika*, 24. Also true outside Europe in cities like Shanghai and Nanjing, see Fu, *Passivity, Resistance, and Collaboration* and Iris Chang, *Rape of Nanking: The Forgotten Holocaust of World War II* (New York: Basic Books, 1997).

[14] Bard E. O'Neill, *Insurgency & Terrorism: From Revolution to Apocalypse* (Washington, DC: Potomac Books, 2005), 71. On urban Serbian insurgent suffering: Prusin, *Serbia under the Swastika*, 79.

Polish independence initiatives.[15] Thus insurgency in Warsaw faced prodigious difficulties from initial cell formation and the setting of strategic goals, through to the development of sabotage and diversion, in its expansion into a mass movement, and especially in its turn to open revolt. Some leaders, especially former members of the Polish Army with combat experience, understood O'Neill's commonsense warnings, and their solution was to delay armed engagement with the enemy as long as possible, but this approach frustrated the impatient.[16] Violent contestation of the occupation regime, whether unified or fractured, risked massive retaliation and significant civilian casualties. These eventually destroyed it – and Warsaw – in 1944.

8.2 Polish Victory Service

Despite risks, individual efforts to depose Nazism by violent means grew straightaway.[17] Loose weapons were hidden; opportunities to disrupt German plans exploited; information hoarded, catalogued, and distributed. Early work was modest and decentralized. Conspiracies grew around networks of familiarity and intimacy, like the clandestine press and secret schools did. In fact, these sometimes ran in tandem with non-violent projects, like when a journal or religious society also formed an armed wing.[18] Prewar political parties, some of them caught in transition, emerged as centers of early conspiracy. But, they could not inspire nationwide or even citywide insurgency, as suspicions ran hot: "the persistence of political divisions after the defeat of 1939," Mikołaj Kunicki explains, "produced a tendency for disparate parties and groups to establish their own private armies." This fractured landscape could be a boon, though. Bolesław Piasecki (1915–79), a leader in the fascist interwar National Radical Movement, was *persona non grata* in most Warsaw political circles by 1939 because of his collaborationist feelers to the Wehrmacht. Still, even he was able to find *some* military willing to include him – and promote him to leadership.[19]

The Gestapo infiltrated violent conspiracies and therefore "private armies" were skittish recruiters: strangers were unwelcome. Prejudice, suspicion, and distrust were intense and "outsiders" excluded.[20] Antisemitism, suspicion of

---

[15] Nowak, *Courier from Warsaw*, 238–239.

[16] In Warsaw demands for violence were local. In Prague the reverse situation operated, with those safely in London requesting insurgency despite reprisals. Bryant, *Prague in Black*, 167–173.

[17] AAN AK Mf 2375–16, s. 203III-113 from 1944.

[18] Conspiracies had "wings" that split and recombined. Kosicki, *Catholics on the Barricades*, 87.

[19] Piasecki burned a lot of bridges but still had friends. Kunicki, *Between*, 59–62.

[20] Fears of Fifth Columnists morphed into fear of infiltrators and collaborators. Urbanek, *Lęk i strach*, 70–71.

newcomers and non-Varsovians, and a preference for known associates ruled the day. A willingness to embrace violence thus resulted in conspiracies, plural, rather than a military underground in the singular.[21] Consolidating independent groups was as tricky as forming initiatives in the first place. Close associations based on trust like families, friends, scouts, parishes, military veterans, or Legionnaires were effective nuclei for early fighters.[22] Army officers who had avoided captivity or escaped POW camps built the first conspiracies, and had expertise that helped them dodge infiltration. They logically recruited their own. Legitimate fears of discovery and persecution meant that surviving intelligentsia military organizations retained elite profiles until the shift toward mass participation, and sometimes thereafter. Codes of conduct – elite conspirators' chivalry – became part of underground army culture, as those who acted out of patriotism distinguished themselves from thugs, bandits, and occupation opportunists.[23]

The seed of the largest armed conspiracy was formed before Warsaw capitulated in 1939. Brigadier-General Michał Karaszewicz-Tokarzewski ("Torwid," 1893–1964), General Juliusz Rómmel's second in command and part of Warsaw's military leadership, created what he called the "Polish Victory Service".[24] Uncertain about the evacuated state and disintegrating army in 1939, Karaszewicz-Tokarzewski vowed to fight on.[25] He seized "responsibility for the organization of both an armed resistance against the occupiers, and also the moral and physical preparation of the country for the launch of an open fight."[26] Karaszewicz-Tokarzewski's goal was "an unrelenting struggle with the invader ... by any means until the liberation of Poland within her prewar borders."[27] His SZP was created before occupation began, in besieged Warsaw: military opposition was early and local.

Occupied Warsaw, however, was also subject to outside intervention. On September 30, 1939, just days after Warsaw's capitulation, Polish evacuees

---

[21] In parallel with occupied France, see Ott, *Living with the Enemy*, 76–77.

[22] KHPSGL, *Polskie Siły Zbrojne*, Tom III: Armia Krajowa (London: Instytut Historyczny im. Gen. Sikorskiego, 1950), 74.

[23] Warsaw was rife with crime and resisters keen to distance themselves from it. Piątkowski, "Przestępczość w okupowanej Warszawie" in *Porządek publiczny i bezpieczeństwo*, 295–308.

[24] He formed the SZP but was dispatched to Lwów and arrested by the NKVD in March 1940. Müller, *If the Walls Could Speak*, 87; AAN 2-88-44 Akta Michała Karaszewicza-Tokarzewskiego, sygn. 138.

[25] Bór-Komorowski, *Armia Podziemna*, 27–28.

[26] M. Tokarzewski-Karaszewicz, *U podstaw tworzenia Armii Krajowej*, "Zeszyty Historyczne," Paris, z.6, 1964, 19–20; *Archiwum Prezydenta Warszawy Stefana Starzyńskiego*, Tom II, ed. Marian Marek Drozdowski (Warsaw: RYTM, 2008), 272).

[27] Nr. 1: „Organizacja, cele i zadania" in *Armia Krajowa 1939-1945: Wybór Źródeł*, ed. Andrzej Chmielarz, Grzegorz Jasiński, and Andrzej Krzysztof Kunert (Warsaw: Wojskowe Centrum Edukacji Obywatelskiej, 2013), 37.

assembled an exile government under French protection. The last president, Ignacy Mościcki, transferred power to a coalition that had escaped to Paris during the September Campaign. This transition was fraught with practical difficulties and conducted under the shadow of military defeat and political collapse, which cast the Second Polish Republic in an exceedingly bad light. The freshly appointed Prime Minister of the new Polish government-in-exile, Władysław Sikorski, took control. (The whereabouts of Commander-in-Chief Marshall Śmigły-Rydz were unknown and he would die in obscurity, never to return to command). Sikorski was an influential opposition politician and an obvious choice for prime minister among the evacuated elite. Still, Sikorski was unelected. He was an outspoken critic of the collapsed Sanacja regime, whose downfall he did not mourn. He concocted a new vision for Polish politics, managed hesitant allies, and "supervised" opposition at home from abroad. Sikorski was particularly keen to eradicate the original sin of the late Second Polish Republic "colonels' regime," which failed to keep political and military power separate.[28] This was a herculean task, especially since early military conspiracies were dominated by professional officers whose politics often favored the old regime and the power it had given them. Sikorski's 1939 decisions promoted friends and curtailed enemies. Karaszewicz-Tokarzewski's group was thus threat and opportunity: if Sikorski controlled it he could lead native opposition, but if it operated independently it might undermine his credibility with the Western Allies.[29] Even as Sikorski negotiated for recognition "at home" based on his government's legitimacy as a continuation of the Second Polish Republic, he was already instituting changes to that Republic.

Sikorski claimed Karaszewicz-Tokarzewski's organization instantly, expanded it, and re-named it the "Union of Armed Struggle" (Związek Walki Zbrojnej, ZWZ), broadcasting to Warsaw that its only legitimate government was in exile, and that its activities would be directed from outside. He dispatched Karaszewicz-Tokarzewski to the borderlands away from Warsaw. Sikorski appointed Kazimierz Sosnkowski (1885–1969), another exile general, to run the new SZP-ZWZ.[30] Sosnkowski was one of Sikorski's rivals (and a candidate for the exile presidency himself). A generation earlier, Sosnkowski had been Piłsudski's political protégé and chief of staff, and no friend of Sikorski, who had taken a different course. Returning to field command during the German invasion, Sosnkowski's best plans were squandered by Śmigły-Rydz's slow-footed leadership style and he was ordered to evacuate. Sosnkowski arrived in France in October 1939 and Sikorski gave him

---

[28] Prażmowska, *Civil War*, 9.
[29] Bór-Komorowski, *Armia Podziemna*, 26; Vetulani, *Poza płomieniami wojny*, 11, 14.
[30] Komenda Główna – Związek Walki Zbrojnej, KG ZWZ. Ney-Krwawicz, *Biuro Generała Sosnkowskiego*, 11–13.

command of all occupation insurgents. Sosnkowski outlived Sikorski and held this post on and off (punctuated by a 1941 resignation – typical among exiles) and ended the war as commander in chief of the Polish Armed Forces. Sikorski brought Karaszewicz-Tokarzewski and Sosnkowski to heel as creatures of the old order who might thwart his new vision.

Sikorski's control did not deter competitors to the SZP-ZWZ in Warsaw, though Western Allied support was a lot to offer. Karaszewicz-Tokarzewski was more aware of this volatility than Sikorski. After all, he was hardly the only escaped officer itching to fight. Younger men like Pilecki and Karski were too, and Pilecki was recruited into another initiative at precisely this moment. Karaszewicz-Tokarzewski wrote to Sikorski about the delicacy of the situation in December 1939:

> Polish territory is teeming with new organizations modeled on the Polish Military Organization.[31] Some allegedly emerge on your [Sikorski's] orders, others on that of the old government. I am liquidating these organizations or incorporating them into the SZP. I am asking for further orders regarding those organizations acting in your name. Here, in the country, only one organization can represent our government and Polish interests.[32]

The SZP-ZWZ did *not* hold a monopoly on military activity, though it would spend the coming years trying to secure one.

Karaszewicz-Tokarzewski and Sosnkowski had the thankless task of publicizing SZP-ZWZ authority to Polish recruits while keeping it secret from the Germans. All anti-Nazi opposition was imbued with this public-secret contradiction. The secrecy – about surnames, commanders, dates and times of meetings, physical addresses, and plans – characterized wartime behavior. The camaraderie of being part of something mysterious and larger than themselves added to the attraction of joining the SZP-ZWZ and its competitors. This sense of open secrecy partially explains the "alphabet soup" of conspiracies built between 1939 and 1940. The thicket of underground acronyms indicates how widespread the elite desire to contest German power was in Warsaw, but also how occupation fragmented society.[33]

---

[31] Polska Organizacja Wojskowa (POW) was an intelligence and sabotage division of the Legions and included in the SS's "enemy organizations" list alongside Catholic Action and the Endecja (BABL R102/II/21, Gouverneur des Distrikts Warschau, "Zusammenstellung der deutschfeindlichen polnischen Organisationen," 3.1.1940, [1]).

[32] Despite ZWZ creation in November 1939 "SZP" was still used (Nr. 2, "Fragmenty Meldunku Dowódcy Głównego SZP Gen. Bryg. Michała Tokarzewskiego-Karaszewicza ('Torwida') do prezesa Rady Ministrów RP i Naczelnego Wodza Gen. Dyw. Władysława Sikorskiego o stanie organizacyjnym SZP," Pt. 5 (*Armia Krajowa 1939–1945: Wybór Źródeł*, 39)).

[33] Acronyms create an impenetrable barrier to understanding underground life, which is why they are avoided here. The SZP, or "Service," was Karaszewicz-Tokarzewski's

Exiles hoped to unify opposition but this was a monumental task.[34] Conspirators used the metaphor of a "jungle" to describe their world, and connections among them were not neatly hierarchical as in a professional military. According to sociologist Feliks Gross, "when Polish territory was overrun by the Germans, the underground movement mushroomed overnight. Poland had had an insurrectionist tradition for nearly a century and a half ... a living tradition ... There was a definite, historically established and accepted pattern of underground struggle."[35] This was not necessarily good news for the London Poles or professional officers, however, as a cultural tradition of insurrection was just as likely to make participants chafe at commands as switch into lock-step under exile or local supervision. SZP-ZWZ leaders leveraged exiles' support both in their struggle against the occupier and in order to tame their own recruits.[36]

The evacuated – or "exiled," from its perspective – government assembled in 1939 legally inherited the Second Polish Republic's authority, and it was recognized by France, Great Britain, and the United States until the end of the war. The SZP-ZWZ demanded control, but the civilian organizations that coalesced into an underground civil society – the *państwo podziemne* – had their own ideas. Those in opposition to Nazi occupation and the exiles abroad in the West together claimed the loyalty and attention of many Poles but were hamstrung by practical difficulties. Though the London exiles' distance undermined their effectiveness in Warsaw, they were convenient for the Western Allies to work with. The regime that had ruled Poland (undemocratically, but that is beside the point) when Germany invaded was, however, disgraced. Evacuated elites built an exile government from the political opposition.[37] They were usurped at the end of the war by the Soviet-backed communist "people's" government, the legitimacy of which they contested. Communists, political radicals, and those particularly disgusted with the Sanacja regime

original intelligentsia officers' conspiracy from September 1939. The SZP-ZWZ was its expansion once Sikorski began directing it from abroad in late 1939. The SZP-ZWZ-AK was the largest organization declared in February 1942 after absorbing other initiatives. The SZP-ZWZ-AK is known as the "Home Army" (AK).

34 Garliński, "The Polish Underground State," 222–223.
35 Feliks Gross, "Some Sociological Considerations on Underground Movements," in *Polish Review* 2 no. 2/3 1957, 33–34; 44.
36 *Armia Krajowa w dokumentach 1939–1945*, Tom I, część 2, wrzesień 1939 – czerwiec 1941, 2nd ed. (Warsaw: IPN, 2015), Nr 163 [Nr 95], 651–656; Andrzej Chmielarz, "Powstanie i rozwój organizacji konspiracyjnych" in *Polska Podziemna, 1939–1945* (Warsaw: Wyd. Szkolne Pedagogiczne, 1991), 80–86.
37 Opposition politicians had grievances against the ousted government (Stefania Zahorska, *Wybór pism: reportaże, publicystyka, eseje* (Warsaw: Instytut Badań Literackich PAN Wydawnictwo, 2010), 28). The Polish Socialist Party was also cautious (*Armia Krajowa w dokumentach 1939–1945*, Tom I, część 2, wrzesień 1939 – czerwiec 1941, February 12, 1941, Nr. 220 [Nr. 137], 842).

disputed the right of their unelected countrymen to govern from London, or simply ignored their efforts to do so. Communists would take power as the war ended courtesy of the Red Army, while the exiles remained indefinitely abroad, endangering by association those who had resisted Nazi Germany in their name and with their support.[38]

The exiles, however, are not the center of this story. In the capital itself political and military conspiracies arose, split, and merged with the vicissitudes of occupation, eventually forming into a fraught intelligentsia-directed collective: a loose underground structure directing civilian and military undertakings, communicating with exiles, and negotiating with allies. Rataj's and Niedziałkowski's fall 1939 efforts were the kernel of a party-based Warsaw governing body, though this was not a state in the commonsense understanding of the term. In 1940 their successors created a parliamentary council and a "delegation" (delegatura) that recognized the London Poles as the successors to the Second Polish Republic and themselves as answerable to London.[39] Stefan Korboński worked out the details with Karaszewicz-Tokarzewski and the man who succeeded him as SZP-ZWZ commander after the Fall of France, Stefan "Grot" Rowecki (1895–1944), a fellow Legionnaire and career officer in hiding. They assimilated disparate conspiracies under London's umbrella with Western Allied backing, and divided civilian efforts from the "purely military organization" (SZP-ZWZ).[40] Korboński and Rowecki hoped "young people active in the parties would gradually enter the ranks of the underground army," turning scouting and youth activism into a shunt for underground military service.[41] Rather than a state, it was a sketch of postwar political visions led by a proto-parliament that dubbed itself the Council of National Unity (Rada Jedności Narodowej, RJN) in 1944, sometimes a source of wartime political-military authority, and often a source of funds for conspirators. The delegation was thus the mainstream civilian face of military opposition and it recognized (and depended upon) the London Poles, but attempted to proceed democratically.[42] It contained representatives of the four major interwar opposition parties, the Peasants' Party (Stronnictwo Ludowe), the Polish Socialist Party (Polska Partia Socjalistyczna, PPS), the National Camp

---

[38] Home Army soldiers emigrated postwar or faced persecution. Rafał Habielski, "Die Soldaten der Heimatarmee in der Emigration," in Die polnische Heimatarmee, 739–751.

[39] Delegation of the Government of the Republic of Poland in the Homeland.

[40] Piotr Majewski, "Konzept und Organisation des 'zivilen Kampfes'" in Die polnische Heimatarmee, 303–323; Aneks nr 14 "Instrukcja Nr 793 Komendanta Głównego ZWZ, Gen. S. Roweckiego o współpracy z innymi organizacjami," Kazimierz Malinowski, Tajna Armia Polska, Znak, Konfederacja Zbrojna: Zarys genezy, organizacji i działalności (Warsaw: Instytut Wydawniczy Pax, 1986), 215–217.

[41] Korbonski, Fighting Warsaw, 22.

[42] Waldemar Grabowski, "Polskie Państwo Podziemne: Aspekty Cywilne" in II Wojna Światowa, 157–185.

(Stronnictwo Narodowe), and eventually the Labor Party (Stronnictwo Pracy). Each had delegation representation, and when Jan Karski went to London in 1942, it was them he spoke for. Karski's reporting detailed how each party (and Jewish leaders) saw the situation, and how well they cooperated. (This meant Sikorski understood mainstream Warsaw politics, not fringe organizations.)

Insofar as the city was being run – with few traditional trappings of governance, such as a concern for public safety – it was by a German civilian-police administration with Wehrmacht participation. Institutions like Śliwiński's SKSS and ROM tried to continue the social provisions of the Second Polish Republic on a shoestring above ground.[43] The delegation was underground. Nevertheless, the delegation's existence simplified conspirators' communication with the exiles.[44] The delegation and its council spoke to Warsaw through the underground press. Its members and leaders double-dipped in other opposition organizations; the alphabet soup of undergound conspiracies masked an inner circle of intelligentsia who had their fingers in most of the pies. They used Kamiński's *Bulletin* and other organs to shape Varsovian behavior: towards petty sabotage, away from collaboration and despair. In the chaos Nazi police persecution created, the underground attempted to re-impose high-level political justice through secret courts. They served as a moral arbiter for behavior that had crossed the wobbling boundary of the acceptable: courts condemned Poles and Germans to death – occasionally in absentia – for crimes against the Polish people. This "secret state" grew alongside secret armies, a loose collective of engaged anti-Nazi intelligentsia who countered German attempts to control Polish Warsaw.

Military resistance proper had a difficult gestation. Early SZP units emerged during the harshest intelligentsia persecution, and arrests, disappearances, and executions kept the first conspirators on the run.[45] Forces were based on five-person cells (*piątki*), each of which recruited others, building a pyramid organization from prewar social, educational, and political networks. Because of the outgrowth from intimate networks, contact among cells was discouraged.[46] Early conspiracies were susceptible to discovery by Nazi police and Polish provocateurs who knew there was money to be made by outing those on the "wrong" side of the occupier.[47] Young men were eager to join the SZP, and many of its first recruits were officers and soldiers of the Polish army.

---

[43] PAN III-59–97 Materiały Artura Śliwińskiego: "Sprawozdania i memoriały Rady Głównej Opiekuńczej," "Memoriał w sprawie stowarszyszeń, [27.XI. 1940], 1–8.

[44] Eberhardt, *Geheimes Schulwesen*, 122–123.

[45] Bennett is incorrect that "infiltration of resistance cells [was] especially effective in 1940 when hastily raised mass membership organizations exercised poor security." In 1940 it was an elite affair. Bennett, *Roots of Counter-Insurgency*, 68.

[46] Sebastian Pawlina, "O kontaktowaniu się słów parę" in *Praca w dywersji:*, 201–211; Garliński, *Survival of Love*, 15.

[47] Motivated by politics or financial gain. Garliński, *Survival of Love*, 16–20.

Some were still armed. To hamper infiltration, messages were coded, the use of real surnames forbidden (hence the elaborate pseudonyms), and espionage and counter-espionage cells monitored information. SZP officers recruited soldiers and found meeting places in which conspirators would be unknown to hosts. The early system required dedicated officers with local connections and still lost members to mistakes and betrayals.[48]

Recruits had to be trained to do something: multiple global insurgencies have collapsed into anarchy when recruit energy was denied an outlet.[49] Small arms were everywhere and German efforts to secure them unsuccessful: caches of weapons regularly surfaced, though they were insufficient to arm growing forces.[50] Once drawn into conspiracy, young people were restive and chafed under Nazi persecution. They were kept busy with some of the earliest para-military work: breaking into German storage depots, diverting supplies, and damaging road and rail.[51] Assaulting "disloyal" Poles with smoke bombs in German-operated cinemas and destroying projection equipment was another favorite pastime. For the more advanced, there was industrial sabotage, steal-ing documents, scrambling accounting, and altering records – for labor con-scription, prisons and camps, and Poles in German service.[52] Attacking German personnel was a no-go because it provoked violent reprisals.[53] The Wawer massacre of December 1939 demonstrated the need for restraint.[54] This and other Nazi atrocities narrowed the "repertoire of violence" available to the SZP-ZWZ and its allies, restricting them primarily to nonlethal means.[55] Other armed groups were bolder, either because they were less committed to protecting civilians or because their assessment of the situation encouraged them to act immediately.[56]

8.3 Scouting's "Grey Ranks"

Scouts (*harcerzy*) were trained in paramilitary skills and among the first conspirators. Scout leader Stanisław Broniewski insisted that scouting

---

[48] Bór-Komorowski, *Armia Podziemna*, 30–32.

[49] Amelia Hoover Green, *The Commander's Dilemma: Violence and Restraint in Wartime* (Ithaca: Cornell University Press, 2018), 28–29. This was also true of collaborationist militias, see Ott, *Living with the Enemy*, 74.

[50] Broniewski, *Całym życiem*, 208–214.

[51] Boot, *War Made New*, 272; Borodziej, *Terror und Politik*, 169.

[52] Henry Witkowski, *"Kedyw:"Okręgu Warszawskiego Armii Krajowej w latach 1939–1944* (Warsaw: Instytut Wyd. Związków Zawodowych, 1984), 160–232.

[53] Witkowski, *Kedyw*, 175–178.

[54] Bór-Komorowski, *Armia Podziemna*, 29–30.

[55] Green, *Commander's Dilemma*, 6–8.

[56] Piasecki's Armed Confederation of "young, right-wing urban intelligentsia" launched Operation Strike in 1942, before SZP-ZWZ-AK went on the offensive. It fared badly. Kunicki, *Between*, 65–66.

conspiracies "began in September 1939 within the walls of besieged Warsaw," simultaneous with the Polish Victory Service, and there is little reason to doubt him.[57] They rescued the elderly, saved art treasures, ran messages, and fought fires during the siege. Most were too young to be caught up in anti-intelligentsia persecution, but they "aged in" to violent opposition. Stanisław Broniewski, Jerzy Braun, and Aleksander Kamiński were all leading lights in underground scouting and served as mentors of those looking to fight.

Kamiński, *Bulletin* editor, wrote voluminously about scouting. He drew from the life of Tadeusz Zawadzki, scout-turned-insurgent, in his propaganda novella *Stones for the Rampart*. The real Zawadzki led Operational Arsenal, the mission that rescued Jan Bytnar from Pawiak in 1943.[58] *Stones* told a quasi-fictionalized tale of "Wojtek," "Czarny," "Stach," and "Antek" – "the Patrol," as the boys called themselves – set during the anti-intelligentsia campaigns. In the story, Wojtek's father, "well known in Warsaw for his social activities and his position as the chief manager of a big industrial concern," was betrayed to the Gestapo, imprisoned in Pawiak, and shot at Palmiry.[59] Wojtek and his buddies, Tannenberg orphans, got revenge. *Stones* demonstrated how tightly scouts' opposition emerged from anti-intelligentsia campaigning and its fallout and was Kamiński's template for how male intelligentsia youth should behave.

The Patrol ferreted themselves into adult conspiracies. They distributed illegal newspapers, mostly *Poland Lives*, the paper Jerzy Hulewicz and Zofia Kossak wrote, and tried to join the "real" fight:[60]

> And then, quite suddenly, they found what they wanted ... They got into contact with the Petty Sabotage Branch [of what is unspecified] which was then in the front line of the fight against the German occupying forces ... For over a year and a half they had worked in the Petty Sabotage Branch ... now [November 1942] other measures were required. The struggle against the occupying powers was to be intensified, and was to be waged with revolver, grenade, and explosive charge ... Wojtek, Czarny, and the other former saboteurs were enlisted in these – not numerous – units of the Armed Forces at Home.[61]

The boys' adventures grew serious: Czarny killed an SS officer, was tortured in Pawiak, rescued, and died; his friends retaliated by killing another German. They witnessed Nazi persecution of their families in 1939; wanted to fight in

---

[57] Broniewski, *Całym życiem*, 12, 27.

[58] Zawadzki's codename, "Zośka," inspired Zośka Battalion. Kamiński, *Zośka i Parasol*, 43.

[59] Kamiński, *Stones*, 49–50, 11–12.

[60] Grey Ranks commanders knew boys saw colportage as "less than" violent resistance and underlined its importance during "Akcja M" in March 1943. Nr 5, "Akcja 'M' – Katechizm 'M'" (Jerzy Jabrzemski, *Harcerze Szarych Szeregów* (London: Studium Polskiej Podziemnej w Londynie, 2010), 249–250).

[61] Violence is portrayed as male though Czarny's girlfriend assists. Kamiński, *Stones*, 14–17; 41; Broniewski, *Całym życiem*, 196–199.

1940; became saboteurs in 1941, and were conscripted into an underground unit and armed in 1942. Details about their neighborhoods, parents' professions, and schooling demarcate them as young intelligentsia. Kamiński's tale was a snapshot of Nazi anti-intelligentsia persecution driving intelligentsia youth radicalization. The boys' frustrations also clarify the implicit hierarchy and gendered nature of underground prestige: despite illegal schooling and newspaper couriering, the boys did not consider themselves "real" resisters – powstańcy – until they were armed and could wield violence.

Though the Polish scouting movement was gender segregated and much of the literature focuses on the exploits of boy scouts-cum-insurgents like Kamiński's patrol, girl scouts (ages 11 to 18) also participated in paramilitary activities and the Nazi regime hunted and killed them for this work.[62] Young women held in Pawiak like Wanda Tumidajska and Eliza Lamert were *harcerki*, girl scouts; Hanna Czaki was, too. Czaki, like the patrol, started moving illegal information and then entered a military conspiracy.[63] Occupation-era care work often fell to girl scouts as nurses, clergy, and families were stretched thin: they nursed in hospitals, organized aid for Pawiak prisoners, taught secret classes, and tended vulnerable children.[64] Zofia Kossakowska (1927–2010), the fifteen-year-old daughter of a prominent surgeon, remembered her scouting well:

> We had different lessons, and we could earn "proficiency" status in them [like badges]. We did military drills, handled weapons, learned Morse code, but the most important part were the nursing skills and the practical lessons in the hospitals. We learned how to give injections, how to make casts for broken hands and legs, how to stop bleeding, and the different ways to bandage limbs and heads. My favorite skill was head bandaging: you had to take a long roll of dressing from both ends and roll it up towards the middle, making an even bandage from the back of the head around both sides in the shape of a turban.[65]

Kossakowska's fondness for bandaging notwithstanding, other girls focused on orienteering: they memorized the city map, including its streets and sewers (*kanały*) so they could direct conspirators, serve as lookouts, and move undetected. Kossakowska used this to thwart the Gestapo, following Kamiński's petty sabotage guidelines: "if a German accosted us on the street

---

[62] Scouts drew heavily from intelligentsia families. Girl scout losses under occupation are approximate but Warsaw units took 47.4 percent of them, with 221 Warsaw Uprising deaths. Zuzanna Stefaniak (inter alia), *Harcerki, 1939–1945* (Warsaw: Państwowe Wyd. Naukowe, 1983), 17, 19, 458–459.

[63] Bartoszewski, *Życie trudne, lecz nie nudne*, 82.

[64] Zawadzka and Zawadzka, *Pełnić służbę*, 45, 50–51, 57–63.

[65] Kossak's relative. Kossakowska's father taught medicine underground. Zofia Kossakowska-Szanajca, *Zapiski dla Wnuków* (Warsaw: Biblioteka Więzi, 2009), 244–255.

and asked after a certain street or a certain address, we would spitefully point him in precisely the opposite direction."[66]

Scouts were initially distinct from the developing SZP-ZWZ because of their age but were incorporated as underground forces expanded. They were designated as the "Grey Ranks" (Szare Szeregi) within the military underground, divided by age, with the Zawisza for ages 12–14, and storm groups or sabotage and propaganda units for boys over seventeen. The Grey Ranks retained their pre-conspiracy structures and codenames and their troop leaders-turned-officers, a merger born of necessity and scout pride. Though Kamiński's story depicted the scouts as seeking resistance, their leaders – themselves members of the intelligentsia – were also pushing it. Stanisław Broniewski negotiated the incorporation of the Union of Polish Scouting (Związek Harcerstwo Polskiego, ZHP) into the Grey Ranks of the SZP-ZWZ-AK in March 1942, shortly after the Home Army's formal consolidation.[67] He thereafter served as their commander from 1943 until the end of the uprising, directing the youngest cohort of armed resisters in the Warsaw underground.[68] Broniewski's efforts and scout enthusiasm added the energy of 2,250 boys to Warsaw's fighting strength by spring 1944.[69]

8.4   Extremes: Left and Right

Youth military activity cropped up across the political spectrum but took distinct forms on the left. Communist groups were in a shifting position during the war since their potential foreign patron and model, the Soviet Union, began the war as an ally of Nazi Germany and co-invader of Poland. After the German invasion of the Soviet Union in 1941, the situation changed and left-wing efforts blossomed, though Moscow directed potential Polish allies with an iron hand. Though they were much smaller numerically than the SZP-ZWZ, left-leaning non-communist Warsaw forces included the Polish People's Independence Initiative (Polska Ludowa Akcja Niepodległościowa, PLAN), Polish People's Army (Polska Armia Ludowa, PAL), and the Peasant Battalions. In October 1939, some of the city's privileged teens built PLAN, which aspired to violent confrontation with the Germans. Michał Wojewódzki, star of the

---

[66] Kossakowska-Szanajca, *Zapiski*, 234. Navigating sewers was vital during the uprising, during which harcerki evacuated soldiers and wounded. Czugajewski, *Na barykadach*, 78–84.

[67] Nr. 2, Rozkaz nr 129 z dnia 16 marca 1942 roku wydany przez Komendanta Głównego PZP. Jabrzemski, *Harcerze Szarych Szeregów*, 240–241.

[68] Jabrzemski, *Harcerze Szarych Szeregów*, 295–307; Tomasz Strzembosz, *Akcje zbrojne podziemnej Warszawy, 1939–1944* (Warsaw: Państwowy Instytut Wydawniczy, 1983), 256–258.

[69] Warsaw had 2,250; the country as a whole 8,188 boy scouts in the Grey Ranks. Jabrzemski, *Harcerze Szarych Szeregów*, xv-xvi.

underground printing world and witness to the ghetto uprising, toyed with joining friends in PLAN in 1939 but opted for another conspiracy instead, which may have saved his life.[70] PLAN was small but drew from socialist leadership and university students, and included Polish-Jewish members. The second issue of their newsletter, *Polska Ludowa* (People's Poland), was in press when the group was denounced and infiltrated by the Gestapo in late 1939.[71] PLAN collapsed because it formed during Tannenberg and its leaders – young left-wing intellectuals involved in scouting – were already targets. One of them was the young Polish-Jewish saboteur named Kazimierz Andrej Kott, the first prisoner to escape from Gestapo clutches on Szuch Boulevard.[72] Kott's escape served as a "provocation" for the roundup of several hundred Polish-Jewish intelligentsia figures. The result was a murderous antisemitic campaign and an elite left-wing rebellion stillborn. After interrogation at Szuch Boulevard and imprisonment at Pawiak, PLAN members died at Palmiry in January 1940.

PLAN was not the only left-wing effort, but most formed late. Polish communists formed PAL in April 1943 – after the first Soviet victory at Stalingrad, buoyed by socialists and PLAN survivors. In late 1943, Henry Borucki (1913–69, "Czarny") took PAL's reins. Borucki had already survived a lot: he had defended Warsaw in 1939, published *Poland Lives*, been arrested and tortured, and spent time in Lublin's Majdanek concentration camp. Borucki led several thousand conspirators by summer 1944, mainly in Warsaw and a few eastern cities. The group had its own politics, ethos, and leadership but accepted subordination to London, joined the SZP-ZWZ for the Operation Heads assassination campaign, and fought alongside it in the 1944 uprising.

PAL cooperated with the Peasant Battalions (Bataliony Chłopskie, BCh), a left-leaning military organization with a rural base outside Warsaw. The BCh was the armed wing of the Peasant Party, Rataj's and Korboński's political home. Most prominent in the countryside and eager to protect peasant economic interests, BCh strength came late: Warsaw units formed in early 1943.[73] BCh participation reached 150,000 (not all combatants) by mid-summer 1944, when its Warsaw units joined the SZP-ZWZ-AK during the uprising.

Soviet-created military organizations of the late occupation formed when the Red Army was moving across Polish territory and Stalin, keen to establish his power there, obscured the efforts of native left-wing groups, filling approved histories in the Polish People's Republic (PRL) with inflated details

---

[70] Wojewódzki, *W tajnych drukarniach*, 85, 89.
[71] Stanisław Izdebowski denounced them. Bartoszewski, *Palmiry*, 29–30.
[72] Domańska, *Pawiak – Kaźń i Heroizm*, 194–195.
[73] Kazimierz Banach, *Z dziejów Batalionów Chłopskich: wspomnienia, rozważania, materiały* (Warsaw: Ludowa Spółdzielnia Wydawnicza, 1967), 366, 350.

of their exploits.[74] Soviet support, however, was never irrelevant: state backing was crucial to successful wartime insurgencies. The most important Soviet-backed group with a Warsaw presence was the People's Guard (Gwardia Ludowa, GL), though its numbers were meager compared to SZP-ZWZ strength. Formed in fall 1940 by the Polish Socialist Party, it moved leftward into the Soviet orbit. With clear Soviet backing after 1942, it harassed the Wehrmacht from its eastern Polish base but had little influence in cities. The People's Guard opted for dramatic destruction and sabotage, provoking reprisals against civilians. Its most important activities in Warsaw included arms and personnel assistance for ghetto fighters in spring 1943, and it included the largest number of Polish-Jewish fighters of any Polish insurgency.[75] Its enduring rejection of SZP-ZWZ hegemony made it the bogeyman of far-right paramilitaries, with which it skirmished in 1943 and 1944. On Stalin's orders the Guard was absorbed into the new Moscow-directed People's Army (Armia Ludowa, AL) in January 1944, when Soviet plans for a communist-friendly Polish postwar state – what became the Lublin Committee (PKWN) in June 1944 – were underway and Soviet communists eager to consolidate their Polish allies for smooth postwar takeover.

On the other side of the political spectrum, sprawling across its center and right with the occasional center-left figure, was the London-backed SZP-ZWZ insurgency.[76] Unlike the hard left, independent right-wing militaries lacked a foreign backer like the Soviet Union – at least once Studnicki's overtures were dismissed – but there were still plenty of them. The Secret Polish Army (Tajna Armia Polska, TAP), for instance, became a sister organization to the SZP-ZWZ.[77] TAP was technically the military wing of the central committee of the Organization for Independence (Centralny Komitet Organizacji Niepodległościowych, CKON), headed by Ryszard Świetochowski (a Sikorskiite rather than a Piłsudskiite) which fused peacefully with the SZP-ZWZ after two years of independent operations, bracketing their differences. TAP began recruiting in November 1939 from the student body of the Warsaw School of Economics (Szkoła Główna Handlowa, SGH) and career military officers, and was infiltrated by the Gestapo in late 1939, though not comprehensively destroyed like PLAN.

---

[74] Główny Zarząd Polityczny WP, *Z dziejów wojny wyzwoleńczej narodu Polskiego, 1939–1945* (Warsaw: Wydawnictwo Ministerstwa Obrony Narodowej, 1960), 310–330, 451–664.

[75] Zimmerman, *Polish Underground*, 69, 210–238; Krakowski, *War of the Doomed*, 149.

[76] Kazimierz Malinowski, who joined TAP in 1939, knew that "all of the documents, writings and publication of TAP ... were destroyed during the Warsaw Uprising or later – in the ruins of Warsaw set on fire by the Hitlerites." Malinowski, *Tajna Armia Polska*, 7.

[77] Kazimierz Malinowski, *Żołnierze łączności walczącej Warszawy* (Warsaw: Instytut Wydawniczy Pax, 1983) 7 n. 1.

Many crucial figures disappeared into Pawiak through 1940, like the physician Zygmunt Śliwicki, an early recruit. Witold Pilecki began his underground career in its ranks and then befriended new colleagues from other competing conspiracies in Auschwitz.[78] Not the creature of one political party, TAP was center-right and strongly religious, counting a Catholic priest among its founders. The phrase "Secret Polish Army" stuck after what remained of TAP merged with the SZP-ZWZ.[79] TAP conspirators joined the Peasant Battalions, PAL, and the NSZ but mainly the SZP-ZWZ after Gestapo infiltration discombobulated them.

On the fascist far right lay the National Armed Forces (Narodowe Siły Zbrojne, NSZ), which resisted incorporation into the SZP-ZWZ until May 1944 and maintained some independence afterward.[80] (Only their moderate wing ever allied, leaving a radical fringe pursuing its own ends). The NSZ was itself a conglomerate of right-wing and national radical militias formed on September 20, 1942. They were virulently anti-communist and antisemitic, positing an ethnic vision of Polishness that excluded Jews and – generally – Ukrainians and Belarusians.[81] The NSZ attacked Polish Jews, Polish communists, and ethnic minorities, defining an enemy bigger than Nazi occupation.[82] Most NSZ members were Catholic though the group was not explicitly religious.[83] The NSZ joined the National Party (Stronnictwo Narodowe) and the ONR to form the National Camp (Obóz Narodowy), a right-wing military conglomerate distinct from and competitive with the SZP-ZWZ. The NSZ focus on Molotov-Ribbentrop Pact betrayal and passionate anti-communism meant any association with the SZP-ZWZ would be uneasy: SZP-ZWZ subordination to the London Poles allied it with the Soviet Union after 1941, which the NSZ abhorred.[84] The National Camp committed itself to Poland's prewar eastern borders – including territory the Soviets seized in 1939 – and excluded "foreigners, and in particular Germans, Jews, and Ukrainians" from its definition of the Polish nation, making all of them

---

[78] Malinowski, *Tajna Armia Polska*, 87–88.

[79] "AAN AK, sygn. 203/I-3, Mf 2368–1, "Memorandum on the Present Activities of the Polish Secret Army and the Estimate of the German Military Situation on the Eastern Front," June 12, 1944, 5–12.

[80] Chodakiewicz attributes their 1942 formation to AK inclusion of left-wing groups. Chodakiewicz, *Narodowe Siły Zbrojne: "Ząb" przeciw dwu wrogom* (Warsaw: Fronda, 1999), 53; Chodakiewicz and Wojciech J. Muszyński, *Narodowe Siły Zbrojne: Dokumenty 1942-1944*, Vol. 1 (Warsaw: Fundacja Kazimierza Wielkiego, 2014), 7–10.

[81] *Not* the Council for Aid to the Jews: Tadeusz Kurcyusz (1881–1944) who led the NSZ from August 1943.

[82] AK units also engaged in antisemitic attacks. Zimmerman, *Polish Underground*, 189, 296, 372.

[83] See documents Nr. 1 and Nr. 2 for prayers. *NSZ: Dokumenty 1942–1944*, Vol. 1, 38–39.

[84] Bohdan Szucki ("Artur"), *Narodowe Siły Zbrojne w moim życiu* (Lublin: Fundacja im. Kazimierza Wielkiego, 2013), 101.

NSZ targets.[85] NSZ strongholds lay in the eastern borderlands, however, not Warsaw. Its units attacked GG personnel, the People's Guard and People's Army, *and* the Red Army when it returned to Polish territory in 1944 – equal-opportunity opposition to its many ideological enemies.[86] Because it pitted itself against other Polish militaries and the Nazi occupation, it contributed to what Anita Prażmowska calls a "long civil war."[87] The NSZ killed and sabotaged Polish leftists to prevent communist domination of Poland from 1942 onward.[88] The violence was mutual, and meant the NSZ, the GL, the AL – most underground militaries – fought against both the local occupier and other competitors for postwar political power. NSZ focus on a ubiquitous communist threat frustrated the SZP-ZWZ because it killed their men – even officers – suspected of communist sympathies.[89] The mature SZP-ZWZ's ability to control the NSZ was limited (especially outside Warsaw), though their overtures toward it became the basis for blanket Soviet condemnation of the entire non-communist underground as fascist in the postwar, a pretense to attack everyone who had opposed Nazism and might be tempted to oppose communism.[90]

Early military conspiracies spanned the political spectrum and drew from myriad civilian and military elites. The ghetto had the Jewish Fighting Organization (ŻOB), and Jerzy Braun's Catholic Unity had its own military wing, complete with colonel and grenade factory. Organizations formed during the anti-intelligentsia years were especially vulnerable to Gestapo infiltration – or even the NKVD, as Karaszewicz-Tokarzewski discovered in Lwów in spring 1940. To survive the most delicate years of elite conspiracy, such ventures had to be lucky, and they needed combatant expertise and outside support in cash, weapons, and advice. Only the NSZ and GL-AL survived until 1944 pursuing domestic *and* foreign campaigns: that collapsed smaller organizations and was a boon for the Gestapo, which could always count on

---

[85] Szucki, *Narodowe Siły Zbrojne*, 103; Nr. 5: Oświadczenie (May 8, 1943) (*NSZ: Dokumenty 1942–1944*, Vol. 1, 45–46).

[86] Chodakiewicz, *NSZ*, 154–156.

[87] Poland, like Greece and Yugoslavia, experienced civil war as a result of occupation. Prażmowska, *Civil War*, 212–215; Mazower, *Inside Hitler's Greece*, xiv.

[88] February 1943 NSZ Declaration claimed it was "leading a conspiratorial struggle with the occupier [Germany] and liquidating communist diversion." Nr. 6: Narodowe Siły Zbrojne Deklaracja (*NSZ: Dokumenty 1942–1944*, Vol. 1, 47; Szucki, *Narodowe Siły Zbrojne*, 55–63).

[89] NSZ assassinated Jerzy Makowiecki ("Malicki"), AK BIP engineer. Bór-Komorowski, *Armia Podziemna*, 206–207. Julian Kulski was also attacked by communist forces and the Home Army attempted to get them to desist. USHMM RG-50.030.0769, AN: 2014.238.1, "Interview with Julian Kulski [Jr.]," 2:10:10–2:11:06. Chodakiewicz underscores competition between SZP-ZWZ, NSZ, and BCh claiming it "never turned bloody." Chodakiewicz, *Between Nazis and Soviets*, 185.

[90] Zimmerman, *Polish Underground*, 372.

denunciation against those who made enemies among their countrymen to keep Pawiak full. Both the SZP-ZWZ and the GL-AL enjoyed foreign support; Soviet support of the GL was essential to its survival despite its small size and frequent targeting by the Gestapo and the NSZ. The destruction of many early organizations demonstrated both the multivalent nature of Polish political-military conspiracy, which no part of the political spectrum monopolized, and the clear independence of such organizations: the fall of PLAN did not collapse the SZP-ZWZ, and it did not destroy left-wing military conspiracy as such, which re-emerged. TAP, PLAN, PAL, and the NSZ were not offshoots of the SZP-ZWZ but peers and competitors and the independence of conspiracies enabled those that were not betrayed to endure.

8.5   Spread of Armed Opposition, 1941–1943

The SZP-ZWZ expanded from its conspiratorial launch and renamed itself the "Home Army" (Armia Krajowa, AK) in February 1942. It was thereafter officially a branch – albeit an unorthodox one – of the Polish Armed Forces (Polskie Siły Zbrojne) and a Second World War belligerent. In its mature form, the Home Army (SZP-ZWZ-AK) included all insurgents willing to subordinate themselves to the London Poles, eventually most formations excepting the communists and the rightmost NSZ fringes.[91] Some groups held out against Home Army incorporation, watching the changing military situation and looking for the best merger deal.[92] Growing in organizational complexity and its domination of the Warsaw insurgency landscape, between mid-1943 and mid-1944 the Home Army conducted a terrorist assassination campaign against German personnel: Operation Heads. In summer 1944 it launched a citywide uprising, the hopeful spark of a nationwide campaign that never materialized. Early elite military conspiracies consolidated into an overarching insurgency of those willing to confront the occupation with violence, expanding dramatically in capacity. Some of these changes were due to internal factors and related to the incorporation of other conspiracies, but the most important shifts were driven by Grand Alliance strategy. Though military conspiracy was some of the first anti-Nazi activity in Warsaw, it became the handmaiden of the larger war. It was thus vulnerable to and dependent on fluctuations in that war in a way that internally focused, civil-society building projects like the information network and underground university were not. This context is crucial to understanding it and differentiating it from other forms of elite-led opposition.

---

[91]   AAN AK s. 203/I-14 Mf 2368–2, "Komendant Główny," 1942–1944, 12, 22.VII.42 on division of duties.

[92]   Piasecki's Cadre Strike Battalions negotiated with Rowecki in 1942 but only allied in August 1943. Kunicki, *Between*, 69.

As the German administration shifted from targeted anti-intelligentsia policy in 1939–40 to general terror, exploiting Warsaw for the bottomless needs of the Wehrmacht, slaughtering its Jewish community, and launching bloody reprisals against conspirators, the space for "normal" life shrank and threadbare protections for civilian non-combatants fell into tatters. Caught between occupation persecution and the increasing strength of various conspiracies, more and more people entered underground life, expanding it beyond its rarified intelligentsia origins.[93] As the scale of insurgency – armed opposition seeking confrontation – expanded, smaller groups merged into an underground front. The Home Army consolidated between 1942 and 1943, and claimed 300,000 members in early 1944: no longer just an intelligentsia effort, though the founders retained leadership positions.[94] Expansion was both problem and opportunity: a larger network was harder to protect and easier for the Gestapo to uncover, but it was also more capable of the large-scale uprising its founders intended.

The mature Home Army vetted recruits ferociously.[95] The original system of vouching for friends was not fully scalable, but even in August 1942 every volunteer took an oath, had his family and work history verified and references checked, and documented how he had made contact. He could then be formally admitted "with the guarantee of two witnesses who were already active members."[96] Such procedures privileged those with intelligentsia connections (and previously uncommitted elites themselves). Still, what started out as an intelligentsia conspiracy dominated by professional officers became something with which much of Warsaw identified by the end of occupation – even if they had reservations about its tactics.

Home Army leadership, nonetheless, carried an elite stamp from its origins until its postwar disbanding.[97] It retained the informality and intimacy which could only come from elite networks of longstanding. In August 1943, still-operating international courier Jan Nowak met with the men running the Home Army in an apartment in Warsaw's Old Town: Brigadier-General Tadeusz Komorowski ("Bór," 1895–1966), the commander in chief, Brigadier-General Tadeusz Pełczyński ("Grzegorz," 1892–1985), his chief of staff, and

---

[93] Home Army history reports underground activities it supported as its own. Eberhardt, *Geheimes Schulwesen*, 173–191.

[94] Komorowski claimed 300,000 in early 1944 and 380,000 by August 1, 1944 (Bór-Komorowski, *Armia Podziemna*, 165); Marek Ney-Krawicz claims 350,000 members in early 1944 and 10,000 officers (Ney-Krawicz, *Armia Krajowa: Siły zbrojne Polskiego Państwa Podziemnego* (Warsaw: Oficyna Wydawnicza RYTM, 2009), 189).

[95] Soviet partisans faced infiltration as their movement democratized. Slepyan, *Stalin's Guerrillas*, 247.

[96] AAN AK s. 203/I-14 Mf 2368-2, "Komendant Główny," 1942–1944, "P.Z.P. Nr. 359," 28. VIII.42, "Sposób przymowania nowych członków," 22.

[97] Ney-Krawicz, *Armia Krajowa*, 200–201.

Jan Rzepecki, head of the Bureau of Information and Propaganda (BIP), whom Nowak called "the chairman." They met Nowak "in shirtsleeves" and "the meeting was friendly, informal, and most unmilitary. We addressed one another without titles or rank, as was the rule in the underground."[98] Nowak was touched to be treated as a familiar by those running Warsaw's largest underground army but the intimacy was sincere: he came from their class and shared their intelligentsia mission.

8.6 Strategic Shifts in the Grand Alliance

The central factor that drove expanding military opposition in Warsaw was the launch of Operation Barbarossa, the German invasion of the Soviet Union in summer 1941. This invasion marked a turning point in the war ideologically, economically, and militarily, so it is hardly a surprise that it drove changes in Warsaw. Simply put, the German expansion of the war eastward changed the meaning of the Polish space, placing new and different burdens on Varsovians, shifting German priorities, and reversing the position of the Soviet Union – which co-invaded Poland in 1939 – from an enemy of Britain and France to their ally. The London Poles had to recognize the change and Sikorski negotiated an anti-German alliance with the Soviet Union, the July 1941 Sikorski–Maisky Agreement, which was not without its vociferous detractors in Warsaw.[99] Varsovian memoirs detail a bevy of opposition motivations after Barbarossa, highlighting patriotism and frustration. Nazi Governor Fischer's reports add the German perspective, identifying six primary factors driving Polish activities. These included Barbarossa, Soviet–Polish rapprochement, the American entry into the war, starvation and forced labor, the Holocaust, and the severing of Polish–Soviet relations over the Katyń incident. The first – the invasion of the Soviet Union – triggered many of the others, but these larger wartime developments unfolded in waves and ballooned violent confrontation.

In spring 1941, Nazi-occupied Poland became a staging ground for the largest military invasion the world had ever seen.[100] Fischer himself declared that "June 1941 was the most difficult month ... in the existence of Distrikt Warschau" because of the "ever-increasing concentration of German Wehrmacht" personnel and equipment. Soviet aerial bombardment reached

---

[98] Nowak, *Courier from Warsaw*, 187.

[99] This lost London Poles Warsaw supporters, who regarded this as accepting the Soviet takeover of eastern Poland in 1939, and gained others who supported a pragmatic Soviet posture. It was a sign of how politics abroad and politics "at home" grew apart. Prażmowska, *Civil War*, 19.

[100] Leonhard, *Pandora's Box*, 90. The Baedeker Guide stated Warsaw was "the most important rail connection in the GG." Karl Baedeker, *Das Generalgouvernement: Reisehandbuch* (Leipzig: Karl Baedeker, 1943), 87.

Warsaw intermittently after June 1941.[101] The "popular mood" varied by ethnicity, and relations among Poles, Germans, Jews, and Ukrainians were tense.[102] The ghetto was "restless" in anticipation of the invasion, favoring a Soviet over a Nazi victory, whereas "the sympathies of the Poles were divided:" elites feared Soviet occupation as much as German, while workers murmured that life "could not be worse under Russian rule."[103] Fischer's reporting oversimplified things: Soviet re-entry into the war was Studnicki's nightmare, and one can imagine radical PAL and NSZ members differing from the "norm." Different hopes divided the city, magnified unrest, and called anew for intelligentsia leadership.

Barbarossa changed calculations in Warsaw and Berlin. As Wehrmacht troops marched east out of Warsaw, Himmler solicited research on long-term eastern European "pacification," back on the Nazi agenda after a year campaigning in western Europe. This planning is now called the "General Plan for the East" (Generalplan Ost, GPO).[104] Himmler had SS researcher Konrad Meyer (1901–73), an expert on human population movement, detail what Germanization of eastern Europe would require.[105] Meyer's GPO draft claimed German settlement necessitated the "relocation" of tens of millions of Slavs and the murder of 31 to 45 million more.[106] Warsaw was one of the main problems for the plan, the largest concentration of Poles in the world and the heartland of anti-Nazi resistance.[107]

Meyer's plan included a list of eastern European cities to be Germanized and estimated "human requirements" and "rebuilding costs" (in millions of marks) for this transition over twenty-five years.[108] The numbers for Warsaw were

---

[101] Czerniaków, *Prelude*, 251, 299.

[102] Jews were discussed under "Ghetto activities." Fischer to Frank June 1941, dated July 12, 1941 (Fischer, *Raporty*, 339–340).

[103] APW (Archiwum Państwowe m. st. Warszawy) 482/II 1552 [Berichte des Gouverneurs des Distrikts Warschau an die Regierung des GG – Jahrgang 1941] – April 1941 report (59); May 1941 (82).

[104] Kershaw, *Hitler*, 669.

[105] Dr. Hans Ehlich & Dr. Konrad Meyer under supervision of Heinrich Himmler, "Generalplan Ost," June 1942: https://ia800602.us.archive.org/19/items/GeneralplanOst/ Generalplan%20Ost.pdf.

[106] Dietrich Eichholtz, "'Generalplan Ost' zur Versklavung osteuropäischer Völker," UTOPIEkreativ, H.167 (Sept. 2004), 801–802; Isabel Heinemann, "Wissenschaft, Planung, Umvolkung: Konrad Meyer und der "Generalplan Ost," Die Berliner Universität und die NS-Zeit: Verantwortung, Erinnerung, Gedenken, Vortragsreihe an der Humboldt-Universität: Die Berliner Universität unterm Hakenkreuz, Vortrag zum 21.5.2003, 8. Mechtild Rossler, ed. (inter alia), *Der 'Generalplan Ost: Hauptlinien der nationalsozialistischen Planungs- und Vernichtungspolitik* (Berlin: Akademie Verlag, 1993).

[107] Meyer, *Generalplan Ost*, 84, 86; Grabowski, *Na posterunku*, 250.

[108] Meyer, *Generalplan Ost*, "Abgrenzung der Siedlungsräume in den besetzten Ostgebieten und Grundzüge des Aufbaues," table titled "Siedlerbedarf und Aufbaukosten in den Siedlungsgebieten und Stützpunkten im Ostraum," 84.

staggering: 1996.0 million marks, half the GG total (4745.7 million marks) and more than any other city. Even in 1942, when anti-intelligentsia campaigning was over and German attention on Soviet defeats, integrating Warsaw into the Third Reich was going to be *three times* costlier than any other conquest. Though the GPO was never realized, some Warsaw elites, especially those with contacts in Kulski's mayoral office, knew about it and feared its implementation.[109] The mentality of disregard for eastern European lives it spawned reached outside planning offices and into Warsaw's occupation administration. A counterinsurgency campaign and bloody reprisals against civilians after 1942, after all, meant little to a regime that was contemplating murdering tens of millions.

Despite Himmler's grandiosity, it would be Germany's enemies that rewrote the European map. New belligerents shifted the Grand Alliance and Warsaw's place in it. Germany declared war on the United States in December 1941 after Pearl Harbor – a development in which Warsaw took "especially great political interest." American participation strengthened hopes for a British victory, and exile fortunes rose with London's.[110] As the conflict globalized, Poland's value fluctuated. Sidelined when the Wehrmacht moved west in May 1940, the German move eastward in 1941 gave Warsaw new importance. The involvement of the Americans, allies of the Poles' allies, buoyed foreign assistance, raising the star of the SZP-ZWZ. Though the *Courier* trumpeted news of Wehrmacht victories, rumors of German defeat were rampant in 1942 and 1943.[111] Varsovians noted their occupier's stumbles.

Though hopes for victory buoyed, war dwindled the scarce resources on which Warsaw subsisted, cut rations, and drove black market food prices wild. A kilogram of beef, which had cost 1.56zl before the war, cost 10.31zl in April 1941, 20zl by February 1942, almost 83zl in July 1943, and 94.23zl in June 1944, *sixty times* its prewar cost. The price of milk, eggs, butter, and flour skyrocketed. A liter of vodka – a wartime staple – was an unthinkable 60zl in February 1942, but a staggering 170zl the next year, incentivizing bootleg distilling.[112] By 1942, most Varsovians "shopped" on the black market, and Fischer's administration faltered, as "the scope and importance of a black market stand in inverse proportion to the power of the state."[113] Poles with relatives in the countryside or even modest garden plots were best situated. Buying produce smuggled from rural areas or growing rabbits for meat became

---

[109] Jan Zachwatowicz knew about the GPO and earlier Pabst Plan. "Jan Zachwatowicz" in *Chronicles of Terror*, 41–42.

[110] Fischer to Frank December 1941, dated January 15, 1942, 431.

[111] Lucjan Dobroszycki, "The Polish-Language Press in Nazi-Occupied Poland, 1939–1945," in *The Polish Review* 16 no. 1 (1971), 22.

[112] Szarota, *Okupowanej Warszawy*, 231.

[113] Mazower, *Inside Hitler's Greece*, 53; Grabowski, *Na posterunku*, 263.

grey-market activities that pushed Varsovians into conflict with the regime.[114] Aleksandra Zaprutko-Janicka, in her study of occupation "from the kitchen," insists that "practically everyone" smuggled despite fines, arrests, and confiscations.[115] People were afraid, hungry, and desperate.

German industry drew manpower from the GG, decreasing the number of mouths to feed, but pulling from the most physically robust parts of the population. Nearly two million Poles were recruited for forced labor, and Warsaw suffered disproportionately high requisition quotas. (It is reasonable to speak of "manpower" since more than 65% of those taken were men.[116]) This was another penalization of the "recalcitrant" city, which was overpopulated with respect to housing and food thanks to German despoliation. Labor conscription intensified in 1941, and doubled between 1942 and summer 1943, when another million Poles went west.[117] Forced labor cannot be differentiated from the war's demands, since Polish laborers replaced Germans in Wehrmacht service.[118] The seemingly limitless demand for Polish labor affected not only the GG economy (and was a point of contention between Frank, Hermann Goering, and Fritz Sauckel), but exacerbated police terror. When the supply of volunteers dried up, Daume's Order Police returned to a Tannenberg tactic: surprise street arrests. From 1942, Varsovians were press-ganged as Reich laborers. Those who resisted were shot, imprisoned, or deported to concentration camps.[119] When quotidian activities like taking the tram to work or queuing for food earned Warsaw's citizens – especially its young men – arrest and deportation, they joined the underground. As aboveground life got more dangerous, underground life, even insurgency, seemed less risky. Because the occupation relied on terror to extract labor from "work-shy" Poles, the narrow space for Polish civilian life collapsed, driving many into an underground existence they had previously avoided for fear of repercussions: when the repercussions of opposition were visited on the

---

[114] Reviving an earlier practice. Richard J. Evans, *Death in Hamburg: Society and Politics in the Cholera Years* (New York: Penguin Books, 1987), 112.

[115] Zaprutko-Janicka, *Okupacja od kuchni*, 65, 120–123, 125–130.

[116] Mark Spoerer and Jochen Fleischhacker, "Forced Laborers in Nazi Germany: Categories, Numbers, and Survivors," *Journal of Interdisciplinary History* 33 no. 2 2002, 186–7. Spoerer and Fleischhacker claim 1.6 million Poles worked. Only the USSR provided more. Dunin-Wąsowicz estimated 52,000 Varsovian laborers died in Germany. Dunin-Wąsowicz, *Warszawa w latach 1939–1945*, 83.

[117] Adam Tooze, *Wages of Destruction: The Making and Breaking of the Nazi Economy* (New York: Viking, 2006), 516–517; Mazower, *Inside Hitler's Greece*, 74.

[118] Daniel Brewing, "'Musimy walczyć' Codzienność zwalczania partyzantów w Generalnym Gubernatorstwie w 1942 r." in *Przemoc i dzień powszedni w okupowanej Polsce*, 57–59.

[119] The April 1942 report mentions "continual difficulties" since "volunteers for work in the Reich are rarer and rarer" (Fischer to Frank April 1942, dated May 12, 1942 (Fischer, *Raporty*, 520)).

city en masse regardless of their behavior, the city joined the anti-Nazi opposition en masse.

Despite the gulf between the ghetto and "Aryan" Warsaw, the Holocaust affected the spread of non-Jewish resistance as well. Ghetto liquidation in late summer 1942 demonstrated that the Germans were willing to ethnically "cleanse" – and kill – whole communities.[120] For non-Jewish Varsovians, the ghetto's emptying provided a terrifying picture of their own possible future.[121] For devoted antisemites, it was a victory that meant postwar Poland would be "ethnically" Polish.[122] But, if the Jewish minority could be carted off and murdered, so could Poles. More important still was ghetto resistance in January and April 1943, when the Jewish Fighting Organization and several other groups, despite a lukewarm Home Army response, attacked German police and inflicted casualties.[123] Joshua Zimmerman has argued that this behavior – unlike the escalating antisemitic persecution that preceded it – was central to Home Army reappraisal of Jewish resistance.[124] Portentously, the behavior of Nazi police in razing the ghetto directly prefigured the razing of the rest of the city after the 1944 uprising. A cycle of opposition and repression was unfolding in which insurgency went hand-in-hand with terror.[125]

Spring 1943 brought multiple catastrophes. On April 13, 1943, Goebbels gleefully announced a horrifying discovery: mass graves filled with Polish corpses outside Smolensk: 21,768 Polish POWs, "around half of the Polish Army's prewar officer corps," men "drawn from some of the most elite segments of Polish society" filled graves outside the village of Katyń.[126] Katyń was thus another intelligentsia blow. News of the Katyń "incident" overshadowed the ghetto uprising that began on April 19, 1943 for many non-Jewish Varsovians; indeed, Nazi propaganda spread antisemitic rumors of "Jewish" communist killers of the officers that were readily believed.[127] It is hard to overestimate the importance of the revelation for Polish behavior and its intertwining with Polish–Jewish relations.[128] The Red Army had arrested the officers after the September Campaign and the Soviet NKVD executed

---

[120] Paulsson, *Secret City*, 73–78.

[121] Whether this was planned is not important; it was feared.

[122] Piasecki's *Nowa Polska* "covered the story of the April 1943 Warsaw Ghetto Uprising like play-by-play commentators at a sporting event, favoring neither side." Kunicki, *Between*, 65.

[123] Jewish prisoners across Europe discussed the ghetto uprising. USHMM RG 02.005.01, "My Deportation," Bernard Nissenbaum, 27–28.

[124] Zimmerman, *Polish Underground*, 227–235, 249.

[125] Yugoslavia is the obvious comparison.

[126] Wallace, *Life and Death in Captivity*, 149; 150–151; USHMM RG-50.012.0044, AN: 1989.67.44, "Interview with Jan Karski," Part 2, 14:00–14:30.

[127] Leociak, *Text*, 225.

[128] Kunicki, *Between*, 67; Gross, *Fear*, 7–10.

them in spring 1940 as the AB-Aktion unfolded in Warsaw.[129] Exacerbating the 22,000 dead was the ham-fisted Soviet cover-up. The London Poles demanded an International Red Cross investigation and Stalin balked, blamed the killings on Germany, and severed diplomatic ties with the exiles. It was one of Warsaw's own elites, Wanda Wasilewska, who announced the split and encouraged Poles to reject the western exiles and turn to Moscow: for all their geographic sprawl, the fight for Polish loyalty retained a Varsovian stamp.[130] The Soviets had leverage despite NKVD guilt; they were vital allies of Britain, France, and the United States: Barbarossa had displaced the Poles as the main eastern European partner of the Western Allies. The fallout of Katyń was that the de facto Soviet enemy became a de jure one and any pretense of Soviet support for Poland collapsed.[131] Soviet backing of left-leaning Polish military conspiracies was also at stake, strengthening the hand of the Home Army. As the Grand Alliance turned to the offensive in 1943–44, Poland lost its footing within the coalition that had formed over its invasion. For some, this was reason to despair; for others, it was reason to fight.

Begun in the fog of war in September 1939, armed opposition rose to encompass much of Warsaw. Ordinary people, however, did not join in large numbers until 1942–43. Both the consolidation of the underground under the Home Army umbrella *and* changing wartime circumstances mushroomed recruiting. Ordinary Poles had chaffed under a draconian administration, but their suffering paled in comparison to the risks of outright opposition, symbolized by the walls of Pawiak. Elites and Polish Jews had had a different experience from the start. As the place of Poland in the alliance system shifted – first with Barbarossa, then the addition of the United States, and finally the Polish–Soviet split over Katyń – Nazi invincibility in eastern Europe crumbled. The all-powerful Nazi occupiers of 1939 and 1940 were worried in 1943. Hunger, arrest, deportation, and forced labor stalked the city. Aerial bombardment destroyed property and lives. The Holocaust raised the specter of mass murder in a manner unthinkable before, though ironically the focused genocide of 1939–40 had been abandoned. The risks of opposition appeared less daunting as daily life deteriorated.[132]

8.7   Conclusion

The growth of intelligentsia-led military activity is unsurprising: it was the response that Himmler and Heydrich expected and launched Tannenberg to

---

[129] Landau, *Kronika*, Tom II, 346.
[130] Shore, *Caviar and Ashes*, 229.
[131] Cienciala, *Katyń*, 207–210.
[132] Soviet partisan demographics also widened during 1942. Slepyan, *Stalin's Guerrillas*, 188–194.

forestall, and it was the time-honored tradition of Warsaw intelligentsia under foreign domination since the late eighteenth century. But, though likely, it was not inevitable, and its fragmentary character, conflicting international loyalties, and slow unification were unique to the Second World War. Despite references to "the underground" in the singular there were always multiple military conspiracies, some of which were ultimately irreconcilable.

Karaszewicz-Tokarzewski's Polish Victory Service and its heirs had an edge over their opponents and contributed to their consolidation into the Home Army: an early start; the elite military background of founders; Sikorski's imprimatur; the assistance of the London Poles and their allies; the mutually supporting relationship with the delegation of the "secret state." It profited from the talents of organizations it absorbed, like the Secret Polish Army (TAP), "Unity" Catholic formations, Peasant Battalion (BCh) soldiers, PLAN refugees, and some of the National Armed Forces (NSZ), most of which were also Warsaw intelligentsia projects. The SZP was the first elite military conspiracy but never the only one. Despite this jungle of fighting organizations, the combined pull that the Home Army eventually exerted – on unaffiliated individuals and other conspiracies, and the push of deteriorating circumstances, which drove men and women into opposition as protection against labor conscription, imprisonment, and execution – made it the most powerful armed force in occupied Warsaw by late 1943.

Home Army on the Offensive

Violence in 1943–1944

Home Army dominance shaped underground civilian society, information trafficking, schools, even the Church. It became the face of Warsaw's opposition in the late occupation, though its founding goal remained elusive. Members of its leadership were still and always remained key figures in the Warsaw intelligentsia, often but not always prewar career officers, steering a now-enlarged underground movement toward more direct confrontation with the occupier: the original Nazi nightmare. Though the anti-intelligentsia campaigns were over, Pawiak was still full, Gestapo men and their informers terrorized the streets, and Generalplan Ost and ghetto liquidation raised anew the specter of mass murder. When 1943 began, Warsaw's situation was bleak and the Wehrmacht undefeated. Between January and April 1943, the ghetto uprisings were brutally repressed, indicating German strength and the costs of rebellion. In April, the Katyń discoveries traumatized the city, underscoring Soviet hostility to Poland and to its military officers in particular. The evolving war offered few comforts, though Polish soldiers were engaged in multiple theaters of the Grand Alliance fight. The Soviet Union had become the *sine qua non* of Grand Alliance coherence and its importance only grew, stifling Western Allied support for Polish resistance. Nevertheless, the Home Army had increasing capacities and its leaders considered how to exploit them, turning to a more confrontational posture.

When the last German Eastern Front offensive foundered in summer 1943 around Kursk, the Home Army launched *its* first offensive, Operation Heads, harnessing the restlessness of its conspirators against Nazi leadership. Operation Heads contributed to a cycle of escalating brutality in which Poles were usually, but not always, the losers, and in which those who considered violence the proper response to German domination had ample opportunity to observe its effects. Intelligentsia who rejected violence saw in this a looming tragedy.

This experience and the coordination of still-independent military efforts was tested in summer 1944, when the strategic situation of the Eastern Front brought the "real" war – the clash of armies from which Varsovians had largely been excluded – back to Poland and raised the question of what victory would bring.[1] The Red Army's behavior as it advanced suggested the Soviets might

---

[1] Also true in western Europe. Ott, *Living with the Enemy*, 80.

occupy rather than liberate Warsaw, which delighted Polish communists. [2]
This forced the Home Army into open revolt (for which Karaszewicz-
Tokarzewski created it) but for which it was unprepared. Caught up in
circumstances which it had exacerbated but not controlled, the Warsaw elite
found itself in the middle of an insurrection in summer 1944. Its members,
especially the remnants of the prewar officer corps in hiding, had built the first
military conspiracies, and had consolidated disparate initiatives under the
Home Army umbrella in 1942, retaining its leadership and connections with
the London Poles. Barbarossa and its fallout stiffened their resolve, but also
pushed them into an uneasy alliance with the Soviet Union, mediated through
the Western Allies. The wartime alliance structure had given their exiled
countrymen a refuge and kept the Polish fate on the agenda of larger powers,
but it also forced Warsaw into decisions contrary to its elite conspirators' local
needs, and which collapsed not only military opposition, but other elite-led
projects.

The last action of the Home Army, the uprising of 1944, was driven by
external events – the approaching Eastern Front – and fulfilled the Polish
Victory Service's initial hopes, but it was unsuccessful. Not only did the Home
Army fail to capture Warsaw, the Germans used the rebellion as an excuse to
implement comprehensive retaliation and destroy the city. Despite consistent
reprisals, it was not the turn to violence that destroyed elite military conspiracies, but the misapplication of that violence: Operation Heads destabilized
occupation, but the circumstances of the Warsaw Uprising cost the Home
Army and allied forces their city. This final action of one initiative – the Home
Army – captured the imagination of much of the intelligentsia but ultimately
destroyed the conditions under which their activities flourished.

9.1   Mature Home Army

The Germans lost their grip on Warsaw between summer 1942 and summer
1944. A growing SZP-ZWZ-AK – hereafter the Home Army – moved from
information gathering, newsletter publishing, and petty sabotage to weapons'
theft, prison breaks, and assassination of German personnel: to terrorism.
They held to Karaszewicz-Tokarzewski's mission to restore Polish independence but hesitated to engage in open revolt since circumstances were so dire. In
September 1940 the SZP-ZWZ had 106 commissioned officers, 131 non-coms,
2,271 soldiers, and 4,000 reservists; in September 1942 the SZP-ZWZ-AK had
126 staff officers, 554 field officers, and 4,000 non-coms. [3] Home Army leaders
nevertheless could not possess anything like fame; members used pseudonyms

---

[2] It disarmed Home Army soldiers in eastern Poland. Anne Applebaum, *Iron Curtain: The
Crushing of Eastern Europe, 1944–1956* (New York: Anchor Books, 2013), 5, 92–94.
[3] Strzembosz, *Akcje zbrojne*, 74.

and there was significant devolution of responsibility.[4] The mature Home Army dominated military activity but did not control it. To situate its development in the model used to evaluate contemporary insurgencies, between late 1942 and summer 1943 the Home Army won its "war of position" in the Polish opposition landscape and achieved hegemon status.[5] Dominant in Warsaw, it was finally prepared to fight terror with terror, and its target was the Nazi occupation.

Spring 1943 was tumultuous; summer 1943 was worse. In Warsaw, Stefan Rowecki ("Grot"), mastermind of SZP-ZWZ diversion operations, led the consolidated Home Army. Rowecki's strategy was to solidify alliances and tame radical fringes.[6] He was also planning a full-scale uprising when he was betrayed to the Gestapo and arrested in June 1943, just before Władysław Sikorski's accidental death in a plane crash over Gibraltar, one of so many Polish conspiracies undermined by other Poles. The double loss of Rowecki and Sikorski was a crushing blow that revealed that the mature Home Army was still very vulnerable. Rowecki was tortured and interrogated for a year. Himmler ordered his execution in August 1944.[7] In London, Stanisław Mikołajczyk (1901–66) replaced Sikorski as prime minister, a post he held until November 1944. Mikołajczyk led Piast, the Polish People's Party (Polskie Stronnictwo Ludowe), and was less charismatic than Sikorski. He also had the unhappy task of repairing Polish–Soviet relations. Despite sincere effort he got few results. Kazimierz Sosnkowski claimed Sikorski's Commander in Chief duties from mid-1943. Tadeusz Komorowski from Krakow replaced Rowecki, and led the Home Army into the Warsaw Uprising. Komorowski was a Galician and a career cavalry officer; opinions on his command talents are sharply divided.[8] He was taken prisoner after the September Campaign and escaped German captivity (common among military conspirators), returning to Krakow to start an officers' conspiracy. His group then joined Karaszewicz-Tokarzewski's Warsaw SZP.[9] Tadeusz Pełczyński, a Varsovian career officer and one of the SZP old guard, served as Komorowski's deputy and chief of

---

[4] AAN AK Mf 2375–16 s. 203/II-119, 25, 29; 203-III-121, 9.

[5] Insurgency literature offers models. Peter Krause insists hegemons become risk averse and are likelier to negotiate with occupier states than weaker groups, but the Home Army became increasingly risk *seeking* as it consolidated. Peter Krause, *Rebel Power: Why National Movements Compete, Fight, and Win* (Ithaca: Cornell University Press, 2017), 9–11.

[6] Borowiec, *Warsaw Boy*, 139–140.

[7] At either Oranienburg or Sachsenhausen. Paul and Mallmann, *Gestapo im Zweiten Weltkrieg*, 360; Bennett, *Roots of Counter-Insurgency*, 68; Nowak, *Courier from Warsaw*, 163, 186.

[8] Zimmerman, *Polish Underground*, 250–251; Włodzimierz Borodziej, *Der Warschauer Aufstand: 1944* (Frankfurt am Main: Fischer Taschenbuch Verlag, 2004), 67–70; Ney-Krwawicz, *Armia Krajowa*, 23–24.

[9] Bór-Komorowski, *Armia Podziemna*, 19–25; 30–32.

staff, and the two shifted the Home Army to an offensive posture while remaining as deferential as they could to Rowecki's vision. None of the 1943 replacements were as good as Sikorski and Rowecki had been.

By the time Komorowski took command in July 1943, the Home Army had branches across Poland with headquarters in Warsaw and possessed a subdivided departmental structure. Its sprawling Bureau of Information and Propaganda (BIP) where Aleksander Kamiński worked was subordinated directly to Komorowski. Rowecki's baby, the Diversion Command (Kierownictwo Dywersji) or "Kedyw," ran sabotage.[10] From January 1941 to summer 1944, Kedyw boasted 28 destroyed German airplanes, 4,326 destroyed military trucks; 122 burned military munitions dumps; 19,058 damaged rail cars; 6,930 damaged locomotive engines; and 732 train transports derailed.[11] The Operations Chief managed combatants – artillerymen, sappers, airmen, sailors, fast-deploy forces, and training facilities – though most specialties were shorthanded. The Organizational Division included women's units and chaplains. In other words, Komorowski's Home Army was an army with a hierarchy (even if the need for secrecy gave lower-level commanders considerable independence), designation of duties, and a support staff feeding the men, bandaging their wounds, and tending to their souls. Units were severely under strength, training was intensive but uneven, nobody was in uniform, financial support from London trickled in, Gestapo infiltration was an ever-present threat, and few combatants had sufficient arms, though not for lack of trying.[12] Secret production facilities fashioned hand grenades and anti-tank explosives; rifles and machine weapons were rare.[13] Money for weapons' purchase and production came from multiple sources: from the British and Americans, from the London Poles, and from an ad hoc blackmail campaign against wealthy Poles, ideally those hobnobbing with Germans who could be shaken down for cash and could not rely on Polish help if they protested.[14] Aristocrats ensconced in country estates could also be targeted but might push back and were sometimes on good terms with German authorities.[15] Funds were tight. Underground arms production employed specialists (Warsaw had forty engineers alone) and the Gestapo regularly raided workshops and executed personnel. At maximum capacity Komorowski had R&D, a testing site, five mechanical workshops, four sites for grenade production, four

[10] Pawlina, *Praca w dywersji*, 51–72.

[11] Bór-Komorowski, *Armia Podziemna*, 179.

[12] The Second Department monitored weapons. Artur Jendrzejewski, *Polsko, ile Ty mnie kosztowałaś* ... (Gdańsk: Muzeum II Wojny Światowej, 2017), 66–69; Bór-Komorowski, *Armia Podziemna*, 169–175.

[13] AAN AK s. 203/I-14 Mf 2368-2, "Komendant Główny," 1942–1944, 24.VIII.43, 35): "Znicz" (Komorowski) received 5,000 nine mms and 10,000 American rifles in August 1943.

[14] Kunicki, *Between*, 66.

[15] Jakubowska, *Patrons of History*, 72–75.

for machine weapons, four for explosives, and one for pyrotechnics. Unfortunately, a spring 1944 Gestapo raid seized his workers and 70,000 of the 320,000 hand grenades stockpiled in Warsaw.[16]

As it expanded, the Home Army shifted demographically. Many young people, especially scouts, aged in. Intelligentsia youth replaced relatives lost or cowed by early persecution. Still, most conspirators remained part-timers until the end. The phenomenon of double and triple lives existed in military conspiracies as in information networks, underground schools, and Catholic projects. The first and most numerous category of conspirators were those who lived double lives with an existence "aboveground" and simultaneous underground work, like Jan Karski's brother Marian Kozielewski.[17] Starzyński's deputy, Julian Kulski, also belonged in this category as he – and his young son – worked with the underground.[18] The physician Zygmunt Śliwicki, using his examining rooms to see patients and "patients" who were really co-conspirators, was a category one conspirator until his arrest. Such people might work in a factory or an office and collect a paycheck – often from the German administration – and also spy for a conspiracy, distribute illegal periodicals, or train in a combat unit.[19] This allowed Home Army reach into factories, workshops, and offices, and disguised its expansion. "Aboveground" existence masked "ordinary" conspirators and their official jobs protected them somewhat from labor roundup. Opposition activities might be occasional, like a priest who heard confessions for conspirators heading out on a sabotage mission, or it could require the majority of a person's time and attention with the "legal" cover a mere fig leaf for a life focused on conspiracy. Category-one conspiracy allowed the intelligentsia to continue to see itself as part of the opposition even when its contributions were perfunctory, a sense that was not inaccurate and that kept many elites "in reserve" to be called on by underground leadership.

The second category were "professional conspirators" who lived entirely underground on false papers. Zofia Kossak – or Zofia Śliwicka, as her Kennkarte read – became a professional conspirator. So was Jan (Kozielewski) Karski. So was Komorowski, who tellingly had multiple aliases.[20] One could professionalize and move from category one to category two, but not back again. The Gestapo continuously hunted category two, who overlapped heavily with the original intelligentsia targets; their arrest endangered whole branches of underground life. The third and last category was the smallest: open partisans who

16 Bór-Komorowski, *Armia Podziemna*, 180–181.
17 Litwiński, "Policja Granatowa" in *Porządek publiczny i bezpieczeństwo*, 112.
18 USHMM RG-50.030.0769, AN: 2014.238.1, "Interview with Julian Kulski [Jr.]," 1:19:00–1:25:11; 2:10:10–2:11:06.
19 Aleksandra Ziolkowska-Bohem, *The Polish Experience through World War II: A Better Day Has Not Come* (Lanham: Lexington Books, 2013), 106.
20 Madaj and Żuławnik, *Proboszcz Getta*, 112.

wore (improvised) uniforms, advertising their insurgent stance publically, and embraced violence from the get-go. The NSZ and People's Guard (GL) favored a category three model more than the Home Army or its predecessors did.[21] In Warsaw, category three was suicidal until the launch of the Warsaw Uprising.[22] The intelligentsia dominated category two, the "professional conspirators," but also had an important presence in category one, and many elites leveraged social or professional clout to filter information to the underground while retaining their "day jobs."

Gender shaped anti-Nazi opposition, and categories two and three were predominantly male, though more because of Nazi persecution than women's lack of commitment. As already explained, women led underground education, and one reason was the departure of male students for the underground militaries, especially during heightened violence. Women's traditional care-giving responsibilities also restricted their underground work – Karski's bachelorhood made him a better courier. Unlike underground education, the Home Army was dominated by men, but there were women's positions in auxiliary units and some combat ones, and numerous female volunteers.[23] Nurses, couriers, and communications personnel were usually women. This gendered division of underground labor might seem obvious, but it bears further consideration. The work of the Home Army and its predecessor and constituent organizations – information collection, agitation, sabotage, weapons collection – were, properly speaking, combat-adjacent auxiliary activities. Most European militaries (and more so insurgencies) included women in auxiliary formations, including Poles.[24] The Home Army absorbed the Women's Military Service (Wojskowa Służba Kobiet, WSK), precisely such an organization.[25] The reason for the organization's predominately male character and commemoration lay more in aspirations than activity: it wished to become a combat organization, and therefore it emphasized men and awarded them more prestige.

Assessments of women's participation has shifted as the understanding of resistance has expanded. Janusz Zawodny, who fought in the uprising, admitted that, "without women, the AK could not have existed" but was also concerned that "women's ability to manipulate the membership of the organization on an informal level was a ... problem" and that female conspirators

---

[21] This fits with movement structure theory on insurgent behavior, in which challengers (NSZ and GL) are more likely to engage in violence knowing repression will disproportionately affect competitors. Krause, *Rebel Power*, 9.

[22] Category three "mainly stayed in the forests." Bór-Komorowski, *Armia Podziemna*, 165–167.

[23] "Wojskowa Służba Kobiet" in *Polskie Siły Zbrojne*, 116; Katja Höger, "Frauen als Kombattanten" in *Polnische Heimatarmee*, 387–410.

[24] Musiał, *Sowieccy partyzanci*, 472–483.

[25] Kunicki, *Between*, 64.

used "tears" and wiles to meddle in strategy, which he believed a male domain.[26] As the hierarchy formalized and combat positions specialized, they were not assigned to women. A May 1942 Home Army report noted women's contributions but not until October 1943 did women gain "equal duties" with men – by exile decree. The most dramatic demonstration of the Home Army's male character was the order to disarm women before the 1944 uprising. Women's weapons were given to "true" soldiers, though female participants were not removed from harm's way.[27]

Formal Home Army restrictions existed on paper despite women's presence in sabotage, diversion, and even combat operations.[28] Elżbieta Zawacka ("Zo," 1909–2009), courier and paratrooper, demonstrated that individual women advanced to considerable responsibility. Zawacka was a dramatic example of the "fighting intelligentsia" in wartime. She was the daughter of a Prussian army officer from a Toruń intelligentsia family subjected to Germanization pressures before the First World War. Zawacka studied mathematics at Poznań University, taught high school, and worked with the Women's Military Training organization (Przysposobienie Wojskowe Kobiet, PWK). She served with the PWK during the September Campaign and joined an early SZP-ZWZ unit in western Poland. A talented athlete who knew German and English, her SZP-ZWZ commander sent her to Warsaw, where she trained alongside couriers Lerski, Nowak, and Karski. In 1940, Zawacka became the deputy director of the SZP-ZWZ international courier service, and then brought it into the Home Army.[29] Rowecki sent her to London to explain 1943 strategy. Using the name Elizabeth Watson, she persuaded Sosnkowski and the London Poles to recognize female Home Army soldiers, and then undertook paratrooper training – one of the "silent and unseen" – to get home. She dropped outside Warsaw in September 1943, the only Polish female paratrooper, and worked at Home Army headquarters until the uprising, during which she fought.[30] Bolesław Szmajdowicz, who commanded an air drop site outside Warsaw, whimsically recalled her landing in the postwar: "The first parachutist takes off his helmet

---

[26] "The ultimate in female weaponry – tears." Zawodny, *Nothing but Honour*, 44, 46–47.

[27] Soviet female partisans suffered this in 1944 when the Red Army disarmed women. Slepyan, *Stalin's Guerrillas*, 203; Höger, "Frauen als Kombattanten," 406.

[28] Female sappers, the Kobiece Patrole Minerskie, formed by Wanda Gertzówna ("Lena," 1896–1958), assisted with the Kutschera Operation. Anna Rojewska, "Grabowska Maria" in *Sylwetki Kobiet-Żolnierzy*, eds. Krystyna Kabzińska, Służba Polek na Frontach II Wojny Światowej – 7 (Toruń: Fundacja Archiwum i Muzeum Pomorskie Armii Krajowej oraz Wojskowej Służby Polek, 2003) 7, 117; Stachiewicz, *Akcja "Kutschera,"* 9–11, 26, 41.

[29] Malinowski, *Żołnierze łączności*, 57; Minczykowska, *Cichociemna Generał Elżbieta Zawacka*, 26–31; 55–57; 82; 119.

[30] She went to Pruszków transit camp, not the POW camp for (male) combatants. Minczykowska, *Cichociemna Generał Elżbieta Zawacka*, 152–155; Ryszard Borowicz, Hanna Kostyło, and Władysława Szulakiewicz, *Elżbieta Zawacka "Zo" – Portret akademicki* (Toruń: Wyd. Naukowe Uniwersytetu Mikołaja Kopernika, 2009).

and – what do I see? Long hair! A woman!"[31] Zawacka was eventually promoted to brigadier general, one of only two women ever to be addressed as *pani generał* in the Polish Army.[32]

Manufacturing and stockpiling weapons; recruiting men and women and training them; retaining officers with combat experience: this force existed, as Karaszewicz-Tokarzewski intended, to launch an "open fight."[33] The mature Home Army did not monopolize Polish violence: it retained competitors, especially on the extreme left and right, and opportunists, thugs, and bandits disrupted Warsaw's streets. Nevertheless, the Home Army kept the undermining of Nazi occupation and the pursuit of postwar independence atop its agenda. Such a fight, however, required a ferociously complex balance, coordinated with Allied strategy, supplied with foreign weaponry, and at the underground's maximum capacities, without Gestapo infiltration. It was the hope for which the elite had created it and why most of its recruits had joined, but it also had to await the right moment.

9.2   Operation Heads

Meanwhile there was the matter of the chaos to which Warsaw was reduced.[34] Komorowski owed his command to continued Gestapo lethality, and in 1943 he decided to give it a taste of its own medicine.[35] A delicious target made a rare visit in fall 1943: Heinrich Himmler. Himmler himself was untouchable – after his deputy Heydrich's Prague assassination his personal security was like a moving fortress – but his family was not. Franz Kutschera, SSPF in Warsaw from September 1943, was engaged to Himmler's sister. The Home Army went after those close to Himmler. In an assassination campaign from late 1943 until August 1944 known as Operation Heads (Akcja Główki), a dedicated attack unit, "Agat" (for "antygestapo"), executed sentences from secret state courts against those who particularly threatened Warsaw.[36] The Grey Ranks and Kedyw supplied many Agat personnel.[37] "Heads" riffed on the Totenkopf, the SS death's head insignia, but also hearkened to the "decapitation" of Polish society in 1939–40.

---

[31] Neither Szmajdowicz nor Zawodny knew her name. Zawodny, *Nothing but Honour*, 45.

[32] By Lech Kaczyński in 2006. Minczykowska, *Cichociemna Generał Elżbieta Zawacka "Zo,"* 293.

[33] Tokarzewski-Karaszewicz, *U podstaw tworzenia Armii Krajowej*, "Zeszyty Historyczne," Paris, z.6, 1964, 19–20.

[34] The tentative German 1943 plans to re-empower Polish elites were of course scrapped in light of growing Polish terrorism. BABL R102/II/11, Gouverneur des Distrikts Warschau, Mai 1943; "Die Polenfrage," Lemberg, den 21. April 1943, 5–6, 12.

[35] Bór-Komorowski, *Armia Podziemna*, 164; Strzembosz, *Akcje zbrojne*, 401.

[36] Stachiewicz, *Akcja "Kutschera,"*24–33; Strzembosz, *Akcje zbrojne*, 401.

[37] Tumidajska-Styrczula, "Ale to już inna historia," *Pawiak był etapem*, 366, 370.

Underground courts drew hard lines around acceptable behavior, first for Poles themselves and then, eventually, for Germans. They sentenced German civilian administrators, policemen (the longest list), Wehrmacht officers, industrialists, judges, propaganda personnel, and Nazi party men to death for crimes against the Polish people.[38] This willingness to kill had been growing: the ZWZ, the Home Army's predecessor, had assassinated Polish and Volksdeutsche targets much earlier, knowing German retaliation would be more muted. The most famous example is the killing of Karol "Igo" Sym (1896–1941), a prominent actor of mixed Austrian and Polish parentage who hobnobbed with occupation officials and even assisted with an anti-Polish Nazi propaganda film. A ZWZ team shot him in his downtown apartment in March 1941 before he could escape to Vienna. Fischer and the Gestapo did respond, arresting over a hundred Poles, including many artists and entertainers, a number of whom died in one of the last Palmiry executions: the ZWZ had miscalculated slightly.[39] Two years later this sort of retaliation was assumed. The 1943 sentences named the most brutal occupiers, and the secret courts' pronouncements asserted the legitimacy of Polish underground society. On the list were Ludwig Fischer, the governor, who would survive Heads to be executed by a postwar Polish court; Franz Kutschera; Wilhelm Koppe; Ludwig Leist, Ludwig Hahn; Ernst Dürrfeld, the director of the urban transit system, and a host of others supervising persecution in Warsaw.

One of the first to fall was the hated Pawiak commandant, Franz Bürkl, on September 7, 1943. "Operation Bürkl" foundered on its first attempt but succeeded two days later. Bürkl's whereabouts were known: he worked in Pawiak, kept an office on Szuch Boulevard, and lived on Polna Street in the "German quarter." He commuted by armored car between these guarded locations. An Agat reconnaissance team selected the intersection of Marszałkowska and Litewska streets for their ambush. Their six-man assassination squad was armed with British submachine guns and homemade hand grenades and opened fire on Bürkl, seated next to his wife and child, killing eight Germans with no Home Army losses.[40] The Home Army was willing to kill bystanders and innocent civilians (whether Bürkl's family, profiting as they were from Polish suffering, was innocent depended on whom one asked) during Heads to force the German administration into retreat. Pawiak

---

[38] Heads targeted *łapanki* directors like Emil Braun. His underling, Friedrich Pabst, author of the Pabst Plan, was killed instead by accident. Strzembosz, *Akcje zbrojne*, 410. Ludwig Fischer was targeted but Ludwig Leist was not; in 1943 the Home Army attacked Leist's vehicle, thinking Fischer inside. USHMM RG-50.030.0769, AN: 2014.238.1, "Interview with Julian Kulski [Jr.]," 1:08:00–1:12:30.

[39] BN Mf. 45816, *BI*, [Rok 1], 13 marca 1941 r., "Warszawa teroryzowana," 1–2, 11; Engelking, "*Szanowny panie gistapo*," 78; Sławomir Koper, *Życie prywatne elit artystycznych Drugiej Rzeczypospolitej* (Warsaw: Bellona, 2010), 95–100.

[40] Strzembosz, *Akcje zbrojne*, 404, 343–346.

prisoners, ever Bürkl's victims, were executed in reprisal for his murder but Varsovians were thereafter spared his distinctive sadism. The city and its occupiers received a clear message about what underground leadership would no longer endure.

Franz Kutschera was the biggest prize. The Kutschera Operation was "the largest armed undertaking of the Underground Army in Warsaw besides Operation Arsenal" before the 1944 uprising.[41] Kutschera was a mass murderer and Himmler's right-hand man in Warsaw, unleashing waves of street arrests and public executions to "quiet" the restive city. In his short tenure his victims numbered between 9,500 and 15,000 people, including women and teenagers.[42] After the conclusion of the anti-intelligentsia campaigns, no Warsaw policeman killed more or faster than he. The Home Army decided "Kutschera had to be killed at any price" because of his staggering body count.[43] After Himmler's visit an eagle-eyed Kedyw spy chanced to notice a parked limousine outside a "private villa on Ujazdowski Boulevard" with a man in full SS uniform inside: Kutschera.[44] After laborious monitoring – how his home was guarded, who formed his security team, what hours he kept, the armament of his car, the vehicles in his convoy, the route he traveled to and from work – the Home Army put together another Bürkl-style assassination team. Kutschera and the Warsaw Gestapo were on high alert after Bürkl's killing, so each attempt escalated considerably in difficulty. A Kedyw execution squad commanded by Emil Fieldorf ("Nil," 1895–1953) pulled it off: they stormed Kutschera's armored limousine and killed him in broad daylight as his car turned off Szuch Boulevard.[45] On February 1, 1944, the dozen-man team ambushed the car convoy and shot Kutschera and his driver, but the shootings drew the attention of German patrolmen, who swarmed the assassins and killed four. In total, Operation Kutschera killed five Germans, including Kutschera, and four Polish assassins with an additional dozen wounded in the shootout. Though it was bloody, Operation Kutschera was a success.[46] From the Kedyw execution squad under "Nil" to the planners, couriers, and spies, Kutschera's killers were young intelligentsia getting revenge.[47] There was a coda to Kutschera's killing, however: 300 civilians were executed in reprisal. New restrictions, including a ban on Poles driving automobiles, followed his death.[48] In early 1944, this was a price the Home Army would pay to stop

[41] Broniewski, *Całym życiem*, 172.
[42] Witkowski, *Kedyw*, 422–423.
[43] Bór-Komorowski, *Armia Podziemna*, 183.
[44] Broniewski, *Całym życiem*, 172.
[45] Later Parasol Battalion. Stachiewicz, *Akcja "Kutschera,"* 5.
[46] Not without consequences: Zbigniew Dębczyński's comrade, "Zabawa," participated and was thereafter "never quite himself." Czajkowski, *Warsaw 1944*, 60.
[47] Stachiewicz, *Akcja "Kutschera,"* 10.
[48] Czugajewski, *Na barykadach*, 8.

Kutschera and send a message to his replacement – Paul Otto Geibel – that he, too, was in danger. With each Operation Heads kill German security tightened and reprisals increased in gruesomeness.[49] But the Home Army had claimed its moment, and was willing to accept staggering retaliation, confident that it would not lose the population's loyalty *and* that it had no choice if it was to seize power when the war ended.

9.3   Domination, Control, and Chaos

The Home Army turn to the offensive, coupled with Wehrmacht deterioration on the Eastern Front, pushed Warsaw out of German control. Fischer's reports to Frank reveal the dissolution of German power, beginning from summer 1941. In August 1941, Fischer called Warsaw "completely loyal" and noted "not one act of sabotage."[50] In September saboteurs tear-gassed cinemas.[51] In October, Germans reported public attacks but the "security situation was not precarious."[52] Spring 1942 saw "intense activity of the Polish resistance movement," including patriotic graffiti and sabotage. Propaganda leaflets were everywhere and Germans nervous.[53] In May, a "stiffening" of the Polish attitude was apparent.[54] In fall 1942, Soviet aerial bombardments killed 239 – but Poles were unfazed. Instead, there were rumors that the "Wehrmacht no longer had the strength to resist enemy attack." Sabotage and "banditry" were rife.[55] In December and January, there was "the shooting of a Luftwaffe officer, the [murder and torture] of a [German] soldier in Mokotów, the murder of a railway inspector in his apartment, the murder of an SD translator, the shooting of an employee of the Ministry of Propaganda ... and the shooting of three other German soldiers."[56] The violence continued with "29 Germans murdered, and 40 ... wounded ... sacrificed to [Polish] enemy elements" over the coming months.[57]

---

[49] Bór-Komorowski, *Armia Podziemna*, 183; Broniewski, *Całym życiem*, 172.

[50] Thanks to Paul Bushkovitch for drawing my attention to this phrasing. Fischer to Frank, August 1941, dated 11 September 1941, quotation 373; APmstW 482/II 1552 [Berichte des Gouverneurs des Distrikts Warschau an die Regierung des GG – Jahrgang 1941]— August 1941, 144.

[51] Fischer to Frank, September 1941, dated October 14, 1941, quotations 393.

[52] Fischer to Frank October 1941, dated November 20, 1941, 413.

[53] Fischer to Frank March 1942, dated April 13, 1942, 491.

[54] Fischer to Frank May 1942, dated June 15, 1942, 526.

[55] APmstW 482/II 1552 [Berichte des Gouverneurs des Distrikts Warschau an die Regierung des GG- Jahrgang 1941], 59; Fischer to Frank Aug./Sept. 1942, dated October 15, 1942, 566–567; Fischer to Frank Oct./Nov. 1942, dated December 10, 1942, 595.

[56] Most were shootings but the German in Mokotów was dismembered. Fischer to Frank, Dec. 1942/Jan. 1943 dated 11 Feb. 1943, 615.

[57] Fischer to Frank Feb./Mar.1943, dated April 12, 1943, 636.

By spring 1943, as the Germans crushed ghetto resistance, violence in "Aryan" Warsaw destabilized the city and "Germans [we]re showing real fear:"[58]

> The extraordinary intensification of the crisis in public safety was without question caused by the conspiratorial acts of sabotage accomplished by bandits and political criminals, the effect of which is that it is no longer possible to secure basic order and day-to-day safety in many parts of the district [of Warsaw]. Since the beginning of April [1943], there has not been either a day or a night all over the city that went without a report of robbery, murder, or acts of sabotage. This is not just a matter of sporadic activities, but of *an increasingly visible and systematic attack* by illegal forces on the life and property of Germans and on the fabric of public administration: an *emerging campaign of terror* against officialdom, German and non-German.[59]

During summer assassinations targeted German civilians, Poles, and Ukrainians.[60] A rumor circulated that "all Germans are to be murdered in October."[61] By late November, 78 Germans were dead and another 72 wounded.[62] Andrew Borowiec, a Grey Ranks scout, noted that "in Warsaw itself we were probably killing about ten Germans a day" and that the occupiers "rarely walked anywhere unless they were part of an armed patrol or in regimental strength."[63]

In early 1944, the Gestapo imposed a retaliation policy for assassinations, further escalating violence. Warsaw was papered with placards warning that for every German killed and all property destroyed, Poles would be shot. The threat was effective initially: the murder rate fell from fifty in December to five in January.[64] But it climbed, with twenty dead in February and forty in March. By this point Poles not only killed Germans: underground activists killed 78 *Poles* that February, and in March 126 non-Germans died as conspirators settled scores and cracked down on rogue activities.[65] Fischer questioned in July if he could hold the city.[66] In August Warsaw was in open revolt.[67]

---

[58] February 28, 1943 diary entry. Julian Kulski, *The Color of Courage: A Boy at War: The World War II Diary of Julian Kulski* (Los Angeles: Aquila Polonica, 2014), 170–171(This is the memoir of the deputy mayor's son).

[59] Fischer to Frank Apr./May 1943, dated June 9, 1943, 653.

[60] German women no longer went out at night. Lehnstaedt, "Codzienność okupanta," 500–503.

[61] Kedyw increased police attacks in October. Witkowski, *Kedyw*, 177.

[62] Fischer to Frank Oct./Nov. 1943 dated Dec. 15, 1943, 710.

[63] Borowiec, *Warsaw Boy*, 143, 157.

[64] Fischer to Frank Dec. 1943/Jan. 1944 dated 10 Feb. 1943, quotations 731.

[65] Fischer to Frank Feb./March 1944 dated 15 Apr. 1944, 756.

[66] Fischer to Frank July 26, 1943, 794.

[67] Fischer to Frank 1–15 August 1944, dated 16 Aug. 1944, 798.

9.4   1944 Uprising

Any examination of the Warsaw intelligentsia's behavior during the war must end with the uprising, the "apocalypse" that destroyed the city. After years of elaborate secrecy, the Home Army grew aggressive in 1943 – but stayed underground. It abandoned cover in summer 1944, believing its best – if not an ideal – moment for insurgency had arrived. Commander Tadeusz Bór-Komorowski launched a citywide uprising on August 1, 1944 at "W Hour," seizing a window of opportunity to reclaim the city before the Red Army, approaching from the east, arrived.[68] The Home Army supplemented its weaponry from caches outside the capital but was poorly armed.[69] A teen's mother held him back from joining his unit, as he was only "half dressed" to fight; he went anyway.[70] Other conspiracies joined in, including the National Armed Forces, the People's Army, and myriad civilians. A handful of ŻOB fighters, rare survivors of the 1943 ghetto uprising, also participated.[71] Yitzhak Zuckerman, who was among them, was proud to fight in 1944: "you have to understand," he remembered, "that we weren't a decisive force, not even an important force; we were only a few dozen; but, morally, we were significant."[72] Varied participants indicated enthusiasm but complicated command and demonstrated that, until the bitter end, different Polish conspirators fought for different visions of Poland.[73] The uprising failed, as the Germans reinforced Warsaw, using the revolt as provocation to attack the population, destroy all opposition, and raze the city. The insurgents were unaided by their erstwhile allies, the British and Americans, who were far

---

[68] Henryk Zamojski called it "tragic." Zamojski, *Jak wywołano Powstanie Warszawskie: tragiczne decyzje* (Warsaw: Bellona, 2014).

[69] Brewing, *Im Schatten*, 269.

[70] Sixteen-year-old Mieczysław Ścieżynski. *Mieszkańcy Warszawy w czasie Powstania 1944* (Warsaw: Dom Spotkań z Historią, 2016), 32.

[71] Within Home Army units or in AL formations or quasi-independently; numbers unclear. Edward Kossoy, "The Gęsiówka Story: A Little-Known Page of Jewish Resistance" in *Polin, Volume Seventeen: The Shtetl: Myth and Reality* (Oxford: Littman Library, 2004), 357; Krakowski, *War of the Doomed*, 276, 280–283. For the most comprehensive account, including Polish-Jewish participation in different fighting groups and among civilians, see: Barbara Engelking and Dariusz Libionka, *Żydzi w powstańczej Warszawie* (Warsaw: Stowarzyszenie Centrum Badań nad Zagładą Żydów, 2009).

[72] Remember he had missed the 1943 uprising. Zuckerman, *Surplus of Memory*, 536. Barbara Engelking and Dariusz Libionka agree but emphasize the diversity of Jewish experience and Polish attitudes towards Jews during the uprising, including continued hostility, see: *Żydzi w powstańczej Warszawie*.

[73] There were 342 Communist and People's Army (AL) troops at the outbreak. Janusz Marszalec, "Armia Krajowa a komuniści i ich stronnicy podczas Powstania Warszawskiego" in Kazimierz Krajewski and Tomasz Łabuszewski, *Powstanie Warszawskie: Fakty i Mity* (Warsaw: IPN, 2006), 62–63.

away, and – this is crucial – by the Soviets, who wished to stifle Polish aspirations as they positioned themselves to rule eastern Europe.[74]

Launched the afternoon of August 1, 1944, insurgents captured the city center – the Old Town, Wola district, and much of Żoliborz – and began their fight with enthusiasm despite mobilization difficulties and a catastrophic weapons shortage. The *Bulletin*, flourishing as a daily, carried Komorowski's August 2, 1944 announcement:

> Soldiers of the capital, today I give the order you have long awaited: an open fight against the eternal enemy of Poland, the German invader. After five years of hard, uninterrupted struggle in underground conspiracy, you stand in the open today, weapons in hand, to restore freedom to your fatherland and punish the German criminals for terror and the crimes they committed on Polish land.

Kamiński's paper reassured the city that, "at last . . . Warsaw is fighting."[75]

Poles outside Warsaw followed events closely, often praising the insurgents as "heroic" but relieved to be spared their suffering.[76] Varsovians generally supported Home Army efforts, even though they were trapped between Polish irregulars and Wehrmacht and SS forces.[77] Within three days, the downtown was in Polish hands, with troubling pockets of German strength in the university campus along Krakowskie Przedmieście and the police complex on Szuch Boulevard.[78] On August 5, soldier-scouts of the Grey Ranks' Zośka Battalion liberated Pawiak. The Gestapo, however, had marched most prisoners west beforehand. After heavy fighting and with the aid of a captured German Panther tank, the scouts freed 348 Greek and Italian Jews – some of whom joined the fight.[79] For several days the *Bulletin* celebrated Polish gains, but the August 6 issue heralded troubling news about "Germans murdering the

---

[74] Stalin airdropped some equipment, mostly onto German-held areas. The consensus is that Stalin's efforts were insincere, though his forces *were* overextended. Paweł Wieczorkiewicz, "Stalin a Powstanie Warszawskie: Próba interpretacji," in Krajewski and Łabuszewski *Powstanie Warszawskie: Fakty i Mity*, 13, 18–20; Richie, *Warsaw 1944*, 181–182.

[75] BN Mf. 45819, *BI*, Rok 6, Warszawa środa 2 sierpnia 1944 r., Nr. 35–242, [1].

[76] Kubalski, *Dziennik*, 341.

[77] The *Bulletin* declared on August 2 that the population's attitude was "excellent." BN Mf. 45819, *BI*, Rok 6, Warszawa środa 2 sierpnia 1944 r., Nr. 36–243, [1]. Janusz Marszalec notes early "euphoria," with falling morale after atrocities. Marszalec, "Porządek i bezpieczeństwo publiczne w Powstaniu Warszawskim" in *Porządek publiczny i bezpieczeństwo w okupowanej Warszawie*, ed. Robert Spałek (Warsaw: IPN, 2018), 260.

[78] Karski, not present, claimed that "within a few hours the center of the city was in their [AK] hands. Soon after, the whole city was." This was untrue. Karski, *Great Powers and Poland*, 415.

[79] These liberated Jewish prisoners had a complicated fate during the uprising. They were rarely armed and some were subject to antisemitic attack; others were praised and valued by Home Army commanders. USHMM RG 02.005.01, "My Deportation," Bernard

civilian population" and, on August 7, "terror." Thereafter news was ever worse.[80] The surprise launch trapped Ludwig Fischer in Brühl Palace, from which the SS painstakingly rescued him on August 8– though not without the Home Army wounding Fischer in the process, a splendid triumph in the second week.[81] Portions of Warsaw, however, never fell to Polish attack: Ochota and Mokotów districts; Praga on the east bank, and the Vistula bridges remained in German hands.[82] Insurgents could not consolidate gains and defended unconnected territory with light weapons and dwindling ammunition. Non-combatants spent two months in basements and behind makeshift barricades, their hopes waxing and waning.[83]

When the Wehrmacht reinforced, the uprising was doomed. Ben Shepherd insists the Wehrmacht escalated violence and that "nowhere . . . did the German occupiers commit depredations more savage than against the Warsaw Uprising." General Heinz Guderian and the Ninth Army leadership, in whose area Warsaw was located, did not protest civilian massacres, not even the feeble gestures Blaskowitz and von Brauchitsch mustered during Tannenberg.[84] Though hardly exonerating the Wehrmacht, Alexandra Richie clarifies that what started as a military operation – a counterinsurgency – became a police-led atrocity. Himmler's police made Warsaw their domain. The man in charge was SS-Obergruppenführer and General of the Waffen-SS Erich von dem Bach-Żelewski (1899–1972), 1944's Jürgen Stroop. Bach-Żelewski left anti-partisan detail on the Eastern Front to lead Warsaw "anti-bandit" operations. He later admitted to a "wild state of anarchy" and the "unnecessary killing of large numbers of the civilian population."[85] The SS executed prisoners, imprisoned civilians in camps, and looted and burned everything. SS Oberführer Oskar Dirlewanger (1895–1945) and SS Brigadeführer Bronislav Kaminski (1899–1944) led brigades that tortured, looted, and conducted mass rapes of Polish women.[86] The Wehrmacht brought equipment in by rail, including some of

Nissenbaum, 30–33; Zimmerman, *Polish Underground*, 392; Domańska, *Pawiak więzienie gestapo*, 492; Finder, "Jewish Prisoner Labour in Warsaw," 325, 345–349.

[80] BN Mf. 45819, *BI*, Rok 6, 6 sierpnia 1944 r., Nr. 43–250, 3; *BI*, Rok 6, 7 sierpnia 1944 r., Nr. 44–260, 2.

[81] Kulski, *Color of Courage*, 297–299.

[82] If the Soviets had helped they would have crossed the Vistula. Richie explains that they never intended aid and thus bridges were irrelevant. Richie, *Warsaw 1944*, 100; Białoszewski, *Memoir*, 126.

[83] Białoszewski, *Memoir*, 86, 37, 67; Zawodny, *Nothing but Honour*, 155, 158; Marszalec, "Porządek i bezpieczeństwo," 255.

[84] Ben Shepherd, *Hitler's Soldiers: The German Army in the Third Reich* (New Haven: Yale University Press, 2016), 486–487; Finder and Prusin, *Justice*, 71.

[85] Nuremberg Trial Proceedings Volume 4, Twenty-Eighth Day, Monday, January 7, 1946, Afternoon Session, 478–481.

[86] Richie, *Warsaw 1944*, 255–307; 308–359; Borodziej, *Warschauer Aufstand*, 113–125; Joanna Kryńska in *Chronicles of Terror: Warsaw*, 236–237.

the most substantial artillery deployed in eastern Europe.[87] By August 25, 1944, Komorowski's subordinate, General Antoni Chruściel ("Monter," 1895–1960), knew the Old Town was indefensible and ordered fighters to evacuate through the sewers.[88] Their escape preserved the command staff and some Home Army strength to fight another month, but it left civilians and the wounded behind to the thin mercy of SS men.[89] The Home Army fought from the city center (Śródmieście) and other isolated pockets throughout September, pleading for Allied help as their holdings shrank. The food situation was dire, sanitation collapsing, and potable water depleted, compounded by sickness and injury that overwhelmed medical facilities.[90] With non-combatants waving white flags and no Soviet help, Home Army command surrendered on October 2, 1944.[91] Its bedraggled soldiers received combatant status from a begrudging Himmler hoping the concession would profit him.[92]

Across the occupation, it was the days between August 1, 1944 and October 2, 1944 that have defined Warsaw's suffering. This formed the second hard bookend of occupation, begun with the failed defense in 1939. Like the siege, uprising destruction was too imprecise to target intelligentsia, despite their leadership of the Home Army and other conspiracies. Intelligentsia shared September 1939 and fall 1944 horrors with other Varsovians, dying alongside them in their beloved city, lamenting two failed efforts. More than 200,000 Varsovians died during the uprising, between 180,000 and 200,000 "civilians" – if that term has significance – and 20,000 insurgents, including 4,500 Polish Jews.[93] SS leadership bragged about a "quarter million" dead.[94] Though this eclipsed the siege and anti-intelligentsia campaigns, historians Daniel Brewing and Alexandra Richie emphasize continuities in how Germans treated Poles: Brewing considers uprising suppression of a piece with the "larger context of German partisan combat in occupied Poland." In the dense urban landscape, the SS and auxiliaries killed more efficiently than in the eastern European countryside.[95] Despite years of violence, 1944 still shocked Warsaw. Forced to abandon the destroyed city, veterans of the uprising, willing and unwilling,

---

[87] Richie, *Warsaw 1944*, 416–418.

[88] Białoszewski, *Memoir*, 135.

[89] Borodziej, *Warschauer Aufstand*, 140–155; Marszalec, "Porządek i bezpieczeństwo," 265.

[90] *Mieszkańcy Warszawy w czasie Powstania 1944*, 35, 41–43, 54–55.

[91] Marszalec, "Porządek i bezpieczeństwo," 264.

[92] Rowinski, *That the Nightingale Return*, 87; Richie, *Warsaw 1944*, 548; BN Mf. 45819, *BI*, Rok VI, 1 października 1944 r., Nr. 99(307), [1–2]; *BI*, Rok VI, 2 października 1944 r., Nr. 100(308), [1].

[93] Zimmerman, *Polish Underground*, 406; Wardzyńska, *Był rok 1939*, 218–220; 236–237; 270–272; Krakowski, *War of the Doomed*, 275–291.

[94] In Krakow figures as high as 265,000 circulated. Kubalski, *Dziennik*, 345.

[95] Brewing, *Im Schatten*, 275.

were relocated to transit camps or drifted across Poland.[96] Hans Frank pursued them in a last-ditch anti-Varsovian action in January 1945; police rounded-up 3,000 "dangerous" Varsovian evacuees across the country;[97] 1,600 people were dragged off to concentration camps and the rest killed to prevent Warsaw from rising again.[98] The city had given out.

Since the uprising failed, much ink has been spilled about why it was launched; had it succeeded the question would be trivial.[99] The Home Army launched an uprising because it wanted Warsaw. Much of its command staff thought an uprising essential to retaining a Polish place in the Grand Alliance, a "political signal" that Warsaw fought on.[100] The bleak 1944 situation, despite drawbacks, seemed unlikely to improve, making waiting unhelpful. Soviet propaganda called on Poles to revolt (an angle Jan Karski, observing from the United States, believed vital), encouraging optimists to think Moscow would support them and pessimists to think that there would be consequences if they did not.[101] Home Army leadership was also under the (mistaken) impression German defenses were in disarray. Even among Polish units fighting with the Red Army, "the rapidity of the Soviet advance had led to complacency and to a strong belief that the Germans were finished as a fighting force."[102] Komorowski decided "in ignorance of the German position at this crucial moment." He had bad information, which was the fault of his subordinates and the London Poles, who were increasingly dishonest about the Grand Alliance's cooling enthusiasm for Warsaw's plans. Komorowski launched an urban uprising under the assumption that his primary enemy, the Wehrmacht, was weak, and that his secondary enemy, the Soviet Union, might support him.[103] He was totally wrong.[104] Some of Komorowski's subordinates anticipated this and tried to prevent

---

[96] Davies, *Rising '44*, 507–576.

[97] Frank waffled. AAN 203VII-6: AK – Komenda Główna Oddział VI – Szef, 1944–45 [Notatka / Atak na RGO – 7.I.45 – "Nowak"], 6; Kubalski, *Dziennik*, 354.

[98] AAN 203VII-6: AK – Komenda Główna Oddział VI – Szef, 1944–45 [Notatka / Atak na RGO – 7.I.45 – "Nowak"], 5).

[99] On still-running debates: Krajewski and Łabuszewski, *Powstanie Warszawskie: Fakty i Mity*.

[100] Tadeusz Pełczyński and Leopold Okulicki particularly. Borodziej, *Warschauer Aufstand*, 97; Krakowski, *War of the Doomed*, 275–276.

[101] Not all communist agitation was external: Warsaw communists were building factory soviets. Karski, *Great Powers and Poland*, 414; Kenney, *Rebuilding Poland*, 58.

[102] Kochanski, *Eagle Unbowed*, 517.

[103] His *Times* obituary called him the man who ordered an uprising "in the foolish hope of setting up a free Polish government before the Russians arrived." TNA DEFE 13/519 Funeral of General Bor-Komorowski commander of the Polish home army during the Warsaw uprising, "Obituary: Gen. Bor-Komorowski: Leader of the Warsaw Uprising of 1944," *Times*, 26-10-66.

[104] GFM 33/681/1698, Political Department V: The Warsaw Uprising, "Abschrift: Auszug aus dem Vertrag über die Einstellung der Kampfhandlungen zwischen den polnischen

it.[105] However, Komorowski was not the only Allied commander who learned in 1944 that retreating German armies were difficult to defeat: his mistake was costly but not unique.[106]

Commanding insurgents was Antoni Chruściel's job, and he also reported to civilian leaders of the "secret state" withdrawn outside Warsaw to the village of Milanówek. Komorowski and Chruściel led Home Army forces – though many units operated in confused independence from command – and are therefore held responsible for failures. Others, too, have shared blame: historian Joshua Zimmerman laments Rowecki's death, seeing it as the beginning of a downward spiral.[107] Historian Włodzimierz Borodziej remarks that conditions looked favorable at the time and disparages ex post facto armchair generaling.[108] Norman Davies blames the Soviets and Stalin. Janusz Zawodny blames Chruściel but saves some ire for Sosnkowski for not securing Allied aid.[109] Richie points out that many blamed Chruściel not for mistakes but for being a peasant: Komorowski was a count and a cavalry officer, Chruściel a "boorish old soldier," "distrustful and crude," unpalatable to the still-rarified circles of opposition leadership.[110] Though Home Army soldiers were no longer exclusively intelligentsia, many were suspicious of the ideas of their social inferiors and blamed them when things went awry. In actual fact, ghastly casualties were the result of SS reprisals, rather than Polish recklessness: to focus on Polish missteps blames the victim.

The Wehrmacht, which rebuffed the initial revolt, blamed Himmler and the SS for the debacle.[111] Himmler disagreed (and was not one to defer to military opinion) and claimed Warsaw would be easier to defend from the Soviets as rubble anyway.[112] Nevertheless, even he acknowledged that the uprising was no German victory. Memoranda between still-functioning GG offices and Berlin in October summarized things: the subjugation of Warsaw was

---

Aufständischen und den deutschen Truppen in Warschau," 10; Borodziej, *Warschauer Aufstand*, 119.

[105] Antoni Chruściel ("Monter," 1895–1960) was an advocate; July 1944 telegrams indicates contentiousness (Zamojski, *Jak wywołano Powstanie Warszawskie*, 139–145; KHPSGL, Polskie Siły Zbrojne, Tom III: *Armia Krajowa*, 657–659) though Borodziej notes that on July 22, 1944 when Komorowski announced the decision his staff had no objections (Borodziej, *Warschauer Aufstand*, 100).

[106] Americans would be surprised by a German attack in the Ardennes in 1944, taking heavy casualties before victory. Antony Beevor, *Ardennes 1944: The Battle of the Bulge* (New York: Viking, 2015); KHPSGL, Polskie Siły Zbrojne, Tom III, 661–666.

[107] Zimmerman, *Polish Underground*, 189, 198, 250–254.

[108] Borodziej, *Warschauer Aufstand*, 111–112.

[109] Zawodny, *Nothing but Honour*, 21, 23, 107, 213–215.

[110] Józef Rybicki's words. Richie, *Warsaw 1944*, 171.

[111] Josef Bühler and SS-Obergruppenführer Stuckart assumed "parts of the intelligentsia" were "not averse" to new arrangements. BABL R58 1002 Neuordnung der Polenpolitik, Anlage 3, "Betr. Kapitulation Warschaus," 25, 25b; Richie, *Warsaw 1944*, 406–407.

[112] Stargardt, *German War*, 459–460.

a Pyrrhic victory and the Germans were in a worse position than in August.[113] The Poles, to German chagrin, no longer believed in final German victory.[114] Little mollified that the advance of the Red Army meant the dashing of Polish hopes, there was a dispirited German consensus that Warsaw was a "Bolshevik victory" alone.[115]

Intelligentsia who fought and observed the uprising were motivated variously, and many were impassioned defenders even after its failure. Their descendants under communism would not settle the question, debating over coffee in Warsaw's communist cafes whether it was "historically correct" or worth the loss of life.[116] Some were overwhelmed with frustration by five years of persecution and could not face replacing a Nazi occupier with a Soviet one without a fight.[117] Some believed the moment genuinely favorable, noting the withdrawal of Wehrmacht and occupation personnel.[118] Some were practical, thinking an uprising important for political and moral reasons, and counting on the Grand Alliance to bail them out. Others remembered the previous war, when Polish military action – in Piłsudski's Legions, within the armies of Germany, Russia, and Austria-Hungary – had resulted (indirectly) in the independent Second Polish Republic and hoped the precedent would hold.[119] The alliance structure of the Second World War, however, did not follow that model: in the earlier conflict, through a combination of battlefield loss, diplomatic bungling, and internal revolution, all three imperial states holding Polish territory lost or withdrew, leaving no victor to claim Poland. In the Second World War, made possible by the Molotov–Ribbentrop Pact between Nazi Germany and the Soviet Union, one state – Nazi Germany – would be defeated but the other, Stalin's Soviet Union, won and claimed Poland as spoils.[120]

The fallout was the worst-case scenario: staggering casualties, a destroyed capital, a humanitarian crisis, a scattered underground, and discredited exiles.

---

[113] This fits with Edelstein's conjecture that most (military) occupations (19 out of 26 since 1815) fail. The exceptionally coercive and anti-nationbuilding aspects of this one contributed to that failure. Edelstein, *Occupational Hazards*, 1–3. BABL R58/1002, "Laufende SD-Bericht," 3. Jan. 1945, 4 (56 of file); 6 (60 of file).

[114] BABL R58/1002, "Abschrift: Anlage 3, Betr. "Kapitulation Warschaus," 4–8 (26–28 of file).

[115] BABL R58/1002, "Abschrift: Bisherige Polenpolitik im GG," 19.10.1944, 19; "Abschrift: Anlage 3, Betr. "Kapitulation Warschaus," 4–6 (26–27 of file).

[116] Brandys, *Warsaw Diary*, 71.

[117] Borodziej, *Warschauer Aufstand*, 126–139; Janusz Marszalec, "Armia Krajowa a komuniści" in *Powstanie Warszawskie*, 61.

[118] Kershaw, *Hitler*, 810–813; Robert M. Citino, *The Wehrmacht's Last Stand: The German Campaigns in 1944-1945* (Lawrence: University Press of Kansas, 2017), 272–312; Edelstein, *Occupational Hazards*, 87–135.

[119] Borodziej, *Warschauer Aufstand*, 95.

[120] Kochanski, *Eagle Unbowed*, 338–339; 394–397.

Figure 9.1 Warsaw uprising capitulation. Home Army Commander Tadeusz Bór-Komorowski (left) meets with Erich von dem Bach-Żelewski (right) outside Warsaw, October 1944.
Wikimedia Commons.

The London Poles emerged looking impotent to Varsovians for failing to support them and incompetent to the Western Allies for being unable to prevent an inconvenient uprising.[121] This was more an international mistake than a national one: after all, the French launched an uprising in Paris the same month, and the American army came to their aid, enabling the French resistance to take power.[122] The Warsaw situation was useful only for the Soviet Union. The uprising's failure was also an intelligentsia loss, as students, scouts, artists, journalists, parliamentarians, priests, lawyers, and Legionnaires died in the fighting. It was more than that: it represented the failure of their wartime opposition, and the end of their collective capacities (Figure 9.1). Home Army consolidation had drawn together the main intelligentsia-led military conspiracies, and it had supported many non-violent conspirators, from the teachers of the "flying" schools to diverse publications and initiatives to aid Jews.

---

[121] Richie, *Warsaw 1944*, 88.
[122] Though the Western Allies were unenthusiastic, still they supported the uprising – in contrast to Red Army treatment of Poles. Paxton, *Vichy France*, 309, 350; Jackson, *France: The Dark Years*, 540–569.

Though it had come a long way from the efforts of Karaszewicz-Tokarzewski and the scouts under siege, the Home Army was the largest intelligentsia-led occupation undertaking. Its behavior drew much of the city in, and its defeat meant the crushing of the elite's national-political hopes.

Intelligentsia activity was revolutionized by the uprising: publications, with the exception of Kamiński's *Bulletin*, shuttered; underground education stopped and students joined the fight; the Church was severed from the Vatican; insurgency had its day. Insurgents, according to Zawodny were "the people of Warsaw. They came from all social strata: the richest and poorest, university professors, students, former governmental officials, artists, priests, unskilled labourers, and some known criminals."[123] Zawodny's list, attempting to indicate the universality of opposition, is still dominated by intelligentsia. Intelligentsia losses were devastating. General Władysław Anders, commanding the Polish 2nd Corps in Italy, called it a "reckless catastrophe" that "destroyed the institutions, the intelligentsia."[124] The uprising – the city pitting its strength against the Germans – made Soviet takeover of Poland easier, and was thus Studnicki's lifelong nightmare.[125] The uprising's "totally needless loss of life" was what Miłosz feared, and why he had disparaged violence (and kept himself out of it). He thought romantic patriotism foolhardy and considered Home Army encouragement of his peers likely to encourage German reprisal. It was "irresponsibly playing with too many human lives."[126] In the case of his friend, Krzysztof Kamil Baczyński ("Jan Bugaj," "Krzysztof," 1921–44), Miłosz was right: Baczyński, the "greatest hope of Polish poetry," was killed by a Wehrmacht sniper on August 4, 1944.[127] A rising star of the left-wing literary scene, envied by Miłosz and Jerzy Andrzejewski, Baczyński studied at the underground university and was drawn into sabotage, fighting in the Parasol battalion in 1944.[128] He left behind a number of half-finished literary works and his young wife, Barbara Drapczyńska (1922–44), pregnant with their child. She, another talent, was killed a month later.[129] The death of the poet – of the entire Baczyński family – has become symbolic of uprising wastage, which much of the intelligentsia joined and in which they died. Still, Baczyński participated not in spite of his poetic talents but because of them: his battalion comrades spent summer 1944

---

[123] Zawodny, *Nothing but Honour*, 16.

[124] Richie, *Warsaw 1944*, 187.

[125] JPI Archiwum Władysława Studnickiego 96:27, "Druga Wojna Światowa: Do rozdziału 'Aneksja i wojna z Sowietami,'" 1, 6.

[126] Franaszek, *Miłosz*, 205–206.

[127] Franaszek, *Miłosz*, 206; Richie, *Warsaw 1944*, 427.

[128] On his legacy: Damian Halik, "'Cudowne przygody pana Pinzla rudego' – K. K. Baczyński powraca," 30 kwietnia 2018, *Exumag*: Sztuka: https://exumag.com /cudowne-przygody-pana-pinzla-rudego/.

[129] Zbigniew Wasilewski (ed.), *Żolnierz poeta czasu kurz ... Wspomnienia o Krzysztofie Kamilu Baczyńskim* (Krakow: Wydawnictwo Literackie, 1979), 7–12, 269, 304.

whistling his "Oh Barbara" as they fought.[130] Nazi policemen and heavy artillery killed indiscriminately, regardless of talent, class, ethnicity, or contributions to the Polish national project. The scope of killing raised questions for intelligentsia survivors about how they "used" the national elite, and whether insurrection was worth the cost. Anders, Studnicki, and Miłosz were elitists: they considered their friends' and colleagues' deaths weightier than others. The point stands, however, that the intelligentsia directed Varsovian opposition to occupation, and 1944 demonstrated how well they had sustained the nation-state project.

9.5   Reappraising Civilian–Military Divisions

Ludwig Fischer's administration collapsed during the uprising; in late 1944 the city was a no-man's land. In September 1939, Varsovians learned they would not be spared Nazi violence. As the dust settled, elites formed a number of distinct projects. These overlapped and intertwined into intricate systems of opposition, some of which were oriented toward politics, education, or cultural initiatives, and others of which organized violence. Violent and non-violent opposition could be two facets of elite life: one for the present, the other for a hoped-for future. This was especially true for the young, whose energy and lack of commitments meant they divided their time among schooling, colportage, scouting, and military training. Other elites specialized as opposition grew in complexity and ambition, focusing in one sector or another. The Home Army's consolidation obscures this specialization, as it coordinated far-flung efforts that predated its 1942 formation and funneled them funds from abroad. Violent opposition became a central, time-consuming endeavor, crowding out others. Male students left study to turn to "army" work; organizations with a military component devoted increasing resources to it; the Home Army made rising demands of Varsovian society. With the launch of the uprising, the Home Army made a violent bid to retake the city and in so doing suspended or redirected other opposition while its work was ongoing.

This does not mean that all elites in Warsaw in summer 1944 literally fought: that would be absurd. Practically speaking, many Home Army insurgents were unarmed, so one should not expect that the violence involved everyone. Still, moving "fronts" and hastily created barricades, the insurgents' need for support, the punishments the SS inflicted – even on women, children, and the elderly – meant that nobody was safe. Varsovians knew this was *their* uprising, and the elite saw in it the culmination of their multi-year efforts, even if it was not the precise culmination all would have chosen. The collapse of the uprising confirmed 1939's lesson: Varsovians themselves defended their city.

Warsaw was unique across Poland in launching a large-scale uprising in 1944, and its subsequent destruction was also unique. The bloodiness of 1944,

---

[130] Dedicated to his wife. Kamiński, *Zośka i Parasol*, 177–178.

like the persecutions suffered after 1939, shaped Varsovians and differentiated them from other Poles. Writer Miron Białoszewski remembered the October evacuation: "all the people getting out of Warsaw then resembled each other and were absolutely unlike other people."[131] Warsaw's wartime experience was exceptionally destructive, rather than representative of a general Polish fate.[132]

9.6 Conclusion

The brutality of Nazi persecution in Warsaw provoked opposition. There was a desire to channel rage into action, to respond to German force with Polish force. The jumble of those willing to fight was slowly and fitfully collected under a single umbrella organization in 1942 called the Home Army, and it placed itself under the authority of the London Poles. The mature Home Army's mission was to direct mainstream Polish opposition from its Warsaw base. This, however, took years of establishing its reputation, persuading partners, and crushing competitors. *Fighting* was key: the willingness to organize violence to overthrow occupation. Metaphorically, much Varsovian behavior was a "fight" or a "struggle," but there were those who literally took up arms. Most of these activities were paramilitary, undertaken by men and women without uniforms and with limited weaponry. They operated in secret and communicated in code. Some had been soldiers of the Polish Army (WP), or had worn scout uniforms – but many were civilians through-and-through. The vast majority were men (or boys), but a number, especially nurses, couriers, typists, and spies, were women.[133] For much of the occupation, they prepared for but avoided open combat: evading capture and infiltration as well as they could, gathering intelligence, distributing information, sabotaging German materiel, stockpiling weapons and supplies, recruiting members, and solidifying internal communication, hierarchy, and discipline in preparation for large-scale insurgency.

Early occupation violence kept conspirators cautious, knowing Nazis would enforce collective responsibility, thousands would die, and their support among the population could falter. This "quiet" period gave birth to numerous small paramilitaries, many of which allied with the SZP-ZWZ during 1941 as Germany went to war against the USSR – though fascists and communists did not. With growing power and London Polish support, in early 1942 the

---

[131] Białoszewski, *Memoir*, 236.

[132] Warsaw was part of Operation Tempest (*Akcja Burza*). The wave of uprisings never materialized; 1944 efforts succumbed to the same failure as 1939: the coordination of fragile plans between its own forces and allies failed for political reasons. Tempest was Rowecki's brainchild. Richie, *Warsaw 1944*, 162–163; KHPSGL, *Polskie Siły Zbrojne*, Tom III, 541–648; Kochanski, *Eagle Unbowed*, 396.

[133] Malinowski, *Żołnierze łączności*, 17.

SZP-ZWZ dubbed itself the Home Army claiming to speak – and fight – on behalf of Poland.

1943 was the heyday of Home Army life. After numerous setbacks including the capture and death of Rowecki, the loss of Sikorski in the west, and the sense that the international situation was in crisis, it adopted an aggressive posture: open terrorism in Operation Heads. This assassination campaign destabilized occupation, which followed its activities with growing alarm. The Home Army was bold enough to attack Pawiak – or rather Bürkl – and created a state of near-anarchy. The German response was massive reprisal shootings and the underground – still underground, but intermingled with the population – was at war with the occupation. The Soviet advance in early 1944 showed the half-exposed Home Army that it faced its own annihilation and the trade of one foreign occupier for another if it miscalculated. Demonstrating that it saw itself as the partner and not the servant of the London Poles, it launched a citywide uprising. Many elites, including leaders of non-violent conspiracies, joined. Others put their plans aside as war overtook the city. Unsurprising in the history of insurgency, the poorly armed Home Army was unable to hold positions against a reinforced enemy. It was also naïve about the London Poles' influence and Grand Alliance strategy. German reprisals killed upwards of 200,000, with the intelligentsia notable among German victims.

The elite's final opposition eclipsed years of less violent efforts and thwarted those committed to seeing Warsaw as the capital of an independent Poland – and hoping to run it. Their 1944 disappointments should not, however, distract from the fact that they undermined the German hold on the city and gave the lie to Nazi assumptions that genocide, segregation, and terror would ensure Poles' quiet incorporation into the New Order. The intelligentsia was fractious and often uncertain; they suffered heavily for their activities, successful and unsuccessful, but they were not docile.

Conclusion

On January 12, 1945, the stalled Red Army offensive lumbered into motion toward Berlin.[1] Soviet soldiers and their allies, who had spent months across the Vistula from Warsaw, advanced into the Polish capital. The Nazi General Government was gone. The Polish intelligentsia had been captured or evacuated; stragglers lived amid the ruins. A member of the Warsaw elite greeted the arrivals: Polish-Jewish pianist Władysław Szpilman, who had survived the anti-intelligentsia campaigns, ghetto liquidation, the ghetto uprisings, the Warsaw Uprising, and the evacuation and demolition of the city. Much the worse for wear, he remembered that unlikely moment:

> Around one o'clock I heard the remaining Germans leaving the building. Silence fell, a silence such as even Warsaw, a dead city for the last three months, had not known before [...] Not until the early hours of the next day was the silence broken by a loud and resonant noise ... Radio loudspeakers set up somewhere nearby were broadcasting announcements in Polish of the defeat of Germany and the liberation of Warsaw. [...] I began slowly coming down the stairs, shouting as loud as I could, "Don't shoot! I'm Polish!" ... The figure of a young officer in a Polish uniform, with the eagle on his cap, came into view beyond the banisters. He pointed a pistol at me and shouted, "Hands up!" I repeated my cry of, "Don't shoot! I'm Polish!" The lieutenant went red with fury. 'Then why in God's name don't you come down?' he roared. "And what are you doing in a German coat?"[2]

Szpilman heard radio in his "dead city" in Polish for the first time since Starzyński's voice had faded from the airwaves. A UNESCO commission sent British and French experts to assess the destruction shortly thereafter. The shocked observers reported that,

---

[1] Warsaw-Poznań Operation of the Vistula-Oder Offensive of Georgy Zhukov's 1st Belorussian Front. The soldier Szpilman encountered was in the 1st Polish Army (Berling Army), subordinated to the 1st Belorussian Front. Antony Beevor, *The Second World War* (Boston: Little, Brown, and Company, 2012), 682–683.

[2] Szpilman, *Pianist*, 183–186.

It is not easy to give any impression of the extent of the devastation in Warsaw. After the Polish rising the whole city was evacuated and then systematically plundered and blown up by the Germans; it is now a vast heap of ruins. The only buildings left standing, until the outskirts of the city are reached, are those which were used by the German authorities or the German troops. The population, formerly 1,200,000, is now said to be under half-a-million. The educational institutions have shared in the general destruction, and most of them are either completely wrecked or only the shells of the buildings remain. [...] Whatever the political or economic considerations, it cannot be conducive of peaceful conditions in Poland, or of understanding between the nations, for the young people of the postwar generation in a country which has suffered so grievously during the war, to grow up largely deprived of educational and cultural facilities; as they must do unless some further means of helping them are found.[3]

Western Europeans saw in Warsaw the work of five long years of Nazi destruction and Polish contestation of it.

The arrival of another occupying army in January 1945 – Red Army "liberation"—obscures the conclusion of the Nazi occupation story, cutting off its loose ends with the sharp scissors of Soviet ideology. An independent Polish state did not materialize. Many Warsaw intelligentsia who had spent the occupation dreaming of independence were demoralized by a second foreign domination. The introduction of a new Moscow-friendly Polish government based on the 1944 communist Lublin Committee answered wartime questions about what would become of Poland, who would run it, and under what sort of regime – but to the satisfaction of few Warsaw elites.[4] The transition from Nazi colony to member state of the communist eastern bloc complicates assessment of what intelligentsia activity achieved in wartime. That assessment is nevertheless necessary: what had Warsaw's intelligentsia accomplished in its opposition to Nazi persecution? A great deal, as it turned out: they had not regained an independent state, but they had formidably maintained national-cultural institutions, some of which outlived the dead.

10.1 Remnants

By the time the Red Army entered Warsaw, Hans Frank, Ludwig Fischer, and the whole General Government was gone. Frank left Krakow the day the

---

[3] Numbers for 1946. UNESCO Archives Paris 361.9 A 20 (438) [Report by the British Members of the Anglo-American Mission of Enquiry into the Requirements of Scientific Instruments and Laboratory Equipment of European Countries: Poland – Extract – Confidential – Ministry of Supply/Ministry of Education [UK]— October 1946], 94–102.

[4] Applebaum, *Iron Curtain*, 8, 23–42; Connelly, *Peoples into Nations*, 502.

Soviets arrived, to be captured by American troops months later. The International Military Tribunal in Nuremberg convicted Frank of crimes against humanity; it hanged him in October 1946.[5] Fischer stood trial before the Supreme National Tribunal (Najwyższy Trybunał Narodowy) along with GG Secretary of State Josef Bühler. The tribunal hanged Fischer for war crimes in Warsaw, where he had committed them, in March 1947 inside Mokotów prison. Himmler, who had supervised the anti-intelligentsia campaigns, the Holocaust, and much of Warsaw's brutal police brutality from Berlin, committed suicide on May 23, 1945 in British custody. His deputy Heydrich, who had directed Tannenberg, was killed in Prague in June 1942. Policeman Lothar Beutel was a Soviet prisoner. Josef Meisinger, Max Daume, and Ludwig Leist all sat in the docks of the Supreme National Tribunal. All three were found guilty of war crimes and crimes against the Polish people, and policemen Meisinger and Daume were executed the day before Fischer. Leist's Polish friends and colleagues served him in good stead: he only got eight years.[6] Kutschera and Bürkl were killed by the Home Army in 1943. Jürgen Stroop was convicted by the United States Military Tribunal at Dachau in 1947 but then extradited to Poland where he was also tried by the Warsaw Criminal District Court for his role in the Warsaw Ghetto liquidation, and he was convicted, sentenced to death, and hanged in March 1952. Erich von dem Bach Żelewski served as a witness for the prosecution against Ludwig Fischer and at Nuremberg and never stood trial himself. He was, however, tried in Germany for a handful of pre-war offenses and died in a Munich prison in 1972.[7]

The Warsaw elite was scattered, but many survived and some continued their intelligentsia mission in exile or under communism. A continuous stream of exiles and refugees followed those who evacuated in 1939. Władysław Studnicki left Warsaw before the uprising (fitting, since he detested violence). He remained abroad, ostracized in Polish émigré circles, and died in London in 1953. Miłosz survived, continued his literary career in communist Poland and then defected, disgusted by the cumulative effects of Nazi and communist totalitarianism. Zygmunt Zaremba left Poland for Paris, where he led Polish socialist émigré circles. Jan Karski had just

---

[5] Finder and Prusin, *Justice*, 53.

[6] USHMM RG-50.030.0769, AN: 2014.238.1, "Interview with Julian Kulski [Jr.]," 1:08:00–1:15:25; Finder and Prusin, *Justice*, 122.

[7] Frank: Winstone, *Dark Heart*, 233–234; 250. Fischer: USHMM RG 15.165M Proces Ludwika Fischera (IPN Sygn. GK 196). Himmler: Longerich, *Heinrich Himmler*, 1–3; 735–736. Heydrich: Gerwarth, *Hitler's Hangman*, 1–13. Stroop: Moczarski, *Rozmowy z katem*, 376–379. Beutel and Meisinger: Mallmann, etc., *Einsatzgruppen in Polen*, 30–33. Leist: Walichnowski, *Rozmowy z Leistem*, 5. Bürkl: Strzembosz, *Akcje zbrojne*, 343–346. Kutschera: Stachiewicz, *Akcja "Kutschera,"* 'Kutschera,' 24–33. Von dem Bach Żelewski: Nuremberg testimony: January 7, 1946, Blue Series; Finder and Prusin, *Justice*, 126.

published *Story of a Secret State* and began doctoral study at Georgetown University, where he taught diplomacy and international relations for decades. Jerzy Lerski was serving as exile Prime Minister Tomasz Arciszewski's secretary, but he joined Karski at Georgetown and made an academic career in the United States. Michał Karaszewicz-Tokarzewski was under Western Allied command and remained in exile in London. Tadeusz Komorowski was a German POW and would emigrate to England after his release. Stanisław Jankowski, who nearly lost his whole family to Pawiak, parachuted back to Warsaw to fight in the uprising and closed the war as a POW like his commanders, spending the rest of his life as a globetrotting urban planner. Antoni Chruściel was also a German prisoner but would be liberated by the Americans, serve with the Polish Armies in the West, and die in the United States.[8]

Many were dead. Pawiak had been emptied and destroyed with the rest of the city after the suppression of the uprising, and its survivors were scattered across Poland, Europe, and the United States. Stefan Starzyński was certainly dead, and had been since perhaps 1940. Marceli Nowakowski, the Endek priest who railed against the Germans, died at Palmiry in January 1940. Maciej Rataj and Mieczysław Niedziałkowski were shot at Palmiry in June 1940. Archbishop Stanisław Gall died in 1942, and was buried in Powązki Cemetery. Stefan Rowecki was in Gestapo hands from mid-1943 and died in a concentration camp on Himmler's orders, likely in late summer 1944. Hanna Czaki, her family, her classmates, and her beloved sociology professor were shot outside Pawiak in early 1944. Tadeusz Dąbrowski, director of the Poniatowski School, died during the Warsaw Uprising. Marceli Godlewski, who smuggled Jewish children from the ghetto, died just before his eighty-first birthday in December 1945.[9]

Polish-Jewish elites were overwhelmingly murdered and survivors exceptional. Szpilman lived. Adam Czerniaków died by his own hand at the beginning of the *Grossaktion* in 1942. Ludwik Landau was caught by the Gestapo in February 1944 on the "Aryan" side after years of life in hiding with Polish friends and killed. Emanuel Ringelblum was caught a month later, betrayed by Polish policemen, having escaped the ghetto with his family, and killed by the Gestapo in March 1944 in Pawiak. His writings and his precious archive

[8] Karski: Karski, *Story of a Secret State*, xxiii, xxx. Lerski: Lerski, *Emisariusz Jur*, 204–241. Karaszewicz-Tokarzewski and Chruściel: Kochanski, *Eagle Unbowed*, 610, 616. Komorowski: TNA DEFE 13/519 Funeral of General Bor-Komorowski commander of the Polish home army during the Warsaw uprising, "Obituary: Gen. Bor-Komorowski: Leader of the Warsaw Uprising of 1944," *Times*, 26–10–66.

[9] Rataj and Niedziałkowski: Domańska, *Pawiak więzienie Gestapo*, 65–68. Starzyński: Drozdowski, *Starzyński prezydent Warszawy*, 324–329. Nowakowski: Bartoszewski, *1859 dni Warszawy*, 105. Miłosz: Franaszek, *Miłosz*, 229, 415–470. Białoszewski: Białoszewski, *Memoir*, viii. Czaki: Domańska, *Pawiak więzienie gestapo*, 407–408; 419–420.

outlasted him. Yitzhak Zuckerman survived the Holocaust and both uprisings and emigrated to Israel.[10]

A few outlived Nazi occupation but withered under a new regime. Witold Pilecki survived Auschwitz and the uprising, but not communism: he was imprisoned in 1947 on charges of treason and spying for foreign governments and executed in 1948. Stefan Korboński, the man who wore a thousand underground hats, was in Milanówek with the government delegation and later imprisoned by communist police for his wartime work. He died in exile in the United States alongside his beloved wife, Zofia, never having returned to Poland. Jerzy Braun was with Home Army leadership, but would end up tortured in communist prison. Braun went into exile in Rome after release and participated in the Second Vatican Council. Elżbieta Zawacka was in Krakow and joined a new patriotic conspiracy which ran afoul of the communist government. Despite arrest, torture, and imprisonment, she survived to build an academic career in Toruń, be promoted to the rank of general, and die in 2009 in the Polish Third Republic.[11]

Some stayed, whether because Warsaw had long been their home regardless of who happened to run it, or because they were young and hoped for the postwar future. Deputy mayor Julian Kulski stayed during the uprising and took up work for the city archive, assembling documentation on the occupation in postwar People's Poland.[12] His son fought in 1944 and both wrote memoirs of their wartime intrigues. Bishop Antoni Szlagowski was in Milanówek waiting out the uprising with the urn holding Frederick Chopin's heart, and returned to preaching at his home parish of St. Barbara's Church. Zofia Kossak was at the Jasna Góra Monastery in Częstochowa. She, too, would return to Warsaw and to writing. Jerzy Andrzejewski wrote and wrote, eventually for film. Miron Białoszewski became a journalist. Aleksander Kamiński laid his *Bulletin* to bed and became the unofficial historian of Polish scouting. Tadeusz Manteuffel stayed at Warsaw University and wrote its occupation history. Czesław Jędraszko, the Prus School director, returned to the classroom to teach Latin grammar. Artur Śliwiński and most of the welfare organizers survived; Śliwiński died an old man in 1953 and was buried at Powązki. Hlond, the cardinal, was freed by American troops and returned to Warsaw to run the Catholic Church.[13]

---

[10] Szpilman: Mazurczak, "Władysław Szpilman's Postwar Career," 219–234. Landau: Landau (Kula), *Kronika*, Tom I, vii. Ringelblum: Kassow, *Who Will Write Our History*, 384–385; Grabowski, *Na posterunku*, 317–318. Czerniaków: Czerniaków, *Prelude*, 23. Zuckerman: Zuckerman, *Surplus of Memory*, vii.

[11] Pilecki: Pilecki, *Auschwitz Volunteer*, liii–liv. Korboński: Korbonski, *Fighting Warsaw*, 415–495. Zawacka: Minczykowska, *Cichociemna Generał Elżbieta Zawacka*.

[12] The phrase indicates the transition of the economy away from capitalism toward communism. Connelly, *Peoples into Nations*, 503; Porter-Szücs, *Beyond Martyrdom*, 186–188.

[13] Gall: BN Mf. 43293, *Prawda*, Wrzesień 1942 r., 8. Szlagowski: Wojdecki, *Arcybiskup Antoni Szlagowski*, 30, 208. Braun: Żychowska, *Jerzy Braun (1901–1975): twórca kultury*

Zygmunt Śliwicki tended to uprising wounded and then married his Pawiak colleague, Anna Czuperska. Leon Wanat had only been out of Pawiak a few months and served as a witness for the prosecution at Josef Meisinger's trial. Regina Hulewicz-Domańska began work documenting Pawiak victims, which she continued for thirty years. Władysław Bartoszewski became one of the earliest postwar chroniclers of Nazi crimes before enduring years of communist imprisonment for his wartime activities. He twice served as Minister of Foreign Affairs in the post-communist Polish Third Republic before his death in 2015.

When the war ended, there were Varsovians in Krakow, London, Moscow, Paris, and the United States, and those serving across the Grand Alliance. Some picked up the fragments of their lives and reassumed roles of leadership and cultural influence – or something like them – in communist Warsaw or other locales. Some experienced persecution under Nazism *and* communism, like Pilecki, Zawacka, Korboński, and Braun. Others became professional survivors of a sort, their postwar lives dominated by their wartime experiences and their authority determined by what they had done between 1939 and 1944, an intensified intelligentsia mission: Regina Domańska, Jan Karski, and Władysław Bartoszewski eventually played such roles. Wartime persecution shaped their identities, and drove them to document and publicize information that had been denied their countrymen under occupation.

10.2 Successes and Failures

Warsaw's occupation legacy was – and is – bitter. The period of focused intelligentsia persecution in 1939–40 killed tens of thousands and befuddled Polish observers until a clearer picture of Nazi policy emerged. While some chose to wait and see and others sought a modus vivendi with the occupiers, substantive Polish underground opposition formed. It formed precisely in response to the botched anti-intelligentsia policies and tangle of restrictions that the occupiers implemented to stifle opposition and "pacify" the population. Though violent opposition started early – and preceded the original capitulation of Warsaw – it matured late, needing until 1942 and really until 1943 to consolidate and move beyond sabotage and diversion toward insurgency. The prewar intelligentsia (particularly the officer corps) played a leading role in it as it developed. Other intelligentsia efforts flourished more quickly, produced tangible results faster, and supported the eventual

harcerskiej i 'Unionizmu, 44–45. Kossak: Bartoszewski, *1859 dni Warszawy*, 642–643. Bartoszewski: Bartoszewski, *Życie trudne*, 166–177. Hlond: Dziurok, *Instrukcje, wytyczne, okólniki*, 286–287. Andrzejewski: Milosz, *Captive Mind*, 98–110. Kamiński: Kamiński, *Zośka i Parasol*, 5–31. Manteuffel: Dobroszycki, *Reptile Journalism*, ix. Jędraszko: Jędraszko, *Łacina na co dzień* (all postwar trace of him). Dąbrowski: https://www .1944.pl/ofiary-cywilne/tomasz-vel-tadeusz-dabrowski,6736.html growth of insurgency. Underground information networks reached into nearly every home, transmitting news from the fronts, patriotic poetry, spiritual counsel, and literary and political feuilletons, despite a never-ending German effort to eradicate them. Indeed, Warsaw was remarkably well informed about its own persecution and the unfolding war. Catholicism, too, inspired sprawling activism, from those who prayed the rosary for German defeat to Unity's military wing, with its grenade factory and ambitions to join a citywide revolt. Despite the silence or absence of the very top of the Polish Catholic hierarchy, priests and lay faithful were active. Some, like Zofia Kossak, made aid to Polish Jews a political and religious matter, saving thousands from certain death. Others defined their faith rigidly and, like Jerzy Braun, implicitly or explicitly supported the Holocaust as benefiting an ethnically homogenous Polish future.

Intertwined with the informational and Catholic networks, the most successful intelligentsia response came from the academy: it was a quintessentially intelligentsia effort, directly combating elite decimation by educating young people to replace the murdered and imprisoned. The underground educational system, from its more modest efforts to teach literature and history to schoolchildren alongside the meager curriculum Goebbels approved, to its secret Warsaw University seminars, dodged a host of German restrictions to train a new educated class. It offered *matura* examinations and granted doctorates and medical degrees to a generation whose careers would continue after 1944, and whose postwar accomplishments demonstrated the value of their efforts.

The pool into which all of these strands of elite activity flowed in the last years of occupation was the burgeoning military opposition: the willingness to contest occupation by force. Indeed, the reason for the mushrooming of this sort of opposition was its inclusion of auxiliary and civilian forces and embrace of their ongoing efforts. Its expanded mission included the delegation and the entire apparatus of the "secret state"; the mature Home Army had a women's section, Catholic priests, a series of cadet schools and training camps, and a formidable publishing apparatus. The early goals of military opposition established by the Polish Victory Service were the overthrow of foreign occupation and the recreation of an independent Poland within its prewar borders. In the heady circumstances of summer 1944, empowered by the dangerous success of Operation Heads, the Home Army and its allies launched the uprising that would subsume the whole city and lead to its destruction.

This uprising failed: the new Polish state established in 1944–45 was hardly independent of Soviet power *and* repugnant to many of those who spent the war in opposition to the German regime. It destroyed the dreams of the exile government, but most of all it destroyed the hopes of many non-communist Varsovians who would return to their city to greet a new foreign army. The failure served the interests of the 1939 co-invader of Poland and the perpetrator of the Katyń massacre, and it maintained the marginalization of the non-communist

Warsaw intelligentsia, empowering a new, Moscow-friendly elite. But, it did succeed in ending the occupation: the fallout of the uprising included the abandonment of German plans to control the Polish capital and its inhabitants. The SS and Wehrmacht destroyed and emptied the city. That acknowledgement – that Warsaw could not be made passive by Nazi policy or terror – had taken more than five years, and cost hundreds of thousands of lives.

The Home Army's 1944 failure has placed Warsaw's multifaceted opposition in a dead end of scholarship. It pays few dividends to military historians preoccupied with the vicissitudes of the alliance war. Political scientists puzzling through insurgency in order to compile lessons for the future derive little profit from the story, as this was not a model to copy. In Poland, Home Army insurgency has produced waves of both critical analysis and deep nostalgia, as some historians construct other victories from the uprising legacy; most of them concentrated on dramatic gestures, patriotic sacrifice, and the betrayal of the Grand Alliance. Understandably, this has not been found useful outside Poland.

The problem is that the Home Army's decision to rise up in August 1944 – and even the Home Army itself – were not synonymous with resistance; they were also not synonymous with Warsaw intelligentsia opposition.[14] Indeed, the uprising was not the sole activity of the Home Army or the diverse insurgent organizations that orbited around it and allied with it. Their most successful behavior lay in their intelligence-gathering and terrorism efforts of 1943–44. The Warsaw intelligentsia and those who joined or aged into it during occupation were busy to the point of fanaticism. Though the allure of violence was always appealing, especially to the young and the strong, this elite concocted multiple durable projects of opposition to their wartime persecution. Why did some fail and others succeed? Timing and leadership were important: projects launched at the height of the anti-intelligentsia campaigns were terribly vulnerable. Individual personality was never irrelevant: some elites thrived as underground conspirators and others wilted. Intimate networks were vital, and provided expertise and support that allowed some projects to flourish and interconnect. Such entanglements also had a dark side, as countless conspiracies were betrayed by Poles themselves, accidentally in a world fraught with danger, tragically under torture, deliberately by rivals and those settling scores.

In these systemic projects of intelligentsia opposition, the Warsaw elite generally succeeded in its internally oriented efforts and failed in external ones: it sustained a nation but could not secure a state. The Warsaw intelligentsia experienced uniquely the two-pronged national and state targeting of Nazi Germany, first articulated in the difference between Case White and Operation Tannenberg. Their actions attempted to contest both attacks,

[14] Dean, "Where Did All the Collaborators Go?" *Slavic Review*, 796.

building opposition systems opposing national and state destruction. Ultimately their efforts at national preservation were much more successful since they depended on the acceptance of their own community – the intelligentsia vanguard – and did not necessitate broader societal let alone international support. Both Church and military opposition were crucially dependent on international recognition and were thus ultimately outside intelligentsia control. Nations, as the Warsaw intelligentsia found out, can be sustained from within even under enormous duress. States require approval from without, and this they could not secure.

10.3   Categorizing Behavior

Most Varsovian agency under Nazi occupation was directed toward routine survival, which was not to be taken for granted in one of the most dangerous places on earth during the war.[15] Jewish Varsovians were subject to particular horrors and their survival least likely; Polish-Jewish intelligentsia efforts were herculean and some succeeded to enrich the Polish, Israeli, and global futures. The non-Jewish intelligentsia behaved variously. Nevertheless, they disproportionately resisted occupation because their doing so was overdetermined and their alternatives few. As the Third Reich attempted to suppress Polish life in the short and long term, any fomenting of Polish national and cultural life – however short-lived – opposed that goal. Behavior that spanned from praying for Wehrmacht defeat to assassinating Nazi personnel could be included in intelligentsia opposition: it ranged widely in danger, audience, and effectiveness.[16] *Risk* was vital to Polish elite patriotic self-conception: opposing Nazi Germany meant putting oneself in harm's way. Profit, on the other hand, seemed to point to collaboration, though in an environment of substantial privation such behavior was ambiguous for elites and ordinary Poles alike. Collective reprisal confused the matter further, killing sloppily and criminalizing the causes and professions that defined the intelligentsia milieu. This infused elite life with danger and mundane activities with political meaning. "Carrying on," as British propaganda advocated, placed Polish elites outside the law. Others sought conspiracy deliberately, taking up activities precisely because of their new meaning.

Nazi policy in Warsaw was brutal but inconsistent. It evolved as the war unfolded and was not the same in 1944 as it was in 1939.[17] Elites collaborated

---

[15] In 2018 revisions to the Institute of National Remembrance act (*Ustawa o Instytucie Pamięci Narodowej*) passed the Polish parliament the 55th article of which stipulated fines and imprisonment for those who "accuse . . . the Polish state or people of involvement or responsibility for the Nazi occupation during World War II." Punishments were reduced amid controversy.

[16] Domańska, *Pawiak był etapem*, 77, 93, 115, 157.

[17] Kunicki posits a "sliding scale between collaboration and resistance." Kunicki, *Between*, 57.

and cooperated with different facets of the Nazi regime in order to sustain their projects – the intelligentsia mission – in the long term. Kamiński's petty sabotage recommendations provide a framework for how his peers imagined acceptable intelligentsia behavior: his 1940 admonitions were the minimum bar for patriotism (resistance being conceived of as something further). It was expected that self-conscious patriots would: "Work [for Germans] as slowly as possible," "Make "mistakes" in all work done for Germans," and undermine the occupation as a general matter.[18] Kamiński – and this is important – recognized that even his peers had to work with and for the occupation regime.

The nature of Nazi German anti-intelligentsia campaigning provoked a variety of elite responses in a matrix that was deadly dangerous. Intelligentsia conspiracies relied on the passivity of those around them; they had to be exceptional initially in order to persevere. Elite opposition could nevertheless not operate in an environment of outright Polish hostility, which would have destroyed efforts stillborn. There had to be some tacit acceptance locally, as secrecy was always imperfect. The demand for secrecy is itself the best proof of the existence of a larger Polish audience which conspirators courted but about which they had to be watchful. The Gestapo was feared and hated but thin on the ground; the Polish blue police and their supporters were much more numerous. Conspirators met in secret, used code names, required passwords, and operated under cover of darkness because they feared betrayal by their own countrymen.[19] There were also activities that implied a silent Polish audience that did *not* betray. Elite opposition – insurgency – attempted secrecy but required a "neutral" matrix within which to operate because participants were bound to slip and occasionally did so deliberately, "performing" their opposition as a model to follow.

Evidence of these silent Varsovians, ordinary Poles the intelligentsia wished to lead, is everywhere. Optimistic intelligentsia curried their support and tried to prompt their patriotism; pessimists knew they were dangerous. Stefan Korboński, years later and long out of danger, called many of his countrymen "fence sitters," watching what way the Gestapo would look or the war would turn.[20] The underground information world had distinct tiers of involvement: writers, editors, printers, couriers, and everyone else. Included in the "everyone else" was a readership who did not generally betray those who provided their bootleg information, though on some occasions they did.[21] Miłosz's complaint about his upstairs neighbor's noisy printing is noteworthy: the

---

[18] BN Mf. 45815, *BI*, 1 listopada 1940 r., 1.
[19] Two examples: PLAN and Rowecki's 1943 arrest. Stanisław Izdebowski betrayed PLAN and Ludwik Kalkstein and Eugeniusz Świerczewski Rowecki: Poles. Bartoszewski, *Palmiry*, 29–30; Bartoszewski, *1859 dni Warszawy*, 410.
[20] USHMM RG-50.012.0046, AN: 1989.67.46, "Interview with Stefan and Sophia Korbonski," Part 2, 22:30–22:45.
[21] Dobroszycki, *Reptile Journalism*, 1–7.

poet – like many neighbors – did not betray the printer, though he worried someone else might. That "someone else" was statistically Polish and not part of the numerically smaller German community. Miłosz's *not betraying* did not mean support of the project. In fact, he thought the printer stupid, though his opinion of Germans was worse still. Still, not betraying could have implicated him: among the Polish elite silence about others' "crimes" was punishable if discovered.[22]

Female couriers engaged in colportage required a guise of "civilianness" to traverse the streets. Their whole operation was premised on the idea that there were women in Warsaw whose behavior was uninteresting to the occupying regime: this was why couriers were predominately women in the first place. If that premise collapsed, couriering became impossible. At moments it did, and the clandestine press took significant casualties, like the 1944 death of Krystyna Idzikowska, the student and Peasant Battalions courier.[23] But the proliferation of publications indicates the premise generally held: Varsovians did not always betray the community that created and distributed clandestine press, a tacit support that points to the ability of intelligentsia opposition to build national community.

Anyone using a pseudonym relied on a larger community of Polish "not resisters" or not-currently-resisting persons to get by. The shorter military nicknames – true *noms de guerre* – like Edward Rydz's "Śmigły," Stefan Rowecki's "Grot," and Elżbieta Zawacka's "Zo" existed in their own world to be used among conspirators safer not knowing each other's identities. These had to be changed frequently.[24] There were also aboveground aliases, like Jan Kozielewski's Jan Karski, Zawacka's British persona Elizabeth Bishop, Zofia Kossak's Zofia Śliwińska, and Jerzy Lerski's Jerzy Gordziewicz. These false surnames (often stolen from the tombstones of the dead) prevented someone from being discovered when addressed informally by acquaintances, and it reinforced the familiarity, the "first name basis" in which Warsaw's intelligentsia functioned. Not being outed required care and good luck, but it also required discretion among those who were suspicious that the person they were encountering had once gone by another name. The acid test was when courier Jerzy Lerski ran into *his own father* in early 1943 on a public street and lived to tell the tale.[25]

Beyond those intelligentsia conspirators who relied on passive support from their countrymen were those whose opposition relied on varying levels of

---

[22] In 1943 residents of Długa Street where *Szaniec* press operated were arrested, the women sent to Majdanek, and "all the men ... none of whom knew anything about the secret press, were taken to Pawiak, and executed." They "knew nothing" like Miłosz did, but this was no protection. Bartoszewski, *Warsaw Death Ring*, 165.

[23] Domańska, *Pawiak więzienie gestapo*, 471, 478.

[24] Kulski, *Color of Courage*, 171.

[25] Lerski, *Emisariusz Jur*, 85–87.

positive interaction and engagement with the occupation. The brunt of this work fell to women as male behavior was more often criminalized, and this gendering of "cooperation" led in Poland – as elsewhere in Nazi-occupied Europe – to allegations of what has charmingly been deemed "horizontal collaboration" and misogynist blame for occupation durability.[26] Aboveground occupation life required a thousand tasks like registration of one's address or obtaining a *Kennkarte*. Visiting an imprisoned friend or family member (when this was permitted) also required interaction with German authorities or blue policemen. Even writing to someone in Pawiak required obtaining the official bilingual card and revealing one's full name and current address. Marceli Godlewski, pastor of All Saints, had an official pass that allowed him to get into and out of the ghetto to work with parishioners – and smuggle out Jewish children. Maciej Piekarski's father had to officially register his boys for school, even if German education personnel had no idea what their actual curriculum was. These were all obtained by interaction with German bureaucrats or their Polish auxiliaries. Most conspirators had forged *Kennkarten* and other falsified "proofs" of identity, but others had genuine occupation documents that they had to maintain and this meant standing in lines, filling out forms, and being polite to Germans. This maintenance of aboveground life to sustain underground life was heavily borne by intelligentsia women, one of many non-violent opposition activities essential to maintaining elite projects in the long term.

Collaboration and resistance coexisted for Varsovian elites as it had across the long century before under partition. Tactical accommodation of German precepts formed the bedrock of opposition; conspirators understood it as something that went without saying. Insurgency, as Poles had been taught across the nineteenth century and young ghetto fighters learned in 1943, required the right moment, and that was late in arriving if it arrived at all. Historian John A. Armstrong offers an understanding of collaboration as "co-operation between elements of the population of a defeated state and the representatives of the victorious power," which does *not* require ideological affinity with the occupier.[27] Persecution and victimhood went hand in glove as occupied people adjusted to enormous Nazi demands.[28] His colleague Klaus-Peter Friedrich

---

[26] In western Europe: Morgan, *Hitler's Collaborators*, 5–6; Rosbottom, *When Paris Went Dark*, 145–151. In Poland: Röger, *Wojenne związki*, 83–185, especially 95, 115, 141–143: Röger notes that Polish women were "significantly younger and less educated than the [German] men"—unlikely intelligentsia.

[27] Armstrong notes that collaborationism – state coordination – characterized the Hungarian Arrow Cross and the Romanians – though not Poland. John A. Armstrong, "Collaborationism in World War II: The Integral Nationalist Variant in Eastern Europe," *Journal of Modern History* Vol. 40, No. 3 (Sep., 1968), 396.

[28] An exchange hosted by the *Slavic Review* in 2005 details this debate including John Connelly's "Why the Poles Collaborated So Little – And Why That Is No Reason for Nationalist Hubris," Klaus-Peter Friedrich's "Collaboration in a 'Land without a Quisling': Patterns of Cooperation with the Nazi German Occupation Regime in

prefers "cooperation" for the Polish context, noting the ubiquity of German-Polish interaction, for which some term is necessary. There was significant "double membership:" intelligentsia who "resisted" and "collaborated" by turns and simultaneously.[29]

Collaboration is rightly associated with western Europe, where there was room for civilian, non-combatant existence, and individuals retained (in many cases) the agency needed to decide to assist their occupiers.[30] Philippe Pétain, France's Quisling and the leader of the Vichy puppet state, offered it as the standard of French behavior toward Berlin.[31] The most muscular form was full-throated collaborationism, an "-ism" if there ever was one, which historian Philip Morgan defines as the posture of "those people who chose to cooperate fully and unequivocally with the Nazi German occupiers, and did so out of a sense of ideological affinity with Nazism."[32] Occupied western Europeans possessed *more* agency and endured *less* coercion than eastern Europeans. Still, Poles – especially Warsaw intelligentsia – possessed *some* agency and did quite a lot with it. Nothing discussed here, however, indicates robust collaborationism with the whole Nazi project, though some Polish elites participated in antisemitic persecution, even the Holocaust, and others followed German anti-communism with interest. Collaboration and related ideas of cooperation and accommodation need nuanced application to Varsovians. Remember that Julian Kulski kept his city hall office, pinned between Gestapo suspicions and Home Army monitoring, ever aware of Starzyński's fate if he should slip. Marian Kozielewski directed the first blue policemen, shepherding what would become one of the nastiest Polish antisemitic institutions in Warsaw, *and* earning him a trip to Auschwitz. Artur Śliwiński and the staff of Warsaw's various charities knew the way to Fischer's and Leist's offices by heart. Tadeusz Dąbrowski dutifully filled out every form his students' studies required, bilingually and in triplicate, and surely delivered them all with a deep bow. Adam Czerniaków worked with GG administration for years as *Judenrat* chairman, his calendar filled with appointments outside the ghetto, trying and failing to protect the Jewish community. Archbishop Szlagowski begged Fischer's mercy for his

---

Poland during World War II" and Dean's "Where Did All the Collaborators Go?" *Slavic Review* 64 no. 4 winter 2005: 711–746; 771–781; 791–798.

[29] James Mace Ward, "Collaboration and Legitimacy: A Reply to Irene Hecht," *Pacific Historical Review* Vol. 81, No. 4 (November 2012), 619.

[30] The ability to refuse is the best criterion for culpability. Though it considers German police, Christopher Browning's study engages this. Christopher Browning, *Ordinary Men: Reserve Police Battalion 101 and the Final Solution in Poland* (New York: Harper Perennial, 1998), 147–190. For French collaboration: Jackson, *France*, 166–212 and Sweets, *Choices in Vichy France*, 7, 82–98.

[31] Jackson, *France*, 81, 140, 168.

[32] Morgan, *Hitler's Collaborators*, 2.

priests and sometimes obtained it, but he knew his own arrest was not impossible. Władysław Studnicki fervently hoped for a substantive cooperation with German leadership – before the Gestapo imprisoned him – but no Varsovian ever established one.

The most important space for elite collaboration with Nazi Germany was in the Holocaust of Warsaw's Jewish community, since it did not target the non-Jewish Polish elite and the GG administration made room for Polish support.[33] Polish response to the Holocaust was dependent on how elites perceived their own victimhood at Nazi hands and on the nature of their antisemitism. Polish elite analysis of Nazi Jewish persecution was filtered through consideration of how it would affect them – "real" – Poles. Polish action and inaction was founded on an accomplished separation of Polish from Polish-Jewish communities in which majority Poles did not see Polish Jews as part of their nation, but as either competitors for territory and resources or those who might be aided if "extra" was available: circumstances that rarely arose.[34] This fight over Polishness, of course, began before 1939 but was exacerbated by Nazi occupation, segregation, and genocide.

Since the 1960s, Polish scholars, some of them Warsaw intelligentsia survivors or their descendants, have argued there was Polish enthusiasm for and participation in the "removal" of their Jewish neighbors.[35] Others have dismissed this, emphasizing Polish victimhood and bloodthirsty Nazi punishments for aiding Jews, which were real indeed. Most supporters of Nazi antisemitism came from the Endecja, adherents of an ethnic definition of Polishness. A number of Varsovians wanted an independent postwar Poland that was *judenrein* and some supported Nazi methods, while others did not.[36] Some Poles, like Franciszek Wyszyński, celebrated the demise of the Polish-Jewish community at Nazi hands or pitched in themselves, betraying, persecuting, and killing their Jewish neighbors. Bolesław Piasecki, Jerzy Braun, and Zofia Kossak imagined Polish futures without Jewish participation – though Kossak opposed Nazi methods and risked her life to thwart them. Two elites with considerable social and cultural power who embraced *ethnic* Polishness, Kossak and Godlewski, were motivated by religious conviction to provide aid

---

[33] Holocaust collaboration cannot be "legitimate collaboration," a moral qualification James Ward has offered, because of the moral stakes. Ward, "Collaboration and Legitimacy," 619.

[34] Kassow, *Who Will Write*, 376–383.

[35] Jan Grabowski details Poles outside Warsaw murdering and robbing Jews (Grabowski, *Hunt for the Jews*). In Warsaw, Barbara Engelking details Gestapo denunciation of Jews by Varsovians: Engelking, *Szanowny panie gistapo*. Erica Tucker discusses Varsovian memory of collaboration: Erica L. Tucker, *Remembering Occupied Warsaw: Polish Narratives of World War II* (DeKalb: Northern Illinois University Press, 2011).

[36] There has been more work on the financial exploitation of *szmalcownicy* and "white collar" gentry collaboration. Paulsson, *Secret City*; Jakubowska, *Patrons of History*, 66–69.

to Jews.[37] Their reactions were due to a combination of their (real and perceived) means, clout in the underground world, and firsthand knowledge of their Jewish neighbors' plight, but such individuals were rare.[38]

Tadeusz Komorowski, the final commander of the Home Army, took the necessity of flexibility between resistance and collaboration for granted because he understood the occupation's murkiness better than analysts who came after him. The tripartite schema offered in his memoirs presumed tactical cooperation with the occupier *and* behavior distinct from that of the Polish masses, who were not in active opposition. His first conspirator category led double lives – above and underground, participating in one or more conspiracies while retaining "legal" employment. The second category was composed of opposition professionals like Komorowski himself, living entirely underground. The last category held open partisans, as Komorowski and his Home Army became on August 1, 1944, but avoided becoming beforehand.[39]

The first category betrays enormous potential for sustained, large-scale Polish cooperation with Nazi plans. Indeed, it meant that many Varsovians were "getting along" and employed by the occupation or in a firm in German hands – as profitable enterprises were. Such people both worked for German interests and contributed to opposition; how their time and sentiments were proportioned is impossible to say. An extremely liberal definition of "collaboration" would include all conspirators in Komorowski's first category, but it would also reveal itself to be irrelevant, as the primary motivations of "doubles" is impossible to assess and Komorowski himself clearly understood such people as his allies. Indeed, to assign collaborator status comprehensively to the first category is to posit that only exclusive or open insurgency behavior – categories two and three – were outside collaboration. In occupied Warsaw, such postures were suicidal. The Home Army commander detailed his countrymen's opposition and his explanation was implicitly premised on the majority of conspirators belonging to the first category: "doubles." The silent majority of Varsovians made sustained elite opposition possible by what they did not always do: betray and denounce opposition behavior to the occupying regime.

10.4   Risks and Consequences

Warsaw intelligentsia were exceptional among Europeans in what they suffered and in how they responded. The war brought them unique horrors but

---

[37] Jan Gross's analysis of the intelligentsia focuses on "progressive," "liberal Catholic," and "left-leaning" figures – not Kossak or Godlewski. Gross, *Fear*, 172, 175, 182.

[38] Nechama Tec claims social "outsiders" were key to rescue but intelligentsia were *not* outsiders. Tec, *When Light Pierced the Darkness*, 7, 64, 69.

[39] Bór-Komorowski, *Armia Podziemna*, 164–167.

their prewar formation also gave them an exclusive vantage point on questions of nation-statehood: they had been the sustainers of a national tradition under partition, beneficiaries of a sovereign state in 1918, and had it taken from them in 1939. They knew states flickered into and out of existence, and they knew what that meant more intimately than other national claimants in Europe. During the war, they experienced the 1939 siege, the combined effects of Tannenberg and AB, and the tortures of Pawiak and Szuch Boulevard. Intelligentsia response was special: it represented an active choice, required risk, and often carried terrible consequences. Intelligentsia took casualties under Nazi occupation disproportionately greater than their numbers; their losses were larger than any comparable group outside of the Roma or, of course, the Jews of eastern Europe, including their own neighbors.[40] No city saw greater material or human losses per capita than Warsaw, Starzyński's "Paris of the East," which was comprehensively destroyed in late 1944. Aleksander Gella, sociologist of the Polish intelligentsia, marks 1945 as the "biological destruction" of the "classical" Polish intelligentsia, by which time "more than 50% of Polish citizens with higher education died."[41]

Outside of besieged Leningrad, Warsaw was the most dangerous place to be a Slav in Europe, and one of the most dangerous places to be Jewish. The occupation's length exacerbated risks and accumulated strain.[42] Warsaw's intelligentsia received special treatment. While Poles elsewhere – like Krakow, Łódź (Litzmannstadt), Białystok, Lublin, and Lwów (L'viv) – suffered during anti-intelligentsia campaigns, their elites were not as viciously targeted, nor as numerous or nationally significant as those in Warsaw. Though there were other persecutions, other prisons, and other conspiracies, Warsaw was the epicenter of Polish opposition, both "traditional" military opposition and Catholic activities and more successful forms like underground education and publishing.[43]

The intelligentsia mission in the Polish capital and its successes and failures were desperately important for the Polish future. Wartime behavior – and the behavior of elites in the capital crucible – has been an issue of great political moment since the Red Army's arrival in 1945, and continues to be today, though with a variety of different "lessons" and a dizzying array of different heroes emphasized, one set replaced by another through changing political regimes. Intelligentsia casualties disappeared possibilities and changed what could be. Warsaw's particular fate, however, is not well known outside of

[40] Radu Ioanid, *The Holocaust in Romania: The Destruction of Jews and Gypsies Under the Antonescu Regime, 1940-1944* (Chicago: Ivan R. Dee, 2000), 289–296.

[41] Gella, *Inteligencja polska*, 107.

[42] Peri, *War Within*, 4–5; Anna Reid, *Leningrad: The Epic Siege of World War II, 1941-1944* (New York: Walker & Company, 2011), 389–397.

[43] "Warsaw was "the point from which all unrest in this land is brought." Richie, *Warsaw 1944*, 152.

eastern Europe, where the specificity of its experience blurs into the confusion of combat and genocidal violence in the space between Nazi Germany and the Soviet Union. Elite Varsovians nevertheless have a great deal to tell us about genocide, agency, and national durability. Their tragedy was local, but it was also more than that: what happened to the Warsaw elite mattered outside their homeland and had spiraling consequences far outside eastern Europe.

Theirs is a story about the possibilities of nation- and statebuilding under duress, the definition of national and ethnic communities, and the limits of imperial control. Nazi rejection of Polish collaboration – even if useful Varsovian collaborators were thin on the ground – ultimately undermined Berlin's ability to control Warsaw – and Poland – in the long term. Elites knew their nation, because it had in many ways been a product of their behavior. They manipulated, cajoled, and coerced their countrymen, and dodged their suspicions, denunciations, and disinterest. They also knew the vulnerabilities of their state, as it evacuated and exiled itself and as they reformed portions of it underground. Nazi personnel, in contrast, were ignorant and blinded by racial ideology and political presumption. Their "new order" looked like uncivilized chaos to educated Varsovians; German *Kultur* was a farce. The opening anti-intelligentsia campaigns and subsequent persecution meant that the leadership of Polish society could never trust the Nazi occupier; immediate if isolated opposition from this group confirmed Nazi fears and meant they would not empower the native elite. Germans in Warsaw created their own nightmare, and they blamed it on the Poles, one of many Nazi "self-fulfilling prophec[ies]."[44] Empire building requires violence and cannot endure without capturing the loyalty of at least some of its subjects: this was true in Warsaw and outside it.[45]

In Warsaw, this vicious gridlock tightened, despite the late closed-door what-ifs of GG administrators who acknowledged anti-intelligentsia policy's failures. Nazi Germany, however, *learned* in Warsaw, and these lessons had consequences: in western Europe from 1940 onward, when local elites were smoothly co-opted to prevent a repeat of the Warsaw disaster; further east where Einsatzgruppen were redeployed, freed from the Tannenberg lists and able to interpret orders for maximum lethality, murdering the Jews of the Soviet Union. West of Warsaw, the city's fate meant fewer horrors for Parisians, east of Warsaw it meant more efficient killing of Nazi Germany's Jewish "enemy."

The intelligentsia community who lost their state and their city, too, learned as they lived. They came to appreciate the importance of *presence* for sustaining community – close-knit elite community or the national community that might emerge from it. Even for the most rarified intellectuals, penning

---

[44] Bartov, *Hitler's Army*, 107.
[45] Prusin, *Serbia under the Swastika*, 55–69, 159.

scientific treatises or writing poetry after curfew, the embodied reality of suffering alongside their countrymen was vital to their legitimacy as national leaders. Meandering lines, bread rationing, aerial bombardment, the absence of window glass, and the scarcity of good paper, combined with the lurking Gestapo and its army of informers were *real*. Hunger and betrayal and torture were intimate and not theoretical matters. A gulf of accumulated horrors separated Varsovians from those who shared their political commitments, educational backgrounds, and national loyalties in Krakow or Łódź or Lwów, and even further from those evacuated or exiled – even if they sought Polish independence in their own way. Varsovians did not have the same war as other Poles or Europeans; their fate was not the same as other belligerents. Their war's chronology, begun with the siege, finished with the uprising, was particularly theirs.

They also came to appreciate the weight of the past and the almost unbearable weight of the future. The Polish elite (among whom were Polish historians, of course) were obsessed with the national past, one of their intelligentsia monopolies. Pawiak prison was filled with ghosts of criminals and freedom fighters and patriots; by 1944 all of Warsaw was haunted, crowded with warnings and precedents and martyrs to a cause of hoped-for independence, a graveyard of elite dreams. Intelligentsia conspirators were often creative, and willing to break with the past and consider different futures. But in occupied Warsaw, they were also deeply conscious of having been preceded in this task by others, a consciousness that romanticized the humdrum and raised the stakes of even fleeting projects. The occupation was also excruciatingly long for young and old: in 1939, men like Rataj, Niedziałkowski, Studnicki, and Starzyński were in charge, preserving the old, and embarking on the new. By 1944 they were long dead. Boys and girls born into an independent Poland grew up and into occupation strictures; they were adults, mature actors in their teens, publishers of feuilletons and teachers and nurses and assassins and soldiers and prison breakers. When they survived until 1945, they carried with them the youthful gravity and sense of urgency of people who had seen the world they knew fall apart, and who understood its terrible vulnerabilities.

The specificity of Warsaw's location and past are local things, but its wartime travails carry a universal significance. The intelligentsia who remained and attempted to contest Nazi domination learned and relearned lessons of durable value. Insurgency requires specific conditions to succeed, and without them it is doomed. Opposition, however, even to a genocidal threat against cultural and civilizational traditions, may be successful if it recruits a new generation with the information and values to sustain the project. Trauma numbs people and provokes others to action; persecution intimidates but also inspires its victims. Patriotism is malleable. Loyalty and identity shift under duress. Left-wing loyalties and right-wing ones often meet in curious places. Faith can stultify and inspire by turns. Suffering makes people myopic and narrow minded and selfish, except when it makes them bold and generous. The recipients of this generosity and the boundaries of national communities are not static in wartime. Elites are self-involved and vain, believing their own actions of outsized consequence, and that "ordinary" people should obey their directives and follow their lead. Even in the absence of conventional state structures, this hubris makes the sustaining of national projects possible.

BIBLIOGRAPHY

Archival Sources

Berlin

Bundesarchiv Berlin-Lichterfelde (BABL)
  NS 19 Persönlicher Stab Reichsführer-SS
R 19 Chef der Ordnungspolizei
  R 52 Regierung des GG
R 58 Reichssicherheitshauptamt (RSHA)
  R102 II: Gouverneur des Distrikts Lublin

Freiburg

Bundesarchiv-Militärarchiv (BAMA)
  RH 53 Militärbefehlshaber im GG
  MSg (Personal Narratives and Memoirs)

Krakow

Archiwum Uniwersytetu Jagiellońskiego (AUJ)
  IDO Institut für deutsche Ostarbeit

London

The National Archives, Kew (TNA)
  FO Foreign Office
  HW Government Communications Headquarters
The Sikorski Institute and Museum (PISM London)
  Ministerstwo Informacji i Dokumentacji: Dział Polski

L'viv

L'viv Regional State Archive (DALO)
  f. P-37 L'vivs'ke mis'ke staroatvo dystryktu "Halychyna" (Galicia)

New Haven

Beinecke Rare Book and Manuscript Library, Yale University
  Czesław Miłosz Papers
Fortunoff Video Archive for Holocaust Testimonies
  Survivor Testimony, various

New York City

Piłsudski Institute (JPI)
  Archiwum Władysława Studnickiego

Paris

UNESCO Archives (UNESCO)
  361.9 UNESCO Reports: Reconstruction (Poland)

Warsaw

Archiwum Akt Nowych (AAN)
  Akta Antoniny Sokolicz-Merkel
  Akta Bogny Lewtak
  Akta Michała Karaszewicza-Tokarzewskiego
  Archiwum Ignacego Jana Paderewskiego
  Armia Krajowa
  Konsulat Generalny RP w Nowym Jorku
  Telewizja Polska S.A. Zbiór wycinków prasowych
  Unia 1943 – organizacja podziemna z siedzibą w Warszawie
  Zbiór monografii i opracowań o partiach, organizacjach politycznych, zawodo-
    wych oraz młodzieżowych
Archiwum Państwowe m. st. Warszawy (APmstW)
  482/II Amt des Gouverneurs des Distrikts Warschau
  Archiwum Stanisława Broniewskiego
  Zbiór Korotyńskich
Archiwum Państwowe m. st. Warszawy w Milanówku (APW-M)
  Państwowe Gimnazjum i Liceum Męskie im. Adama Mickiewicza w Warszawie

Państwowe Gimnazjum i Liceum Męskie im. Księcia Józefa Poniatowskiego w Warszawie

Prywatne Gimnazjum Męskie im. Bolesława Prusa w Warszawie

Biblioteka Narodowa (BN)

    Konsp IIegz Magazyn Czasopism

      Biuletyn Informacyjny

      Prawda

    Dział Rękopisów

    Adam Chętnik

Biblioteka Uniwersytecka w Warszawie-Gabinet Rękopisów (BUW)

    Uniwersytet Warszawski w latach 1939–1945

Instytut Pamięci Narodowej (IPN)

    GK (Główna Komisja) 704–19

    GK 162–770

    GK 162–770

Polska Akademia Nauk (PAN)

    Materiały Aleksandra Kamińskiego

    Materiały Artura Śliwińskiego

Washington, DC

National Archives and Records Administration (NARA)

    Berlin Document Center

    Records of Headquarters, German Army High Command

    SA Personnel Files

    SS Officer Personnel Files

United States Holocaust Memorial Museum (USHMM)

    Proces Ludwika Fischera

    Ringelblum Archive (Oneg Shabbat)

    Oral History Interviews

Collections and Databases

Biblioteka Śląska Cyfrowa

Narodowe Archiwum Cyfrowe

Powstańcze Biogramy (Muzeum Powstania Warszawskiego)

Published Primary Sources

Andrzejewski, Jerzy. *Wielki Tydzień*. Warsaw: Czytelnik, 1983.

Bartoszewski, Władysław. *Życie trudne, lecz nie nudne: ze wspomnień polaka w xx wieku*. Commentator. Andrzej Friszke. Krakow: Wydawnictwo Znak, 2010.

Berg, Mary. *The Diary of Mary Berg: Growing up in the Warsaw Ghetto*. New York: Oneworld Oxford, 2007.

Białoszewski, Miron. *A Memoir of the Warsaw Uprising*. Trans. Madeline G. Levine. New York: New York Review Books, 2014.

Borowiec, Andrew. *Warsaw Boy: A Memoir of a Wartime Childhood*. New York: Penguin Books, 2014.

Bór-Komorowski, Tadeusz. *Armia Podziemna*. Ed. Andrzej Krzysztof Kunert. Warsaw: Wydawnictwo Bellona, 1994.

Broniewski, Stanisław. *Akcja pod Arsenałem*. Warsaw: Książka i Wiedza, 1972.

Całym życiem: Szare Szeregi w relacji naczelnika ("Stefan Orsza"). Warsaw: Państwowe Wyd. Naukowe, 1983.

Buczyński, Eugeniusz. *Smutny wrzesień: Wspomnienia*. Krakow: Wydawnictwo Literackie, 1985.

Centkowska, Elżbieta. *Na tajnych kompletach*. Warsaw: Wydawnictwa Szkolne i Pedagogiczne, 1974.

Chmielarz, Andrzej, Grzegorz Jasiński, and Andrzej Krzysztof Kunert, eds. *Armia Krajowa 1939–1945: Wybór Źródeł*. Warsaw: Wojskowe Centrum Edukacji Obywatelskiej, 2013.

Chodakiewicz, Marek J., Wojciech J. Muszyński, and Leszek Żebrowski, eds. *Narodowe Siły Zbrojne: Dokumenty 1942–1944*. Vol. 1. Lublin/Warsaw: Fundacja Kazimierza Wielkiego, 2014.

Chu, Winson. *The German Minority in Interwar Poland*. New York: Cambridge University Press, 2012.

Cieplewicz, Mieczysław and Eugeniusz Kozłowski, eds. *Obrona Warszawy 1939: we wspomnieniach*. Warsaw: Wyd. Ministerstwa Obrony Narodowej, 1984.

Wrzesień 1939 w relacjach i wspomnieniach. Warsaw: Wyd. Ministerstwa Obrony Narodowej, 1989.

Czajkowski, Zbigniew. *Warsaw 1944: An Insurgent's Journal of the Uprising*. Trans. Marek Czajkowski. Barnsley: Pen & Sword Military, 2012.

Czerniaków, Adam. *The Warsaw Diary of Adam Czerniaków: Prelude to Doom*. Trans. Stanislaw Staron. New York: Stein and Day Publishers, 1979.

Czuperska-Śliwicka, Anna. *Cztery lata ostrego dyżuru: Wspomnienie z Pawiaka 1940–1944*. Warsaw: Czytelnik, 1965.

Czuperska-Śliwicka, Anna, et al., eds. *Wspomnienia więźniów Pawiaka*. Warsaw: Ludowa Spółdzielnia Wydawnicza, 1964.

Dembowski, Peter F. *Memoirs: Red and White: Poland, the War, and After*. South Bend: University of Notre Dame Press, 2015.

Detkens, Edward. *Wielkie serce ks. Edward Detkens: jego życie i droga męczeńska: grypsy z Pawiaka oraz listy z obozów koncentracyjnych Sachsenhausen-Oranienburg i Dachau*. Ed. and intro. Dariusz Kaczmarzyk. Warsaw: Instytut Wydawniczy Pax, 1985.

Domańska, Regina, ed. *Pawiak był etapem: Wspomnienia z lat 1939–1944*. Warsaw: Ludowa Spółdzielnia Wyd., 1987.

Pawiak: Więzienie Gestapo: Kronika 1939–1944. Warsaw: Książka i Wiedza, 1978.

Donimirska-Szyrmerowa, Halina. *Był taki świat . . . Mój Wiek XX.* Warsaw: Wyd. Cyklady, 2007.

Drozdowski, Marian Marek, ed. *Archiwum Prezydenta Warszawy Stefana Starzyńskiego.* Tom II. Warsaw: RYTM, 2008.

Fischer, Ludwig. *Raporty Ludwiga Fischera Gubernatora Dystryktu Warszawskiego, 1939–1944.* Warsaw: Książka i Wiedza, 1987.

Frank, Hans. *Das Diensttagebuch des deutschen Generalgouverneurs in Polen, 1939–1945.* Ed. Werner Präg and Wolfgang Jacobmeyer. Stuttgart: Deutsche Verlags-Anstalt, 1975.

Garliński, Józef. *Fighting Auschwitz: The Resistance Movement inside the Concentration Camp.* Trans. Jarosław Garliński. Los Angeles: Aquila Polonica, 2018.

The Survival of Love: Memoirs of a Resistance Officer. Oxford: Basil Blackwell, 1991.

Główna Kwatera Harcerzy. *Szare Szeregi: Związek Harcerstwa Polskiego w czasie II wojny światowej: Główna Kwatera Harcerzy "Pasieka."* London: Polonia Book Fund, 1982.

Główny Urząd Statystyczny (GUS). *Mały Rocznik Statystyczny 1939.* Warsaw: Nakładem Głównego Urzędu Statystycznego, 1939.

Goebbels, Joseph. *The Goebbels Diaries, 1939–1941.* New York: G. P . Putnam's Sons, 1983.

Grzymała-Siedlecki, Adam. *Sto jedenaście dni letargu: wspomnienie z Pawiaka z lat 1942/1943.* Krakow: Wydawnictwo Literackie, 1965.

Hoess, Rudolf. *Commandant of Auschwitz.* London: Phoenix Press, 2000.

Instytut Historii Polskiej Akademii Nauk. *Cywilna Obrona Warszawy we wrześniu 1939 r.* Warsaw: Państwowe Wydawnictwo Naukowe, 1965.

Instytut Historyczny im. Gen. Sikorskiego, ed. *Polskie Siły Zbrojne w drugiej wojnie światowej*, tom III: Armia Krajowa. London: Instytut Historyczny im. Gen. Sikorskiego, 1999.

Jankowski, Stanisław. *Z fałszywym ausweisem w prawdziwej Warszawie: Wspomnienie 1939–1946*, 2 vols. Warsaw: Państwowy Instytut Wydawniczy, 1985.

Jarausch, Konrad. *Reluctant Accomplice: A Wehrmacht Soldier's Letters from the Eastern Front.* Princeton: Princeton University Press, 2011.

[Kamiński, Aleksander]. *Kamienie na szaniec.* 9th ed. Ill. Jerzy Brzoza. Katowice: Wyd. Śląsk, 1978.

Stones for the Rampart: The Story of Two Lads in the Polish Underground Movement. London: Polish Boy Scouts' and Girl Guides' Association, 1945.

Zośka i Parasol: Opowieść o niektórych ludziach i niektórych akcjach dwóch batalionów harcerskich. Warsaw: Wyd. Iskry, 1970.

Kaplan, Chaim A. *Scroll of Agony: The Warsaw Diary of Chaim A. Kaplan.* Trans. Abraham I. Katsh. New York: The Macmillan Company, 1965.

Karski, Jan. *Story of a Secret State: My Report to the World.* Washington: Georgetown University Press, 2013.

Kermish, Joseph, ed. *To Live with Honor and Die with Honor: Selected Documents from the Warsaw Ghetto Underground Archives "O.S."* Jerusalem: Yad Vashem, 1986.

Komisja Historyczna Polskiego Sztabu Głównego w Londynie. *Polskie Siły Zbrojne w Drugiej Wojnie Światowej,* Tom III: *Armia Krajowa.* London: Instytut Historyczny im. Gen. Sikorskiego, 1950.

Polskie Siły Zbrojne w Drugiej Wojnie Światowej, Tom I: *Kampania Wrześniowa 1939.* London: Instytut Historyczny im. Gen. Sikorskiego, 1959.

Korbonski, Stefan. *Fighting Warsaw: The Story of the Polish Underground State, 1939–1945.* Trans. F. B. Czarnomski. London: George Allen & Unwin, Ltd., 1956.

W imieniu Rzeczypospolitej. Warsaw: Wydawnictwo Bellona, 1991.

Kossak, Zofia. *Z otchłani.* Częstochowa: Wydawnictwo Księgarni Wł. Nagłowskiego, 1946.

Kossakowska-Szanacja, Zofia. *Zapiski dla Wnuków.* Warsaw: Biblioteka Więzi, 2009.

Krausnick Helmut. *Hitlers Einsatzgruppen: die Truppe des Weltanschauungskrieges, 1938–1942.* Frankfurt: Fischer Taschenbuch Verlag, 1985.

Krawczyńska, Jadwiga. *Zapiski Dziennikarki Warszawskiej, 1939–1947.* Warsaw: Państwowy Instytut Wydawniczy, 1971.

Kubalski, Edward. *Niemcy w Krakowie: Dziennik, 1 IX 1939 – 18 I 1945.* Ed. Jan Grabowski and Zbigniew R. Grabowski. Krakow: WydawnictwoAusteria, 2010.

Kulski, Julian. *Stefan Starzyński w mojej pamięci.* Warsaw: Państwowe Wyd. Naukowe, 1990.

Z minionych lat życia, 1892–1945. Warsaw: Państwowy Instytut Wydawniczy, 1982.

Kwiatkowski, Eugeniusz. *Dziennik: Lipiec 1939 – sierpień 1939.* Rzeszów: Wyższa Szkoła Informatyki i Zarządzania, 2003.

Landau, Ludwik. *Kronika Lat Wojny i Okupacji.* 3 vols. Warsaw: Państwowe Wydawnictwo Naukowe, 1962.

Lato, Stanisław, ed. *Maciej Rataj we wspomnieniach współczesnych.* Warsaw: Ludowa Spółdzielnia Wydawnicza, 1984.

Lemkin, Raphael. *Axis Rule in Occupied Europe: Laws of Occupation – Analysis of Government – Proposals for Redress.* Washington, DC: Carnegie Endowment for International Peace, 1944.

Lerski, Jerzy. *Emisariusz Jur.* Warsaw: Oficyna Wydawnicza Interim, 1989.

Lipiński, Wacław. *Dziennik: Wrześniowa obrona Warszawy 1939 r.* Warsaw: Instytut Wydawniczy Pax, 1989.

Lipski, Józef. *Diplomat in Berlin, 1933-1939: Papers and Memoirs of Józef Lipski, Ambassador of Poland.* New York: Columbia University Press, 1968.

Mallmann, Klaus, Jochen Boehler, and Juergen Matthaeus, eds, *Einsatzgruppen in Polen: Darstellung und Dokumentation*. Darmstadt: Wissenschaftliche Buchgesellschaft, 2008.

Manteuffel, Tadeusz. *Uniwersytet Warszawski w latach 1915/16–1934/35*. Warsaw: Imprint of the Piłsudski University (UW), 1936.

Uniwersytet Warszawski w latach wojny i okupacji: Kronika 1939/40–1944/45. Warsaw: Uniwersytet Warszawski Imprint, 1948.

Milosz, Czeslaw. *The Captive Mind*. Trans. Jane Zielonko. New York: Vintage International, 1990.

New and Collected Poems, 1931–2001. New York: Ecco Paperbacks, 2003.

Moczarski, Kazimierz. *Rozmowy z katem*. Warsaw: Wyd. Naukowe PWN, 1993.

Muszyński, Wojciech J., Rafał Sierchuła, and Leszek Żebrowski, eds. *Narodowe Siły Zbrojne: Dokumenty NSZ-AK 1944-1945*. Vol. 2. Lublin/Warsaw: Fundacja Kazimierza Wielkiego, 2015.

Nałkowska, Zofia. *Dzienniki czasu wojny*. Warsaw: Czytelnik, 1970.

Nowak, Jan. *Courier from Warsaw*. Detroit, MI: Wayne State University Press, 1982.

Paratroops of the Polish Home Army. *The Unseen and Silent: Adventures from the Underground Movement*. Trans. George Iranek-Osmecki. London: Sheed and Ward, 1954.

Pawełczyńska, Anna. *Dary losu*. Łomianki: Wydawnictwo LTW, 2013.

Pilecki, Witold. *The Auschwitz Volunteer: Beyond Bravery*. Trans. Jarek Garlinski. Los Angeles: Aquila Polonica, 2012.

Polish Labor Group. *Obrona Warszawy: Lud Polski w obronie stolicy (Wrzesień, 1939 roku)*. New York: Polish Labor Group, 1942.

Polish Ministry of Information. *The German Invasion of Poland: Polish Black Book Containing Documents, Authenticated Reports, and Photographs*. London: Hutchinson & Co., 1940.

The German New Order in Poland: [Black Book, Volume II]. London: Hutchinson & Co., 1942.

Porwit, Marian. *Komentarze do historii polskich działań obronnych 1939 r.* 3 vols. Warsaw: Czytelnik, 1969–1978.

Obrona Warszawy wrzesień 1939 r.: Wspomnienia i fakty. Warsaw: Czytelnik, 1979.

Reicher, Edward. *Country of Ash: A Jewish Doctor in Poland, 1939–1945*. Trans. Magda Bogin. New York: Bellevue Literary Press, 2013.

Regulska, Halina. *Dziennik z oblężonej Warszawy: Wrzesień – październik – listopad 1939 r.* Warsaw: Instytut Wydawniczy Pax, 1978.

Ringelblum, Emmanuel. *Kronika getta warszawskiego, wrzesień 1939- styczeń 1943*. Warsaw: Czytelnik: 1983.

Polish-Jewish Relations during the Second World War. Jerusalem: Yad Vashem, 1974.

Rowinski, Leokadia. *That the Nightingale Return: Memoir of the Polish Resistance, the Warsaw Uprising and German P.O.W. Camps*. Jefferson, NC: McFarland & Company, 1999.

Szatkowska, Anna. *Był dom . . . Wspomnienia*. Krakow: Wydawnictwo Literackie, 2013.

Szpilman, Władysław. *Pianista: Warszawskie wspomnienia, 1939–1945*. Krakow: Wyd. Znak, 2000.

Szucki, Bohdan *"Artur." Narodowe Siły Zbrojne w moim życiu*. Lublin: Związek Żołnierzy Narodowych Sił Zbrojnych/Fundacja im. Kazimierza Wielkiego, 2013.

Szymańska, Magda, ed. *Mieszkańcy Warszawy w czasie Powstania 1944*. 2nd ed. Warsaw: Dom Spotkań z Historią, 2016.

Szymańska-Szwąder, Magda, and Jarosław Pałka, eds. *Warszawa okupowana: relacje mieszkańców*. Warsaw: Dom Spotkań z Historią, 2011.

Śliwicki, Zygmunt. *Meldunek z Pawiaka*. Warsaw: Państwowe Wydawnictwo Naukowe, 1974.

Umiastowski, Roman. *Dziennik Wojenny, 18.IX.1939 – 19.IX.1945*. Ed. Przemysław Marcin Żukowski. Warsaw: Wyd. DiG, 2009.

Vetulani, Adam. *Poza płomieniami wojny: internowani w Szwajcarii, 1940–1945*. Warsaw: Wydawnictwo Ministerstwa Obrony Narodowej, 1976.

Wanat, Leon. *Za murami Pawiaka*. Warsaw: Książka i Wiedza, 1967.

Wat, Aleksander. *My Century: The Odyssey of a Polish Intellectual*. Trans. Richard Lourie. Foreword Czesław Miłosz. New York: New York Review Books, 1988.

Watowa, Ola. *Wszystko co najważniejsze . . .* Warsaw: Agora, 2011.

Witold Pilecki Center for Totalitarian Studies. *Chronicles of Terror Warsaw*. Warsaw: Witold Pilecki Center for Totalitarian Studies, 2017.

Wojewódzki, Michał. *W tajnych drukarniach Warszawy, 1939–1944: Wspomnienia*. Warsaw: Państwowy Instytut Wydawniczy, 1976.

Wyszyński, Franciszek. *Dzienniki z lat 1941–1944*. Ed. Jan Grabowski and Zbigniew R. Grabowski. Warsaw: Mówią Wieki, 2007.

Zahorska, Stefania. *Wybór pism: reportaże, publicystyka, eseje*. Warsaw: Instytut Badań Literackich PAN Wydawnictwo, 2010.

Zaremba, Zygmunt. *"Żeby chociaż świat wiedział:" Obrona warszawy 1939; Powstanie sierpniowe 1944*. Warsaw: Bellona, 2010.

Żórawski, Zdzisław. *Dziennik obrońcy Warszawy*. Intro. Tomasz Szarota. Warsaw: Oficyna Wydawnicza RYTM, 2011.

Zuckerman, Yitzhak. *A Surplus of Memory: Chronicle of the Warsaw Ghetto Uprising*. Berkeley: University of California Press, 1993.

Selected Secondary Sources

Applebaum, Anne. *Iron Curtain: The Crushing of Eastern Europe, 1944–1956*. New York: Anchor Books, 2013.

Arad, Yitzhak. *Belzec, Sobibor, Treblinka: The Operation Reinhard Death Camps*. Bloomington: Indiana University Press, 1987.

Banach, Kazimierz. *Z dziejów Batalionów Chłopskich: wspomnienia, rozważania, materiały.* Warsaw: Ludowa Spółdzielnia Wydawnicza, 1967.

Baranowski, Shelley. *Nazi Empire: German Colonialism from Bismarck to Hitler.* New York: Cambridge University Press, 2011.

Bartoszewski, Władysław. *1859 dni Warszawy.* Krakow: Wydawnictwo Znak, 1974.

ed. *Doświadczenia lat wojny, 1939–1945: fakty, postawy, refleksje.* 2nd ed. Krakow: Wydawnictwo Znak, 2009.

Palmiry. Warsaw: Wyd. Książka i Wiedza, 1969.

Dni walczącej Stolicy: Kronika Powstania Warszawskiego. Warsaw: Świat Książki, 2004.

Warsaw Death Ring, 1939–1944. Krakow: Interpress Publishers, 1968.

Bartoszewski, Władysław and Marek Edelman. *I była dzielnica żydowska w Warszawie.* Warsaw: Literatura Faktu PWN, 2010.

Bartoszewski, Władysław T., and Antony Polonsky, eds. *The Jews in Warsaw: A History.* Cambridge: Basil Blackwell, 1991.

Bartov, Omer. *Hitler's Army: Soldiers, Nazis and War in the Third Reich.* New York: Oxford University Press, 1992.

Becker, Annette. *Messagers du désastre: Raphael Lemkin, Jan Karski et les génocides.* Paris: Fayard, 2018.

Beckett, Ian F. W., ed. *The Roots of Counterinsurgency: Armies and Guerrilla Warfare, 1900–1945.* London: Blandford Press, 1988.

Bemporad, Elissa. *Legacy of Blood: Jews, Pogroms, and Ritual Murder in the Lands of the Soviets.* New York: Oxford University Press, 2019.

Bikont, Anna. *The Crime and the Silence: Confronting the Massacre of Jews in Wartime Jedwabne.* Trans. Alissa Vales. New York: Farrar, Straus and Giroux, 2015.

Sendlerowa w ukryciu. Wołowiec: Wydawnictwo Czarne, 2017.

Bjork, James, Tomasz Kamusella, Timothy Wilson, and Anna Noviko, eds., *Creating Nationality in Central Europe, 1880–1950: Modernity, Violence, and (Be)longing in Upper Silesia.* New York: Routledge, 2016.

Blobaum, Robert, ed. *Antisemitism and Its Opponents in Modern Poland.* Ithaca: Cornell University Press, 2005.

Blobaum, Robert. *A Minor Apocalypse: Warsaw during the First World War.* Ithaca: Cornell University Press, 2017.

Rewolucja: Russian Poland, 1904–1907. Ithaca: Cornell University Press, 1995.

Borodziej, Włodzimierz. *Der Warschauer Aufstand: 1944.* Frankfurt am Main: Fischer Taschenbuch Verlag, 2004.

Terror und Politik: Die deutsche Polizei und die polnische Widerstandsbewegung im Generalgouvernement, 1939–1944. Mainz: Verlag Philipp von Zabern, 1999.

Borodziej, Włodzimierz, et al. *Polska Podziemna, 1939–1945.* Warsaw: Wyd. Szkolnej Pedagogiczne, 1991.

Borowicz, Ryszard, Hanna Kostyło, and Władysława Szulakiewicz. *Elżbieta Zawacka "Zo"—Portret akademicki.* Toruń: Wydawnictwo Naukowe Uniwersytetu Mikołaja Kopernika, 2009.

Bourdieu, Pierre. *Distinction: A Social Critique of the Judgement of Taste.* Cambridge: Harvard University Press, 1984.

Böhler, Jochen. *Auftakt zum Vernichtungskrieg: Die Wehrmacht in Polen 1939.* Frankfurt/Main: Fischer Taschenbuch Verlag, 2006.

Breitman, Richard. *The Architect of Genocide: Himmler and the Final Solution.* New York: Alfred A. Knopf, 1991.

Brenner, Rachel Feldhay. *The Ethics of Witnessing: The Holocaust in Polish Writers' Diaries from Warsaw, 1939–1945.* Evanston: Northwestern University Press, 2014.

Brewing, Daniel. *Im Schatten von Auschwitz: Deutsche Massaker an polnischen Zivilisten, 1939–1945.* Darmstadt: Wissenschaftliche Buchgesellschaft, 2016.

Broszat, Martin. *Nationalsozialistische Polenpolitik, 1939–1945.* Stuttgart, Deutsche Verlags-Anstalt, 1961.

Browning, Christopher. *Ordinary Men: Reserve Police Battalion 101 and the Final Solution in Poland.* New York: Harper Perennial, 1998.

   The Origins of the Final Solution: The Evolution of Nazi Jewish Policy, September 1939–March 1942. Lincoln: The University of Nebraska Press, 2004.

   Remembering Survival: Inside a Nazi Slave Labor Camp. New York: W. W. Norton & Co., 2010.

Bryant, Chad. *Prague in Black: Nazi Rule and Czech Nationalism.* Cambridge: Harvard University Press, 2007.

Brykczynski, Paul. *Primed for Violence: Murder, Antisemitism and Democratic Politics in Interwar Poland.* Madison: The University of Wisconsin Press, 2016.

Bukey, Evan Burr. *Hitler's Austria: Popular Sentiment in the Nazi Era, 1938–1945.* Chapel Hill: The University of North Carolina Press, 2000.

Burleigh, Michael. *Germany Turns Eastwards: A Study of* Ostforschung *in the Third Reich.* New York: Cambridge University Press, 1988.

   Sacred Causes: The Clash of Religion and Politics, from the Great War to the War on Terror. New York: HarperCollins, 2007.

Chiari, Bernhard, ed. *Die polnische Heimatarmee: Geschichte und Mythos der Armia Krajowa seit dem Zweiten Weltkrieg.* Munich: Oldenbourg, 2003.

Chodakiewicz, Marek Jan. *Between Nazis and Soviets: Occupation Politics in Poland, 1939–1947.* Lanham, MD: Lexington Books, 2004.

   Narodowe Siły Zbrojne: "Ząb" przeciw dwu wrogom. 2nd ed. Warsaw: Fronda, 1999.

Cienciala, Anna M. *Katyń: A Crime without Punishment.* New Haven: Yale University Press, 2007.

Clark, Christopher. *Iron Kingdom: The Rise and Downfall of Prussia, 1600–1947.* Cambridge: Belknap Press, 2006.

Connelly, John. *From Peoples into Nations: A History of Eastern Europe.* Princeton: Princeton University Press, 2020.

Cornwell, John. *Hitler's Pope: The Secret History of Pius XII.* New York: Viking Books, 1999.

Cüppers, Martin. *Wegbereiter der Shoah: Die Waffen-SS, der Kommandostab Reichsführer-SS und die Judenvernichtung 1939–1945.* Darmstadt: Wissenschaftliche Buchgesellschaft, 2005.

Czaputowicz, Jacek. *Administracja cywilna Polskiego Państwa Podziemnego i jej funkcje w okresie powstania warszawskiego.* Warsaw: KSAP, 2011.

Czubaty, Jarosław. *Warszawa, 1806–1815: Miasto i ludzie.* Warsaw: Wyd. Neriton, 1997.

Daszkiewicz, Krystyna. *Niemieckie ludobójstwo na narodzie polskim (1939–1945).* Toruń: Wydawnictwo Adam Marszałek, 2009.

Davies, Norman. *Heart of Europe: The Past in Poland's Present.* New York: Oxford University Press, 2001.

Rising '44: Battle for Warsaw. New York: Viking, 2003.

White Eagle, Red Star: The Polish-Soviet War 1919–1920 and the Miracle on the Vistula. London: Random House, 2003.

Dean, Martin. *Robbing the Jews: The Confiscation of Jewish Property in the Holocaust, 1933–1945.* New York: Cambridge University Press, 2008.

Dembowski, Peter. *Christians in the Warsaw Ghetto: An Epitaph for the Unremembered.* South Bend: University of Notre Dame Press, 2005.

Dębski, Jerzy. *Kadra dowódcza SZP-ZWZ-AK w Konzentrationslager Auschwitz 1940–1945.* Katowice/Oświęcim: Oddział Instytutu Pamięci Narodowej/ Państwowe Muzeum Auschwitz- Birkenau, 2009.

Dobroszycki, Lucjan. *Reptile Journalism: The Official Polish-Language Press under the Nazis, 1939- 1945.* New Haven: Yale University Press, 1994.

Domańska, Regina. *A droga ich wiodła przez Pawiak.* Warsaw: Książka i Wiedza, 1981

Pawiak - Kaźń i Heroizm. Warsaw: Książka i Wiedza, 1988

Pawiak: Więzienie Gestapo: Kronika 1939–1944. Warsaw: Książka i Wiedza, 1978.

Drozdowski, Marian Marek and Andrzej Zahorski. *Historia Warszawy.* Warsaw: PWN, 1981.

Drozdowski, Marian Marek. *Jan Karski Kozielewski (1914–2000).* Warsaw: Oficyna Wydawnicza Aspra, 2014.

Starzyński: Legionista, Polityk, Gospodarczy, Prezydent Warszawy. Warsaw: Wyd. Iskry, 2006.

Dunin-Wąsowicz, Krzysztof. *Na Żoliborzu, 1939–1945.* Warsaw: Książka i Wiedza, 1984.

Warszawa w czasie pierwszej wojny światowej. Warsaw: Państwowy Instytut Wydawniczy, 1974.

Warszawa w latach 1939–1945. Warsaw: PWN, 1984.

Dwork, Deborah and Robert Jan van Pelt. *Auschwitz.* New York: W. W. Norton & Company, 1996.

Holocaust: A History. New York: Norton & Company, 2002.

Dziurok Adam, Józef Marecki, Filip Musiał, eds. *Instrukcje, wytyczne, okólniki dyrektor Departmentu V MBP dotyczące działań przeciwko Kościołowi katolickiemu w latach 1945-1953*. Krakow: Wydawnictwo Avalon/IPN, 2012.

Eberhardt, Christiane. *Geheimes Schulwesen und konspirative Bildungspolitik der polnischen Gesellschaft im Generalgouvernement, 1939-1945*. Frankfurt am Main: Peter Lang, 2003.

Edelstein, David. *Occupational Hazards: Success and Failure in Military Occupation*. Ithaca: Cornell University Press, 2008.

Engelking, Barbara and Jacek Leociak. *Getto Warszawskie: Przewodnik po nieistniejącym mieście*. Warsaw: Stowarzyszenie Centrum Badań nad Zagładą Żydów, 2013.

Engelking, Barbara. *Holocaust and Memory: The Experience of the Holocaust and Its Consequences: An Investigation Based on Personal Narratives*. London: Leicester University Press, 2001.

"*Szanowny panie gistapo:*" *Donosy do władz niemieckich w Warszawie i okolicach w latach 1940-1941*. Warsaw: Wyd. IFiS PAN, 2003.

Engelking, Barbara, Jacek Leociak, and Dariusz Libionka, eds. *Prowincja noc: Życie i zagłada Żydów w dystrykcie warszawskim*. Warsaw: Wydawnictwo IFiS PAN, 2007.

Engelking, Barbara and Jan Grabowski. *Dalej jest Noc: Losy Żydów w wybranych powiatach okupowanej Polski*. Warsaw: Stowarzyszenie Centrum Badań nad Zagładą Żydów, 2018.

'*Przestępczość' Żydów w Warszawie 1939-1942: 'Żydów łamiących prawo należy karać śmiercią!'* Warsaw: Stowarzyszenie Centrum Badań nad Zagładą Żydów, 2010.

Epstein, Catherine. *Model Nazi: Arthur Greiser and the Occupation of Western Poland*. New York: Oxford University Press, 2010.

Fijałkowski, Zenon. *Kościół katolicki na ziemiach polskich w latach okupacji hitlerowskiej*. Warsaw: Książka i Wiedza, 1983.

Finder, Gabriel and Alexander Prusin. *Justice behind the Iron Curtain: Nazis on Trial in Communist Poland*. Toronto: University of Toronto Press, 2018.

Friedländer, Saul. *Nazi Germany and the Jews, Volume I: The Years of Persecution, 1933-1939*. New York: Harper Perennial, 1998.

Friedrich, Klaus-Peter. *Der nationalsozialistische Judenmord und das polnisch-jüdische Verhältnis im Diskurs der polnischen Untergrundpress (1942-1944)*. Marburg: Verlag Herder Institut, 2006.

Fritzsche, Peter. *An Iron Wind: Europe under Hitler*. New York: Basic Books, 2016.

Gałęzowski, Marek. *Pułkownik 'Żegota:' życie i pisma pułkownika dypl. Tadeusza Münnicha*. Warsaw: Instytut Pamięci Narodowej, 2009.

Garlicka, Aleksandra and Jerzy Jedlicki, eds. *Inteligencja polska XIX i XX wieku: materiały z wystawy i sesji naukowej*. Warsaw: Galeria Sztuki Współczesnej Zachęta, 1997.

Garlicki, Andrzej. *Józef Piłsudski, 1867–1935.* Brookfield: Ashgate Publishing Company, 1995.

Garliński, Józef. *Niezapomniane lata: Dzieje Wywiadu Więzionnego i Wydziału Bezpieczeństwa Komendy Głównej Armii Krajowej.* London: Odnowa, 1987.

Gerlach, Christian. *Extremely Violent Societies: Mass Violence in the Twentieth-Century World.* New York: Cambridge University Press, 2010.

Gerwarth, Robert. *Hitler's Hangman: The Life of Heydrich.* New Haven: Yale University Press, 2011.

Głowacki, Ludwik. *Obrona Warszawy i Modlina na tle kampanii wrześniowej.* Warsaw: Wydawnictwo Ministerstwa Obrony Narodowej, 1963.

Główna Komisja Badania Zbrodni Hitlerowskich w Polsce. *Struktura i obsada rządu Generalnej Guberni oraz władze administracji cywilnej dystryktów.* Nr. 5, 1968. Warsaw: Min. Sprawiedliwości, Główna Komisja Badania Zbrodni Hitlerowskich w Polsce, 1968.

Główny Zarząd Polityczny WP. *Z dziejów wojny wyzwoleńczej narodu Polskiego, 1939–1945.* Warsaw: Wydawnictwo Ministerstwa Obrony Narodowej, 1960.

Grabowski, Jan. *Hunt for the Jews: Betrayal and Murder in German-Occupied Poland.* Bloomington: Indiana University Press, 2013.

Na posterunku: Udział polskiej policji granatowej i kryminalnej w zagładzie Żydów. Wołowiec: Wydawnictwo Czarne, 2020.

Grabowski, Waldemar. *Polska tajna administracja cywilna, 1940–1945.* Warsaw: Instytut Pamięci Narodowej, 2003.

Greble, Emily. *Sarajevo, 1941–1945: Muslims, Christians, and Jews in Hitler's Europe.* Ithaca: Cornell University Press, 2011.

Gröning, Gert, ed. *Planung in Polen im Nationalsozialismus.* Berlin: Hochschule der Künste, 1996.

Gross, Jan T. *Fear: Anti-Semitism in Poland after Auschwitz.* New York: Random House, 2007.

Neighbors: The Destruction of the Jewish Community in Jedwabne, Poland. New York: Penguin Books, 2002.

Polish Society under German Occupation. Princeton: Princeton University Press, 1979.

Guesnet, François, Howard Lupovitch, and Antony Polonsky, eds. *Polin Vol. 31: Poland and Hungary: Jewish Realities Compared.* Liverpool: Liverpool University Press, 2019.

Gutman, Yisrael, ed. *Anatomy of the Auschwitz Death Camp.* Washington, DC: United States Holocaust Memorial Museum, 1994.

Gutman, Israel. *Resistance: The Warsaw Ghetto Uprising.* Boston: Houghton Mifflin, 1994.

Gutschow, Niels and Barbara Klein. *Vernichtung und Utopie: Stadtplanung Warschau, 1939–1945.* Hamburg: Junius Verlag, 1994.

Heinemann, Isabel. *"Rasse, Siedlung, deutsches Blut:" Das Rasse- und Siedlungshauptamt der SS und die rassenpolitische Neuordnung Europas.* Göttingen: Wallstein Verlag, 2003.

Helm, Sarah. *Ravensbrück: Life and Death in Hitler's Concentration Camp for Women*. New York: Anchor Books, 2015.

Heuser, Beatrice and Etian Shamir, eds. *Insurgencies and Counterinsurgencies: National Styles and Strategic Cultures*. New York: Cambridge University Press, 2016.

Hirshaut, Julien. *Jewish Martyrs of Pawiak*. New York: Holocaust Library, 1982.

Horwitz, Gordon. Ghettostadt: *Łódź and the Making of a Nazi City*. Cambridge: Belknap Press, 2008.

Housden, Martyn. *Hans Frank, Lebensraum, and the Holocaust*. New York: Palgrave Macmillan, 2003.

Jabrzemski, Jerzy. *Szare Szeregi: Harcerze, 1939–1945*. 3 vols. Warsaw: Państwowe Wyd. Nauk, 1988.

Jakubowska, Longina. *Patrons of History: Nobility, Capital and Political Transitions in Poland*. New York: Routledge, 2016.

Janowski, Maciej. *Birth of the Intelligentsia, 1750–1831, A History of the Polish Intelligentsia Part I*. Frankfurt/Main: Peter Lang, 2014.

Janus, Piotr. *W Nurcie Polskiego Etatyzmu: Stefan Starzyński i Pierwsza Brygada Gospodarcza, 1926- 1932*. Krakow: Wyd. Avalon, 2009.

Jastrzębski, Włodzimierz. *Terror i Zbrodnia: Einsatzkommandos terminacja ludności polskiej i żydowskiej w rejencji bydgoskiej w latach 1939–1945*. Warsaw: Wyd. Interpress, 1974.

Jaworska, Janina. *Polska sztuka walcząca, 1939–1945*. Warsaw: Wydawnictwa Artystyczne i Filmowe, 1976.

Jedlicki, Jerzy. *A Suburb of Europe: Nineteenth-Century Polish Approaches to Western Civilization*. Budapest: CEU Press, 1999.

   The Vicious Circle, 1832–1864, A History of the Intelligentsia- Part 2. Frankfurt am Main: Peter Lang, 2014.

Julian, Jackson. *France: The Dark Years, 1940–1944*. New York: Oxford University Press, 2001.

Kabzińska, Krystyna, ed. *Służba Polek na Frontach II Wojny Światowej – 7*. Toruń: Fundacja Archiwum i Muzeum Pomorskie Armii Krajowej oraz Wojskowej Służby Polek, 2003.

Karski, Jan. *The Great Powers and Poland, 1919–1945: From Versailles to Yalta*. Lanham: Rowman & Littlefield, 2014.

Kassow, Samuel D. *Who Will Write Our History? Rediscovering a Hidden Archive from the Warsaw Ghetto*. New York: Vintage Books, 2007.

Kauffman, Jesse. *Elusive Alliance: The German Occupation of Poland in World War I*. Cambridge: Harvard University Press, 2015.

Kay, Alex J. and David Stahel, eds. *Mass Violence in Nazi-Occupied Europe*. Bloomington: Indiana University Press, 2018.

Kaźmierska, Janina. *Szkolnictwo warszawskie w latach 1939–1944*. Warsaw: Państwowe Wydawnictwo Naukowe, 1980.

Kenney, Padraic. *Dance in Chains: Political Imprisonment in the Modern World*. New York: Oxford University Press, 2017.

Kershaw, Ian. *Hitler: A Biography*. New York: W. W. Norton, 2008.

Kertzer, David I. *The Popes against the Jews: The Vatican's Role in the Rise of Modern Anti-Semitism*. New York: Vintage Books, 2001.

Kieniewicz, Stefan. *Trzy powstania narodowe: kościuszkowe, listopadowe, styczniowe*. Warsaw: Książka i Wiedza, 1994

Kirszak, Jerzy and Daniel Koreś, eds. *Kampania Polska '39: Militarne i polityczne aspekty z perspektywy siedemdziesięciolecia*. Wrocław: Oddział Instytutu Pamięci Narodowej, 2011.

Kochanski, Halik. *The Eagle Unbowed: Poland and the Poles in the Second World War*. Cambridge, MA: Harvard University Press, 2012.

Komorowski, Krzysztof. *Armia Krajowa: rozwój organizacyjny*. Warsaw: Wyd. Bellona, 1996.

Konwinski, Norbert, *The Mayor*. Posen, MI: Diversified Enterprises, 1978.

Koper, Sławomir. *Życie prywatne elit artystycznych Drugiej Rzeczypospolitej*. Warsaw: Bellona, 2010.

Kopstein, Jeffrey S. and Jason Wittenberg. *Intimate Violence: Anti-Jewish Pogroms on the Eve of the Holocaust*. Ithaca: Cornell University Press, 2018.

Kosicki, Piotr H. *Catholics on the Barricades: Poland, France, and the "Revolution," 1891–1956*. New Haven: Yale University Press, 2018.

Koskodan, Kenneth J. *No Greater Ally: The Untold Story of Poland's Forces in World War II*. Oxford: Osprey Publishing, 2009.

Krajewski, Kazimierz and Tomasz Łabuszewski, eds. *Powstanie warszawskie: fakty i mity*. Warsaw: Instytut Pamięci Narodowej, 2006.

Krajewski, Kazimierz and Magdalena Pietrzak-Merta, eds. *Warszawa miasto w opresji: Warszawa nie?pokonana*. Warsaw: Instytut Pamięci Narodowej, 2010.

Krakowski, Shmuel. *The War of the Doomed: Jewish Armed Resistance in Poland, 1942–1944*. New York: Holmes & Meier Publishers, 1984.

Krause, Peter. *Rebel Power: Why National Movements Compete, Fight, and Win*. Ithaca: Cornell University Press, 2017.

Kucha, Ryszard and Ulla Johansson, eds. *Gender and Secondary Education in Poland and Sweden in the Twentieth Century*. Lublin: Marie Curie-Skłodowska University Press, 2002.

Kunert, Andrzej Krzysztof and Zygmunt Walkowski. *Kronika kampanii wrześniowej 1939*. Warsaw: Edipresse Książki, 2005.

Kunert, Andrzej Krzysztof. *Oskarżony Kazimierz Moczarski*. Warsaw: Wydawnictwo Iskry, 2006.

  ed. *Polacy – Żydzi: 1939–1945: Wybór źródeł = Polen – Juden: 1939–1945: Quellenauswahl = Poles – Jews: 1939–1945: A Selection of Documents*. Warsaw: Rada Ochrony Pamięci RYTM, 2001.

Kunicki, Mikołaj Stanisław. *Between the Brown and the Red: Nationalism, Catholicism, and Communism in 20th-Century Poland – The Politics of Bolesław Piasecki*. Athens, OH: Ohio University Press, 2012.

Lehnstaedt, Stephan. *Occupation in the East: The Daily Lives of German Occupiers in Warsaw and Minsk, 1939–1944*. New York: Berghahn Books, 2010.

Leociak, Jacek. *Text in the Face of Destruction: Accounts from the Warsaw Ghetto Reconsidered.* Trans. Emma Harris. Warsaw: Żydowski Instytut Historyczny, 2004.

Lewandowska, Stanisława. *Prasa okupowanej Warszawy, 1939–1945.* Warsaw: Instytut Historii PAN, 1992.

Liulevicius, Vejas Gabriel. *The German Myth of the East, 1800 to the Present.* New York: Oxford University Press, 2009.

   War Land on the Eastern Front: Culture, National Identity, and German Occupation in World War I. New York: Cambridge University Press, 2000.

Longerich, Peter. *Goebbels: A Biography.* Trans. Alan Bance, Jeremy Noakes, and Lesley Sharpe. New York: Random House, 2015.

   Heinrich Himmler. Trans. Jeremy Noakes and Lesley Sharpe. New York: Oxford University Press, 2012.

Lower, Wendy. *Nazi Empire-Building and the Holocaust in Ukraine.* Chapel Hill: University of North Carolina Press, 2005

Madaj, Karol and Małgorzata Żuławnik. *Proboszcz getta.* Warsaw: IPN, 2010.

Madacjzyk, Czesław. *Polityka III Rzeszy w okupowanej Polsce.* 2 vols. Warsaw: Państwowe Wydawnictwo Naukowe, 1970.

Majer, Diemut. *"Non-Germans" under the Third Reich: The Nazi Judicial and Administrative System in Germany and Occupied Eastern Europe, with Special Regard to Occupied Poland, 1939–1945.* Trans. Peter Thomas Hill, et al. Baltimore: The Johns Hopkins University Press, 2003.

Malinowski, Kazimierz. *Żołnierze łączności walczącej Warszawy.* Warsaw: Instytut Wydawniczy Pax, 1983.

Mallmann, Klaus-Michael and Bogdan Musial, eds. *Genesis des Genozids: Polen 1939–1941.* Darmstadt: Wissenschaftliche Buchgesellschaft, 2004.

Mazower, Mark. *Hitler's Empire: How the Nazis Ruled Europe.* New York: Penguin Books, 2009.

   Inside Hitler's Greece: The Experience of Occupation, 1941–1944. New Haven: Yale University Press, 1993.

Micińska, Magdalena. *At the Crossroads, 1865–1918: A History of the Polish Intelligentsia, Part 3.* Frankfurt am Main: Peter Lang, 2014

Milewski, Jan Jerzy and Anna Pyżewska, eds. *Początek wojny niemiecko-sowieckiej i losy ludności cywilnej.* Warsaw: Instytut Pamięci Narodowej, 2003.

Minczykowska, Katarzyna. *Cichociemna: Generał Elżbieta Zawacka "Zo," 1909–2009.* Warsaw: Oficyna Wydawnicza Rytm, 2014.

Moorhouse, Roger. *Poland 1939: The Outbreak of World War II.* New York: Basic Books, 2020.

Morgan, Philip. *Hitler's Collaborators: Choosing between Bad and Worse in Nazi-Occupied Western Europe.* New York: Oxford University Press, 2018.

Mosse, George. *Nazi Culture: Intellectual, Cultural, and Social Life in the Third Reich.* New York: Schocken Books, 1966.

   Toward the Final Solution: A History of European Racism. New York: Howard Fertig, 1997.

Mórawski, Karol and Wiesław Głębocki. *Warszawa: przewdonik turystyczny.* Warsaw: Krajowa Agencja Wydawnicza, 1982.

Murzański, Stanisław. *Sojusz nieczystych sumień: inteligencja polska i jej elity na przełomie XX i XXI wieku.* Krakow: Wyd. Arcana, 2010.

Müller, Anna. *If the Walls Could Speak: Inside A Women's Prison in Communist Poland.* New York: Oxford University Press, 2018.

Naimark, Norman M. *Fires of Hatred: Ethnic Cleansing in Twentieth-Century Europe.* Cambridge: Harvard University Press, 2001.

Ney-Krwawicz, Marek. *Biuro Generała Sosnkowskiego: Komenda Główna Związku Walki Zbrojnej we Francji: listopad 1939 – czerwiec 1940.* Warsaw: Wydawnictwo Naukowe/Semper, 1996.

Osica, Janusz, Andrzej Sowa, and Paweł Wieczorkiewicz. *1939: Ostatni rok pokoju, pierwszy rok wojny.* Poznań: Wyd. Zysk i S-ka, 2009.

Ossibach-Budzyński, Andrzej. *Pawiak: więzienie polityczne, 1880–1915.* Warsaw: Wyd. Aspra, 2016.

Paczkowski, Andrzej. *The Spring Will Be Ours: Poland and the Poles from Occupation to Freedom.* University Park: Penn State University Press, 1995.

Paehler, Katrin. *The Third Reich's Intelligence Services: The Career of Walter Schellenberg.* New York: Cambridge University Press, 2017.

Paulsson, Gunnar S. *Secret City: The Hidden Jews of Warsaw, 1940–1945.* New Haven: Yale University Press, 2002.

Pawlina, Sebastian. *Praca w dywersji: Codzienność żołnierzy Kedywu Okręgu Warszawskiego Armii Krajowej.* Gdańsk: Muzeum II Wojny Światowej, 2016.

Pawłowicz, Jacek. *Rotmistrz Witold Pilecki (1901–1948).* Warsaw: IPN, 2008.

Pawłowski, Edward and Zbigniew Wawer. *Losy Polski i Polaków w okresie II Wojny Światowej.* Warsaw: Wyd. Bellona, 2009.

Paxton, Robert O. *Vichy France: Old Guard and New Order, 1940–1944.* New York: Alfred A. Knopf, 1972.

Peri, Alexis. *The War Within: Diaries from the Siege of Leningrad.* Cambridge, MA: Harvard University Press, 2020.

Persak, Krzysztof and Paweł Machcewicz, eds. *II Wojna Światowa. Polski Wiek XX.* Warsaw: Bellona/Muzeum Historii Polski, 2010.

Peszke, Michael A. *The Polish Underground Army, the Western Allies, and the Failure of Strategic Unity in World War II.* Jefferson, NC: McFarland, 2005.

Pietrzykowski, Jan. *Akcja AB w Częstochowie: AB-Aktion.* Katowice: Wyd. Śląsk, 1971.

Piotrowski, Mirosław, ed. *Na przełomie stuleci: Naród – kościół – państwo w XIX i XX wieku.* Lublin: Klub Inteligencji Katolickiej, 1997.

Polonsky, Antony, ed. *Polin Studies in Polish Jewry, Vol. 17: The Shtetl: Myth and Reality.* Liverpool: Liverpool University Press, 2004.

Porter-Szücs, Brian. *Faith and Fatherland: Catholicism, Modernity, and Poland.* New York: Oxford University Press, 2011.

Poland in the Modern World: Beyond Martyrdom. West Sussex: Wiley Blackwell, 2014.

Prażmowska, Anita J. *Civil War in Poland, 1942–1948.* New York: Palgrave Macmillan, 2004.

Prochwicz, Jerzy. *Arcybiskup Stanisław Gall (1865–1942): Biskup polowy Wojsk Polskich.* Warsaw: Ordynariat Polowy, 2018.

Prusin, Alexander. *Serbia under the Swastika: A World War II Occupation.* Urbana: University of Illinois Press, 2017.

Rees, Laurence. *The Holocaust: A New History.* New York: Public Affairs, 2017.

Rosbottom, Ronald C. *When Paris Went Dark: The City of Light under German Occupation, 1940–1944.* New York: Little, Brown & Company/Back Bay Books, 2014.

Rossino, Alexander B. *Hitler Strikes Poland: Blitzkrieg, Ideology, and Atrocity.* Lawrence: University Press of Kansas, 2003.

Rothschild, Joseph. *East Central Europe between the Two World Wars.* Seattle: University of Washington Press, 1977.

Piłsudski's Coup d'Etat. New York: Columbia University Press, 1966.

Röger, Maren. *Wojenne związki: Polki i Niemcy podczas Okupacji.* Trans. Tomasz Dominiak. Warsaw: Świat Książki, 2016.

Rutherford, Phillip T. *Prelude to the Final Solution: The Nazi Program for Deporting Ethnic Poles,1939–1941.* Lawrence: University Press of Kansas, 2007.

Rybicki, Roman W., ed. *"Piękna Zosia:" Pamięci Zofii Korobońskiej.* Warsaw: Wydawnictwo RYTM/Fundacja im. Stefana Korbońskiego w Warszawie, 2011.

Sadurska, Wanda. *Kobiety w łączności Komendy Głównej i okręgu warszawskiego ZWZ-AK.* Warsaw: Wydawnictwo Comandor, 2002.

Schenk, Dieter. *Hans Frank: Hitlers Kronjurist und Generalgouverneur.* Frankfurt/Main: S. Fischer Verlag, 2006.

Krakauer Burg: Die Machtzentrale des Generalgouverneurs Hans Frank, 1939–1945. Berlin: Ch. Links Verlag, 2010.

Sesja Historyczna 50-lecia Duszpasterstwa Akademickiego przy Kościele św. Anny w Warszawie 23–25 IX 1978. Warsaw: Rektorat Kościoła Akademickiego św. Anny, 1981.

Sheffer, Edith. *Asperger's Children: The Origins of Autism in Nazi Vienna.* New York: W. W. Norton & Company, 2018.

Shore, Marci. *Caviar and Ashes: A Warsaw Generation's Life and Death in Marxism, 1918–1968.* New Haven: Yale University Press, 2009.

Slepyan, Kenneth. *Stalin's Guerrillas: Soviet Partisans in World War II.* Lawrence, University Press of Kansas, 2006.

Snyder, Timothy. *Bloodlands: Europe between Hitler and Stalin.* New York: Basic Books, 2010.

Sketches from a Secret War: A Polish Artist's Mission to Liberate Soviet Ukraine. New Haven: Yale University Press, 2005.

Solarczyk, Hanna. *Doświadczenia edukacyjne kobiet w Polsce i w Niemczech: Raport z badań biograficznych*. Toruń: Biblioteka Edukacji Dorosłych, 2002.

Spałka, Robert, ed. *Porządek publiczny i bezpieczeństwo w okupacyjnej Warszawie*. Warsaw: Instytut Pamięci Narodowej, 2018.

Stachiewicz, Piotr. *Akcja "Kutschera."* Warsaw: Książka i Wiedza, 1982.

Stanek, Piotr. *Stefan Korboński (1901–1989): Działalność polityczna i społeczna*. Warsaw: Instytut Pamięci Narodowej, 2014.

Stargardt, Nicholas. *The German War: A Nation under Arms, 1939–1945: Citizens and Soldiers*. New York: Basic Books, 2017.

Strzembosz, Tomasz. *Akcje zbrojne podziemnej Warszawy, 1939–1944*. Warsaw: Państwowy Instytut Wydawniczy, 1983.

Szarota, Tomasz. *Okupowanej Warszawy Dzień Powszedni*. Warsaw: Czytelnik, 1988.

Tec, Nechama. *When Light Pierced the Darkness: Christian Rescue of Jews in Nazi-Occupied Poland*. New York: Oxford University Press, 1987.

Tomasevich, Jozo. *War and Revolution in Yugoslavia, 1941–1945: Occupation and Collaboration*. Stanford: Stanford University Press, 2001.

Tooze, Adam. *Wages of Destruction: The Making and Breaking of the Nazi Economy*. New York: Viking, 2006.

Tucker, Erica L. *Remembering Occupied Warsaw: Polish Narratives of World War II*. DeKalb: Northern Illinois University Press, 2011.

Urbanek, Joanna. *Lęk i strach: Warszawiacy wobec zagrożeń Września 1939 r.* Warsaw: Oficyna Wydawnicza Aspra, 2009.

Wachsmann, Nikolaus. *KL: A History of the Nazi Concentration Camps*. New York: Farrar, Straus & Giroux, 2015.

Walicki, Andrzej. *Poland between East and West: The Controversies over Self-Definition and Modernization in Partitioned Poland*. Cambridge, MA: Harvard Ukrainian Research Institute, 1994.

Walicki, Michał. *Muzeum Narodowe w Warszawie: Przewodnik po dziale malarstwa obcego*. Warsaw: Nakł. Muzeum Narodowego w Warszawie, 1936.

Walker, Jonathan. *Poland Alone: Britain, SOE and the Collapse of the Polish Resistance, 1944*. Stroud: Spellmount Publishers, 2010.

Ward, James Mace. *Priest, Politician, Collaborator: Jozef Tiso and the Making of Fascist Slovakia*. Ithaca: Cornell University Press, 2013.

Wardzyńska, Maria. *Był rok 1939: Operacji niemieckiej policji bezpieczeństwa w Polsce: Intelligenzaktion*. Warsaw: Instytut Pamięci Narodowej, 2009.

Wasilewski, Witold, ed. *Zagłada polskich elit: Akcja AB - Katyń*. Warsaw: Instytut Pamięci Narodowej, 2006.

Weigel, George. *Witness to Hope: The Biography of John Paul II, 1920–2005*. New York: Harper Perennial, 2005.

Weitbrecht, Dorothee. *Der Exekutionsauftrag der Einsatzgruppen in Polen*. Tübingen: Markstein Diskursiv, 2001.

Westermann, Edward. *Hitler's Police Battalions: Enforcing Racial War in the East*. Lawrence: University Press of Kansas, 2005.

Wildt, Michael. *An Uncompromising Generation: The Nazi Leadership of the Reich Security Main Office.* Trans. Tom Lampert. Madison: The University of Wisconsin Press, 2003.

Winiarz, Adam. *Gender and Secondary Education in Poland and Sweden in the Twentieth Century.* Lublin: Marie Curie-Składowska University Press, 2002.

Winstone, Martin. *The Dark Heart of Hitler's Europe: Nazi Rule in Poland under the General Government.* London: I. B. Tauris, 2015.

Wood, E. Thomas and Stanisław M. Jankowski. *Karski: How One Man Tried to Stop the Holocaust.* New York: John Wiley & Sons, 1994.

Wojdecki, Waldemar. *Arcybiskup Antoni Szlagowski: Kaznodzieja Warszawy.* Warsaw: Wydawnictwo Archidiecezji Warszawskiej, 1997.

Wysocki, Wiesław Jan, ed. *Kapelani wrześniowi: służba duszpasterska w Wojsku Polskim w 1939 r.: dokumenty, relacje, opracowanie.* Warsaw: Oficyna Wyd. RYTM, 2001.

   Rotmistrz Witold Pilecki, 1901–1948. Warsaw: Oficyna Wydawnicza RYTM, 2009.

Wysznacki, Leszek. *Warszawa Zbrojna: 1794–1918, 1939–1945.* Warsaw: Krajowa Agencja Wydawnicza, 1979.

Załęski, Grzegorz and Krzysztof Załęski. *Satyra w konspiracji, 1939–1944.* Warsaw: Wydawnictwo LTW, [2011].

Zamojski, Henryk. *Jak wywołano powstanie warszawskie? Tragiczne decyzje.* Warsaw: Bellona, 2013.

Zawodny, J. K. *Nothing but Honour: The Story of the Warsaw Uprising, 1944.* Stanford: Hoover Institution Press, 1978.

Zeller, Guillaume. *The Priest Barracks: Dachau, 1938–1945.* San Francisco: Ignatius Press, 2017.

Zimmerman, Joshua D., ed. *Contested Memories: Poles and Jews during the Holocaust and Its Aftermath.* New Brunswick: Rutgers University Press, 2003.

   The Polish Underground and the Jews, 1939–1945. New York: Cambridge University Press, 2015.

Żaryn, Jan, ed. *Lista strat osobowych ruchu narodowego, 1939–1955.* Zeszyt 1. Warsaw: Instytut Pamięci Narodowej, 2008.

Żurawicka, Janina. *Inteligencja warszawska w końcu XIX wieku.* Warsaw: Państwowe Wydawnictwo Naukowe, 1978.

Żychowska, Maria. *Jerzy Braun (1901–1975): Harcerz, poeta, filozof, publicysta,* Nr. 4. Warsaw: Zespół Historyczny GK ZHP, 1983.

   Jerzy Braun (1901–1975): twórca kultury harcerskiej i 'Unionizmu.' Tarnów: Harcerska Pracownia Archiwalno-Naukowa, 2003.

INDEX